Using Freelance Graphics® Release 2.0 for Windows™

STEPHEN W. SAGMAN

Using Freelance Graphics Release 2.0 for Windows

Library of Congress Catalog No.: 93-60613

ISBN: 1-56529-259-6

96   10 9 8

Interpretation of the printing code: the rightmost double-digit number is the year of the book's printing; the rightmost single-digit number is the number of the book's printing. For example, a printing code of 93-1 shows that the first printing of the book occurred in 1993.

Screens reproduced in this book were created using Collage Plus from Inner Media, Inc., Hollis, NH.

This book is based on Freelance Graphics Release 2.0 for Windows.

Publisher: David P. Ewing

Associate Publisher: Rick Ranucci

Operations Manager: Sheila Cunningham

Publishing Plan Manager: Thomas H. Bennett

Marketing Manager: Ray Robinson

For Eric

CREDITS

Title Manager
Don Roche, Jr.

Acquisitions Editor
Sherri Morningstar

Product Director
Joyce J. Nielsen

Production Editor
Virginia Noble

Editors
William A. Barton
Barb Colter
Jane A. Cramer

Technical Editor
Christopher Denny

Book Designer
Amy Peppler-Adams

Production Team
Claudia Bell
Danielle Bird
Julie Brown
Laurie Casey
Brad Chinn
Brook Farling
Heather Kaufman
Bob LaRoche
Jay Lesandrini
Michael Mucha
Wendy Ott
Caroline Roop
Linda Seifert
Sandra Shay
Amy Steed
Marcella Thompson
Tina Trettin
Michelle Worthington

Indexers
Michael Hughes
Joy Dean Lee

Composed in *Cheltenham* and *MCPdigital* by Que Corporation

Stephen W. Sagman is the president of a company that provides training, courseware, documentation, and user interface consulting. Mr. Sagman writes about personal computing in *PC/Computing*, *PC Week*, *Computer Shopper*, and *PC Magazine* and gives classes and seminars nationwide on desktop publishing, graphics and presentation graphics, and multimedia. Mr. Sagman is the author of *Using Harvard Graphics 3.0*, *Using Windows Draw*, and *1-2-3 Graphics Techniques* from Que; the author of *Getting Your Start in Hollywood*; and a contributor to *Mastering CorelDRAW! 3*. He can be reached via CompuServe (72456,3325) or at CMM, Inc., 140 Charles St., New York, NY, 10014.

ACKNOWLEDGMENTS

The author would like to thank Allison Parker, Freelance Product Manager, for her assistance, and Karla Fisk for her contributions to Chapters 11 and 14.

The author is also grateful to Ginny Noble, Joyce Nielsen, and the technical and copy editors at Que for their consummate manuscript development and editing. Sherri Morningstar, Acquisitions Editor, should win a medal for being firm, but gentle.

Trademarks

CONTENTS AT A GLANCE

V Working with Presentations

VI Customizing Freelance Graphics

Appendixes

TABLE OF CONTENTS

II Using SmartMaster Sets

III Adding Charts to Pages

IV Adding Text and Graphics to Pages

V Working with Presentations

Introduction

You have a presentation to make, and you haven't got much time. You need something polished and professional, but you can't learn complex, new software in just a few hours. So where do you turn? To Freelance Graphics Release 2.0 for Windows, and this book, of course.

Freelance Graphics Release 2.0 for Windows is designed for presentation makers who need top-of-the-line slides, overheads, and handouts quickly and easily, and with enough flexibility to make their presentations both communicative and memorable.

Freelance manages to satisfy all of these needs. Creating basic "dog and pony" shows is shockingly simple, but the automatic presentations that come out of Freelance are hardly bare-boned. Instead, they are fully realized, tastefully designed, and attractively coordinated sequences of slides, pages, or animated screens. And if you are willing to get under the hood and modify a few easily controlled options, you can customize a chart, table, or drawing so that it expresses virtually any message.

The ease of using Freelance comes from several key features. Freelance offers dozens of presentation designs, each of which includes a complete set of page layouts. Simply select an overall design and a page layout and then fill in the blanks with your text or numeric data. Freelance creates the presentation pages, attending to such details as their background design, the text styles used, and the formatting of charts and tables.

Whenever you must make a design decision, such as the type of chart to create, Freelance provides numbered steps to follow on its screens. And when it comes time for you to decide among alternatives, Freelance displays them visually. You see the colors that you can use in pie slices, for example, or the typefaces that you can select for text. Freelance is so easy to use that you will be up and running—creating basic presentations in no time.

Who Should Read This Book?

Using Freelance Graphics Release 2.0 for Windows is written and organized both for new users of Freelance Graphics and for experienced veterans of other presentation graphics programs who are upgrading to Freelance Graphics Release 2.0 for Windows. Most of the information will be relevant to users of Freelance Graphics Release 1.0 for Windows also.

To make your earliest experiences with Freelance positive, the first three chapters of this book take you on a brief tour of the program and then teach the few concepts and procedures you must know in order to create presentations. With these skills under your belt, you will be able to create presentations that will inform and impress your audience.

Later in the book, you will learn to embellish the basic Freelance presentations with special charts and tables, symbols, drawings, and imported graphics files. Before you finish, you will learn to create printed or slide output, create screen shows, and customize Freelance so that it will work the way you like best.

The Organization of This Book

By browsing the pages of this book, you can get a good sense of its organization. The topics are presented in the order in which you are likely to need them when both learning and using Freelance Graphics Release 2.0 for Windows.

Part I: Getting Started

Chapter 1, "Understanding the Freelance Window," takes you on a tour of the parts of the Freelance window, including the buttons, controls, and tools it contains. This chapter introduces the names for these elements that you need to know as you learn Freelance.

Chapter 2, "A Quick Tour," takes you on a brief tour of the program and gives you a hands-on opportunity to create a presentation. You'll see how easy using Freelance really is.

Part II: Using SmartMaster Sets

Chapter 3, "The Essential Steps," introduces you to the three basic steps that you need to follow to create any presentation. These steps serve as the building blocks for all the work you do in Freelance.

Chapter 4, "Making Basic Changes to the Presentation," teaches you how to quickly accomplish the most elemental changes to the presentation. With Chapters 3 and 4 under your belt, you'll be able to create sophisticated, polished presentations.

Chapter 5, "Using Page Sorter View," describes the three views you can use to examine and edit your work in Freelance and concentrates on the capabilities of Page Sorter view.

Part III: Adding Charts to Pages

Chapter 6, "Adding a Data Chart," describes how to create charts and graphs that can depict numbers visually. You learn to distinguish among data chart types, start a data chart, and enter the numbers that Freelance needs so that it can construct the chart for you.

Chapter 7, "Formatting a Data Chart," shows you how to make changes to the appearance of the data charts that Freelance creates.

Chapter 8, "Importing the Data for a Data Chart," describes how to pull in the data for a chart from another program or from a file on disk so that you don't have to retype the numbers into Freelance by hand.

Chapter 9, "Creating Organization Charts," tells you everything you need to know about creating charts that depict the structure of an organization.

Chapter 10, "Creating Table Charts," teaches you to create tables that can contain text or numbers.

Part IV: Adding Text and Graphics to Pages

Chapter 11, "Adding and Formatting Text Blocks," shows you how to add additional text to text blocks on pages and how to format those text blocks to customize their appearance.

Chapter 12, "Drawing Objects," teaches you to use the drawing tools of Freelance to embellish presentation pages with graphic shapes.

Chapter 13, "Editing Objects," shows you how to edit individual drawing objects that you have created and how to arrange groups of drawing objects.

Chapter 14, "Using Symbols," describes how to incorporate in your presentation pictures, or symbols, that come with Freelance in the extensive symbol library.

Chapter 15, "Adding Bitmap Images," shows you how to incorporate in your presentations images that have been created with painting programs or scanning software.

Chapter 16, "Importing and Exporting Drawings and Charts," shows you how to use drawings from other programs in your presentations and how to export a presentation for use in other Windows applications.

Part V: Working with Presentations

Chapter 17, "Managing Presentations," shows you how to use the features of Freelance that give you overall control of a presentation. For example, you learn to spell-check a presentation, change to a different color palette, and copy pages from one presentation to another.

Chapter 18, "Using the Outliner To Organize a Presentation," teaches you to use the Outliner view of Freelance, which displays the text content of your presentation, and lets you enter, edit, and reorganize the topics of the presentation without regard to the presentation design.

Chapter 19, "Creating Screen Shows," gives you the knowledge you need to create on-screen presentations that can include slides that build, as well as transition effects as each slide is drawn.

Chapter 20, "Creating Output," shows you how to create the several different forms of printed output that Freelance can create and how to create 35mm slides.

Part VI: Customizing Freelance Graphics

Chapter 21, "Editing SmartMaster Sets," describes how to customize the presentation designs that come with Freelance and how to create your own presentation designs.

Chapter 22, "Using and Editing Color Palettes," teaches you to select and modify the color palettes that control the colors of all objects in the presentation.

Chapter 23, "Modifying the Default Settings," shows you the controls, commands, and settings that let you alter, to your liking, the way Freelance works.

Appendixes

Appendix A, "SmartMaster Sets," identifies the SmartMaster sets from which you can choose. You can scan the pages of this appendix rather than preview the SmartMaster sets on-screen one by one.

Appendix B, "The Symbol Library," identifies the symbols you can select from the symbol library. As with the SmartMaster sets, you can scan this appendix to see all the symbols instead of combing tediously through the many categories of symbols in the symbol library.

Conventions Used in This Book

A number of conventions appear in *Using Freelance Graphics Release 2.0 for Windows* to help you learn the program. This section includes examples of these conventions to help you distinguish among the different elements in Freelance Graphics Release 2.0 for Windows.

Special typefaces in this book include the following:

Typeface	Meaning
italic	New terms or phrases when initially defined
boldface	Information you are asked to type; menu and dialog box options that appear underlined on-screen
`special type`	Direct quotations of words that appear on-screen or in a figure

In most cases, keys are represented as they appear on the keyboard. The arrow keys are usually represented by name (for example, the up-arrow key). The Print Screen key is abbreviated PrtSc, Page Up is PgUp, Insert is Ins, and so on. On your keyboard, these key names may be spelled out or abbreviated differently.

When two keys appear together with a plus sign, such as Shift+F9, you are to press and hold down the first key and then press the second key.

The function keys F1 through F10 are used for special situations in Freelance. You also can use the Alt, Ctrl, and Shift keys with certain function keys as shortcut keys to perform commands or tasks in Freelance.

NOTE

This paragraph format indicates additional information that may help you avoid problems or that should be considered in using the described features.

TIP

This paragraph format suggests easier or alternative methods of executing a procedure or discusses advanced techniques related to the topic described in the text.

CAUTION

This paragraph format warns the reader of hazardous procedures (for example, activities that delete files).

Icons, such as the File New icon beside this paragraph, appear in the margin to indicate that the procedure described in the text includes instructions for using the appropriate SmartIcons or toolbox icons in Freelance Graphics Release 2.0 for Windows.

Finally, although the full name of the product covered in this book is Freelance Graphics Release 2.0, the short form of *Freelance* or *Freelance Graphics* is used throughout the chapters.

Getting Started

Understanding the Freelance Window

Freelance's clear and logical on-screen controls are a key ingredient to the program's ease of use and the power it bestows. Before you take the guided tour in Chapter 2, you should take a few moments to peruse this chapter to become familiar with the menus, icons, buttons, and bars that you see on-screen while working in Freelance. Some of these are common to all Windows programs, such as the title bar and menu bar, and some are special to Freelance, such as the SmartIcons and the toolbox. In later chapters, you learn to use these on-screen controls to accomplish specific tasks.

The Title Bar

The *title bar*, which appears at the top of the Freelance window (see fig. 1.1), identifies the Freelance Graphics window and includes the file name of the current presentation. If you have not yet named the presentation, [Untitled1] appears. At the right end of the title bar, the indicator displays Ready in green or Wait in red, depending on whether the program is ready for you to work or still carrying out your last command.

Fig. 1.1

The Freelance Graphics window.

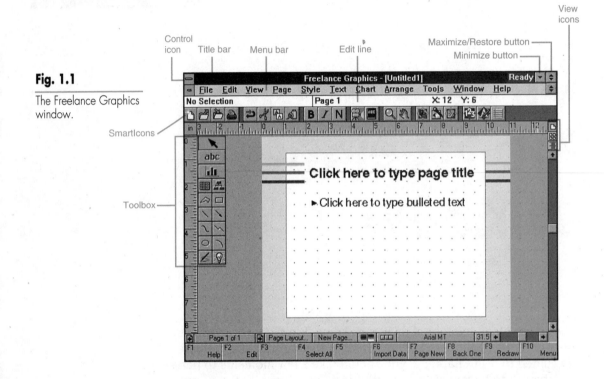

Clicking the Minimize button (the down-arrow button at the right end of the title bar) minimizes the Freelance window to an icon. Clicking the Restore button (the double-arrow button at the right end of the title bar) reduces the size of the window so that it floats on the screen instead of fully occupying it. After the window is restored, you can drag the window's borders to resize it. You can also click the Maximize button (the up-arrow button at the right end of the title bar) to maximize the Freelance window so that it again occupies the entire screen. Clicking the Control icon at the left end of the title bar summons the Control menu, which displays menu items that enable you to minimize, maximize, restore, and close the Freelance window. (Double-clicking the Control icon also closes the Freelance window.) If an open presentation has not been saved, you will be asked whether to save it before closing the Freelance window.

The Menu Bar

The *menu bar* includes the menu options **F**ile, **E**dit, **V**iew, **P**age, **S**tyle, **T**ext, **C**hart, **A**rrange, Too**l**s, **W**indow, and **H**elp. The underlined letter in each menu name is the accelerator key that you can use with the Alt key to pull down the menu.

> **TIP**
>
> To see a description of each menu in the title bar, click the menu name and hold down the left mouse button. Or press Alt and the accelerator key for the menu.

Clicking the Control icon at the left end of the menu bar pulls down a menu of commands that you can use to control the window within the Freelance window that holds the current presentation. **Mi**nimize converts the currently selected presentation window into an icon. **R**estore converts the presentation window to a window that you can move and resize within the Freelance window. (The Restore button at the right end of the menu bar also performs this function.) Ma**x**imize fills the Freelance window with the selected presentation window. **C**lose closes the currently selected presentation window.

The Edit Line

The *edit line*, located just below the menu bar, displays information about the current work you are performing in Freelance. The edit line describes the object you've selected, the name of the page you're working on, and, if you've chosen to display the cursor coordinates, the location of the cursor. The cursor coordinates constantly show the distance of the cursor from the upper-left corner of the page.

To show the cursor coordinates, choose **V**iew Preferences from the View menu. Then choose **C**oordinates from the Display group of settings. You learn about the other View Preferences settings in Chapter 23, "Modifying the Default Settings."

The SmartIcons

A row of SmartIcons appears just below the edit line. Each SmartIcon offers a shortcut alternative to one or more menu selections.

The default set of SmartIcons includes shortcuts for the most common menu selections, but you may want to select additional SmartIcons from the comprehensive collection that comes with Freelance. If you frequently use pie charts, for example, you can add a pie chart SmartIcon to the SmartIcon palette so that you can start a pie chart with a single click. The controls for changing which SmartIcons appear as well as the location and size of the SmartIcons on the screen reside under SmartIcons on the Tools menu.

The Toolbox

The *toolbox*, which appears on the left side of the screen, holds the tools you use to create and edit objects such as charts, graphic shapes, and symbols. The toolbox holds icons that represent the tools (see fig. 1.2).

TIP

To see a description of each tool in the toolbox, click and hold down the right mouse button while you point to the tool.

Fig. 1.2

The Freelance toolbox.

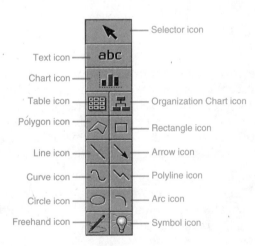

Selector icon
Text icon
Chart icon
Table icon — Organization Chart icon
Polygon icon — Rectangle icon
Line icon — Arrow icon
Curve icon — Polyline icon
Circle icon — Arc icon
Freehand icon — Symbol icon

The tools in the toolbox have the following uses:

Tool	Description
Selector tool	Produces an on-screen arrow that you use to point to and select menu commands, SmartIcons, and other tools from the toolbox. You use the Selector tool also to select objects to modify.
Text tool	Adds a free-form text block anywhere on a page or selects for editing the text you've already added.
Chart tool	Adds a new chart to a page. If you select an existing chart, clicking the Chart icon opens the data window for the chart.
Table tool	Adds a new table to a page. If you select an existing table, clicking the Table icon opens the Table Choices dialog box so that you can change the design of the table.
Organization Chart tool	Adds a new organization chart to a page. If you select an existing table, clicking the Organization Chart icon opens the Organization Chart Entry List dialog box so that you can change the contents or design of the chart.
Polygon tool	Draws a closed object with three or more sides.
Rectangle tool	Draws a rectangle or square.
Line tool	Draws a straight line.
Arrow tool	Draws a line with an arrowhead at one or both ends.
Curve tool	Draws a curving line.
Polyline tool	Draws a line with more than one segment.
Circle tool	Draws a circle or ellipse.
Arc tool	Draws an arc.
Freehand tool	Draws a freehand shape.
Symbol tool	Accesses the Add Symbol to Page dialog box, which you use to select a symbol from the Freelance symbol library for placement on a presentation page.

The View Icons

The three icons at the right edge of the screen, just above the scroll bar, determine which view of the presentation you see (see fig. 1.3). One of the three icons is always pressed.

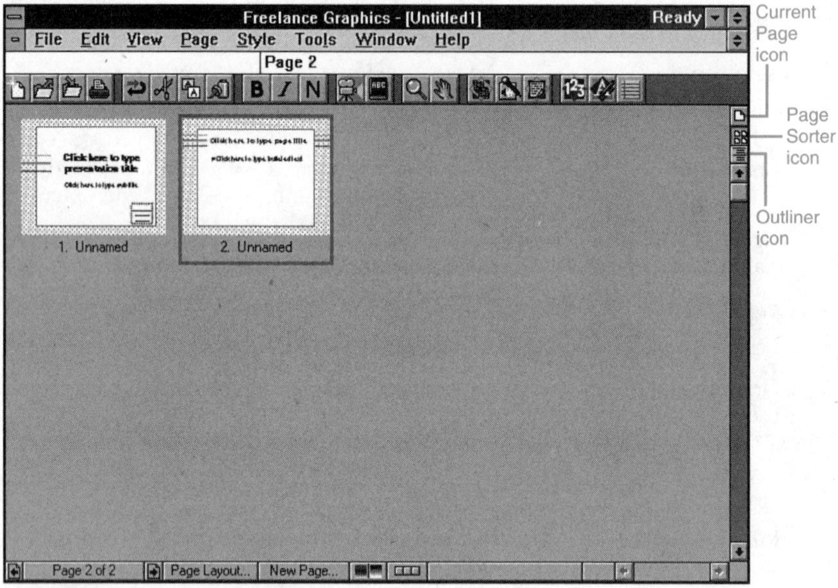

Fig. 1.3

The View icons.

The following list describes the View icons:

- The *Current Page icon* causes Freelance to show the current presentation page.

- The *Page Sorter icon* switches to Page Sorter view.

- The *Outliner icon* switches to Outliner view.

The Status Bar

The *status bar* is a narrow band near the bottom of the screen and just above the function key panel, as shown in figure 1.4. The controls that appear in the status bar perform a variety of functions (see fig. 1.5).

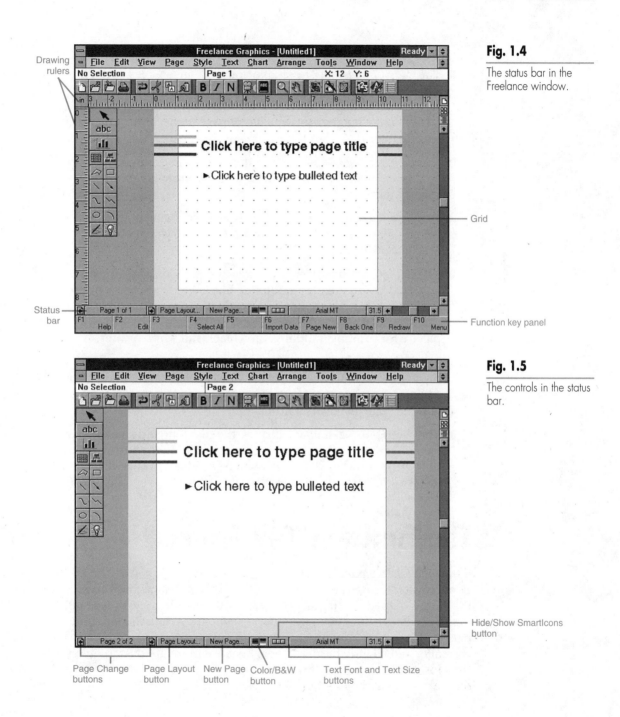

Fig. 1.4

The status bar in the Freelance window.

Fig. 1.5

The controls in the status bar.

The following list describes the buttons in the status bar:

■ The *Page Change buttons* enable you to change pages in the presentation. Click the right- or left-arrow symbol to turn a page forward or back, respectively. Click the button that displays the current page number to see a list of page names from which you can choose.

■ The *Page Layout button* leads to the Choose Page Layout dialog box, from which you can select a different page layout for the current page.

■ The *New Page button* leads to the New Page dialog box, from which you can select a page layout for the new page that Freelance will add.

■ The *Color/B&W button* enables you to switch instantly from a color palette to the corresponding black-and-white palette and back. After you create a color presentation for color slides, you can click this button to switch to the matching black-and-white palette for printing handouts on a black-and-white printer.

■ The *Hide/Show SmartIcons button* enables you to turn on or off the display of the SmartIcons. When the SmartIcons are hidden, you can no longer use them, but the screen is a little less cluttered, and the page display is a little larger.

■ The *Text Font/Size buttons* display the text font and size for a selected text block. If no text block is selected, these buttons display the text font and size that will be used if you click the Text icon to add a free-floating text block.

The Function Key Panel

If the *function key panel* is turned on (refer to fig. 1.4), you see an additional row of buttons at the bottom of the screen. These buttons show the names of the first 10 function keys. You can either click these buttons or press the function keys on the keyboard. When the function key panel is turned on, it leaves less space for the page display, so the page is smaller and slightly harder to see. Because there are on-screen controls for nearly all the function key commands, you may want to turn off the display of the function key panel.

To turn on the function key panel, choose **V**iew Preferences from the **V**iew menu and then choose **F**unction Key Panel from the Display group of settings. Click OK to leave the dialog box.

The Drawing Rulers

Another option in the View Preferences dialog box, **D**rawing Ruler, turns on or off a set of rulers running across the top and down the left edges of the page display (see fig. 1.4). An indicator within the drawing rulers shows the location of the cursor. When an object is selected, the rulers show the locations of the edges of the object. When multiple objects are selected, the drawing rulers show the locations of the edges of the group.

The measurement units of the drawing rulers are determined by the Units & Grids settings. To change the Units & Grids settings, choose **U**nits & Grids from the **V**iew menu. Then choose **M**illimeters, **C**entimeters, **I**nches, **P**oints, or Pic**a**s from the Units group of settings.

The Grid

When the *grid* is turned on, it appears as a pattern of dots across the page display (refer to fig. 1.4). You can use these dots to visually align objects, or you can cause objects to be pulled to the nearest dot as they are being drawn. To change the grid, choose **U**nits & Grids from the **V**iew menu. Then choose **D**isplay Grid to turn on or off the grid, and **S**nap To Grid to turn on or off the pulling effect of the grid dots. You use the **H**orizontal Space and **V**ertical Space text boxes to enter a new number for the spacing of the dots in the grid. The number's unit of measurement is determined by the Units setting in the same dialog box. To display grid dots one inch apart, for example, enter **1.0** for both **H**orizontal Space and **V**ertical Space and then set the Units to **I**nches.

Summary

Now that you've had a chance to become familiar with the Freelance window, you are prepared to begin working with Freelance. The next chapter takes you on a quick tour of the many features of Freelance.

A Quick Tour

Trial and error may be the way most people learn new tasks, but trial without error is an even better approach. The tutorial in this chapter gives you a step-by-step, controlled, and error-free exposure to the basic commands and functions of Freelance. By following these steps, you quickly get an overview of this truly remarkable software and see for yourself how easy it can be to create a professional-looking presentation. You also see the broad range of presentation designs from which you can choose in Freelance and the wide array of charts, tables, and graphic designs you can create.

Whenever possible, Freelance guides you with step-by-step instructions on-screen. You often see these steps on-screen during this tutorial. Later, when you are on your own and are unsure of how to use a command or control, look for a question mark button on-screen to click. There's always one in the upper-right corner of every dialog box, and the icon always summons Help information about the options that are currently on-screen. If you cannot find a question mark button, press F1 or click **Help** in the menu.

Allow yourself 20 minutes of undisturbed time with this chapter, and try to follow the steps of the entire tutorial in one sitting and without interruptions. Later in the book, you learn about all the unexplained options and commands you may encounter along the way, and you get the chance to practice using them in more focused and detailed exercises.

About the Presentation

For the purposes of this tutorial, imagine that you plan to give a presentation to the local planning board on the impact of allowing an ecologically sensitive area to be developed.

Your presentation will include several charts and graphs that detail the numeric results of scientific studies, but the presentation will start with a title page and an executive summary of the key findings, both in text form.

Fortunately, Freelance does not require that you decide before you begin the presentation how the eventual output will be created. Right now, you plan to create an on-screen presentation called a *screen show* so that the presentation pages appear on-screen one by one, but you can easily switch to 35mm slides or black-and-white printed output later, or even create all three kinds of output.

Starting a New Presentation and Choosing Its Look

To begin creating a new presentation, start Freelance Graphics Release 2.0 for Windows by double-clicking its icon in the Program Manager. After the Freelance Graphics window opens, a dialog box appears, labeled Choose a Look for Your Presentation. An on-screen instruction in this dialog box tells you to Choose a look for your presentation by selecting a SmartMaster set. Follow the instruction by clicking a SmartMaster set name on the list and then examining the preview of the presentation design it holds. Click several of the SmartMaster sets and examine their previews. You also can press the down-arrow key on the keyboard to highlight and preview each SmartMaster set sequentially.

As you will learn, SmartMaster sets hold background designs for presentations, as well as the formatting and placement of text, charts, tables, and symbols on pages. After you select a SmartMaster set, you can enter the data for the presentation (the text and numbers) and get a finished and polished presentation in almost no time.

As you scroll down the list of SmartMaster sets, the set named FOREST.MAS may catch your eye. The Forest SmartMaster set is ideal for a presentation with an ecological theme. To use this set, make sure

that FOREST.MAS is highlighted, as shown in figure 2.1, and then click
OK or press Enter.

> As a shortcut, you can press the letter F on the keyboard to jump to the
> first SmartMaster set on the list that begins with an F. Then you can scroll
> down one entry to FOREST.MAS.

TIP

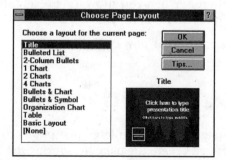

Fig. 2.1

Selecting the
SmartMaster set named
FOREST.MAS.

Selecting a Page Layout

The next dialog box to appear, shown in figure 2.2, asks you to choose
a page layout. The Choose Page Layout dialog box lists 11 layouts and
shows a preview of each layout that you click. Each SmartMaster set
contains 11 of these page layouts that set the size and positioning of
presentation elements on the page. The page layout called Bulleted
List, for example, creates a page with a page title and a list of bulleted
text points below the title. The page layouts also set the text attributes,
such as the point size and typeface, of the text elements on the pages.

Fig. 2.2

The Choose Page Layout
dialog box.

Although each SmartMaster set has only 11 page layouts, you are likely to find a page layout for just about any presentation need. If you need a special page design, you can always arrange the elements on the page manually or create a new, custom page layout. You learn about both of these techniques later in this book.

Your presentation, like most, will start with a title page, so choose the Title page layout and then click OK. The Title page layout appears full-screen.

Filling in the Blanks with "Click here..." Blocks

As you can see by examining the Title page layout, a *page layout* is an arrangement of boxes in the background that you can click to create presentation elements. These boxes are called "Click here..." blocks because each asks you to "Click here" to create a presentation element such as a page title or subtitle, a chart, or a table. The Title page layout has three "Click here..." blocks—two that create text titles and one that enables you to select a symbol from the symbol library.

To type the presentation title, click the "Click here to type presentation title" text block, type **Environmental Impact**, and click OK. To enter the subtitle, click the "Click here to type subtitle" text block, type **Mecox Farms Area**, and click OK. The presentation page then appears as shown in figure 2.3.

You still have not used the third "Click here..." block to add a symbol to a page, but this presentation does not require a symbol. The background design is so rich that a symbol to emphasize the environment theme might be overkill. Just ignore the final "Click here..." block. The box and the prompt text inside the box appear only while you are working on the presentation. When you show the presentation as a screen show or print the presentation, they do not appear.

The first presentation page is now complete.

Adding a Second Page

Next, you need a page that uses bulleted text points to present the key findings of this report. Create the page by clicking the New Page button

near the bottom of the Freelance window. The New Page dialog box
opens, as shown in figure 2.4.

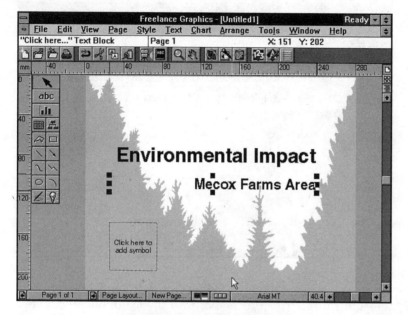

Fig. 2.3

The presentation page
after entering a title and
subtitle.

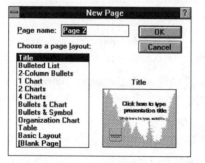

Fig. 2.4

The New Page dialog
box.

In the **P**age Name text box, type as much of the name **Executive Summary** as will fit. This entry replaces the default page name of Page 2.
Then click the Bulleted List page layout and examine the preview in the
dialog box. The preview shows a page title at the top of the page and
the first of a series of bulleted text points. To use the Bulleted List page
layout, click OK or press Enter. The Bulleted List page layout appears,
as shown in figure 2.5.

Fig. 2.5

The Bulleted List page
layout.

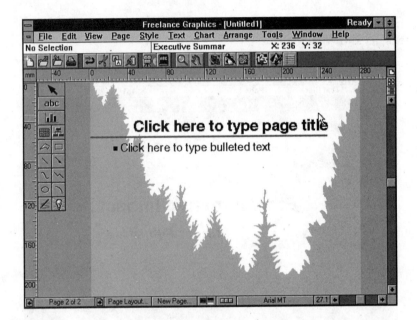

The Bulleted List page layout contains only two "Click here..." text
blocks—one for the page title and one for the list of bulleted text
points.

Click the page title "Click here..." text block and enter the title **Executive Summary**. Then press the down-arrow key to move to the next
"Click here..." block. The typing cursor appears next to the first bullet.

Type **Ecosystem depends on balance of wooded and open areas.** and
press Enter. Then type the following three sentences, pressing Enter
after each:

> **Development proposal opens 30% of wooded areas.**
>
> **Recommend 10% wooded areas to be opened, maximum.**
>
> **Cluster siting mandatory.**

Click OK to finish the Bulleted List page. Figure 2.6 shows the completed page.

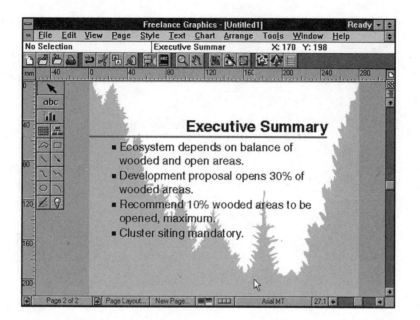

Fig. 2.6

The completed Bulleted List page.

Adding a Data Chart Page

Next, you add a page with a data chart that can show the measured impact on a similar ecosystem of cluster versus spread siting of homes. To begin, add a new page to the presentation by clicking the New Page button at the bottom of the Freelance window. Type **Siting Chart** as the page name. Then choose the 1 Chart page layout from the Choose Page Layout dialog box.

The 1 Chart page layout offers a "Click here..." text block that you can use to enter a page title, and a "Click here..." data chart block that you can click to begin the process of creating a chart. The "Click here..." data chart block also indicates the positioning of the chart you will create. Figure 2.7 shows the 1 Chart page layout as it appears in the Freelance window.

Click the "Click here to type page title" block and then type **Cluster vs Spread Siting** as the page title. Click anywhere outside the text block (even on the gray area around the page) to place the text on the page. Next, you use the other "Click here..." block to create the data chart.

Fig. 2.7

The 1 Chart page layout.

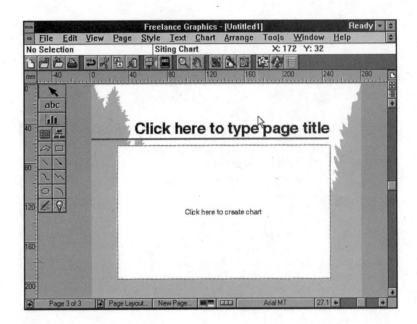

Click the "Click here to create chart" block. The Chart Gallery dialog box opens, as shown in figure 2.8.

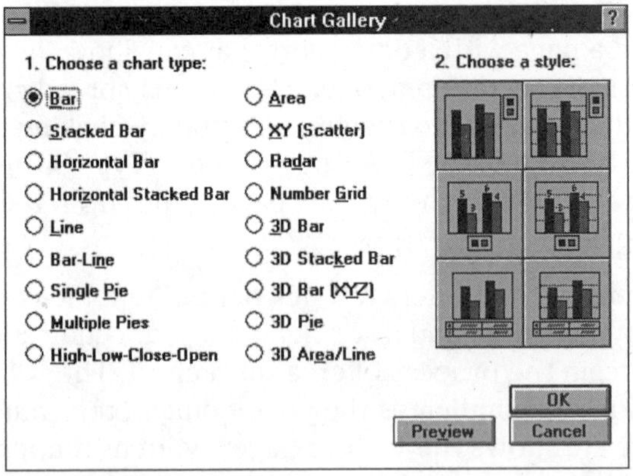

Fig. 2.8

The Chart Gallery dialog box.

Notice that the dialog box displays two numbered steps. Whenever possible, Freelance numbers the steps you should follow to respond to a dialog box. Complete the first step by clicking one of the chart type buttons. In this case, click the Line button to create a line chart. (A line chart is appropriate because you want to show how results change over time.) Notice that the display of chart styles on the right changes to show different line chart styles. You will create a line chart with a number grid below the chart, so click the third button in the second column.

The next step is to enter the numbers to chart. Freelance opens the Chart Data & Titles dialog box and displays a spreadsheet-like grid into which you can enter the data for the data chart. Text and an arrow in the window point to the first column as the destination for Axis Labels. More text and another arrow points to the first two rows as the destination for Legend entries. The sequences of numbers that you must supply to create a chart are arranged in columns below each Legend entry.

Use the arrow keys to move the highlight from cell to cell in the Chart Data & Titles dialog box. You also can click a cell with the mouse pointer to "jump" the highlight directly to a cell.

Notice the Import button on the left. If you keep your data in another software program on your system (for example, Lotus 1-2-3), you can import the data rather than retype it in Freelance. The data that you need to enter for this chart is short, however, so type the data manually.

Move the highlight around the Chart Data & Titles dialog box and type entries into each cell until you have completed the data, as shown in figure 2.9.

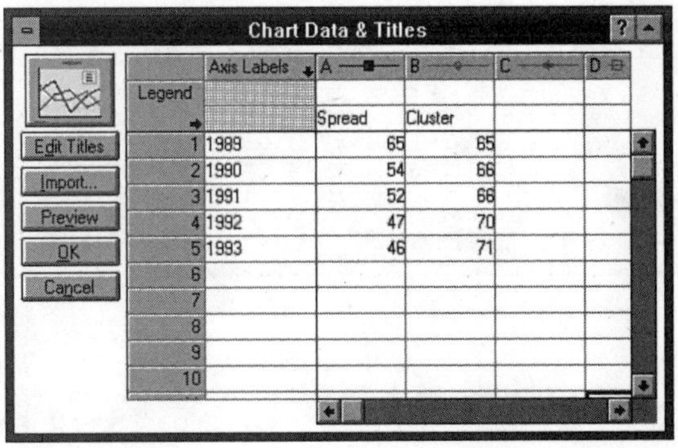

Fig. 2.9

The completed Chart Data & Titles dialog box.

Then click the Edit Titles button so that you can enter a chart heading. In the first Headings text box, type **Ecosystem Viability**, as shown in figure 2.10.

Finally, click OK to have Freelance create a chart based on the data you have entered. Figure 2.11 shows this chart.

Fig. 2.10

Entering a chart heading.

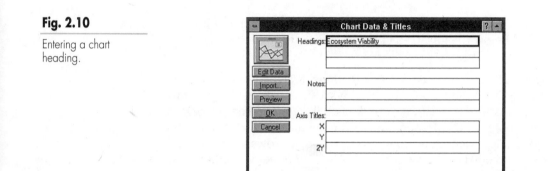

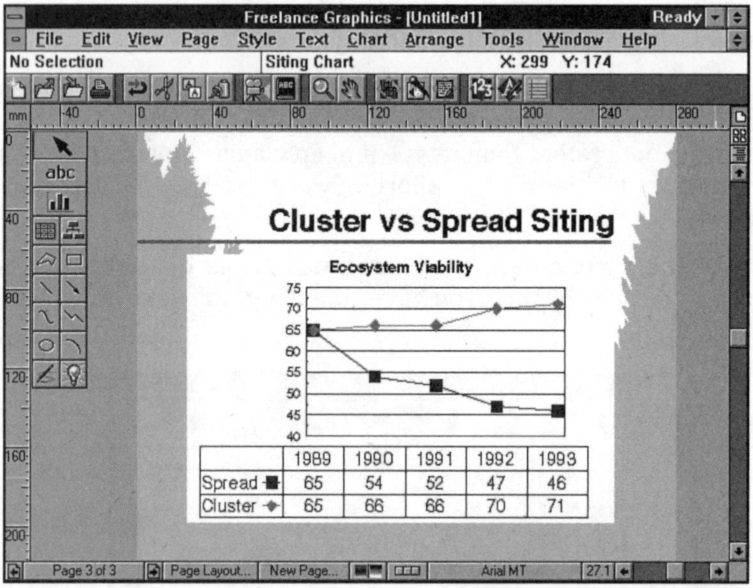

Fig. 2.11

The completed data chart.

Changing an Object's Attributes

Every object that you create—whether it is a text block, chart, table, or drawn object—has a set of attributes that control its appearance. To change the attributes, place the mouse pointer on the object and click the right mouse button. A pop-up menu appears with options that are specific to the object you have selected. One of the options is always Attributes. If you choose Attributes, a dialog box appears with special settings that change the appearance of the object. As usual, Freelance offers several other ways to accomplish the same thing. You can access the Attributes dialog box for any object by choosing **Attributes** from the **S**tyle menu after you select an object. You also can access the Attributes dialog box by double-clicking many objects (except charts).

To see the attributes for the data chart you have just finished, click the chart with the right mouse button and then choose Attributes from the pop-up menu. The Line Chart Attributes dialog box appears, as shown in figure 2.12.

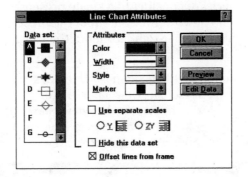

Fig. 2.12

The Line Chart Attributes dialog box.

You can use this dialog box to change the color and width of the lines in the chart, for example, and to make many other changes to the appearance of the chart. Try using the settings in the dialog box by clicking the line sample shown next to **W**idth and then choosing a wider line width from the menu. To see the effect of the change, place the cursor on the Preview button and then press and hold down the mouse button. While you hold down the mouse button, the dialog box disappears so that you can see the results of the new attribute setting reflected on the chart. When you release the mouse button, the dialog box reappears.

To increase the width of the second line in the chart, click Data Set B at the left and then use the **W**idth control to choose the same wider line. You can make other changes to the attributes if you want, or click OK to close the Line Chart Attributes dialog box.

Modifying the Presentation in Page Sorter View

Now that you have completed the first three pages of your presentation, you can turn back and forth among the pages by pressing the PgUp or PgDn key or by clicking the Page Change buttons on either side of the current page number display at the lower-left corner of the Freelance window. You also can click the current page number and choose a different page from the pop-up list.

Examining presentation pages like this, however, allows you to see only one page at a time. One of the strengths of Freelance is that all the pages you create are part of the same presentation file, unlike other presentation graphics programs that store each page in a separate file. Because all the pages are considered a single presentation, Freelance offers three different views of the content of the presentation. Each view has an icon at the upper-right corner of the viewing area, just above the scroll bar on the right.

At the moment, the Current Page icon is selected, so Freelance is in Current Page view. You also can view a number of pages at once by clicking the Page Sorter icon; Page Sorter view shows tiny pages arranged in a grid. Try clicking the Page Sorter icon. Figure 2.13 shows the presentation as it appears in Page Sorter view.

Fig. 2.13

The presentation in Page Sorter view.

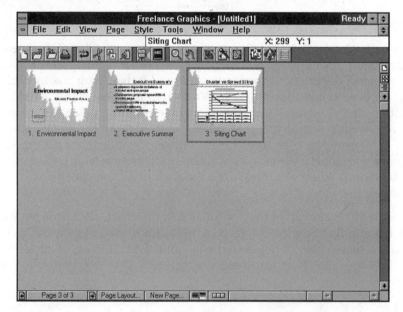

In Page Sorter view, you can see the consistency of design that the SmartMaster set imposes on the presentation. The title page has one design, and the other pages have a second design that is related to the title page. You also see the page titles below each page.

In Page Sorter view, you can get an overall view of a presentation. You can also change the SmartMaster set attached to a presentation, rearrange the order of pages, and duplicate pages that have contents you want to copy. You can even arrange two presentations that are in Page Sorter view in side-by-side windows and then copy the contents of a page from one presentation to another. You learn about all these techniques in Chapter 5, "Using Page Sorter View."

For now, try rearranging the order of the pages by clicking page 3 to select it and then dragging it between pages 1 and 2. When you release the mouse button, the page appears in the new position.

Another thing to try is duplicating a page. Select the page with the data chart and either choose **D**uplicate from the **P**age menu or press Alt+F7. You then have two sequential data charts in the middle of the presentation, as shown in figure 2.14.

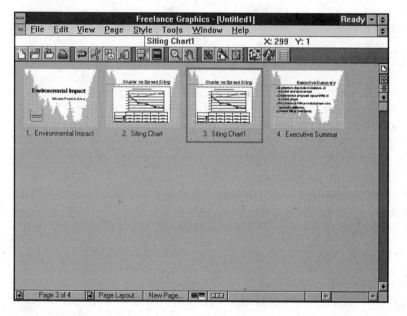

Fig. 2.14

The duplicated data chart page.

Double-click the second data chart page to view it in Current Page view. Then, by double-clicking the data chart, you can open its Chart Data & Titles dialog box so that you can modify the numbers to create a second data chart related to the first. If you have opened the Chart Data & Titles dialog box, you can click **OK** to view the updated chart, or click Ca**n**cel to return to a view of the original chart.

Switch back to Page Sorter view by clicking the Page Sorter icon so that you can try one other technique. In Page Sorter view, click the first data chart page to select it. Then press and hold down the Shift key and select the second data chart page. Place the pointer on either page and drag the two pages to the end of the presentation. A dark vertical bar then appears where the pages will drop when you release the mouse button. Click somewhere in the blank area of the Freelance window to deselect the second data chart page. Then click only the second data chart page (page number 4 in the presentation). Make sure that only the second data chart page is selected before continuing.

With the second data chart page selected, press the Del key on the keyboard. The page disappears. If you have deleted the wrong page, you can immediately choose Undo Delete Page(s) from the Edit menu.

Working with the Presentation in the Outliner

The Outliner in Freelance offers a third view of a presentation. This view shows only the text content of the presentation pages so that you can concentrate on the content of the presentation rather than the design of the pages. To switch to Outliner view, click the Outliner icon at the right edge of the Freelance window. Figure 2.15 shows the three-page presentation in Outliner view.

Notice that the text of the presentation appears on what looks like a yellow legal pad. Next to each page is a page icon. The page icon for the third page shows a data chart to indicate the contents of the page.

In Outliner view, you can edit the text contents of pages by editing the text on the Outliner legal pad. You can also rearrange the order of pages and of bulleted text points on Bulleted List pages. Just as in Page Sorter view, you can duplicate pages and delete extraneous pages too.

To try rearranging the pages in Outliner view, click the page icon to the left of the third page. A border appears around the page, as shown in figure 2.16.

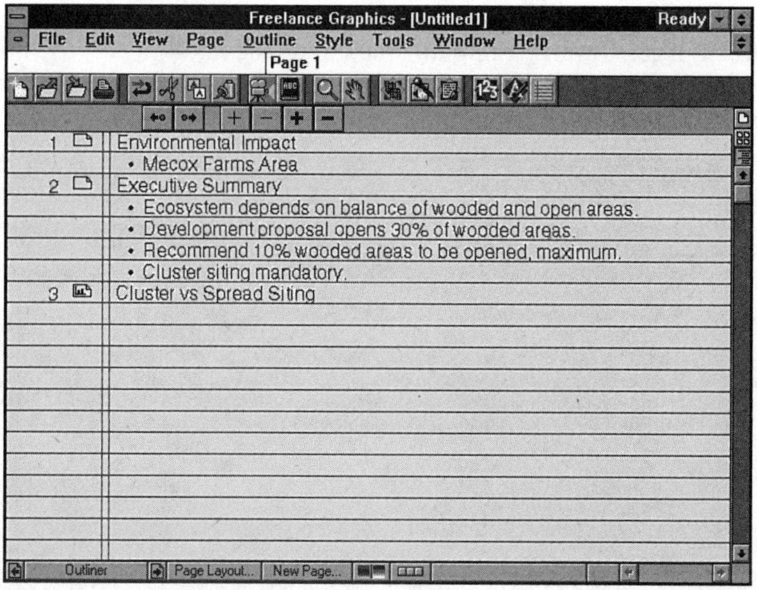

Fig. 2.15

The presentation in Outliner view.

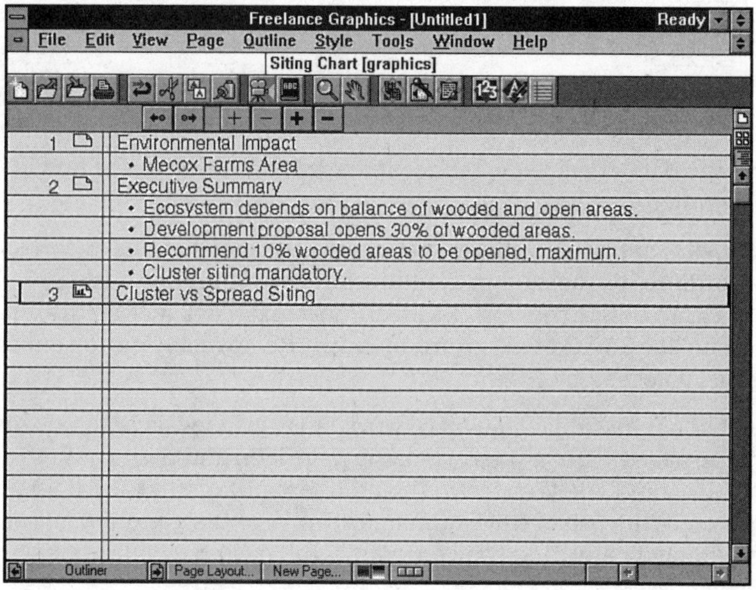

Fig. 2.16

A selected page in Outliner view.

Drag the page icon up the page while holding down the mouse button. A dark horizontal bar appears where the page will drop if you release the mouse button. Release the mouse button when the bar appears between pages 1 and 2. The data chart then becomes page 2, as shown in figure 2.17. If you switch to Page Sorter view, you will see the data chart page in its new position.

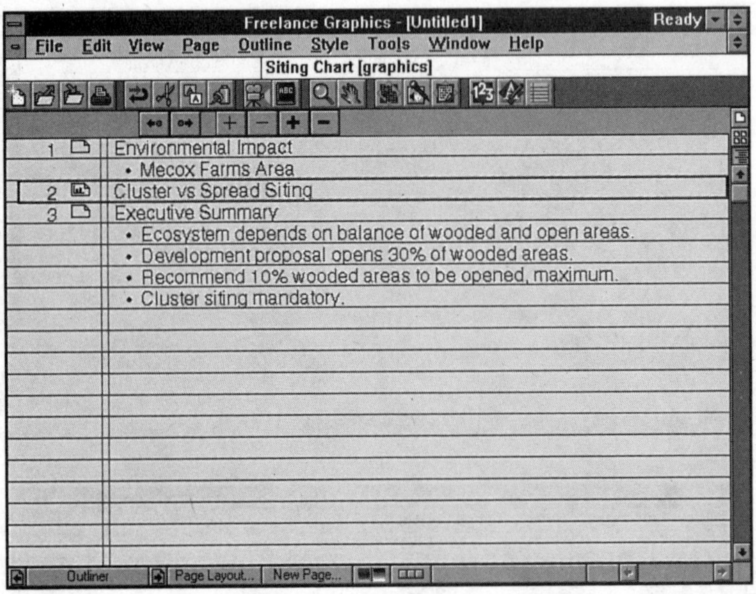

Fig. 2.17

The data chart page
after it is moved.

Move the data chart page back to its correct position at the end of the presentation.

To try editing text in Outliner view, move the mouse pointer across the words to be opened in the third bulleted text point of page 2. Then press Del to delete the text. To insert new text, click just before 10% in the same line and type the word **opening**. Remove any extra spaces in the line, if necessary.

The Outliner also enables you to work at varying levels of detail. To see only the page title of a page, click the page icon and then press the gray minus key on the keyboard (in the number pad) or click the light gray plus icon at the top of the Outliner screen. A plus sign to the left of the page icon indicates that the contents of the page are collapsed under the page title.

To see only the page titles of all pages, click the dark gray minus icon at the top of the Outliner screen. This action does not delete the entries under the page titles. It just hides them so that you can consider the flow of the main topics of the presentation. Figure 2.18 shows the contents of all the pages collapsed under the page titles. Click the dark gray plus icon to expand all the pages once again.

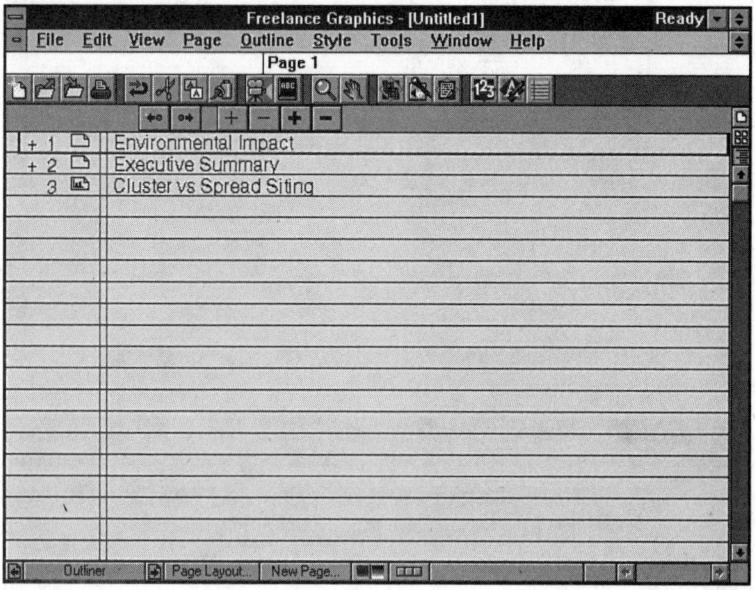

Fig. 2.18

The page contents collapsed under the page titles.

You also can add a page while in Outliner view by simply typing into the Outliner as though you were typing on the yellow legal pad. To add a new page to this presentation, put the cursor at the end of the last line. (You can press the down-arrow key to move the cursor to the last line, and then press the End key to move the cursor to the end of the line.) Then press Enter to move down a line. A new bullet appears as though you planned to enter a new bulleted line on the page. To start a new page, press Shift+Tab. A new page icon appears. Type **Conclusion** and then press Enter. Then type **Cluster siting will preserve Mecox Farms ecosystem.** Figure 2.19 shows how the page appears in Outliner view.

To see the actual presentation page you have created, click the Current Page icon. Figure 2.20 shows the page in Current Page view.

Fig. 2.19

The new page in
Outliner view.

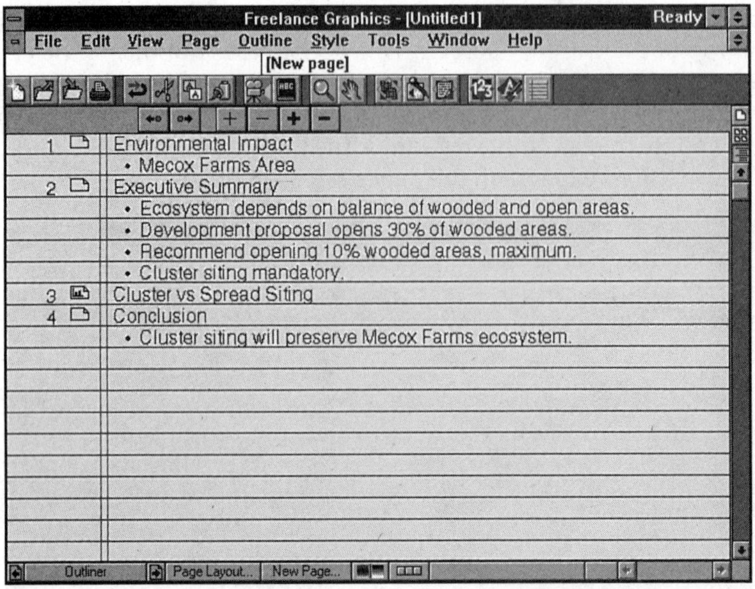

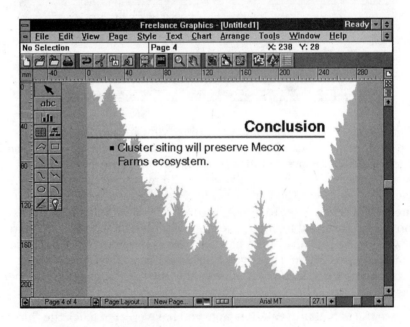

Fig. 2.20

The new page in
Current Page view.

Viewing the Presentation as a Screen Show

You have had the chance to view miniatures of the pages in Page Sorter view and the text content of the pages in Outliner view. Fortunately, Freelance offers yet another way to view a presentation. You can have the pages appear one after another, with fancy transition effects between pages, in an on-screen production called a *screen show*.

To create the screen show, choose **S**creen Show from the **V**iew menu and then choose **R**un from the pop-out menu. You also can press Alt+F10 to start the show. After a moment, the first page of the show appears full-screen. To advance to the next page, press Enter or click the left mouse button. Continue advancing through the screen show until you have seen all four pages.

The default screen show uses a simple transition effect to change from one page to the next. The new page replaces the preceding page by wiping down the screen. This is only one of the many transition effects you can use to change from page to page, though, and you can assign a different transition effect for each page. You also can have the pages advance automatically or have the show run continuously if it will be running as part of a display in a store window, company lobby, or trade show booth.

To change the transition effects of the screen show, choose **S**creen Show from the **V**iew menu and then click E**d**it Effects from the pop-up menu. The Edit Screen Show dialog box appears, as shown in figure 2.21.

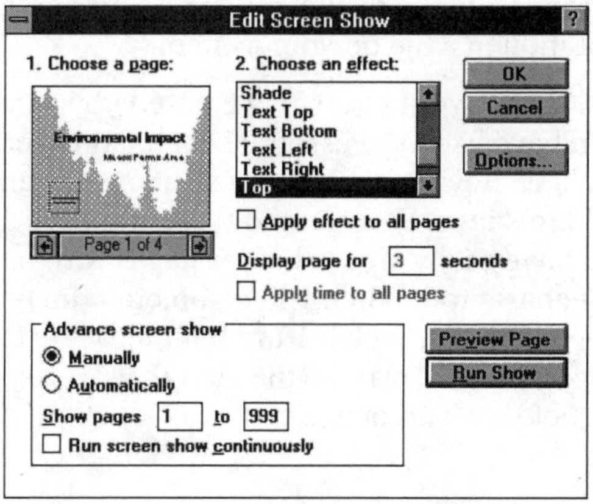

Fig. 2.21

The Edit Screen Show dialog box.

To assign an effect to a page, follow the numbered steps in the Edit Screen Show dialog box. First choose a page by pressing the left- or right-arrow button under the page preview, or by clicking the current page number button and then selecting a page from the list. Then choose an effect from the scrollable list of effects.

For this show, choose page 1 and the Curtains effect. Then choose page 2 and the Fade effect, page 3 and the Checkerboard effect, and page 4 and the Box Out effect.

Click **Au**tomatically under Advance Screen Show and then enter **2** in the **D**isplay Page For *n* Seconds text box. Click the check box next to Apply Time to All Pages.

To see the show, click the **R**un Show button and then sit back and relax.

To improve the show, you may want to try one last technique. In Current Page view, turn to the page with the Executive Summary. Then, from the **P**age menu, choose Cr**e**ate Build. Freelance adds three additional pages to the presentation that gradually build to the Executive Summary page. Next choose **S**creen Show from the **V**iew menu and then choose **E**dit Effects from the pop-out menu. For all four pages that build the Executive Summary, choose the Top effect and then run the Screen Show again. You will see the Executive Summary build point by point during the show.

Saving the Presentation

To make a permanent record of the presentation you have just completed, choose **S**ave from the **F**ile menu. Type **tour** and press Enter to save the presentation in a file on your system.

Congratulations. You have successfully created your first presentation. Even though you have used the essential commands and techniques of presentation making, however, you have seen only a sampling of the many powers of Freelance. You created two text pages and a data chart page. You could have easily created other pages with organization charts and table charts too. When you completed the presentation, you could have used the Spell Check feature built into Freelance to eliminate obvious typographical errors (the kind that are especially obvious when displayed before an audience).

Freelance offers many other features too. By using the drawing tools, you can embellish pages you have created with freehand drawings or with symbols pulled from the extensive symbol library. You can also draw diagrams and illustrations from scratch.

To assist the speaker who will be giving the presentation, you can create speaker notes that display the presentation page on the upper half of a printed page and display speaking topics on the lower half. You can print audience notes to hand out to an audience; the notes show the presentation on the top half of a page but leave the bottom half clear for the audience's notes and doodles. You can also print handout pages that show two-, four-, or six-page miniatures on each printed page. You learn how to accomplish these tasks and many others in the remaining chapters of this book.

Summary

In this quick tour, you had the opportunity to create a short, sample presentation. You completed the essential steps you must follow to create a sequence of presentation pages. In the next chapter, you delve into these basic steps in detail.

Using SmartMaster Sets

The Essential Steps

One solution to your charting and graphing needs is a graphics program that creates a chart and saves it in a file. After you finish a series of files, you have the sequence of visuals required for a presentation, but this approach leaves you with the onus of using a similar design in every chart you create.

Freelance Graphics Release 2.0 for Windows offers a better approach. Instead of creating each chart in a separate file, Freelance produces a series of pages, all in the same file. The pages share a common design that ensures a visual consistency from one end of a presentation to the other. The presentation looks custom-designed rather than thrown together from charts and graphs that you happened to have lying around.

Understanding SmartMaster Sets

The SmartMaster set is the key to the way Freelance works. When you start a Freelance presentation, you select an overall design, or SmartMaster set, for the presentation. Freelance provides 65 of these

SmartMaster sets, designed by professional artists. Each SmartMaster set provides a background design for all the pages in the presentation. One such background design, found in the SmartMaster set called Blocks, shows floating three-dimensional blocks on a blue background, and a rectangle filled with a color wash of blue to black. Figure 3.1 shows the background design of the Blocks SmartMaster set.

Fig. 3.1

The background design of the Blocks SmartMaster set.

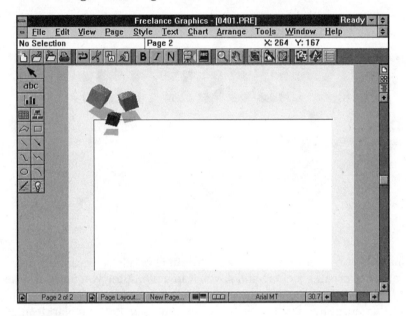

The same SmartMaster set also provides page layouts for all the different page designs you might need. Bulleted List, the page layout for a page with a bullet chart, sets the page title in yellow and places it just to the right of the floating blocks. The Bulleted List page layout also sets the bulleted text items in white and aligns them with the left edge of the rectangular color wash. This page layout is shown in figure 3.2. Bulleted List is just one of the page layouts in the Blocks SmartMaster set. Each set has 11 page layouts and one blank page design.

After you have selected a SmartMaster set, adding a presentation page is simply a matter of selecting a page layout for the type of charts you want to place on the new page and then filling in the blanks with your text and numbers. In other words, the process of creating a Freelance presentation boils down to three basic steps: selecting a SmartMaster set, picking a page layout, and filling in the blanks. These steps are discussed in the following sections. In later chapters, you learn to change the SmartMaster set, modify page layouts, and create the charts and graphs that go on each page.

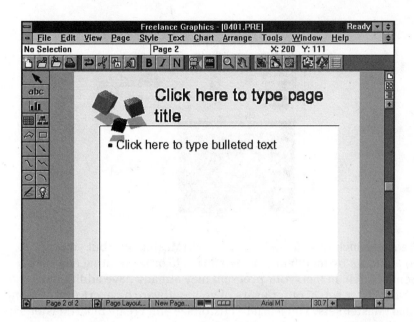

Fig. 3.2

The Bulleted List page layout.

Step 1: Establishing the Presentation Design—Choosing a SmartMaster Set

When you start a new presentation by choosing New from the File menu, Freelance displays the SmartMaster set dialog box. This dialog box, shown in figure 3.3, holds a scrollable, alphabetical list of SmartMaster sets and a preview of the SmartMaster set that is highlighted on the list. The preview enables you to see each design before you choose it. The name of the SmartMaster set being previewed appears just above the preview.

NOTE

If the SmartMaster set dialog box is not displayed when you start a new presentation, the user setup for Freelance has been changed to make a blank page display first. If you see a blank page without the SmartMaster set dialog box, choose Choose **S**martMaster Set from the **S**tyle menu to get the SmartMaster set dialog box; you can then select a SmartMaster set. To learn how to modify the user setup, refer to Chapter 23, "Modifying the Default Settings."

Fig. 3.3

The SmartMaster set dialog box.

Freelance includes 65 ready-made SmartMaster sets, but you can create more by modifying the existing sets or by creating new sets from scratch. In fact, your program may already have additional SmartMaster sets if other users of your software have created custom SmartMaster sets. You learn to customize and create SmartMaster sets in Chapter 21, "Editing SmartMaster Sets."

To find a SmartMaster set you like, click a SmartMaster set name on the list and then examine the preview. To see more SmartMaster sets, use the scroll bar to the right of the list. When you find a SmartMaster set, click OK or press Enter.

TIP

If you know the name of the SmartMaster set you want, you can get to it quickly by pressing the first letter of its name. If you want the SmartMaster set called Circle, for example, press the C key on the keyboard. The first SmartMaster set name that starts with the letter C (CANADA.MAS) is highlighted. CIRCLE.MAS appears just below CANADA.MAS.

One SmartMaster set, called Blank, has a blank background design and simple, unformatted text. To create a completely undesigned presentation, you can select BLANK.MAS from the list or click the **S**martMaster with Blank Background check box. Either way, you get the BLANK.MAS SmartMaster set.

When you examine the SmartMaster set list, you will see that each SmartMaster set has the file extension MAS. If you do not see the SmartMaster set that you need, click **D**irectory and use the options in the Directory dialog box to open the directory where the SmartMaster set that you want is stored. By default, the SmartMaster sets are stored in a subdirectory called MASTERS under the directory in which you have installed Freelance (\FLW).

Step 2: Setting Each Page Design—Picking a Page Layout

After you choose a SmartMaster set, the Choose Page Layout dialog box appears. This dialog box lists the 11 page layouts in the SmartMaster set and gives you the chance to see each layout design. The preview shows the currently highlighted page layout. To see another page layout previewed, you can click its name, or you can click the first name on the list and then scroll down the list with the down-arrow key to preview each page layout. Figure 3.4 shows the 11 page layouts in the BLOCKS.MAS SmartMaster set.

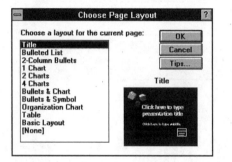

Fig. 3.4

The Choose Page Layout dialog box.

In addition to choosing one of the 11 page layouts, you can choose [None] from the list to work on an absolutely blank page. You might want to draw a diagram with the drawing tools on such a page, for example.

Each page layout, except [None], holds a different arrangement of "Click here..." blocks, which are the keys to the ease of using Freelance. By clicking a "Click here..." block, you can easily add a title, a list of bulleted points, or a chart. You learn about taking advantage of the "Click here..." blocks in the next section of this chapter.

When you decide which page layout you want, double-click its name, or click its name once and press Enter. The page layout appears in the Freelance window.

After you have finished entering the contents of the page (described in the following section), you are ready to add a new page by clicking the New Page button at the bottom of the Freelance window. In the New Page dialog box that appears, you can choose a page layout for the next page as well as enter a page name. The New Page dialog box is shown in figure 3.5.

Fig. 3.5

The New Page dialog box.

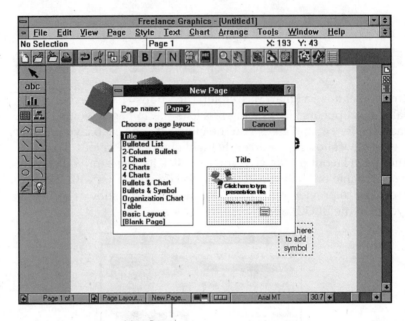

New Page button

Step 3: Filling in the Blanks— Using "Click Here..." Blocks

When you examine the list of page layouts in the New Page dialog box, you see that each page layout contains the background design and a particular arrangement of "Click here..." blocks. The page layout called 1 Chart has a "Click here to type page title" block at the top and a "Click here to create chart" block at the bottom. The page layout called Table has the same "Click here to type page title" block at the top, but it has a "Click here to create table" block at the bottom.

"Click here..." blocks make it easy to add to each page the elements you need. You don't need to remember a command for starting a graph chart, for example. Just click the "Click here to create chart" block, and Freelance automatically launches into chart making.

You are shown a dialog box in which you can select a chart style. Figure 3.6 shows the dialog box you see. Just about any graph chart type that you might want to make is displayed.

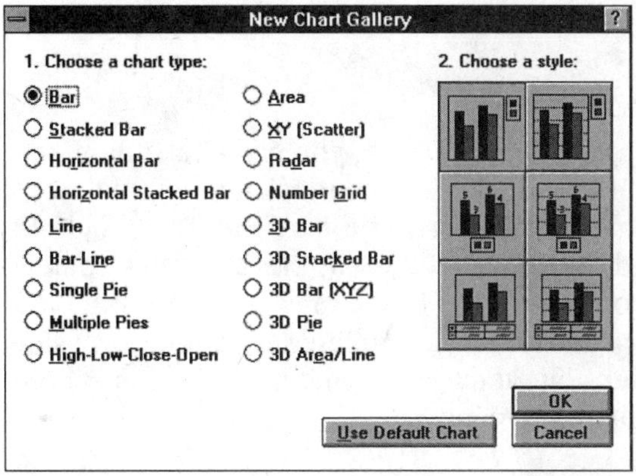

Fig. 3.6

The New Chart Gallery dialog box.

Numbered steps at the top of the dialog box tell you what to do next. Step 1, on the left, instructs you to choose a chart type. You do so by clicking one of the 18 buttons. Samples of the chart type that you select appear at the right. Step 2, on the right, instructs you to choose a style. Simply click one of the buttons on the right. The buttons are a visual menu of six chart styles. Figure 3.7 shows the New Chart Gallery dialog box when the 3D Pie button is selected.

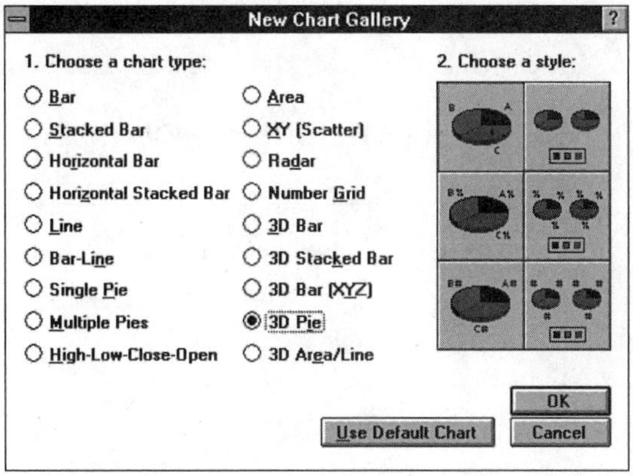

Fig. 3.7

The chart styles available on the right when the 3D Pie button is selected.

After you select a chart type and chart style, click OK or press Enter.

NOTE

Instead of clicking a chart style and chart type with the mouse, you can use the arrow keys to move the highlight to a chart type, tab over to the chart styles, and then use the arrow keys to move the highlight to the style you want. Then press the space bar to "press" the highlighted style button.

If you want to add text to a page, you can click one of the "Click here..." blocks for that text. Just click the block and immediately begin typing. If the block says "Click here to type a page title," click the block, type a page title, and then click a different block or click somewhere else on the page to continue. If the block says "Click here to type bulleted text," click the block and then type bulleted text lines, pressing Enter after each line. After you type the last line, click a different block or click anywhere else on the page.

TIP

After you type text in a text block, you can press the down-arrow key to move to another text block on the same page.

Figure 3.8 shows the Bulleted List page layout as it initially appears. Figure 3.9 shows the page layout after you have typed the page title and begun typing bulleted text lines.

Fig. 3.8

The Bulleted List page layout.

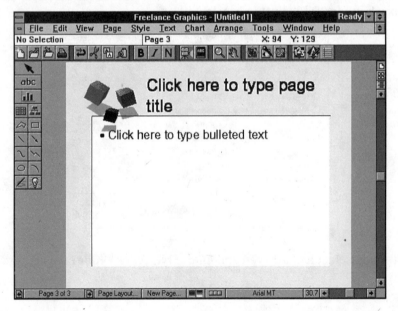

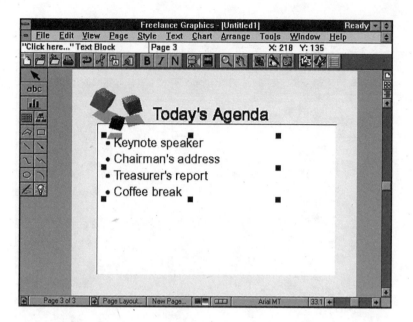

Fig. 3.9

The Bulleted List page after you type a few bulleted text lines.

Adding New Pages to a Presentation

Creating the sequence of pages in a presentation is simply a matter of repeating steps 2 and 3 until you have created as many pages as you need. To start a new page and select a page layout, click the New Page button at the bottom of the window. Then click the "Click here..." blocks to add page titles, bulleted lists, charts, and symbols.

Browsing the Presentation

Freelance offers several ways to access other pages in the presentation. To examine the presentation pages you have already created, press the PgDn key to turn forward a page or press the PgUp key to turn back a page. You also can click the Page Change buttons—the left- and right-arrow symbols next to the Page Number button at the lower-left corner of the Freelance window (see fig. 3.10).

Fig. 3.10

The Freelance window.

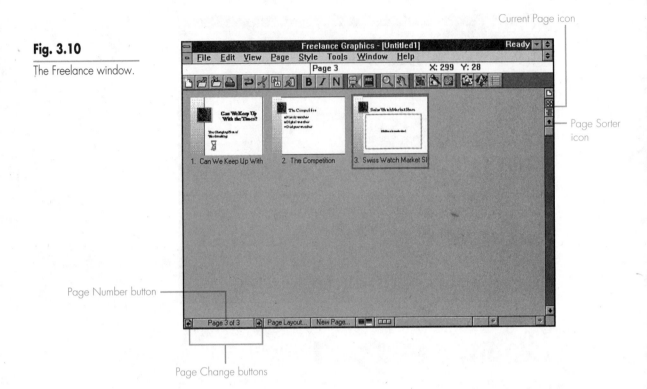

Current Page icon

Page Sorter icon

Page Number button

Page Change buttons

To jump to a specific page in the presentation, click the Current Page icon (see fig. 3.10). When the list of presentation pages appears, click the name of the page you'd like to see.

TIP

Another way to view a specific page is to switch to Page Sorter view, which displays miniatures of the pages in the presentation. To switch to Page Sorter view, click the Page Sorter icon. Then double-click the miniature of the page you want to see. Chapter 5, "Using Page Sorter View," describes Page Sorter view in detail.

Exercise: Creating a Few Presentation Pages

To get a firsthand feel for the three steps described in this chapter, you may want to try this exercise. It will give you a chance to create a short presentation, select a SmartMaster set and page layouts, and even use a few "Click here..." blocks.

In this exercise, you create a three-page presentation for the Watch-makers Association of SpringStadt—a small, picturesque, and entirely fictional mountain village in Switzerland. The presentation will have a title page, a bulleted list, and a page with a chart. You don't actually create the chart, but you set up a page for it.

Creating the Title Page

Begin by starting a new presentation in Freelance. From the **File** menu, choose **New**.

 To start a new presentation, you also can click the File New SmartIcon at the left end of the row of SmartIcons.

TIP

When the Choose a Look for Your Presentation dialog box appears, scroll down the list of SmartMaster sets until you find the SmartMaster set called MARBLE.MAS. Figure 3.11 shows the MARBLE SmartMaster set previewed in the dialog box. Double-click MARBLE.MAS or click OK to load the SmartMaster set.

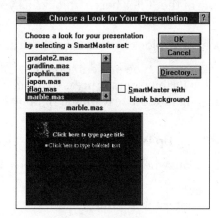

Fig. 3.11

Previewing the MARBLE SmartMaster set.

The Choose Page Layout dialog box then appears. Title is already high-lighted in the list of layouts and appears as a preview within the dialog box. The first page of your presentation will be a title page, so click OK to use the Title page layout on the first page. The Title page layout appears (see fig. 3.12).

Fig. 3.12

The Title page layout on the first presentation page.

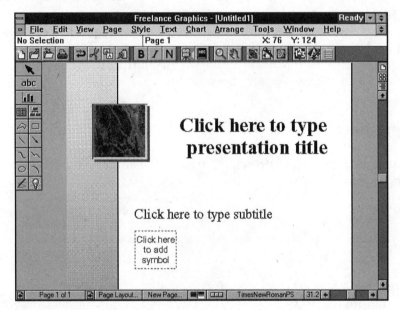

The title page of your presentation shows three "Click here..." blocks: one for the presentation title, one for a subtitle, and one for a symbol. You can use as many of the "Click here..." blocks as you want. If you ignore a block, it will not print or appear in a screen show.

Use the first "Click here..." block by following these steps:

1. Click the "Click here to type presentation title" block. A text entry box opens with a flashing cursor pressed against the right side of the box (indicating that the text will be right-aligned within the box).

2. Type **Can We Keep Up With the Times?**

3. Click OK or click anywhere outside the text box. The title appears on the page.

   Now it's time to enter the subtitle.

4. Click the "Click here to type subtitle" block.

5. Type **The Changing Face of Watchmaking** in the text box that opens.

6. Click OK or click anywhere outside the text box. The subtitle appears on the page. Ordinarily, you might take a moment to format the title so that it does not word-wrap to a second line, but you learn about formatting text in another chapter.

Finally, you add a symbol to complete the page.

7. Click the "Click here to add symbol" block. The Add Symbol to Page dialog box opens.

8. Select TIME.SYM from the list of symbol categories, as shown in figure 3.13.

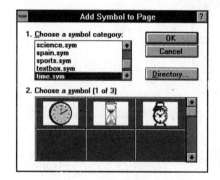

Fig. 3.13

The Add Symbol to Page dialog box.

9. Double-click the symbol of an hourglass, or click it once and click OK. The hourglass symbol appears on the page, as shown in figure 3.14.

The title page is now complete. To create the next page—a bullet chart—click the New Page button at the bottom of the Freelance window.

Adding a Bullet Chart Page

When you click the New Page button, the New Page dialog box appears. Selecting the next page layout is easy. Follow these steps:

1. From the list of layouts, select Bulleted List and click OK. You see two "Click here..." blocks on the bulleted list page.

2. Click "Click here to type page title."

3. Type **The Competition**.

Fig. 3.14

The completed title page.

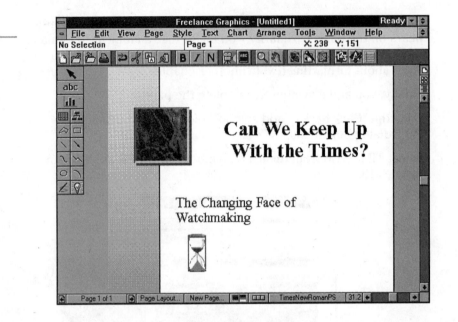

4. Press the down-arrow key to move to the "Click here to type bulleted text" block. The cursor is positioned next to the first bullet.

5. Type **Plastic watches** and press Enter.

6. Type **Digital watches** and press Enter.

7. Type **Designer watches**.

8. Click anywhere else on the page or click OK to finish entering the bulleted list.

Now you are ready to add the final page—the page for a graph chart.

Adding a Graph Chart Page

Click the New Page button to start a third page. Then follow these steps to add a graph chart page:

1. Select the 1 Chart page layout from the New Page dialog box. The 1 Chart page has only two "Click here..." blocks, one for a page title and one for a chart.

2. Click "Click here to type page title."

3. Type **Swiss Watch Market Share**.

4. Click OK.

If you were ready to create the chart on page 3, you would click the "Click here to create chart" block; Freelance then would guide you in the process of creating a graph chart. The chart would show how the market share of classic Swiss watches had fared against the new up-start competition of the last few years. You learn about creating graph charts in Chapter 6, "Adding a Data Chart."

Viewing the Entire Presentation

To examine miniatures of the presentation pages, click the Page Sorter icon on the right side of the Freelance window.

Notice that the three presentation pages share a common design and common text colors. The SmartMaster set ensures the consistency you see. Figure 3.15 shows the Page Sorter view of the presentation. To return to working on a single page, double-click any of the miniatures, or click any miniature once and then click the Current Page icon. You find more information about the many tasks you can accomplish in Page Sorter view in Chapter 5, "Using Page Sorter View."

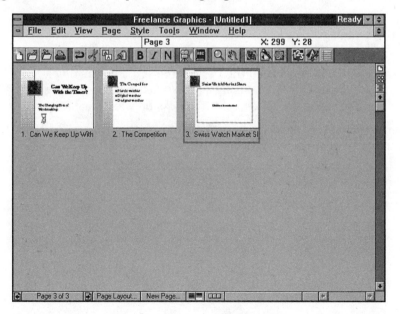

Fig. 3.15

The presentation in Page Sorter view.

To continue creating the presentation, you add new pages one by one, select a page layout for each, and continue clicking the "Click here..." blocks to add the text and graphs you need.

Saving the Presentation

You can save the sample presentation by following these steps:

1. From the **File** menu, choose Save **As**.

2. Enter a file name, containing one to eight characters, for the presentation. Freelance adds a PRE file extension at the end of the file name.

3. Click OK.

You can confirm that the presentation is saved by examining the title bar at the top of the window. The new presentation name should appear next to the window name (Freelance Graphics).

You can abandon the presentation by choosing **Close** from the **File** menu. Choose **No** when Freelance displays the prompt Do you want to save window before closing?

Summary

In this chapter, you learned the basic three steps in creating a Freelance presentation: choosing a SmartMaster set, selecting page layouts, and using the "Click here..." blocks on each page.

The next chapters describe how to customize the text and graphic charts you create on each page.

Making Basic Changes to the Presentation

After you have accomplished the steps described in the preceding chapter (selecting a SmartMaster set, choosing page layouts, and using the "Click here..." blocks), the presentation you obtain is likely to meet your basic needs. No presentation is perfect after the first go-around, however. You probably will notice editing corrections that should be made, pages that could benefit from page subtitles, and charts and bulleted lists that would look a little better if they were repositioned on the pages. You may even decide that a different SmartMaster set would give a presentation a more desirable look. The minor revisions, adjustments, and formatting changes your presentation may need are the subject of this chapter.

Naming the Pages

When you click the Page Number button at the lower-left corner of the Freelance window, a list of page names appears. Freelance gets these names from the page titles unless you enter a specific name for a page. If you have not yet entered a page name or a page title, the page is labeled Unnamed.

You can enter your own page names in two ways. To first create a page, you click the New Page button and choose a page layout. When the New Page dialog box opens, the new page name is highlighted, as shown in figure 4.1. Simply type a page name into the **P**age Name text box before choosing a page layout. Remember that when text is highlighted in Windows, typing something replaces what is highlighted. When the page layout you've chosen appears on-screen, the new page name appears in the list of page names and in the status bar.

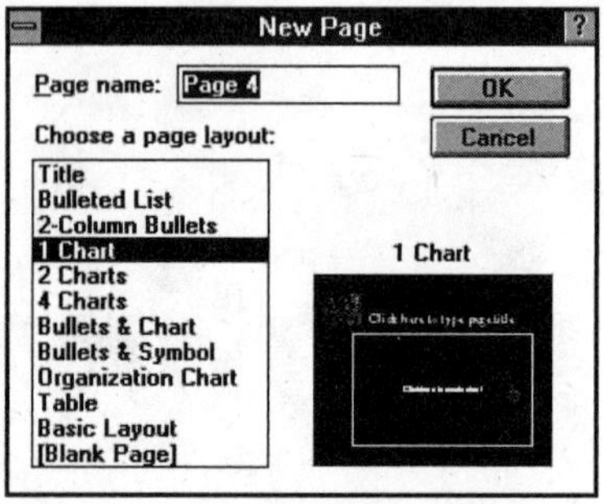

Fig. 4.1

The page name highlighted when the New Page dialog box opens.

To change the name of a page, view the page and then drag across the current name in the edit line to highlight it. Type a new name and either press Enter or click the green check mark button. The new name then immediately appears in the edit line and in the list of page names, as shown in figure 4.2.

Changing SmartMaster Sets

After you create a presentation, you may decide that a different SmartMaster set would give it a better look. A slightly more conservative design might befit a particular presentation, or the SmartMaster set created for a new client could be applied to an old presentation to make it look custom-tailored.

Changing the SmartMaster set for a presentation is easy. Simply follow these steps:

1. From the **S**tyle menu, choose Choose **S**martMaster Set.

2. Choose a SmartMaster set from within the Choose SmartMaster Set dialog box (see fig. 4.3). Click once on a SmartMaster set name to preview it, or double-click the name to choose it.

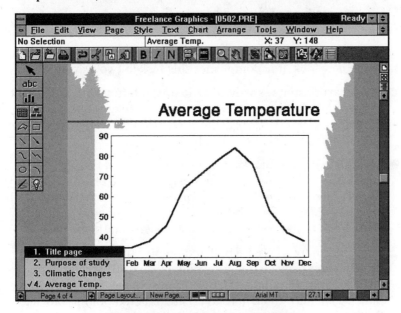

Fig. 4.2

The new page name in both the edit line and the list of names.

Fig. 4.3

The Choose SmartMaster Set dialog box.

After a moment, the presentation is reformatted according to the design of the new SmartMaster set. The text fonts, the colors, and the placement of objects on the pages change.

TIP

If the Choose SmartMaster Set SmartIcon has been added to the SmartIcon palette, you can click the icon rather than choose Choose **S**martMaster Set from the **S**tyle menu.

Changing the SmartMaster set for a presentation gives the overall presentation a new look. It accomplishes this task in two ways:

- The SmartMaster set provides the presentation with a different background design, which can include a background color, graphic shapes, a drawing, and even a company logo. A variation of the background is used for the title page.

- The "Click here..." blocks in the page layouts of the new SmartMaster set have different designs for the text and charts you have created on the page. The corresponding page layouts in the new SmartMaster set take over; the new "Click here..." blocks change the fonts, colors, and chart designs on the pages.

  The "Click here to create bulleted points" block in the new Bulleted List page layout, for example, gives the bulleted points yellow text at 14 points, the New Times Roman font, and white bullets. The old "Click here to create bulleted points" block in the Bulleted List page layout gave the bulleted points white text at 16 points, the Arial font, and cyan bullets. Each new page layout affects all the pages with the corresponding old page layout. The new 1 Chart page layout redesigns all pages that use the old 1 Chart page layout, the new Organization Chart page layout redesigns the old Organization Chart page layout pages, and so on.

In addition to applying different designs to the objects you have created from "Click here..." blocks, the new page layouts try to reposition any objects you move. If you have already moved objects created from "Click here..." blocks when you attempt to switch SmartMaster sets, Freelance displays the warning message shown in figure 4.4. If you move the page title on any page or change the position of a chart, for example, this warning message appears.

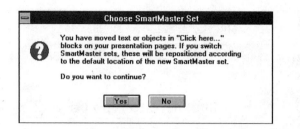

Fig. 4.4

Freelance warns that moved objects will be repositioned.

This warning informs you that Freelance will reposition moved objects when you change SmartMaster sets. The program places all objects in the default positions predetermined by the new SmartMaster set. If you have moved objects to accomplish a specific arrangement, they are moved again by the new SmartMaster set, and your arrangement may be spoiled. To let Freelance rearrange the objects and apply the new SmartMaster set, click Yes within the message box. The result is a default presentation with everything on the pages arranged the way the particular SmartMaster set requires it to be. To leave the existing SmartMaster set and preserve the custom arrangements you have created, click No. Unfortunately, you cannot both change SmartMaster sets and preserve your custom page arrangements.

Changing Page Layouts

In addition to changing the overall design of the presentation by changing SmartMaster sets, you can change a particular presentation page by choosing another page layout for it. The new page layout contains a different combination of "Click here..." blocks that can apply other formatting to the existing text and charts created from "Click here..." blocks.

A page can have the Bulleted List page layout, for example, but only two "Click here..." blocks (see fig. 4.5). To change the design so that the page contains both a bulleted list and a chart, you can change the page layout to Bullets & Chart. The new page layout has three "Click here..." blocks; the "Click here to type bulleted points" block is now positioned on the left half of the page, leaving room for the "Click here to create chart" block on the right (see fig. 4.6). Figures 4.7 and 4.8 show the effects of two different page layouts on a page.

Fig. 4.5

The Bulleted List page
layout.

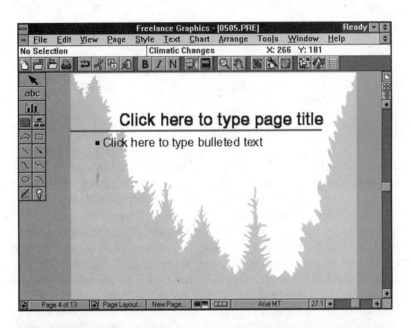

Fig. 4.6

The Bullets & Chart
page layout.

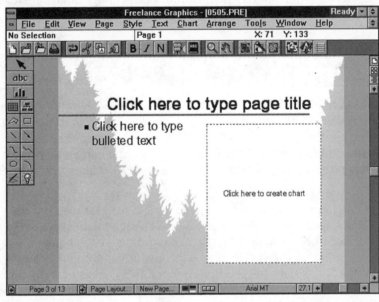

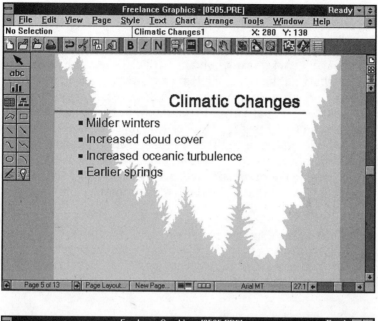

Fig. 4.7

The Bulleted List page layout with data.

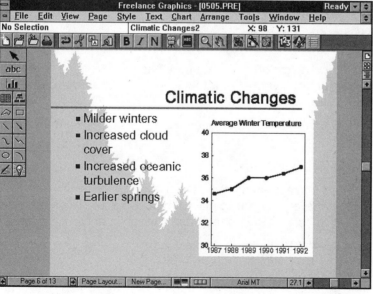

Fig. 4.8

The Bullets & Chart page layout with data.

To change the layout of a page, click the Page Layout button at the bottom of the Freelance window and then choose a different page layout from the Choose Page Layout dialog box.

If the new page layout doesn't contain a "Click here..." block for a block of text or a chart on the page, the text or chart remains in its current position with its current formatting. If you've created a bullet chart with the Bulleted List page layout and you want to change the chart to the Organization Chart page layout, for example, the new page will still display the bulleted points in their original position but also will include a "Click here to create organization chart" block. You may need to manually resize the organization chart that you make so that it doesn't overlay an area taken by the bulleted points.

TIP

If you do not see the Organization Chart and Table Chart page layouts on the list of available layouts, you may be using a SmartMaster set from the earlier release of Freelance Graphics for Windows, Release 1.0. SmartMaster sets provided with Release 2.0 include all the layouts.

Editing Text

You can edit any text on a presentation page—correcting or deleting text that is already entered or adding new text to existing blocks. To edit text, follow these steps:

1. To select the block, click once on the text block containing the text.

2. Pause a split second.

3. When a box appears around the text block, click again on the text block where you want to place a typing cursor. The typing cursor will be placed at the point of text closest to the arrow cursor.

Figures 4.9 and 4.10 illustrate these steps.

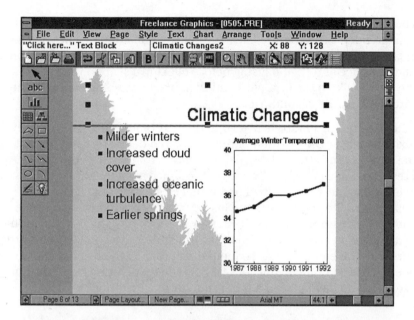

Fig. 4.9

Clicking a text block to
edit the text.

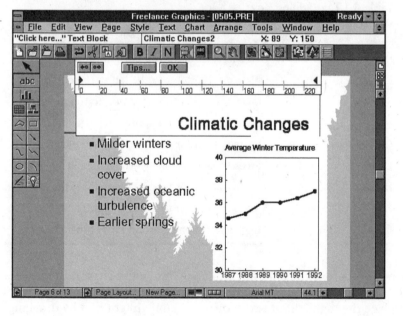

Fig. 4.10

Clicking again to place
a typing cursor.

The split-second pause in step 2 is to ensure that Freelance knows that you intended two separate clicks rather than one double-click. Double-clicking on most text blocks brings up the Paragraph Styles dialog box. Clicking once and then pausing before clicking a second time selects the text block on the first click and then places a typing cursor in the text block on the second click.

When the typing cursor is placed in the text block, you can enter new text, starting at the position of the cursor. To delete text to the right of the cursor, press the Del key. To delete text to the left of the cursor, press the Backspace key. To toggle Freelance from insert mode to overtype mode so that typed text replaces existing text rather than pushes it to the right, press the Ins key once. To add new text to the end of the text block, move the cursor to the end of the last line of the text and begin typing. You can press the End key to quickly "jump" the cursor to the end of a line. To jump the cursor to the beginning of a line, press the Home key. Table 4.1 lists the text-editing keys you can use after you have placed a typing cursor in a text block.

Table 4.1 Text-Editing Keys

Key(s)	Action
Del	Deletes a character to the right of the cursor
Backspace	Deletes a character to the left of the cursor
→	Moves the cursor one position to the right
←	Moves the cursor one position to the left
Ctrl+→	Moves the cursor one word to the right
Ctrl+←	Moves the cursor one word to the left
Home	Moves the cursor to the beginning of the line
End	Moves the cursor to the end of the line
Ins	Toggles between insert and overtype modes

When you press the Shift key while you move the cursor, the text that the cursor passes across is highlighted. You can then type new text to replace the highlighted text. You also can highlight text by dragging across it with the mouse.

The easiest way to replace a page title is to click it once to select it, click again at the beginning of the line, press Shift+End to highlight the entire line, and then type a new title. Click elsewhere on the page to finish editing the text block.

You can edit text in any of the text blocks created from "Click here..." text blocks. You can also use the same steps to edit the text in tables, organization charts, and graph charts.

You also can click a text block once and then press the F2 key to edit the text in the text block. Yet another approach is to right-click a text block and then choose Edit from the pop-up commands menu.

Changing the Size and Font of Text Blocks

Freelance offers several methods to change the size and font of text in text blocks. You can use the Text Font and Text Size buttons, or you can access the Font dialog box. These methods are described in the following sections.

Using the Text Font and Text Size Buttons

The easiest way to change the entire text block is to select it and then use the Text Font and Size buttons in the status bar at the bottom of the Freelance window. To use this method, follow these steps:

1. Click once on the text block to select it.

2. Click either the Text Font button or the Text Size button.

3. From the pop-up list of options, select the text font or text size you want.

When you select a text block, the name of the current font of the selected text appears on the Text Font button. The Text Size button displays the current point size of the text. When you click the Text Font button, you see a list of alternative fonts for the selected block. If you have installed more fonts in Windows than can fit in the pop-up menu, you must click **M**ore Fonts on the pop-up menu to get a larger, scrollable list of fonts in the More Fonts dialog box.

Figure 4.11 shows a sample pop-up menu that appears when you click the Text Font button. Figure 4.12 shows the scrollable list that appears in the More Fonts dialog box when you click **M**ore Fonts.

Fig. 4.11

The text font pop-up menu that appears when you click the Text Font button.

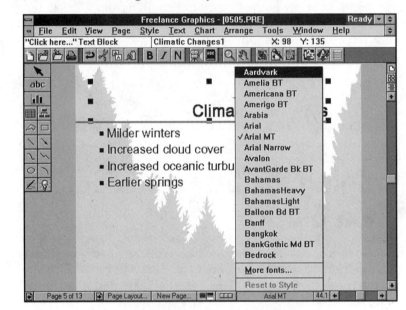

Fig. 4.12

The More Fonts dialog box.

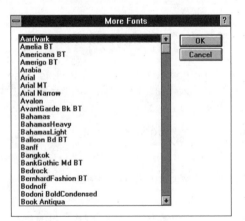

Figure 4.13 shows a sample pop-up menu that appears when you click the Text Size button. The current point size of the selected text appears in brackets next to the word Size on the menu. If the point size that you want does not appear on the list, click Size to display the Text Size Other dialog box. In this dialog box, you can enter the point size you want. Figure 4.14 shows the dialog box that appears when you click Size.

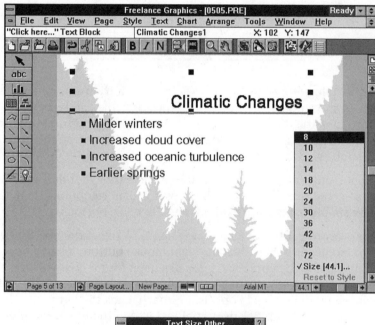

Fig. 4.13

The text size pop-up menu that appears when you click the Text Size button.

Fig. 4.14

The Text Size Other dialog box.

You can use the same buttons to change the font or size of only part of the text in a text block. Simply highlight only the text that you want to change before you click the Text Font or Text Size button. To highlight the text, drag the mouse cursor across it, or hold down the Shift key while using the keyboard to move the cursor across the text.

Using the Font Dialog Box

A second way to choose a different font and point size for text is to select the text and then choose Font from the Text menu. The Font dialog box appears (see fig. 4.15).

Fig. 4.15

The Font dialog box.

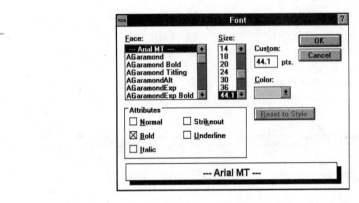

The Font dialog box enables you to select a font from a scrollable list of typefaces and a point size from a second scrollable list. A preview at the bottom of the dialog box shows the selected font (but not the selected point size). If the point size that you want is not on the list, you can type the size in the Custom text box.

The Font dialog box also allows you to change the color and attributes of the selected text. This dialog box gives you more options than you have by simply using the Text Font and Text Size buttons.

Another way to get to the Font dialog box is to select the text that you want to modify and then click the right mouse button. A small pop-up menu displaying the commands you use most frequently with text then appears (see fig. 4.16). Among those commands is Font, which leads to the same Font dialog box. For this approach, click the left mouse button to select the text block or partial text within the block and then click the right mouse button to get the pop-up commands menu.

If more than one text block is selected and the blocks have different fonts and sizes, the font is listed as Mixed, and the point size also is Mixed when you bring up the Font dialog box. Choosing a different font or point size changes all the selected text blocks simultaneously.

TIP

If the Change Font SmartIcon has been added to the SmartIcon palette, you can click that icon after you select text. The Font dialog box then appears.

Changing the font and size of text overrides the text font and size that is determined by the SmartMaster set. The changes are preserved even when you apply a different SmartMaster set to the presentation.

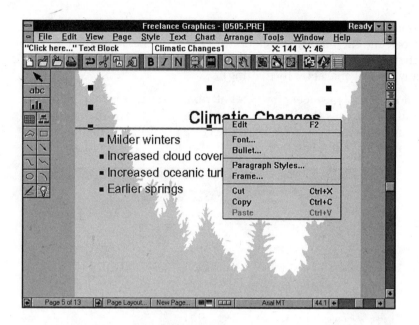

Fig. 4.16

The pop-up commands menu for text.

Changing the Character Attributes of Text

To give text special emphasis, you may want to apply character formatting to it—making it bold, underlined, or italicized. As usual, Freelance offers several ways to accomplish this. The easiest way is to highlight the text to be formatted and then use one of the character-attributes accelerator keys. Table 4.2 lists these keys.

Table 4.2 Character-Attributes Accelerator Keys

Key(s)	Description
Ctrl+B	Bold text
Ctrl+I	Italic text
Ctrl+U	Underlined text
Ctrl+N	Normal text (no bold, italic, or underlined)

Remember that you must first select a text block or select text within a block and then use the accelerator keys. To remove all the character attributes you've applied to text, use Ctrl+N (Normal is the absence of any special character formatting).

Another way to select character attributes for text is to select the text and then access the **Text** menu, which lists all the available attributes. Simply choose one of the attributes directly from the menu. Figure 4.17 shows the **Text** menu.

Fig. 4.17

The **T**ext menu showing the character attribute options.

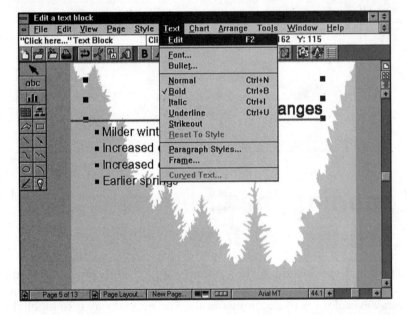

The character attribute options are available in the Font dialog box also. To get this dialog box, choose **F**ont from the Text menu, or right-click on the selected text and then choose Font from the common commands pop-up menu. When you use the Font dialog box, you also can choose Strikeout, which draws a horizontal strikeout line through the text.

Yet another way to apply character attributes is to select the text and then use the Text Normal, Text Bold, Text Italic, and Text Underline SmartIcons.

TIP

The character attributes that you apply to text will be preserved even if you change SmartMaster sets. You can italicize a word in a page title, for example, and the word remains highlighted after you choose a different SmartMaster set.

Justifying Text

Another easy change that you can make in a presentation is to change the justification of a text block. Most page titles are left-aligned, for example, but you can easily center or right-align a title to change the look of a page.

The fastest way to change justification is to select the text block and then press Ctrl+L to left-align the block, Ctrl+R to right-align the block, or Ctrl+E to center the block. All text within the text block will be affected. You can even select more than one block and use these accelerator keys to affect all the selected blocks simultaneously. Figure 4.18 shows the same text block with the three different justification settings.

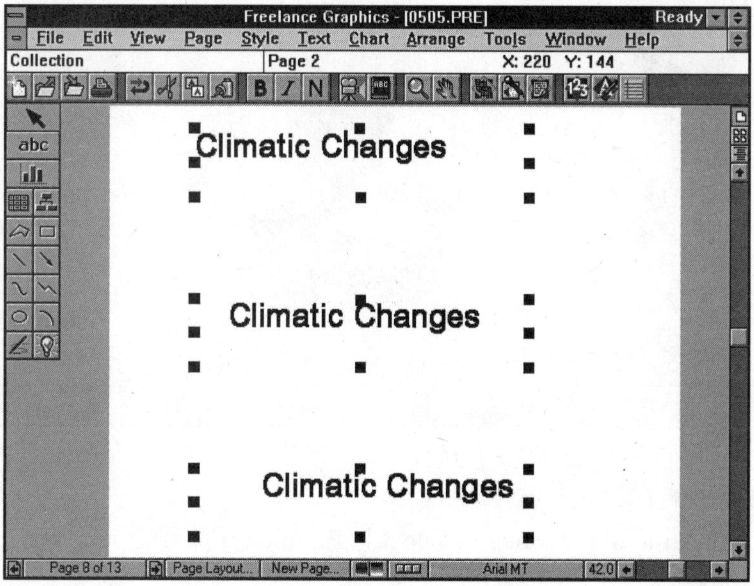

Fig. 4.18

A text block with different justification settings.

Text justification settings, unlike character attribute settings, override only the current SmartMaster set. If you change SmartMaster sets, the new SmartMaster set will have jurisdiction over the justification of all text blocks. Any justification changes you have made will be lost.

Moving and Resizing Objects

You may want to reposition and resize the objects you've created from "Click here..." blocks. In Freelance, it's simply a matter of selecting which object to move or resize and then using the object's handles.

Handles are the eight small squares that appear in a rectangle around objects. Four handles appear at the corners of the rectangle and four appear at the sides. Figure 4.19 shows the handles that appear around a selected text block.

Fig. 4.19

The handles surrounding a text block.

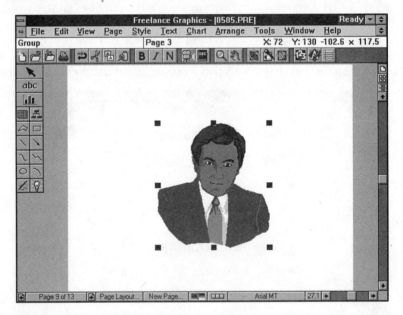

To move an object, follow these steps:

1. Click the object once to select it. Handles appear around the object.

2. Place the cursor anywhere within the rectangle formed by the handles.

3. Click and hold down the left mouse button and then drag the mouse.

4. Release the mouse button when the object is at the new position.

As you move the mouse, a dashed box moves on the page to indicate where the block will drop when you release the mouse button. Figure 4.20 displays such a box.

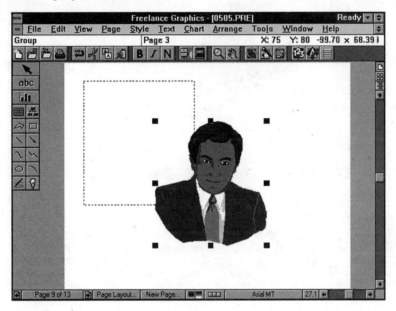

Fig. 4.20

Moving an object.

To resize an object, follow these steps:

1. Click the object once to select it. Handles appear around the object.

2. Place the point of the cursor on one of the handles.

3. Click and hold down the left mouse button and then drag the mouse.

4. Release the mouse button when the object is correctly resized.

To stretch an object horizontally, use a handle at the right or left side of the object. To stretch an object vertically, use a handle at the top or bottom of the object. To stretch the corner of an object diagonally, use a handle at a corner of the object. Figure 4.21 demonstrates an object that is being stretched by its corner handle.

Fig. 4.21

Stretching an object by
its corner handle.

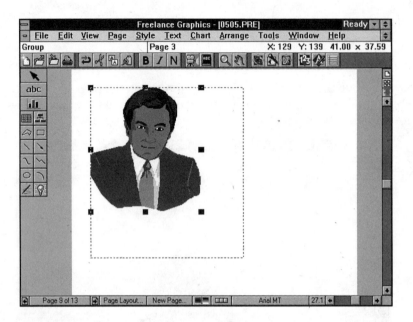

 TIP

To resize an object without changing its shape, press and hold down
the Shift key while dragging a corner handle. The object will resize
proportionately.

Duplicating "Click here..." Blocks

Page layouts come with a preset number and arrangement of "Click
here..." blocks, but sometimes you may need an extra block to complete a page. A second "Click here..." text block at the top of the page
can provide a page subtitle, for example.

After you have filled in an existing "Click here..." block by clicking it and
then creating the text or graphic chart, you can drag away the text or
chart that results from the block and leave behind a duplicate of the
original "Click here..." block. Follow these steps:

1. Press and hold down the Ctrl key.

2. Place the mouse pointer on text or a chart created from a "Click here..." block and then click and hold down the mouse button.

3. With the button still pressed, move the mouse, dragging away a duplicate of the block. Now you can click the original "Click here..." block to add another text block or chart to the page.

As you begin dragging away the object created from the "Click here..." block, a dashed rectangle appears along the border of the block. Figure 4.22 shows this rectangle. As soon as the cursor passes outside the rectangle, the rectangle disappears. While the cursor remains within this boundary of control, the original "Click here..." block determines the positioning of the object. When you release the mouse button, the text or graph snaps back to its original position. You must move the cursor outside the rectangle and release the mouse button to drop the object in a new position. When the cursor moves outside the rectangle, the original block returns the control of the object to you.

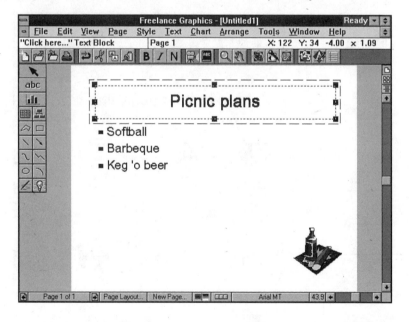

Fig. 4.22

The boundary of control of a "Click here..." block.

The text or chart that you drag away from a text block retains its formatting, and the additional text or chart created from the "Click here..." block gets the same formatting.

Understanding how "Click here..." blocks control the formatting and positioning of objects within their reach will help you as you create presentations. Not only can you use these blocks to create objects, but you also can use them to format objects you have already created. After you add text to a page, for example, you can drag the text within the boundaries of a "Click here..." text block, and the text is formatted and positioned by the "Click here..." block. You can delete a page title created by filling in a "Click here to type page title" block, for example, and then move another text object on top of the original "Click here..." block. As soon as the cursor moves within the rectangle of the "Click here..." block, the block formats and positions the text object, and the text snaps into place as a title. Figures 4.23 and 4.24 show a text object before and after it has been dragged onto a page title "Click here..." block.

Fig. 4.23

Text to be dragged onto a page title "Click here..." block.

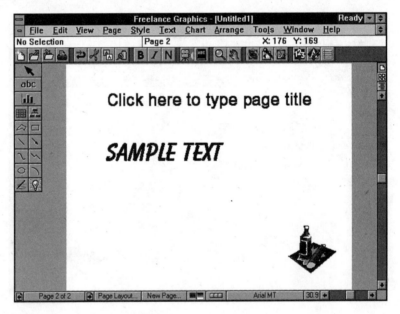

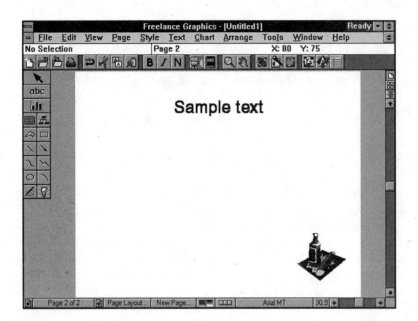

Fig. 4.24

Text dragged onto a page title "Click here..." block.

Changing the Attributes of Objects

The text, tables, and charts that you create for presentation pages are a combination of their contents and the attributes that govern their appearance (the *content* is what's in them, and the *attributes* are how they look). When you first create an object, you have the opportunity to supply its content, but the appearance attributes are contributed by the SmartMaster set. You can change the attributes that determine an object's appearance, however, and override the attributes selected by the SmartMaster set. Changing the attributes of an object is usually just a matter of double-clicking.

To change the attributes of simple objects like text, a table, or a graphic object drawn with a drawing tool, double-click the object rather than click it once. An Attributes dialog box appears, displaying controls that govern the object's appearance. Figure 4.25 shows the Attributes dialog box with attribute controls for a drawn circle or an ellipse.

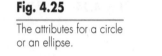

Two more complex objects—graph and organization charts—are composed of many parts. You must first select the part of the chart that you want to change before double-clicking to bring up an Attributes dialog box. To select a particular part of the chart, click that part; both the chart part and the entire chart are then selected. (A selected part of a selected chart has a second, smaller set of handles around it.) Figure 4.26 shows the result of clicking the top box of an organization chart. Notice that large handles appear around the entire organization chart; smaller handles appear around the top box. To access the Attributes dialog box for the selected top box, double-click the box. The Attributes dialog box for the selected box is shown in figure 4.27.

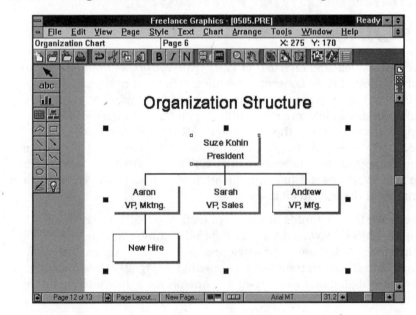

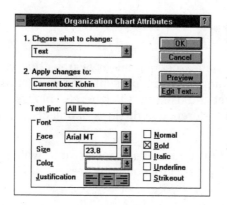

Fig. 4.27

The Attributes dialog box for the selected box in the chart.

Similarly, you can click a pie chart slice to select the entire pie and also select one slice. To select a different slice, click that slice. When you double-click a selected slice, the Attributes dialog box for a pie slice appears, as shown in figure 4.28.

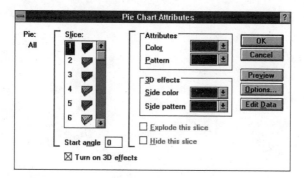

Fig. 4.28

The Attributes dialog box for a pie slice.

In addition to clicking individual pie slices, you can click any of the slice labels or percentages to select all the labels or percentages. When you double-click one of these, an Attributes dialog box for the selected chart part appears.

Other graph chart types have even more parts. You can select many different parts of a bar chart, for example.

Summary

In this chapter, you learned a number of steps that you may want to take after examining the basic presentation you get when you apply a SmartMaster set and use the "Click here..." blocks. These steps make a dramatic difference in the look of objects you've placed on the pages.

The next chapter introduces Page Sorter view, which provides a way to gain an overall perspective on your presentation and make still more changes.

Using Page Sorter View

Viewing pages one at a time gives you the detailed scrutiny necessary to hone the presentation to perfection. But it doesn't give you a sense of the overall flow of a presentation. That's why Freelance Graphics for Windows includes Page Sorter view, which displays the pages of your presentation on the screen as miniatures.

Page Sorter view displays as many miniature pages as can fit in the Freelance window. Each page looks just as it does when examined in Current Page view, complete with text, graphics, and the background provided by the SmartMaster set.

Viewing the sequence of pages in a presentation is only one of the benefits provided by Page Sorter view. You also can rearrange the order of pages, apply a new SmartMaster set and change page layouts, and duplicate pages that are especially useful or remove pages that are no longer necessary.

TIP

Arranging the Page Sorter views of two presentations side by side is excellent for copying pages from one presentation to another. You'll learn how in Chapter 17, "Managing Presentations."

This chapter covers all you can do in Page Sorter view.

Understanding the Three Presentation Views

Page Sorter view is only one of three views of the content of a presentation:

- Current Page view displays a single page in the Freelance window. To see the next page, press the Page Down (PgDn) key. This view lets you work in detail on a single page. Figure 5.1 displays a page in Current Page view.

- Page Sorter view displays as many miniature pages of the presentation as will fit in the Freelance window. This view enables you to see all or most of the pages at once, rearrange the order of pages, duplicate pages, and remove pages you no longer need. You cannot work with the objects on pages, though. Figure 5.2 displays a presentation in Page Sorter view.

- Outliner view displays the text of the presentation in outline form. You can easily create and organize the text content of the presentation, checking and correcting the flow of ideas. Figure 5.3 displays the same presentation in Outliner view.

Switching from one view to another gives different perspectives on the presentation and allows you to perform different actions.

Fig. 5.1

A page from a presentation in Current Page view.

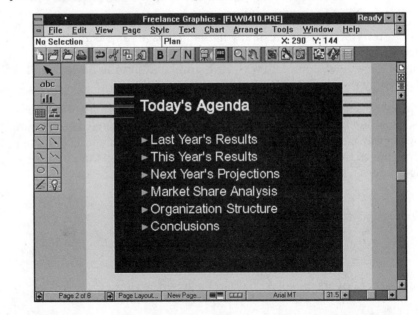

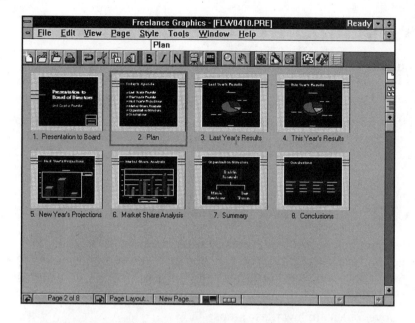

Fig. 5.2

The presentation in Page Sorter view.

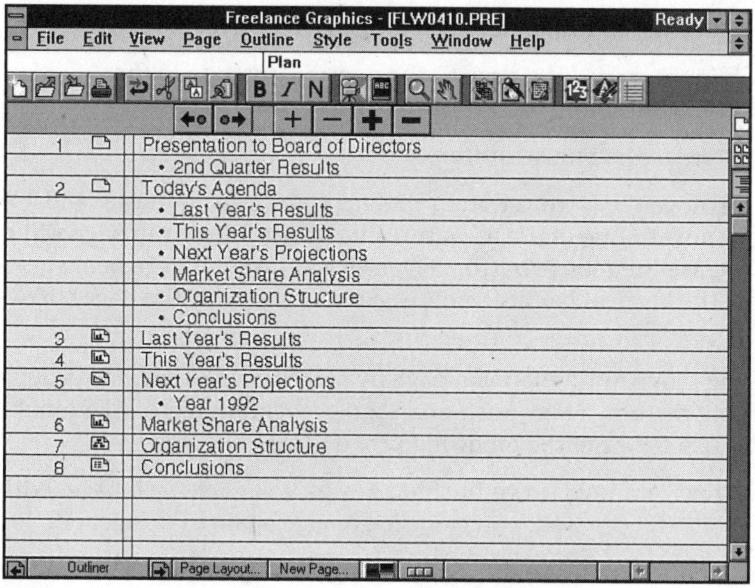

Fig. 5.3

The same presentation in Outliner view.

Switching to Page Sorter View

You can change to Page Sorter view any time by clicking the Page sorter icon at the right edge of the Freelance window. An alternative path to Page Sorter view is to choose **P**age Sorter from the **V**iew menu.

In Page Sorter view, Freelance draws the entire presentation in miniature pages. If you cannot see all the pages in the current presentation, use the scroll bar at the right to scroll down to the next set of pages.

Rearranging the Order of Pages

One common use for Page Sorter view is to rearrange the order of pages in the presentation. You may decide to cover a topic earlier in a presentation, and Page Sorter view provides an easy way to move the corresponding page.

To move a page, follow these steps:

1. Place the mouse pointer on the page to move.

2. Click and drag the page to the desired position in the presentation.

3. Release the mouse button.

As you move the page, a dotted outline of the page appears, and a vertical bar next to one of the miniatures indicates where the page will go if you release the mouse button. Figure 5.4 shows the page being moved. Notice the vertical bar at the chosen destination for the page (between pages 2 and 3).

You can move more than one page by selecting multiple pages before dragging them to a new position in the presentation. To select multiple pages, use either of the following procedures:

■ Press and hold down the Shift key as you click each page. With Shift still pressed, you can click a page again to deselect it.

■ Use the pointer to draw a box that entirely encloses the pages you want in the group. To draw the box, move the cursor to the corner of an imaginary rectangle that would surround the group, hold down the left mouse button, and then move the cursor diagonally to the far corner of the rectangle. When you release the mouse button, all pages entirely within the rectangle you created are selected. Figure 5.5 demonstrates the drawing of a rectangle to select a group of pages.

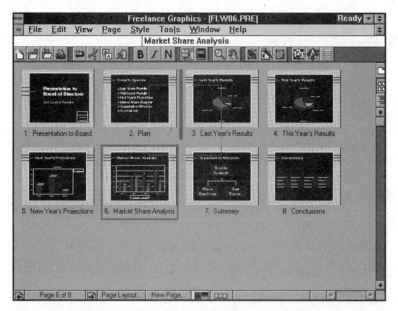

Fig. 5.4

Moving a page in Page Sorter view.

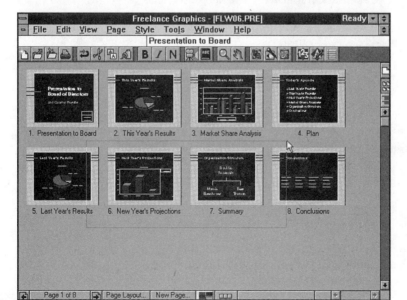

Fig. 5.5

Using the pointer to draw a rectangle around multiple pages.

To add more pages to the group, hold down the Shift key and click each page one by one. After you've selected multiple pages, place the cursor on any page, hold down the left mouse button, and move the cursor to the new position for the pages in the presentation.

Duplicating a Page

Another easy task to accomplish in Page Sorter view is to duplicate a page. Suppose that you need a series of pie charts, all alike except for one of the slices. Or perhaps you have created on a page a special diagram that you want to repeat at the start of each new section of a presentation. After you have created a model page in Current Page view, switch to Page Sorter view, copy the page, and then paste it back into the presentation as many times as necessary.

To duplicate a page in Page Sorter view, follow these steps:

1. Select a page or pages. (Click the page or pages.)

2. Press Ctrl+C or Ctrl+Ins to copy the page.

3. Click the page that the duplicate(s) should follow.

4. Press Ctrl+V or Shift+Ins to paste the duplicate(s) into the presentation following the selected page.

TIP

Another way to duplicate a page is to select the page and then either choose **D**uplicate from the **P**age menu or press Alt+F7. You can use the **D**uplicate command in Current Page view too.

Changing SmartMaster Sets and Page Layouts in Page Sorter View

Page Sorter view is useful for seeing the effects of different Smart-Master sets on a presentation. While in Page Sorter view, you can use the Choose **S**martMaster Set command on the **S**tyle menu to select a different SmartMaster set. You'll see the new SmartMaster set revise every page in the presentation, and you can easily spot particular pages that need special attention without having to peruse the presentation a page at a time.

You can even change the page layout for a page by selecting the page and then using the Page Layout button at the bottom of the Freelance window. You can decide to add a second chart to a page by clicking the page, clicking the Page Layout button, and then choosing the 2 Charts layout from the Choose Page Layout dialog box.

Examining a Page in Current Page View

To return to Current Page view and examine one page closely, you can use any of these methods:

- Double-click the page.
- Click the page and then click the Current Page icon.
- Use the arrow keys to move the dark border to the page, and then press Enter.

The page will appear in Current Page view.

Summary

In this chapter, you learned to switch to Freelance's Page Sorter view. In Page Sorter view, you can reorganize the pages of a presentation. In Part III of this book, you learn to add graphic data charts to presentation pages.

Adding Charts to Pages

PART

III

OUTLINE

Adding a Data Chart

Whenever the information that you need to present is numeric, you may want to show it graphically in a data chart. A data chart can make clear a short-term change, a long-term trend, a comparison, a breakdown of a total, or even a simple aberrant result in a way that a table of numbers simply cannot.

Freelance makes it easy to create a data chart from a set of numbers. In this chapter, you learn how to start a data chart, enter your numbers, and then examine the chart that Freelance creates. In the next chapter, you learn how to modify the appearance of the data chart.

Adding a Chart Page

The easiest way to create a page containing a data chart is to select a page layout that includes a chart "Click here..." block. Then click the

"Click here to create chart" block to access the New Chart Gallery dialog box, and follow the procedure described in this chapter to create the chart.

Follow these steps to add to your presentation a page containing a chart "Click here..." block:

1. Click the New Page button. The New Page dialog box appears.

2. From the New Page dialog box, choose the 1 Chart, 2 Charts, 4 Charts, or Bullets & Chart page layout. A page containing the layout you choose appears on-screen.

3. Click a "Click here to create chart" block. The New Chart Gallery dialog box appears.

Figures 6.1 through 6.4 show the four page layouts that include "Click here..." blocks for creating charts.

Fig. 6.1

The 1 Chart page layout.

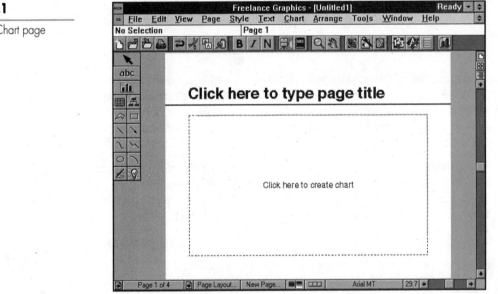

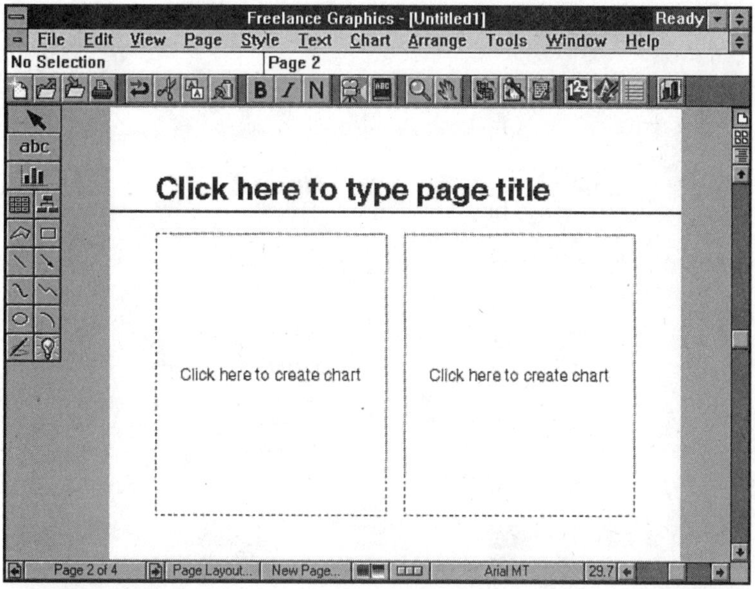

Fig. 6.2

The 2 Charts page layout.

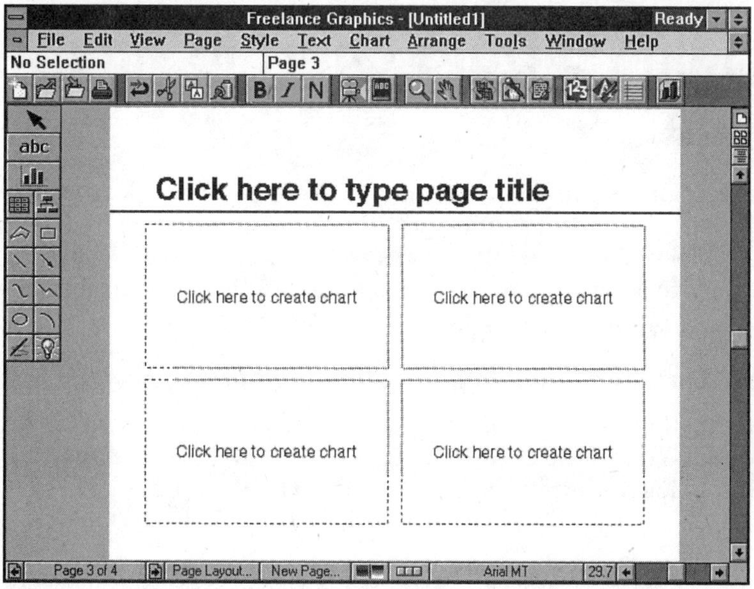

Fig. 6.3

The 4 Charts page layout.

Fig. 6.4

The Bullets & Chart page layout.

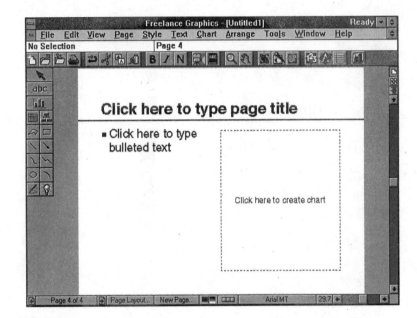

Adding a Data Chart to Any Page

Freelance offers two ways of adding data charts to any page in a presentation, even a page that does not include a "Click here to create chart" block. To create a chart on a page, first turn to the page where you want to add the chart, and then follow either of these methods:

- ■ Click the Chart icon in the toolbox.

- ■ From the **Chart** menu, choose **New** and then **Data Chart**.

Either method accesses the New Chart Gallery dialog box, as shown in figure 6.5. You can select a chart type and chart style from the choices in this dialog box, or you can select the default chart design.

Selecting a Chart Type and Style

As in nearly all Freelance dialog boxes, the selections available in the New Chart Gallery dialog box are both numbered and clearly described. The first selection (Choose a Chart Type) asks you to choose one of the 18 radio buttons on the left side of the dialog box. This selection determines the chart's category. The second selection (Choose a Style) asks you to choose one of the six buttons showing chart designs. These buttons change to show variations of the chart type you select. After you choose a chart type and style, press Enter.

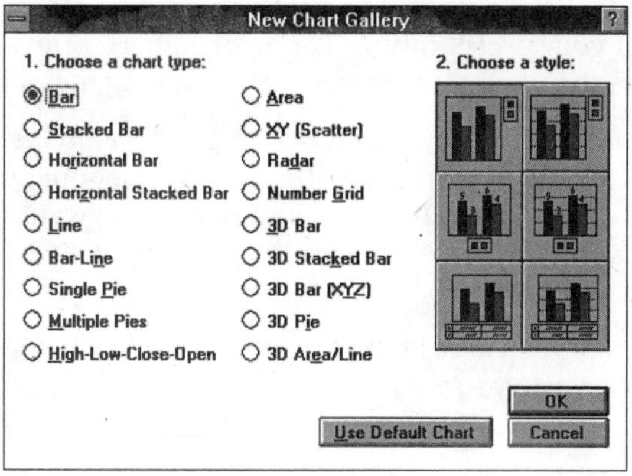

Fig. 6.5

The New Chart Gallery dialog box.

If you have defined a chart as the default chart, you can create that chart on your new page by clicking the **Use Default Chart** button. To define a particular chart as the default chart, you must first create a chart design. Then choose Replace **D**efaults from the **C**hart menu. This newly defined chart remains the default chart while you work in the current presentation. If you switch to a different presentation, the default chart switches back to the original Freelance default chart.

After you select a chart type and style, the Chart Data & Titles dialog box opens (see fig. 6.6). You can type the contents of the chart—its text labels and numbers—directly into this dialog box, or you can import the contents from another file. After you enter the chart's data, Freelance takes care of the appearance of the chart, representing the data in the exact format of the chart type and style you selected.

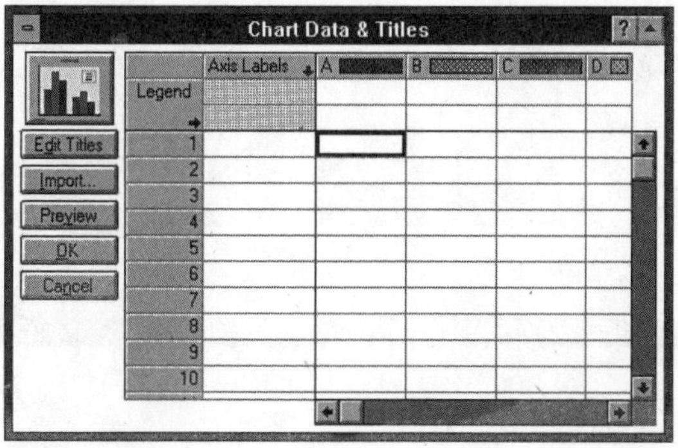

Fig. 6.6

The Chart Data & Titles dialog box.

Choosing an Appropriate Chart Type

Choosing the best chart type for your particular needs may be the hardest part of creating a presentation with Freelance. The appropriate chart can enhance the meaning of a set of numbers, increasing the persuasiveness of your presentation. The wrong chart, or even the right chart designed the wrong way, can send the wrong message entirely.

The first step in creating crystal-clear charts, therefore, is to select a suitable chart for the job. To make the correct selection, you first must understand the job. Ask yourself what message you want to convey. Then try to match that message with the message delivered best by each different chart type.

The following sections may help you determine which chart type best matches the message you want to convey.

Bar

A *bar chart* compares numbers by using side-by-side bars. Bar charts are best used for comparisons of numbers at specific moments in time. Figure 6.7 shows a bar chart.

Fig. 6.7

A bar chart.

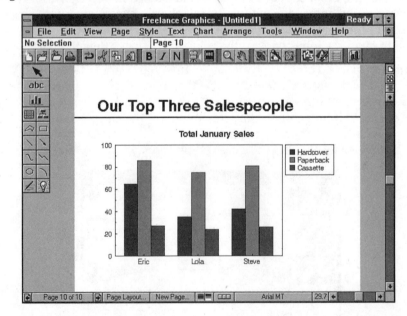

Stacked Bar

A *stacked bar chart* stacks bars on top of one another. This type of chart displays the grand total of each set of bars and the breakdowns of these totals. The colors or patterns of the stacked bars enable you to distinguish among them. Figure 6.8 shows a stacked bar chart.

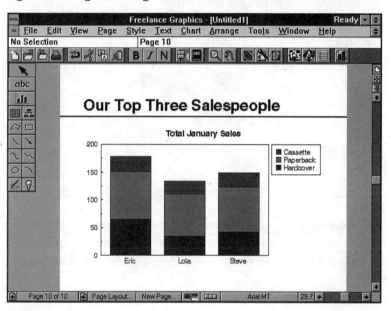

Fig. 6.8

A stacked bar chart.

Horizontal Bar

A *horizontal bar chart* is just like a standard bar chart except that this chart type switches the positions of the horizontal and vertical axes, and all the bars run horizontally rather than vertically. A horizontal bar chart suggests progress toward a goal, accomplishment, or distance traveled. This chart also is useful if axis labels are unusually long. Figure 6.9 shows a horizontal bar chart.

Horizontal Stacked Bar

A *horizontal stacked bar chart* is similar to a stacked bar chart except that this chart type stacks its bars horizontally. This type of chart best demonstrates cumulative progress or movement across a distance. Figure 6.10 shows a horizontal stacked bar chart.

Fig. 6.9

A horizontal bar chart.

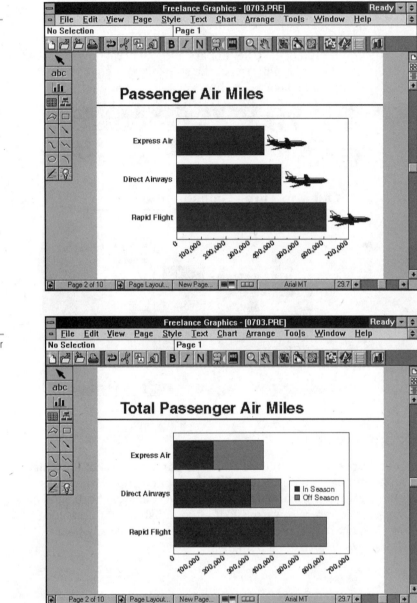

Fig. 6.10

A horizontal stacked bar chart.

Line

A *line chart* represents a series of numbers by using a line that runs from data point to data point. Line charts emphasize continuous change or a trend over time rather than values at discrete intervals. A line chart is appropriate for census data, for example, to represent a continuously increasing population. Figure 6.11 shows a line chart.

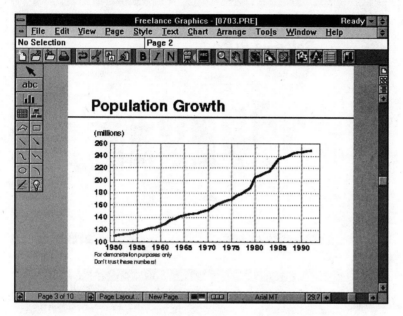

Fig. 6.11

A line chart.

Bar-Line

A *bar-line chart* displays both bars and lines in the same chart. Data sets A and B are shown as bars. Data sets C and D are shown as lines. Bar-line charts are useful for emphasizing certain data sets or depicting two different types of data in the same chart. You may show sales volume with bars, for example, and selling price with a line. Figure 6.12 shows a bar-line chart.

Single Pie

A *single pie chart* portrays the breakdown of a total. The size of each pie slice represents the percentage of each component. Use this type of chart only if you can add all the numbers in a data set to create a meaningful total. Figure 6.13 shows a single pie chart.

Fig. 6.12

A bar-line chart.

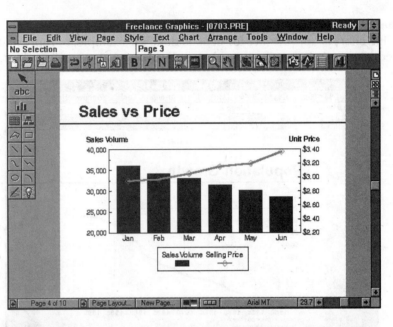

Fig. 6.13

A single pie chart.

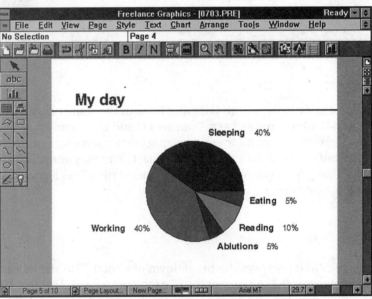

Multiple Pies

A *multiple pies chart* draws more than one pie on a page so that you can compare two breakdowns or see how a breakdown changes over time.

Figure 6.14 shows a multiple pies chart drawn with two pies. You can have up to four pies in a multiple pies chart.

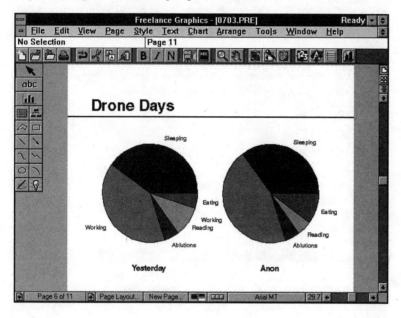

Fig. 6.14

A multiple pies chart.

High-Low-Close-Open

A *high-low-close-open (HLCO) chart* is most often used to track the performance of stocks, but this type of chart also can be used for any measurement that fluctuates during intervals, such as daily high, low, and average temperatures. Each vertical line portrays the extents of the values measured during the interval. A tick mark at the left side of the line shows the opening value. A tick mark at the right side shows the closing value. HLCO charts also can include a set of bars to represent the volume of transactions during the day. Figure 6.15 shows a high-low-close-open chart.

Area

An *area chart* displays a data set as a line with the area underneath filled in by a color or pattern. The data sets are stacked. Like a line chart, an area chart demonstrates change over time. The filled areas below the lines emphasize volume (such as sales volume). Figure 6.16 shows an area chart.

Fig. 6.15

A high-low-close-open (HLCO) chart.

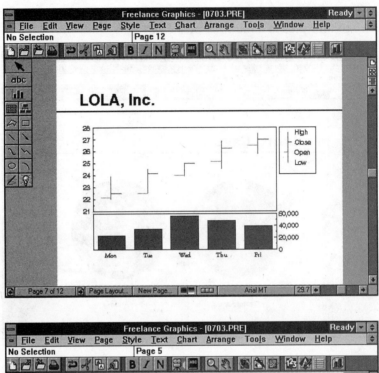

Fig. 6.16

An area chart.

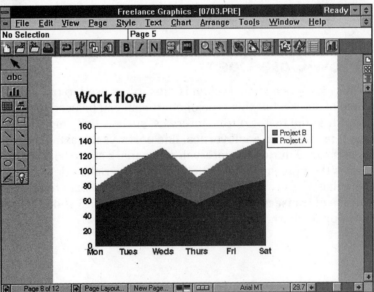

XY (Scatter)

An *XY (scatter) chart* displays the correlation between two data sets. Data values are plotted on the chart as points. Both the x-axis and y-axis are numeric. The more the points clump together in a line, the more closely are the two sets of data correlated. An XY (scatter) chart may show the correlation between home sales and mortgage interest rates, for example. Figure 6.17 shows an XY (scatter) chart.

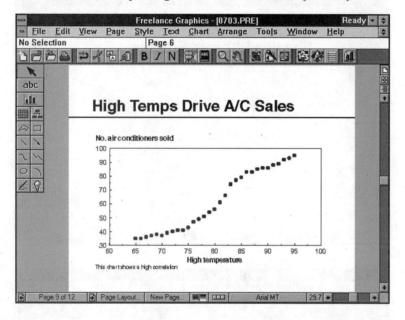

Fig. 6.17

An XY (scatter) chart.

Radar

A *radar chart* depicts different measurements relating to a subject on different axes that radiate from a center point. A line connects the data set values on the axes. This type of chart is applicable if each number in a data set measures a different aspect of a subject. A single radar chart can display more than one data set. A single radar chart, for example, can show the following measurements for several health clubs (with each measurement on a different axis extending from the center): number of visitors, number of instructors, number of hours open each day, and average weight lifted by all muscle builders. Figure 6.18 shows a radar chart.

Number Grid

A *number grid chart* displays a number table. This type of chart is useful if you want to show actual numbers rather than a graphic representation of the numbers. A number grid chart is applicable if the message is clear from the numbers alone; interpreting the numbers with data is not necessary. Figure 6.19 shows a number grid chart.

Fig. 6.18

A radar chart.

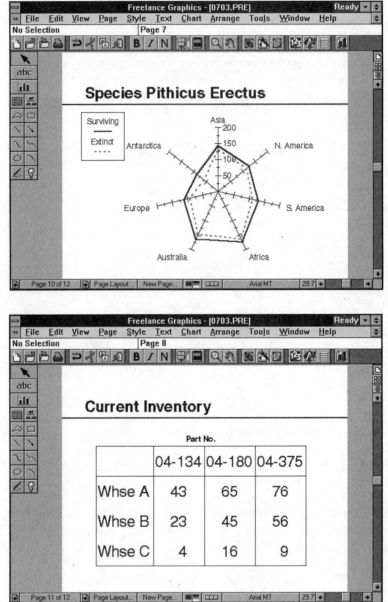

Fig. 6.19

A number grid chart.

3D Bar

A *3D bar chart* is essentially the same as a bar chart, but the bars are shown with depth for visual interest. Figure 6.20 shows a 3D bar chart.

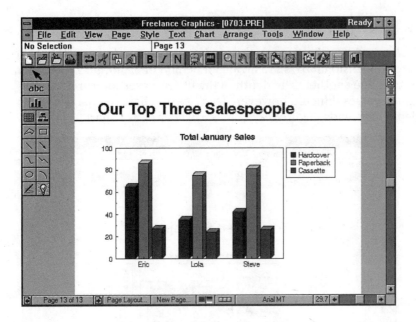

Fig. 6.20

A 3D bar chart.

3D Stacked Bar

A *3D stacked bar chart* serves the same purpose as a stacked bar chart, but the bars are shown with depth. Figure 6.21 shows a 3D stacked bar chart.

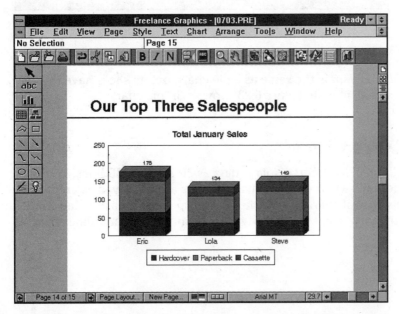

Fig. 6.21

A 3D stacked bar chart.

3D Bar (XYZ)

A *3D bar (XYZ) chart* serves the same purpose as a bar chart, but the three-dimensional bars are arranged behind one another rather than next to one another. The depth of the chart makes interpreting individual values difficult, however. This type of chart is most useful for depicting trends. Figure 6.22 shows a 3D bar (XYZ) chart.

Fig. 6.22

A 3D bar (XYZ) chart.

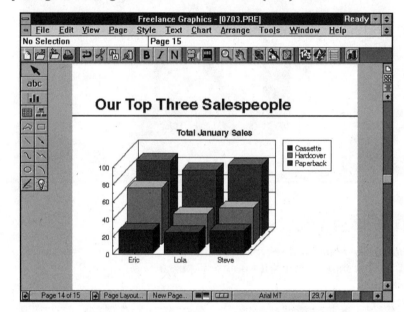

3D Pie

A *3D pie chart* is the same as a pie chart, but its slices have thickness for visual interest. Figure 6.23 shows a 3D pie chart.

3D Area/Line

A *3D area/line chart* displays data as 3D areas or 3D lines. You can determine whether individual data sets are displayed as areas or lines. This type of chart serves the same purpose as area and line charts, but with more visual interest. Figure 6.24 shows a 3D area/line chart.

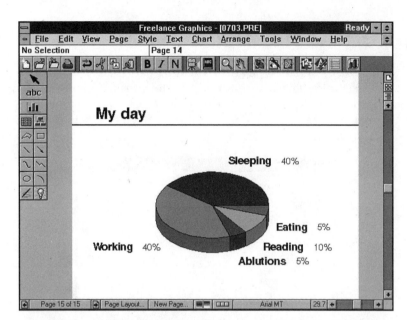

Fig. 6.23

A 3D pie chart.

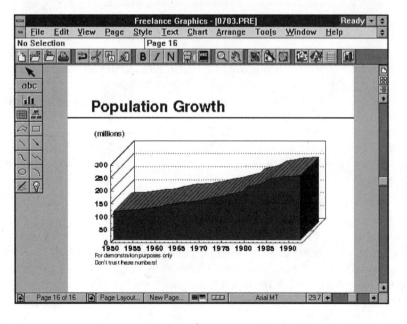

Fig. 6.24

A 3D area/line chart.

Entering the Data

After you select a chart type and style, the Chart Data & Titles dialog box opens within the Freelance window. The appearance of the Chart Data & Titles dialog box, which provides space for you to type the chart's data and text labels, depends on the chart type you select. Figure 6.25 shows the Chart Data & Titles dialog box for a basic bar chart.

Fig. 6.25

The Chart Data & Titles dialog box for a bar chart.

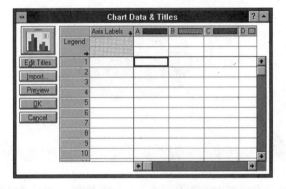

At the upper-left corner of the window, a large button displays a sample of the chart type you selected. To select a different chart type, click this button to return to the New Chart Gallery dialog box. Other buttons along the left edge of this dialog box enable you to create titles, import numbers, and preview your work in progress. You learn about creating titles in the section "Supplying Titles" later in this chapter, and you learn about previewing charts in the section "Previewing the Chart." Chapter 8, "Importing the Data for a Data Chart," shows you how to use the Import button. The rest of this dialog box is occupied by the grid into which you enter the data for the chart.

The grid, arranged in lettered columns and numbered rows of cells, looks much like a spreadsheet grid. Its function is to hold, but not calculate, data. Each lettered column holds one data set—a related sequence of numbers, such as the month-by-month sales total for a particular product. Next to each column letter is a small bar, line, area, or pie slice in the color to be used for that data set. The far-left column is reserved for entering the labels that appear along an axis of the chart (usually the x-axis). The first two rows are reserved for the descriptive labels to appear in the chart's legend. If the column is to hold the sales figures for a product, for example, you enter the product name at the top of the column.

TIP

The two spaces at the top of each column enable you to enter a two-line legend. To label a column with only one word, enter the word in either space.

To enter the contents of a chart, you move the highlight from cell to cell and enter labels and data for the chart into the highlighted cells. To move the highlight, click the destination cell for the highlight or use the arrow keys to move cell by cell. You also can press the Tab key to move the highlight to the right. To move your view of the grid one window's length in any direction, hold down the Ctrl key while you press an arrow key. To move the highlight to the bottom of the window, press the PgDn key. Press Home to return the highlight to cell A1.

Pressing the End key and then an arrow key moves the highlight to the last cell in a group filled with data in the direction of the arrow key you press. Pressing End and the down-arrow key, for example, moves the highlight to the last cell in the column that is filled with data. If there is no more data in the row or column, pressing End and then an arrow key moves the highlight to the end of the row or bottom of the column. Press Home to return to the top-left corner of the data area. To move the highlight to a specific cell, press F5 (Goto) to access the Goto dialog box, and type the cell address (column letter and row number) in the Cell Goto text box, as shown in figure 6.26. Then click OK or press Enter.

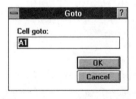

Fig. 6.26

The Goto dialog box.

TIP

To see more data at one time, you can resize the Chart Data & Titles dialog box by stretching its borders with the mouse.

Entering the Data for a Line, Bar, or Area Chart

After you select any line, bar, or area chart type and style, the Chart Data & Titles dialog box displays as many columns as can fit in the current window size. The total number of columns is 26, labeled A through Z, and the total number of rows is 4,000—so you can enter 4,000 values in each of 26 data sets. You actually use only a tiny portion of those available cells, however, because you are likely to have only a small amount of data to chart. And trying to include too much data, especially too many data sets, can make a chart cluttered and incomprehensible. Figure 6.27 shows the Chart Data & Titles dialog box. The same dialog box is used for line, bar, and area charts.

Fig. 6.27

The Chart Data & Titles dialog box for a line, bar, or area chart.

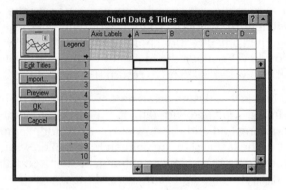

The Axis Labels column is blank but ready to hold the labels that are to appear along the x-axis of the chart. These labels often mark the passage of time, listing successive days, weeks, months, or years, but you can type any text into the Axis Labels column. To chart the popularity of three television game shows, for example, you can enter their names in the Axis Labels column. Make sure that you keep the axis labels as short as you can so that the labels fit easily along the axis.

TIP

Freelance provides a method called Date Fill to enter a series of successive dates automatically. You learn about this method in the section " Entering Axis Labels Automatically," later in this chapter.

The best approach to entering data into the Chart Data & Titles dialog box is to provide the axis labels and legend entries first, setting up the structure of the data, and then to enter the columns of numbers in the data area.

To type an entry, move the highlight to the cell for the entry and begin typing the text. As you type, the text appears both in the cell and in the edit line near the top of the Freelance window. Use the Backspace key to delete errors. After you finish typing, follow any of these actions:

- Press Enter.

- Press an arrow key to move the highlight to the next cell.

- Click a different cell.

- Click the green check mark button that appears in the edit line while you are typing an entry.

TIP

You can determine whether pressing Enter will move the highlight to the cell below or leave the highlight in the current cell. Choose the **O**ptions command from the **C**hart menu and then choose **K**eyboard from the **O**ptions pop-out menu. Choose the highlight movement option that you want from the Chart Keyboard Options dialog box that appears.

Figure 6.28 shows a completed set of data in the Chart Data & Titles dialog box. The data plots the sales of three salespeople over six months. Figure 6.29 shows the resulting chart.

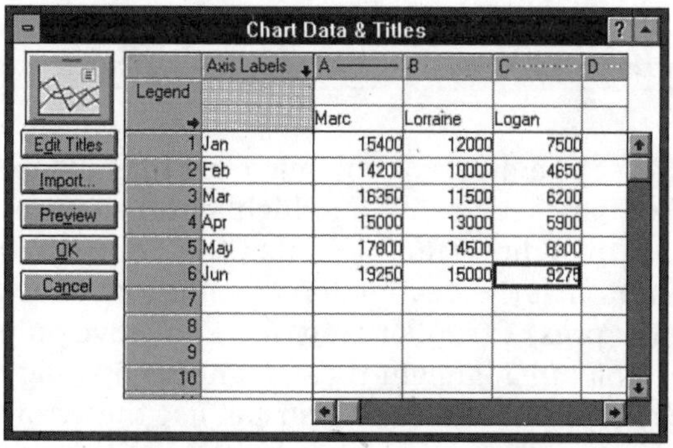

Fig. 6.28

A complete set of data entered in the Chart Data & Titles dialog box.

	Axis Labels	A	B	C	D
Legend		Marc	Lorraine	Logan	
1	Jan	15400	12000	7500	
2	Feb	14200	10000	4650	
3	Mar	16350	11500	6200	
4	Apr	15000	13000	5900	
5	May	17800	14500	8300	
6	Jun	19250	15000	9275	
7					
8					
9					
10					

Buttons: Edit Titles, Import..., Preview, OK, Cancel

TIP

An easily understood bar, area, or line chart should include no more than six data sets.

Editing, Copying, and Moving the Data

To edit a text label or number, move the highlight to the cell containing the label or number and then type a new label or number into that cell.

The new entry replaces the current entry. You also can move the high-light to a cell and press F2 (Edit). This brings the contents of the cell to the edit line. Type a correction in the edit line and then either press Enter or click the green check mark button.

Fig. 6.29

The chart based on the data shown in figure 6.28.

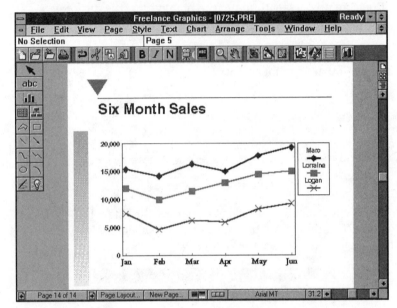

To move a data set to a different column, click the column letter button at the top of that data set's column to highlight the entire column. Choose Cut from the Edit menu (or press Ctrl+X or Shift+Del), click the column letter button at the destination column, and choose **Paste** from the Edit menu (or press Ctrl+V or Shift+Ins). To move only some of the numbers in the column, highlight those numbers by dragging across them with the mouse pointer. (You also can use the arrow keys to move the highlight to the first number, hold down the Shift key, and then move the highlight to the last number.) Then choose Edit Cut, move the highlight to the destination for the first of the numbers, and choose Edit Paste.

Moving data sets enables you to rearrange the order of lines, bars, or areas in a chart. To copy a data set, highlight the set and choose **Edit Copy** instead of **Edit Cut** (or press Ctrl+C or Ctrl+Ins).

TIP

To give the chart additional meaning, you can order the bars or areas from largest to smallest or from smallest to largest. Figures 6.30 and 6.31 show two charts, one before and one after ordering the data.

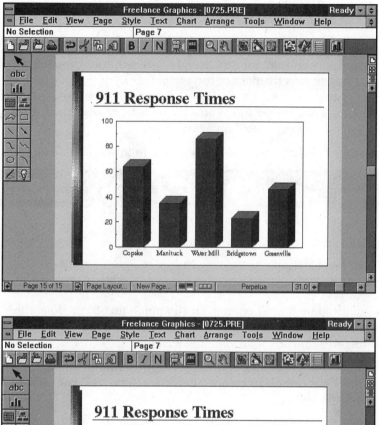

Fig. 6.30

Before ordering the data in a chart.

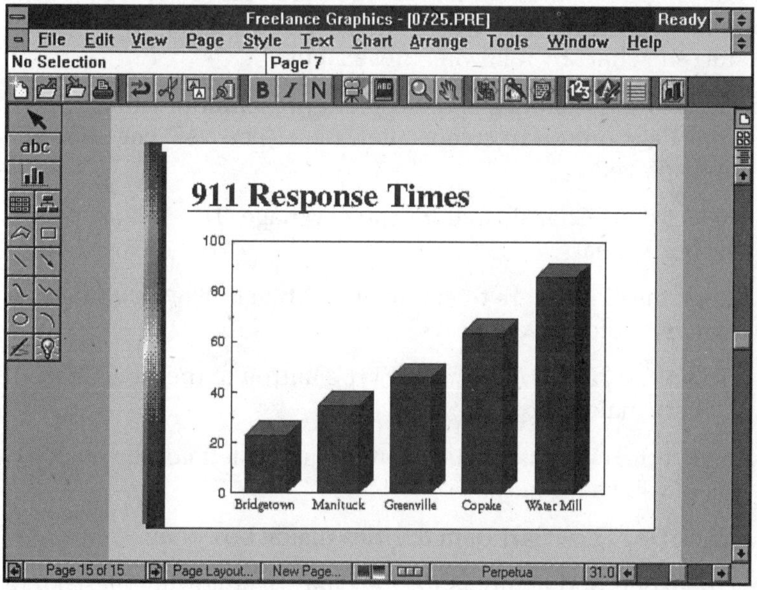

Fig. 6.31

After ordering the data in a chart.

If you make a change to the data in the Chart Data & Titles dialog box but then decide to revert to the original data, choose the **Undo Edit Chart** command from the **Edit** menu or press **Ctrl+Z**. Undo Edit Chart, however, remembers only the *last* change you made to the data.

Exercise: Creating a 3D Bar Chart

To practice entering data for a 3D bar chart, follow the steps of this exercise. Suppose that, for an upcoming presentation, you need a chart comparing the effectiveness of three community programs for two years. Because your emphasis is to compare the measurements at two discrete intervals rather than show the variations over time, a bar chart is more appropriate than a line chart.

You gather the data and come up with the following numbers:

Program	Participants This Year	Participants Last Year
Adopt-A-Road	42	36
Community Clean Up Week	51	49
Senior Helping Hand	73	68

The full program names contain far too much text to fit along the x-axis, so you must enter abbreviations instead. Create a page for the chart and start the chart by following these steps:

1. Turn to the last page of the current presentation and click the New Page button to create a new page. The New Page dialog box is displayed.

2. Select the 1 Chart layout for the new page. The 1 Chart page layout appears.

3. Click the "Click here to create chart" block. The New Chart Gallery dialog box appears.

4. Select the 3D Bar (XYZ) chart type button in the New Chart Gallery dialog box.

5. Select the chart style button at the upper-left corner (a chart displaying a legend).

6. Click OK. The Chart Data & Titles dialog box opens.

Enter the labels and numbers for the chart by following these steps:

1. In rows 1 through 3 of the Axis Labels column, type **Adopt Road**, **Clean Up**, and **Helping Hand**.

2. In the Legend cells of the A and B data sets, type **This Year** and **Last Year**.

3. Enter the numbers into their respective cells. (Pressing Enter after typing each number moves the highlight to the cell below. To begin the second column of numbers, you must move the highlight to the top of that column by using the arrow keys or mouse.) Figure 6.32 shows the completed data window.

Fig. 6.32

The completed Chart Data & Titles dialog box for the sample 3D bar chart.

Now preview the chart you created by placing the mouse pointer on the Preview button and holding down the mouse button. You quickly see that the bars for this year's data hide last year's bars, as shown in figure 6.33.

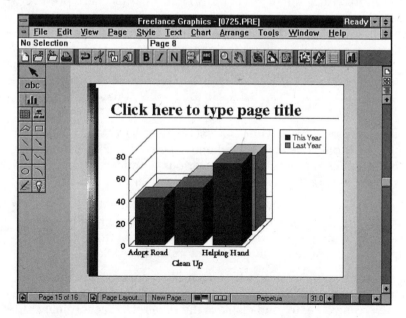

Fig. 6.33

The chart that results from the data shown in figure 6.32.

To solve this problem, you need to switch data sets A and B in the Chart Data & Titles dialog box. Follow these steps:

1. Release the mouse button to finish previewing the chart and return to the Chart Data & Titles dialog box.

2. Click the button labeled A at the top of the data set in column A.

3. Press Ctrl+X to cut the data set.

4. Click the button labeled C at the top of column C.

5. Press Ctrl+V to paste the data set into column C.

6. Place the cursor on the button labeled B and drag the mouse across the button on top of column C so that both columns are selected.

7. Press Ctrl+X again to cut both data sets.

8. Click the button labeled A at the top of column A.

9. Press Ctrl+V to paste the data sets into columns A and B. The data sets have now switched columns from where they were originally located.

Click and hold down the Preview button again to see the revised chart. Notice that the smaller bars are now in front of the larger bars. You may want to reduce the depth of the 3D effect in this chart, however, to make comparing the two sets of bars easier. The next chapter describes how to change the 3D depth, among other modifications to the appearance. Figure 6.34 shows the revised chart.

Entering the Data for Pie Charts

If you select Single Pie as your chart style, the Chart Data & Titles dialog box holds only one data set column, labeled Pie A. This data set holds the values represented by the various pie slices. Figure 6.35 shows the Chart Data & Titles dialog box for a single pie chart.

You enter slice labels, which identify the pie slices, in the Slice Labels column of the chart. You enter a Pie Title for the pie chart in the first two spaces of the Pie A column. The row number buttons to the left portray each pie slice and show the colors of these slices.

You enter the actual numbers that each slice represents in the Pie A column. Do not enter percentages. Freelance calculates percentages from the data you enter and displays the slices sized accordingly.

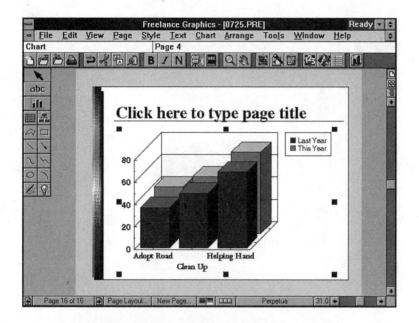

Fig. 6.34

The completed 3D bar chart.

Fig. 6.35

The Chart Data & Titles dialog box for a single pie chart.

Figure 6.36 shows the single pie chart that results from the data displayed in figure 6.35.

TIP

Use six or fewer slices in a pie chart. More than six slices can make a pie chart hard to interpret. If you have more than six components in a total, give the five largest components their own slices and add the remaining components together to represent the total of these components as a sixth slice labeled All Others. You can show the breakdown of the All Others slice in a second pie if necessary.

Fig. 6.36

The single pie chart that results from the data in figure 6.35.

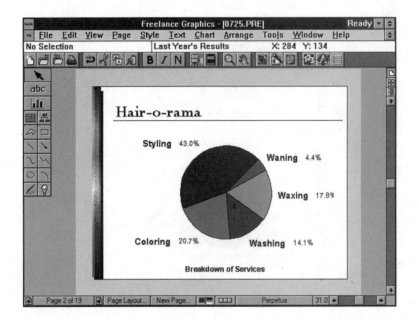

If you need to compare two or more breakdowns or depict how a breakdown changes over time, you can create more than one pie on a page by selecting **M**ultiple Pies as the chart type. Freelance then provides enough columns to enter up to four data sets in the Chart Data & Titles dialog box one data set for each pie. Instead of labeling each slice in each pie, Freelance creates a legend that identifies the slices in all four charts. Figure 6.37 shows the Chart Data & Titles dialog box for four pies. Figure 6.38 shows the resulting pies and the legend that applies to all pies. No percentage figures appear around the pies in the multiple pies chart because the chart style without percentage figures was chosen to create this chart. You can turn on percentage figures by selecting a different chart style, though.

TIP

As you create multiple pies, make sure that you enter the Pie Titles in the upper of the two spaces available for them at the top of the data sets. This places the Pie Titles closer to the bottom of the pies in the resulting chart.

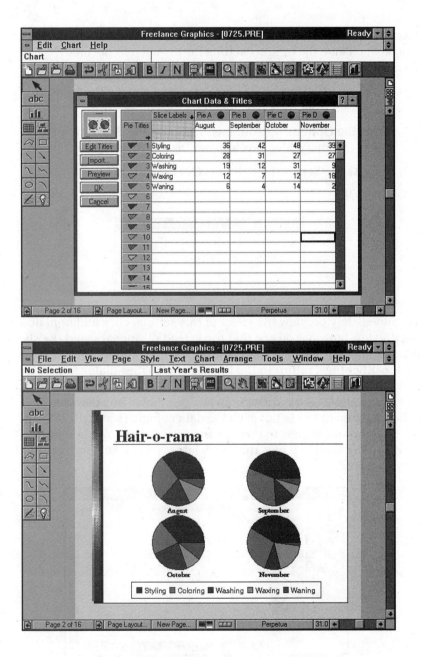

Fig. 6.37

The Chart Data & Titles dialog box for a multiple pies chart.

Fig. 6.38

The four pies that result from the data shown in figure 6.37.

To omit the legend and enter individual labels for the slices instead, you must change the options setting for the current pie chart. To change the options setting, follow these steps:

1. Make sure that the chart is selected and choose the **O**ptions command from the **C**hart menu.

2. From the **O**ptions pop-out menu, choose **Pie**. The Multiple Pie Chart Options dialog box appears, as shown in figure 6.39.

3. Choose the Se**p**arate Attributes (No Legend) button.

4. Click OK.

Fig. 6.39

The Multiple Pie Chart Options dialog box.

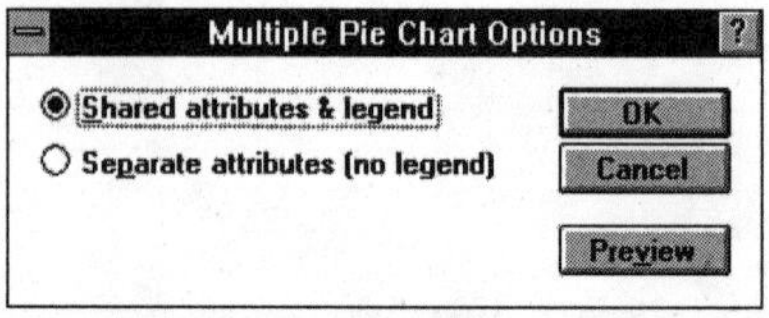

To immediately preview the effect of this setting, click and hold down the Preview button. You see that the legend disappears, and the slice labels apply only to Pie A (at the upper left). To supply slice labels for the other pies, return to the Chart Data & Titles dialog box. After you select Se**p**arate Attributes (No Legend) in the Multiple Pie Chart Options dialog box, the Chart Data & Titles dialog box displays a Labels column to the left of each Pie data column (see fig. 6.40). Figure 6.41 shows two pies that result from the data shown in figure 6.40. (Giving more than two pies their own labels can make your screen very cluttered.)

Fig. 6.40

The Chart Data & Titles dialog box after Se**p**arate Attributes (No Legend) is selected.

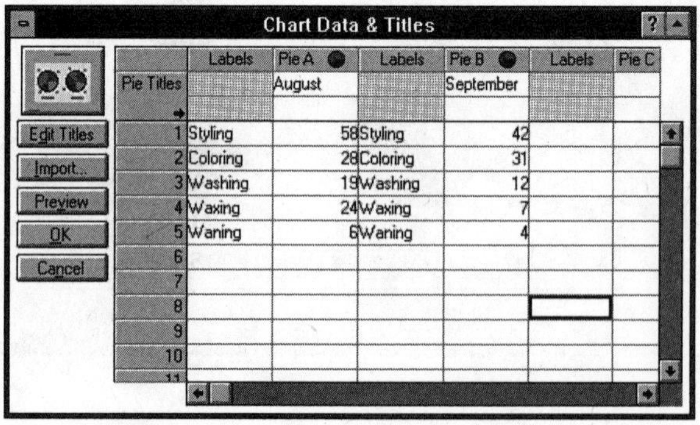

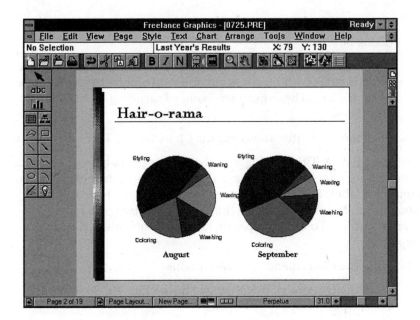

Fig. 6.41

The pies created from
the data shown in
figure 6.40.

Exercise: Creating a Pie Chart

In this exercise, you create a chart to depict last year's total sales in
the small but growing chain of nine health food stores you manage.
The stores had varying successes last year, and you want a chart that
shows each store's contribution to the total sales for the group. A pie
chart is the best way to show such a breakdown, but nine slices are too
many for a single pie. To solve this problem, you can show two pies
side by side. The left pie will have six slices: five for the five largest
stores and a sixth slice for the total of the smallest stores. The right pie
will show a breakdown of the sixth slice.

To begin, create a new page in the current presentation by clicking the
New Page button. Select the 1 Chart page layout in the New Page dialog
box. (Although you plan to show two pies, you create only one chart
that shows both pies.) Then follow these steps to begin creating the
pie:

1. Click the "Click here to create chart" block on the page layout.
   The New Chart Gallery dialog box appears.

2. Select **M**ultiple Pies as the chart type in the New Chart Gallery dialog box.

3. Click the first button in the second row of chart style buttons to select a chart with no slices cut and with a percentage figure next to each slice. (These buttons change depending on the chart type you choose.)

4. Click the OK button to access the Chart Data & Titles dialog box.

The Chart Data & Titles dialog box that now appears has only one column for Slice Labels, which means that every pie in the chart has the same slice label. The chart you need, however, must have separate labels around each pie because the slices in the two pies represent different stores. To create separate labels for each pie, follow these steps:

1. From the **C**hart menu, choose **O**ptions.

2. From the **O**ptions pop-out menu, choose **P**ie. The Multiple Pie Chart Options dialog box opens.

3. Select Se**p**arate Attributes (No Legend).

4. Click OK.

Now you can begin entering the data. The following list shows the data for each store (by store manager name), in descending order of sales:

Store Manager's Name	Sales (in Thousands)
Brent	59
Brock	57
Helga	48
Rocky	42
Trevor	31
Christie	24
Biff	22
Archer	20
Star	16

You chart the five largest stores and the total of the other four stores in Pie A, and you chart the four smallest stores in Pie B. To accomplish this, type data in the Chart Data & Titles dialog box as shown in figure 6.42. The resulting pie is shown in figure 6.43. Notice that Pie B shows a breakdown of the All Others slice in Pie A.

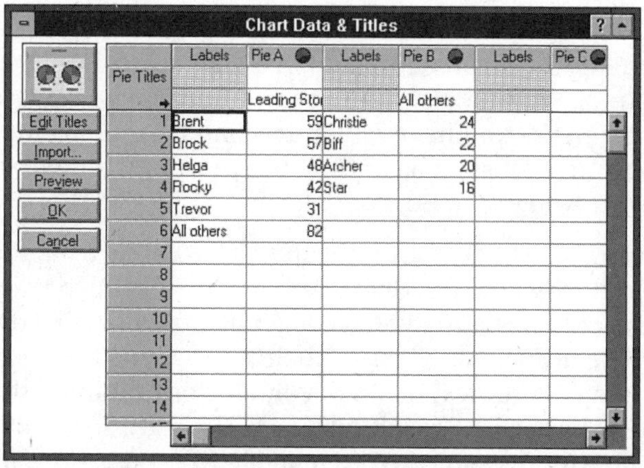

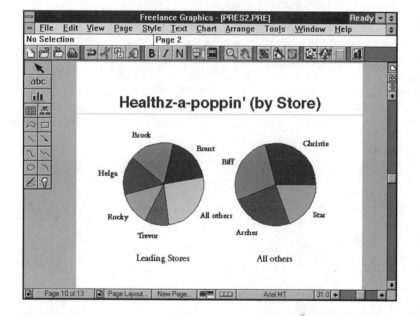

Fig. 6.42

The data entered correctly for the multiple pies chart.

Fig. 6.43

The multiple pies chart that results from the data shown in figure 6.42.

Unfortunately, you cannot enter formulas into the cells of the Chart Data & Titles dialog box, even though the cells look like those of a spreadsheet. You must calculate the Pie B slices manually and then place the total in the All Others slice of Pie A.

Entering the Data for a High-Low-Close-Open Chart

High-low-close-open (HLCO) charts track the performance of stocks and other financial instruments that have high, low, closing, and opening prices during set periods. HLCO charts also can be used to track other measurements that have minimums and maximums during successive time intervals, such as barometric pressure, temperature, or even the mood swings of a boss.

After you select an HLCO chart type and a chart style from the New Chart Gallery dialog box, the Chart Data & Titles dialog box opens. The first four data columns already have legend entries (High, Low, Close, and Open). The fifth column is not labeled, but if you type numbers into this column (to represent stock volume, for example), these numbers appear as bars in the resulting chart. The sixth series of numbers entered in the window is plotted as a line in the chart. (You may want to use this line to plot the average selling price.)

Figure 6.44 shows a typical collection of data for an HLCO chart. Notice that the Axis Labels indicate the time intervals during which activity is depicted by the vertical lines. Notice also that the stock prices must be entered in decimal form. The number 24 7/8, for example, must be entered as 24.875, because the Chart Data & Titles dialog box does not accept fractions. The day-to-day volume figures for the stock have been entered in Column E. Figure 6.45 shows the chart that results from the data shown in figure 6.44.

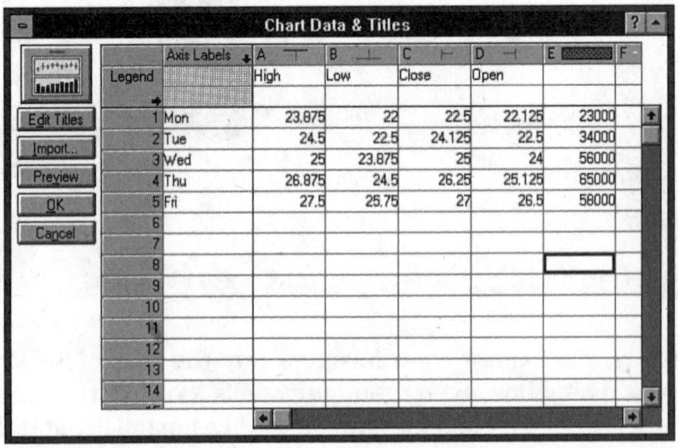

Fig. 6.44

A typical set of data for an HLCO chart, as entered in the Chart Data & Titles dialog box.

	Axis Labels	A High	B Low	C Close	D Open	E	F
Legend							
1	Mon	23.875	22	22.5	22.125	23000	
2	Tue	24.5	22.5	24.125	22.5	34000	
3	Wed	25	23.875	25	24	56000	
4	Thu	26.875	24.5	26.25	25.125	65000	
5	Fri	27.5	25.75	27	26.5	58000	
6							
7							
8							
9							
10							
11							
12							
13							
14							

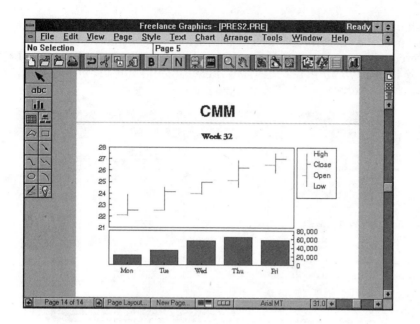

Fig. 6.45

The HLCO chart that results from the data shown in figure 6.44.

Entering the Data for a Radar Chart

Each row of data in the Chart Data & Titles dialog box for a radar chart is another axis that extends from the center of the chart. You enter Axis Titles in the far left cell of each row.

Each column of numbers is represented by a line that extends from axis to axis in a rough circle around the center. Each column letter button at the top of the window displays the color and line type of that line.

Figure 6.46 shows a sample set of data entered in the Chart Data & Titles dialog box for a radar chart. Figure 6.47 shows the chart that results from the data shown in figure 6.46.

Previewing the Chart

After you finish entering the data for any chart in the Chart Data & Titles dialog box, you can view the chart that Freelance draws by pressing and holding down the Preview button in the Chart Data & Titles dialog box. As long as you hold down the Preview button, the chart remains on-screen, reflecting the data you have entered. You can inspect the chart for any irregularities. If you have inadvertently entered too many zeros for one number, for example, the error should be obvious as you preview the chart. Releasing the mouse button returns you to the Chart Data & Titles dialog box.

Fig. 6.46

A sample set of data for a radar chart.

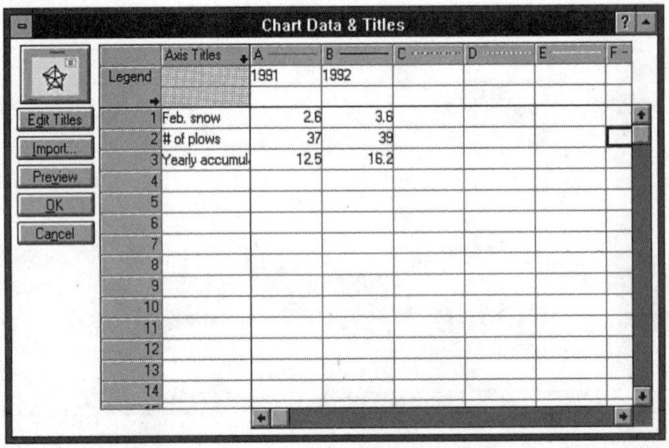

Fig. 6.47

The radar chart that results from the data shown in figure 6.46.

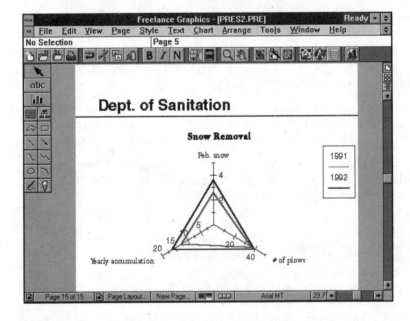

If the preview seems fine, you can leave the Chart Data & Titles dialog box by clicking OK. You can always return to the chart's data to make changes by following any of these steps:

- Select the chart and then click the Chart icon in the toolbox.

- Double-click the chart.

- Click the chart with the right mouse button and then choose Edit Data & Titles from the pop-up commands menu.

- Select the chart and then choose **Edit** from the **Chart** menu.

Supplying Titles

After you enter the content of the chart, you may want to add text for the chart's titles. You can specify up to three lines of text (headings) for the top of the chart, three lines of small text notes at the bottom, and axis titles. Figure 6.48 identifies these titles on a sample chart.

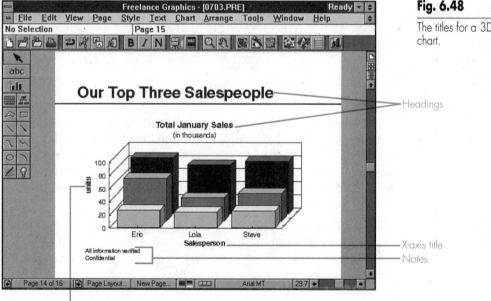

Fig. 6.48

The titles for a 3D bar chart.

To enter the titles for a chart, click the E**d**it Titles button in the chart's Chart Data & Titles dialog box. Text boxes appear in which you can enter the text for each title. Press the Tab key to move from one entry to the next; press Shift+Tab to move back to the preceding entry. Figure 6.49 shows the completed Chart Data & Titles dialog box for the chart shown in figure 6.48.

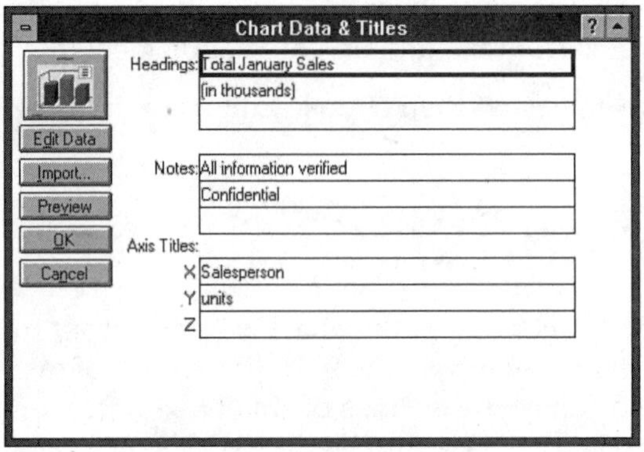

Fig. 6.49

The Chart Data & Titles dialog box displaying titles for the chart shown in figure 6.48.

TIP

Remember that you can press and hold down the Pre**v**iew button to see how the titles you enter appear on the chart.

To return to the view of the Chart Data & Titles dialog box that shows the data for the chart, click the E**d**it Data button.

To add titles to a completed chart or to edit the existing titles, you must double-click the chart to access the Chart Data & Titles dialog box. Then, if necessary, you can click the E**d**it Titles button. Another way to edit the titles of a chart is to select the chart and then choose **H**eadings & Notes from the **C**hart menu. After the Chart Headings & Notes dialog box appears, click its E**d**it Text button.

The titles you enter appear on the chart in preset fonts and colors. You can edit both the content and appearance of the titles just as you can any other text in a presentation. The next chapter describes how to change the appearance of a chart's titles.

Entering Axis Labels Automatically

If a chart requires a sequence of dates along the x-axis or in the legend, you can take advantage of Freelance's Date Fill command, which automatically enters into the Chart Data & Titles dialog box a series of dates. To use Date Fill, you must open the Chart Data & Titles dialog box and then follow these steps:

1. Move the highlight to the cell in the Labels column or the Legend row where you want the sequence of dates to begin.

2. From the Chart menu, choose Options.

3. From the Options pop-out menu, select Date Fill. The Chart Options Date Fill dialog box opens, as shown in figure 6.50.

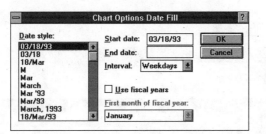

Fig. 6.50

The Chart Options Date Fill dialog box.

 You can click the Chart Date Fill icon to access the Chart Date Fill dialog box (instead of following steps 2 and 3) if you have added that SmartIcon to the SmartIcon palette.

4. Click any of the date styles from the scrollable Date Style list at the left of the dialog box.

5. Select from the Interval list box an interval (Weekdays, Days, Weeks, Months, Quarters, or Years).

6. Enter the starting and ending dates you need in the Start Date and End Date text boxes. (In these text boxes, you must use the date format specified in the International Date User Setup dialog box. A sample, showing the current date, appears in the Start Date text box. See Chapter 23, "Modifying the Default Settings," for

information about changing the International Date format.) If you need to enter month names in these text boxes, any date that includes the name of the month that you need will work. (To start with the month name July, for example, you can enter any date in July.)

If you selected a date style that includes quarters (such as Q1 or 1st Qtr) but your fiscal years do not start in January, choose the **U**se Fiscal Years check box and then enter the first month of the fiscal year in the text box labeled **F**irst Month of Fiscal Year.

7. Click OK or press Enter. If the cursor is in a Labels column, as many date labels as you have specified are entered into the column. If the highlight is in the Legend row, the date entries appear across the row.

Figure 6.51 shows a Chart Data & Titles dialog box with the Axis Labels column filled with weekly dates.

Fig. 6.51

Weekly dates are automatically filled into the Axis Labels column by Freelance's Date Fill option.

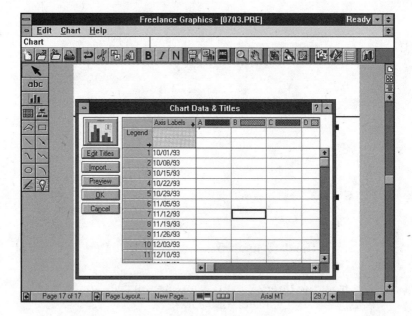

You also can use Date Fill to automatically fill a data set in a number grid. You must set the object type of the data set to Text rather than Number by following these steps:

1. From the **C**hart menu, choose Num**b**er Grid. The Number Grid Chart dialog box opens.

2. Click the **D**ata Style button.

3. From the Data Set list, select the data set to be set as Text.

4. Choose the **T**ext button under Object Type.

Changing the Chart Type

After you create a chart, you may decide that another chart type better represents the data. You can easily switch chart types even after you complete a chart. As usual, Freelance offers several ways to do this.

First, you can click the button showing the sample chart in the upper-left corner of the Chart Data & Titles dialog box. This accesses the New Chart Gallery dialog box from which you can select a different chart type and style. You also can choose **G**allery from the **C**hart menu to access the New Chart Gallery dialog box.

Another way to change the chart is to click the SmartIcon for the chart type you need. The chart immediately changes to the new type after you click that type's SmartIcon. (This option is available only if you have added the appropriate SmartIcon to the SmartIcon palette.)

> **TIP**
>
> To supply two perspectives in the presentation of a set of data, you may want to duplicate the page containing a chart in Page Sorter view and then change the chart type on one of the pages. One page can show the data as a bar chart, for example, to emphasize comparisons at discrete intervals. Another page can show the same data as a line chart to emphasize how the data changes over time. For more information, refer to Chapter 5, "Using Page Sorter View."

Summary

In this chapter, you learned to choose the appropriate chart type and style and to supply the content for the charts you need. In the next chapter, you learn to modify that design to make it clearer, more expressive, or simply more attractive.

Formatting a Data Chart

The default chart formatting settings in Freelance can give you attractive, professionally designed data charts. With Freelance, however, you can easily change the formatting of any chart to fit a particular presentation need or to correspond with your own aesthetic sense.

In this chapter, you learn to use the data chart formatting commands and controls to format bar, line, area, XY, pie, and HLCO charts. You learn also to set the formatting you design as the default for the current presentation and to ungroup a chart so that you can work with a picture of a data chart as a group of drawing objects.

Formatting Bar, Line, Area, and XY Charts

Bar, line, area, and XY charts share most features, so the steps to follow in formatting them are very similar. As with all charts and most objects in Freelance, you select the portion of the chart to format, and you then double-click it, bringing up a dialog box with settings tailored for that chart portion.

You can click the labels along the y-axis of a bar chart to select them, for example, and then double-click the labels. A Chart Axis Labels dialog box opens, displaying settings that format the axis labels in the current chart.

Changing the Color of a Data Set

The colors of the bars, lines, or areas in a chart are set by the presentation's color palette to fit well with the design of the presentation background, but you can override these settings.

To change the color of a data set (one set of bars, one line, or one area), click any bar in the data set or click the line or area. Handles then appear around the chart; a second set of handles appears along or within the selected bar, line, or area. Then double-click at the same spot. An Attributes dialog box opens, similar to the one shown in figure 7.1. (This Attributes dialog box is the same one that appears when you select a chart, click the right mouse button, and then choose Attributes from the pop-up menu.) After you make changes to the settings in this dialog box, you can move the cursor to Preview, press and hold down the Preview button, and examine the changes. When you release the mouse button, the dialog box reappears. You can make more changes, or click OK to accept the changes you've made.

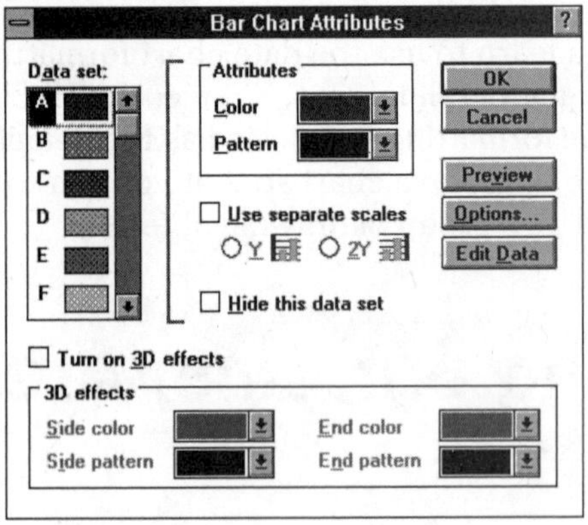

Fig. 7.1

The Bar Chart Attributes dialog box.

Along the left side of the dialog box, a scrollable Data Set list displays each data set's color. Click a data set on the list. To choose a color from the color palette, click the pull-down button next to Color and then click any of the colors in the current palette. If you are using a black-and-white palette, it has shades of gray rather than colors.

If the data set is represented by bars, another control under **Color** enables you to choose a pattern that fills the bars of the current data set. If the data set is represented by a line, controls for **Width**, **Style** (line style), and **Marker** (a graphic shape that appears at each data point) appear rather than **Pattern**. If the data set is represented by areas, an **Edge** color control appears so that you can make the color of the edge of the area different from its fill.

To change the color of the lines surrounding each bar, click **Options** in the Bar Chart Attributes dialog box and then use the Bar Edges section of the Bar Chart Options dialog box shown in figure 7.2. The settings in this dialog box affect all the data sets in the chart.

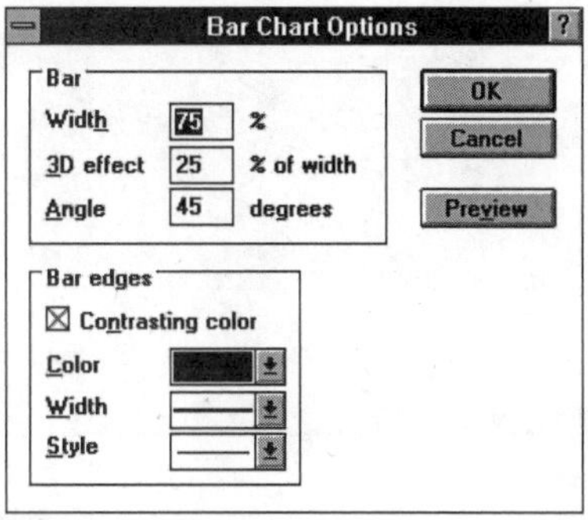

Fig. 7.2

The Bar Chart Options dialog box.

If the **Co**ntrasting Color check box is checked, the **Color** option becomes available so that you can change the color of the edges of the bars. If this box is not checked, the bar edges will be the same color as the interior of the bars. The **Width** and **Style** options let you change the appearance of the line surrounding each bar.

The Wid**th** control, in the group of controls labeled Bar, changes the width of all the bars in the chart. The number entered is a percentage of the total width available for that data set. If you enter 100%, the bars take up 100% of the space along the x-axis that is available for them; they touch one another (see fig. 7.3).

Changing the 3D Effect of a Bar Chart

When you choose one of the 3D bar chart types from the chart gallery as you begin a data chart, Freelance automatically turns on a 3D effect for the bars. You can turn this effect on or off in any bar chart (whether it was 3D initially or not) by clicking any set of bars, double-clicking to get the Bar Chart Attributes dialog box, and then clicking the Turn on **3**D Effects check box.

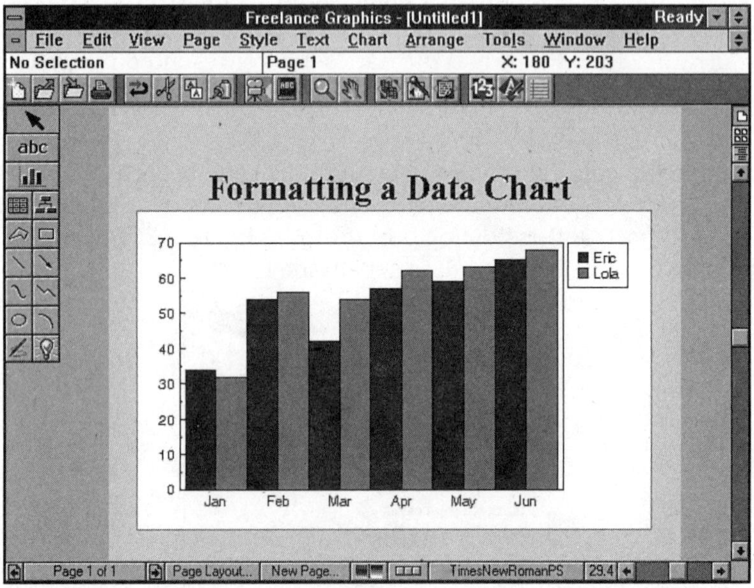

Fig. 7.3

A bar chart with the bar width set at 100%.

When 3D effects are turned on, a group of settings labeled 3D Effects becomes available. These settings let you choose a color and pattern for the sides of the 3D bars and for the ends. Appropriately shaded colors are already chosen by Freelance, but you can change them by choosing different colors from the color palette. Click the pull-down button next to each setting to see the color palette.

To change the depth and angle of the 3D effect, click **O**ptions in the Bar Chart Attributes dialog box. The **3**D effect setting enables you to change how much of the bar width is used for the 3D effect. Increasing this setting increases the depth of the effect. The **A**ngle setting enables you to change the angle at which the 3D effect extends from the bar. Zero degrees is equivalent to the 3 o'clock position; 135 degrees extends the 3D effect diagonally up to the left, as shown in figure 7.4.

Hiding Data Sets

Occasionally, you may need to hide one or more data sets in a chart—and not necessarily because a data set displays poor results. You may have 12 groups of data in the Chart Data & Titles dialog box of a chart but you wisely plan to compare only three or four data sets in each chart to prevent clutter.

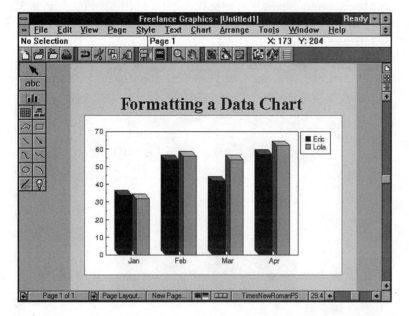

Fig. 7.4

A 3D bar chart with the bar angle set to 135 degrees.

To hide a data set, click the chart, click the data set, and then double-click to open the Attributes dialog box for the chart. Make sure that the correct data set is selected from the list and then click the **H**ide This Data Set check box. A gray box then appears around the data set name on the list. Freelance will not display the data set in the chart or in the legend. Figure 7.5 shows a standard area chart with only three data sets showing. Figure 7.6 shows a chart made from the same data but with those data sets hidden and other data sets showing.

Setting Up a Second Y-Axis

When you create a vertical or horizontal bar chart, you can plot certain data sets against a second y-axis. The second y-axis, which appears on the opposite side of the chart from the first y-axis, can have different formatting and different scaling.

Using a second y-axis is helpful when you want to compare two data sets that have different units of measure or vastly different high and low ranges. You can plot the rising and falling value of two foreign currencies in one chart by setting up a second y-axis, for example. Against the first y-axis, you plot the rising and falling value of the U.S. dollar. The first y-axis is formatted in dollars and ranges from $0.5 to $1.5. Against the second y-axis, you plot the value of the Japanese yen. The second y-axis is formatted in yen and ranges from 15¥ to 75¥. Figure 7.7 shows such a chart.

Fig. 7.5

A chart that shows only three data sets.

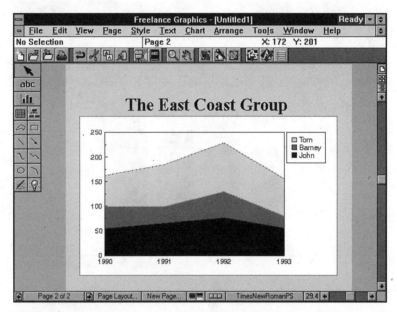

Fig. 7.6

A chart that shows different data sets from the same data.

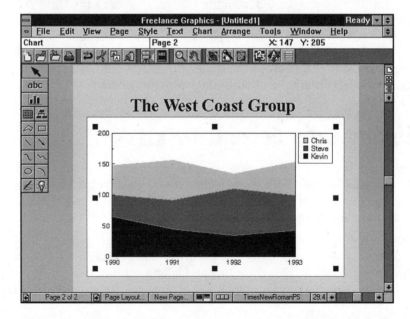

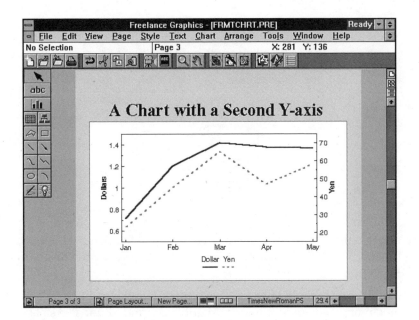

Fig. 7.7

A chart with a second
y-axis.

To add a second y-axis to a chart, click the right mouse button to select
the chart, and then choose Attributes from the pop-up menu. You also
can double-click any bar in the chart or choose **A**ttributes from the
Chart menu. Then click the **U**se Separate Scales check box. From the
list of data sets at the left, choose a data set to be plotted against the
second y-axis and then click **2**Y. If another data set should be plotted
against the second y-axis, click it and then click **2**Y again. You can plot
as many data sets against the second y-axis as you want.

When you change the formatting of the axis labels, you now are able
to choose whether to format the x-axis labels, the y-axis labels, or the
second y-axis labels. In addition, you are able to set different scales for
the y- and second y-axes. You learn about scaling axes and formatting
axis labels next.

Formatting the Axes

With all charts that have axes (pie charts are a notable exception), you
can change the appearance of the axes by selecting the chart and then
choosing **S**cale from the **C**hart menu. The Chart Scale dialog box appears, as shown in figure 7.8.

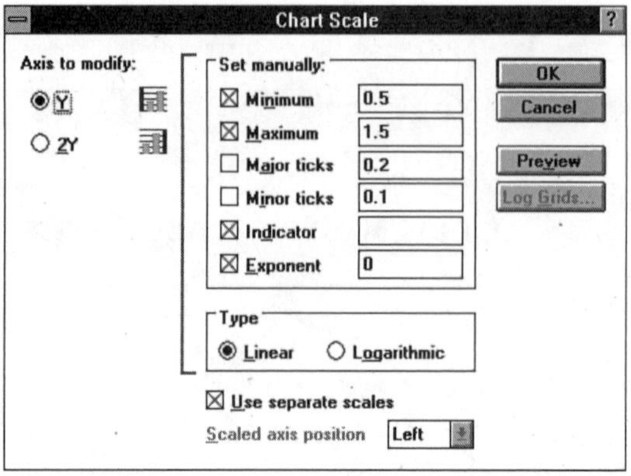

Fig. 7.8

The Chart Scale dialog
box.

To use this dialog box, first select an axis by clicking one of the buttons
on the left. Then use the controls at the right to change the formatting
of the axis.

Minimum and Maximum change the minimum and maximum values at
the beginning and end of the axis. Major Ticks and Minor Ticks set the
intervals along the axis at which tick marks appear. (*Tick marks* are
small lines like the marks along a ruler that register intervals along the
axis.) Axis labels appear at major ticks. Minor ticks are evenly spaced
between major ticks. Figure 7.9 shows one group of settings for Minimum, Maximum, Major Ticks, and Minor Ticks. Figure 7.10 shows these
settings on the y-axis of a chart.

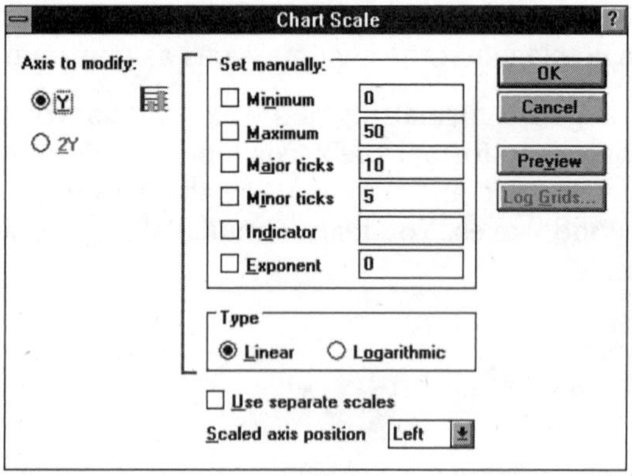

Fig. 7.9

Sample settings for
Minimum, Maximum,
Major Ticks, and Minor
Ticks.

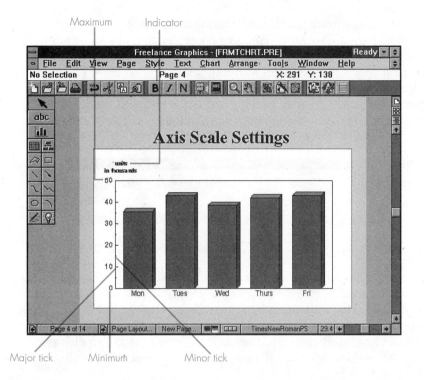

Fig. 7.10

The y-axis that results
from the settings shown
in figure 7.9.

You should always set the Mi**n**imum of a bar chart to 0 because you
cannot gauge the relative heights of bars unless you can see their entire
lengths. A bar chart with the minimum set to anything other than 0 is
inaccurate and deceptive.

To place a second text line underneath the Axis Scale Settings title,
click the check box next to In**d**icator in the Chart Scale dialog box and
then type the text into the In**d**icator text box. Figure 7.10 shows the
indicator that appears when you type **in thousands** in the In**d**icator
text box.

To multiply or divide the values along an axis by a power of 10, enter
the power of 10 into the **E**xponent text box in the Chart Scale dialog
box. This can make very high or very low numbers easier to interpret.
If the data has numbers that are all in millions, for example, enter **3** to
display thousands along the axis. If you use an exponent, be sure to
add text to the chart that explains this. In the previous example, "in
thousands" has been added to the indicator to show that the numbers
were entered in thousands even though they are displayed in tens.

To use a logarithmic rather than linear scale, click the L**o**garithmic button in the Chart Scale dialog box. Each successive value along the selected axis will be 10 times the previous value. Use logarithmic axis scaling only if the variation within the data is very large. When you choose Logarithmic axis scaling, you can choose the position of the logarithmic grid lines by clicking Log **G**rids in the Chart Scale dialog box. The Log Grids dialog box, shown in figure 7.11, lets you enter the number of grid lines (up to 20) and the placement for each grid line.

Fig. 7.11

The Log Grids dialog box.

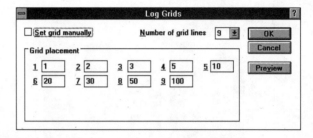

If you are using only one y-axis, you can use the **S**caled Axis Position control in the Chart Scale dialog box to determine whether the axis should appear along the left or right side of the chart, or along both. You can also turn on or off a second y-axis by clicking the **U**se Separate Scales check box.

Formatting Axis Titles and Labels

If you entered axis titles at the same time you entered the data for the chart, you can make some minor changes to the appearance of the titles. (If you have not entered axis titles, you can do so by double-clicking the chart to get to the Chart Data & Titles dialog box and then clicking E**d**it Titles.)

Freelance offers two methods for changing the appearance of a title or the labels that appear along an axis. You can double-click the title or the labels, or you can choose A**x**is Titles and Labels from the **C**hart menu and then choose either **T**itles or **L**abels from the pop-out menu.

Changing the Appearance of Axis Titles

After you choose to format a title, the Chart Axis Titles dialog box appears, as shown in figure 7.12.

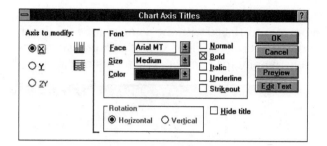

Fig. 7.12

The Chart Axis Titles dialog box.

This dialog box controls two groups of settings: Font and Rotation. Use the Font settings to change the title of the axis you select at the left. The Face setting enables you to choose from among the available typefaces installed in your copy of Windows. With the Size setting, you can choose from among five sizes—Tiny, Small, Medium, Large, and Extra Large. To change the actual point size represented by each of these names, choose All Chart Text from the Chart menu. A dialog box enables you to change the default point size settings for each name and to change the default font for all the text in the chart.

The Rotation settings are available only if you can rotate the title. A vertical y-axis or second y-axis title appears rotated 90 degrees along the axis. A horizontal y-axis or second y-axis title sits at the top of the axis. Click the Hide Title check box to turn off the display of the selected axis title. Turning off the titles when the descriptions of the axes are obvious can leave more space on the page for the graphic part of the chart.

To edit the title text, click the Edit Text button to jump to the Chart Data & Titles dialog box.

Formatting Axis Labels

When you double-click the labels along an axis or choose Labels after choosing Axis Titles & Labels from the Chart menu, the Chart Axis Labels dialog box appears, as shown in figure 7.13.

To change the font of the axis labels, select the axis to modify at the left, and then use the Font settings. Below the Font group are six other settings you can use to change the x- or y-axis labels.

The Number of Places setting, available only when you select a y-axis to format, determines the number of decimal places to which the numbers are displayed. You can choose any number from 0 to 5. All numbers are rounded to the nearest decimal place. The default setting, Auto, displays numbers up to 10,000 with the same number of decimal places entered in the Chart Data & Titles dialog box. Freelance does not display the decimal point for numbers greater than 10,000.

Fig. 7.13

The Chart Axis Labels dialog box.

The Format setting, available only when you select a y-axis to format, determines the style used to display the numbers. Here are the possible settings for Format:

- *Fixed* displays the numbers with the chosen number of decimal places.

- *Scientific* displays the numbers in scientific notation. Scientific notation is always used when the number is greater or equal to 1×10^{11} or smaller than 1×10^{-4}.

- *Currency* displays a currency sign before the numbers and a separator between thousands and hundreds. The currency sign that is used depends on the Tools User Setup International setting.

- *, (comma)* places a comma between the thousands and hundreds digits in the numbers and encloses negative numbers in parentheses.

- *General* displays the numbers with as many decimal places as entered. No separator appears between the thousands and hundreds digits.

- *Percent* shows the numbers as percentages with percent signs. The number entered is multiplied by 100. For example, 0.12 becomes 12%.

- *X suffix* places an X as a factor symbol after every point value.

You use the Hide Axis Labels check box to turn off the display of axis labels in the chart. You can use this control when you want to convey the general growth or decline of data shown by a set of bars or lines without attempting to depict the actual values.

The Adjustments setting, available only when you are formatting x-axis labels, enables you to change the appearance of the x-axis labels when they are crowded along the axis. Slant sets the labels at an angle along the axis. Stagger alternates labels on two rows underneath the axis. Shrink reduces the size of the labels so that they fit the line. When a number grid is displayed under the chart, Shrink is automatically used no matter which setting is chosen.

By using Skip Factor, you can display alternate labels along an x-axis. You can display every other year or every third month, for example. When you enter a Skip Factor other than 1, the Set Skip Factor Manually check box is automatically checked.

Figure 7.14 shows a data chart with slanted x-axis labels and y-axis labels displayed with Currency formatting. Figure 7.15 shows a chart with staggered x-axis labels and with y-axis labels displayed as percentages.

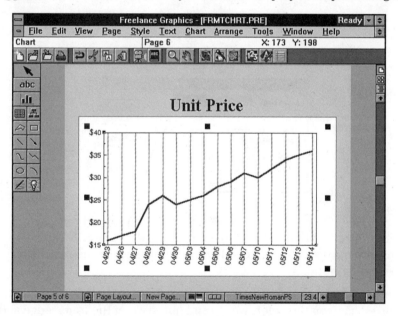

Fig. 7.14

A data chart with slanted x-axis labels and y-axis labels with the Currency format.

Setting the Chart Frame

The frame for a chart is a box that encloses the graphic portion of the chart. When you double-click the frame or choose Frame from the Chart menu, the Chart Frame dialog box appears, as shown in figure 7.16.

Fig. 7.15

A data chart with staggered x-axis labels and with y-axis labels formatted as percentages.

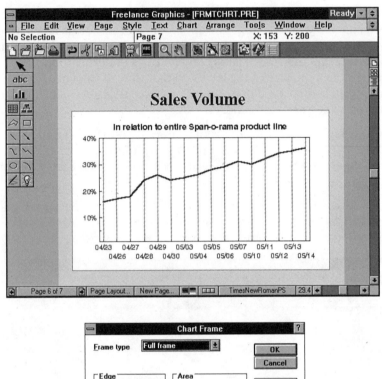

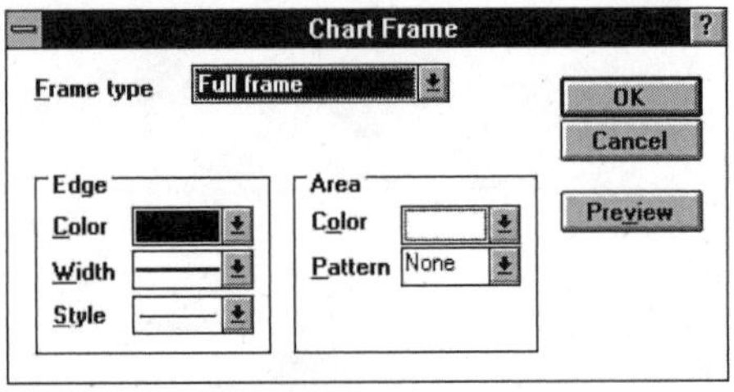

Fig. 7.16

The Chart Frame dialog box.

The **Frame Type** setting enables you to place a frame all the way around the chart (Full Frame), along the x- and y-axes only (X and Y), or along either axis (X or Y). You also can choose not to display the frame by selecting None.

With the Edge and Area settings, you can change the appearance of the frame—changing the color, width, and line style of the frame edge and the color and pattern of the frame area (the interior). Figure 7.17 shows a chart with an X and Y frame type.

When the chart is a high-low-close-open chart, the Chart Frame dialog box shows an additional control, **H**eight for Volume Bars Frame. You can use this setting to change the percentage of the overall height of the chart that will be used by the lower portion of the chart that shows bars representing volume.

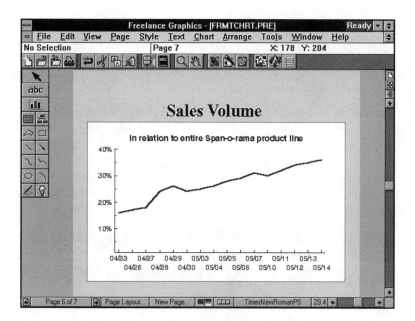

Fig. 7.17

A chart with an X and Y frame type.

Changing the Chart Grid

Grid lines are the horizontal and vertical lines that run across and down the background of a data chart. They help visually align bars, lines, and areas with the x- and y-axes. To change the appearance of the grid lines and tick marks along the axes, double-click any grid line, or select the chart and then choose Grid from the Chart menu. The Chart Grid dialog box appears (see fig. 7.18).

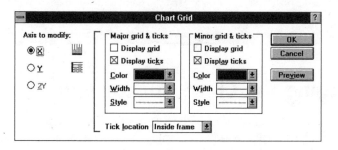

Fig. 7.18

The Chart Grid dialog box.

The Chart Grid dialog box holds separate settings for each axis in the chart. Select an axis at the left and then use the two groups of settings to the right—Major Grid & Ticks and Minor Grid & Ticks. The Major

Grid & Ticks settings refer to the grid lines that appear at the intervals you specified when you set the scale of the axis. Major ticks have axis labels beside them. Major grid lines extend from the ticks to the other side of the chart. Minor grid lines and ticks appear evenly spaced between major grid lines and ticks.

You can choose whether to display the grid and ticks for each axis by clicking the check boxes. In addition, you can choose a color, width, and line style for major and minor grids independently. With the Tick Location option, you can specify whether ticks should extend inside the frame or outside the frame, or whether they should cross the frame. Figure 7.19 shows a chart with solid y-axis grid lines, dotted x-axis grid lines, and major and minor ticks located outside the frame.

Fig. 7.19

A chart with solid y-axis grid lines, dotted x-axis grid lines, and major and minor ticks located outside the frame.

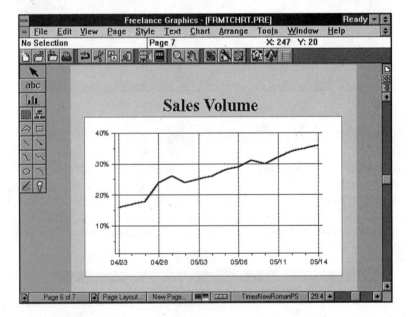

Changing the Chart Background

By default, the background of a chart (a rectangle on which the chart sits) is usually not displayed. To display the background, you must choose Background from the Chart menu. The Chart Background dialog box appears (see fig. 7.20). Click the check box labeled **D**isplay to turn on the background. By clicking the **S**hadow check box, you also can display a subtle shadow behind the background to give it a raised appearance.

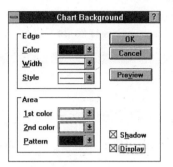

Fig. 7.20

The Chart Background dialog box.

Use the Edge and Area settings to change the look of the edge of the background and its interior. You can fill the background with a color gradient, for example, by choosing different **1**st and **2**nd Color settings and then choosing a gradient style for the **P**attern. Figure 7.21 shows a chart with a gradient background and a shadow behind the background.

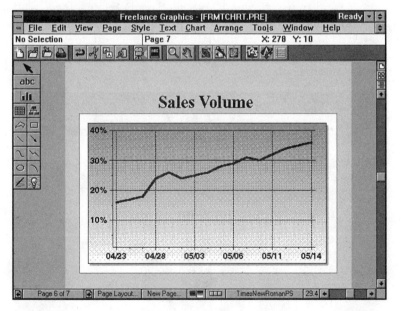

Fig. 7.21

A chart with a shadowed, gradient background.

Creating and Formatting the Legend

Most charts that you create display a legend automatically. The legend helps you distinguish among the data sets in the chart. When you double-click the legend or choose **Legend** from the **Chart** menu, the Chart Legend dialog box appears (see fig. 7.22).

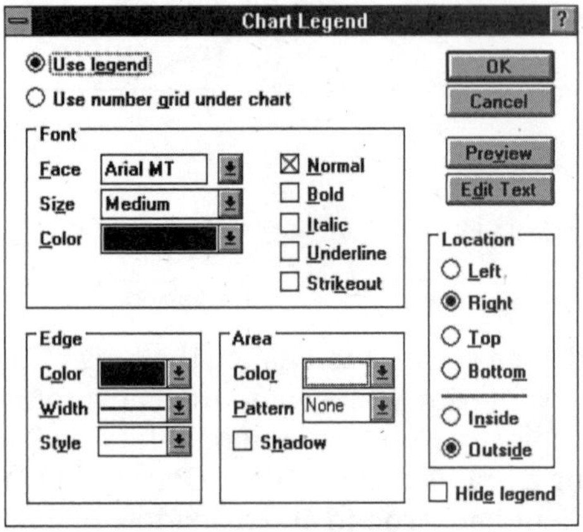

Fig. 7.22

The Chart Legend dialog box.

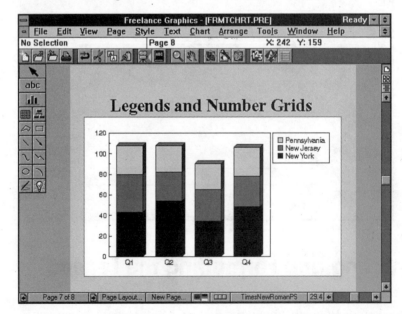

If you don't want to use a legend, you can have Freelance place a number grid under the chart to display the numbers represented by bars, lines, or areas and to identify the data sets as a legend does. Figure 7.23 displays a chart with a standard legend. Figure 7.24 shows the same chart with a number grid.

Fig. 7.23

A chart with a standard legend.

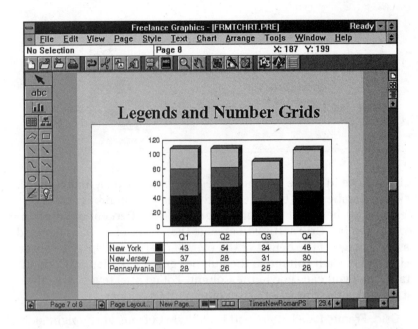

Fig. 7.24

A chart with a number grid.

> **TIP**
>
> To turn off the box surrounding the legend, choose None as the Edge Style.

After you choose Use Legend (the default setting), you can use the Font settings to change the appearance of the text in the legend. You can use the Edge and Area settings to change the appearance of the box surrounding the legend.

With the Location settings, you can determine the position for the legend on the chart. Choose Left, Right, Top, or Bottom, and choose whether the legend will be Inside or Outside the chart.

To turn on or off the legend, click the Hide Legend button.

Formatting a Number Grid

You can turn on a number grid in the Chart Legend dialog box, or you can select the chart and then choose Number Grid under Chart from the Chart menu. The Number Grid Under Chart dialog box appears (see fig. 7.25). If you have already turned on the number grid, you can double-click the number grid to get to this dialog box so that you can change the appearance of the grid.

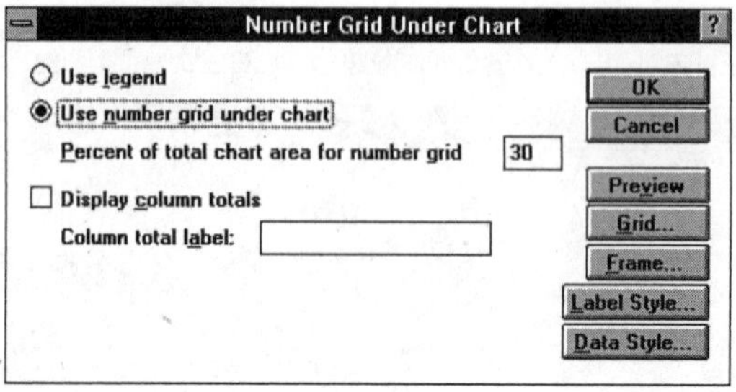

Fig. 7.25

The Number Grid Under
Chart dialog box.

Click Use **L**egend to use a standard legend rather than a number grid. Click Use **N**umber Grid Under Chart to display the number grid. To determine the height of the number grid, use the **P**ercent of Total Chart Area for Number Grid setting to change the height of the number grid as a percentage of the height of the overall chart. To display totals at the bottom of each column in the number grid, click Display **C**olumn Totals. Then you can type in the Column Total La**b**el text box a label that identifies the row where the column totals appear.

The **G**rid, **F**rame, **L**abel Style, and **D**ata Style buttons at the right side of the dialog box lead to four other dialog boxes with which you can set the appearance of different aspects of the number grid. When you click **G**rid, the Number Grid Style dialog box shown in figure 7.26 appears.

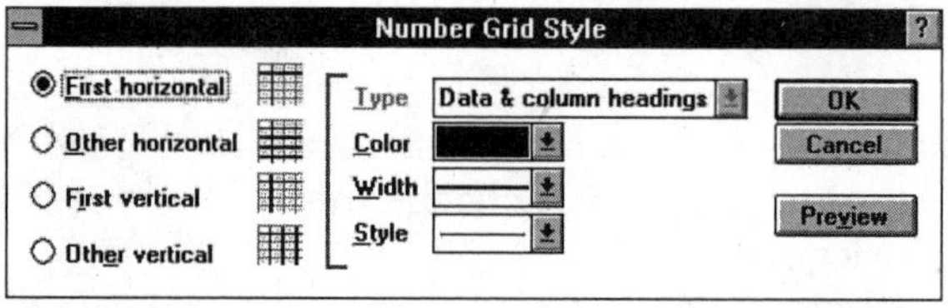

Fig. 7.26

The Number Grid Style
dialog box.

In this dialog box, choose the grid lines you want to format from the four choices at the left, and then use the settings on the right to choose a format. When you choose to format vertical grid lines, you can use the **T**ype setting to determine whether the grid lines will appear in the data and column headings area, only the data area, or only the column heading area.

When you click **F**rame in the Number Grid Under Chart dialog box, the Number Grid Frame dialog box appears, as shown in figure 7.27.

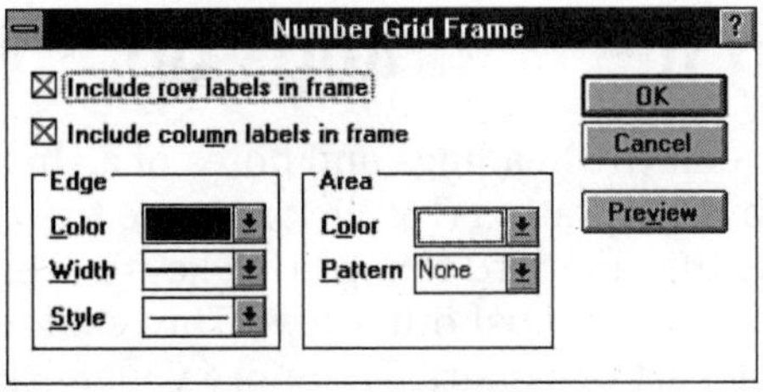

Fig. 7.27

The Number Grid Frame dialog box.

Click the Include **R**ow Labels in Frame check box if you want the frame to extend out and include the row labels to the left of the frame. Click the Include Colu**m**n Labels in Frame check box if you want the frame to extend up and include the column headings in the frame. Then use the Edge and Area settings to change the edge and interior of the frame.

To change the appearance of the labels at the top and left edge of the grid, click **L**abel Style in the Number Grid Under Chart dialog box. In the Number Grid Label Style dialog box, click either Colu**m**n or **R**ow to choose which group of labels to format, and then select text-formatting choices from the options to the right (see fig. 7.28).

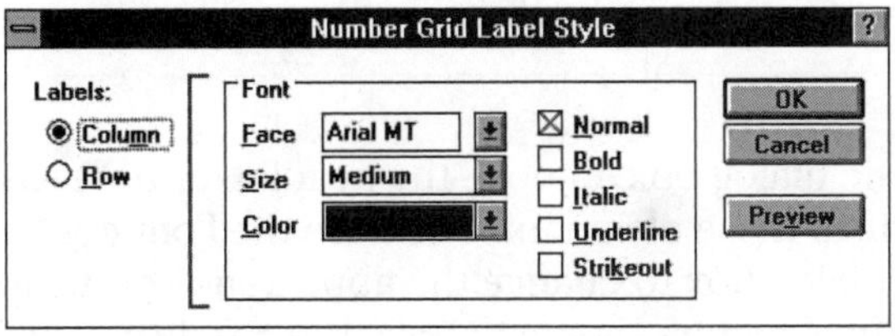

Fig. 7.28

The Number Grid Label Style dialog box.

To change the appearance of the numbers in the number grid, click **D**ata Style in the Number Grid Under Chart dialog box. Use the settings in the dialog box shown in figure 7.29 to change the font, number of decimal places, and formatting of the numbers.

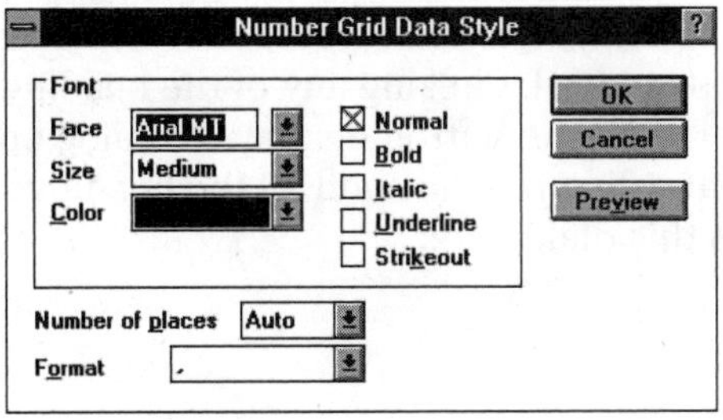

Fig. 7.29

The Number Grid Data Style dialog box.

Formatting the Headings and Notes

Although you can edit the headings and notes of a chart as you would any other text in a presentation (by clicking once to place a typing cursor and then using the standard text-editing keystrokes), you cannot format the text as you can most other text. The text for headings and notes is an integral part of a chart. Therefore you must format this text with the same techniques you use to format any other chart element. You must double-click a heading or note or select the chart, and then choose **H**eadings & Notes from the **C**hart menu to open a dialog box with format settings. Figure 7.30 shows the Chart Headings & Notes dialog box.

Fig. 7.30

The Chart Headings & Notes dialog box.

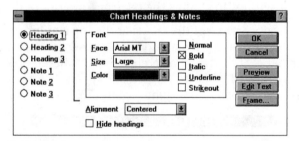

At the left of the dialog box, choose the heading or note to format. Figure 7.31 identifies these elements. Then use the Font controls in the middle of the dialog box to change the appearance of the text. The **A**lignment setting centers the text above the chart (headings) or below the chart (notes) or aligns the text with the left or right side. To turn off the display of all the headings or all the notes but leave the text still available in the Chart Data & Titles dialog box, select a heading or note and then click the **H**ide Headings or **H**ide Notes check box.

Clicking the E**d**it Text button on the right side of the dialog box accesses the Chart Data & Titles dialog box where you can edit the headings and notes you entered. Clicking any of the heading or note buttons and then clicking the F**r**ame button displays a dialog box you can use to design a frame that will appear around all the headings or all the notes. Figure 7.32 shows this dialog box.

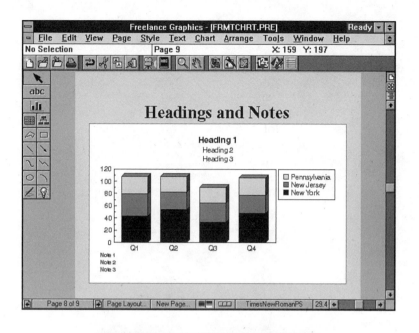

Fig. 7.31

Annotated chart
headings and notes.

Fig. 7.32

The Chart Headings &
Notes Frame dialog box.

Figure 7.33 shows a chart with a shadowed frame around the headings.

Setting Up Value Labels

You can place on the chart the actual numbers that bars and lines represent by adding value labels. Value labels appear at the data points along lines or at the tops of bars, as shown in figure 7.34. You can turn the labels on and change their formatting by choosing **V**alue Labels from the **C**hart menu. The Chart Value Labels dialog box appears (see fig. 7.35).

Fig. 7.33

A chart with a shadowed frame around the headings.

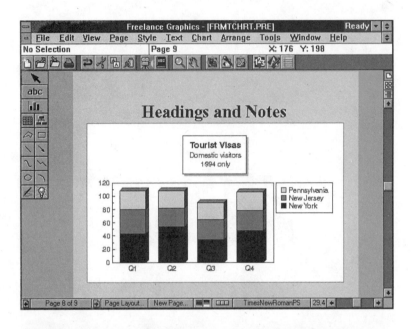

Fig. 7.34

A bar chart with value labels.

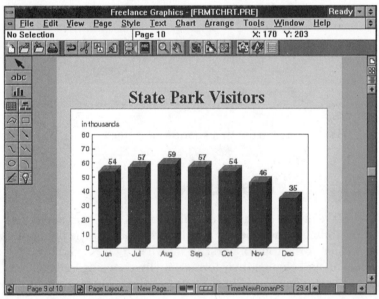

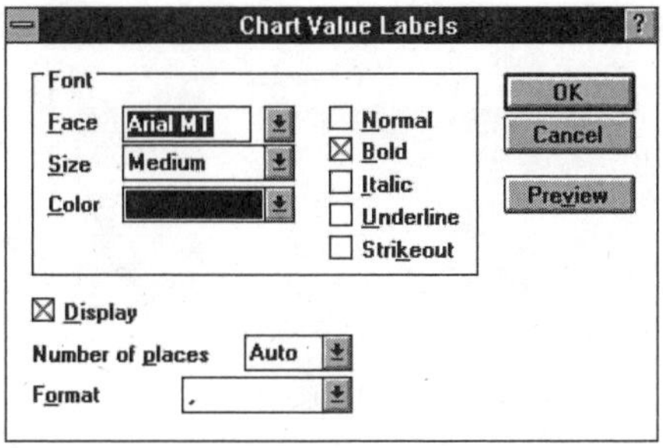

Fig. 7.35

The Chart Value Labels dialog box.

Turn on the display of value labels by clicking the check box next to **D**isplay. The value labels then appear, and the dialog box displays the Font, Number of **P**laces, and F**o**rmat settings. Change any of these settings to change the appearance of the value labels. For information about using the Number of places and format settings, refer to "Formatting Axis Labels" earlier in this chapter.

Formatting Pie Charts

Because pie charts lack the axes, frame, grid, and number grid of bar charts, they have fewer formatting options. Nevertheless, Freelance offers quite a few formatting controls for pie charts.

Changing Slice Colors

Many of the formatting controls for pie charts are in the Pie Chart Attributes dialog box, as shown in figure 7.36. To open this dialog box, double-click a pie chart, right-click a chart and then choose Attributes from the pop-up menu, or select the chart and then choose **A**ttributes from the **C**hart menu.

The Pie Chart Attributes dialog box shows the pie slices with their actual colors in a column at the left (the slices are three-dimensional if you've created a 3D pie). To the right are two sets of controls. The Attributes controls let you change the color and pattern used within the selected slice. The controls for the 3D effects let you change the color and pattern of the sides of 3D pie slices. These controls are available only when the Turn on 3D E**ff**ects check box, also in this dialog box, is checked.

Fig. 7.36

The Pie Chart Attributes
dialog box.

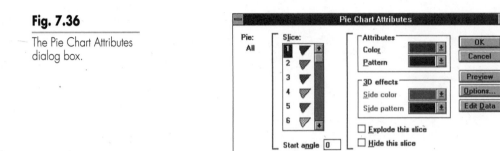

If the pie is not 3D (the Turn on 3D Effects check box is unchecked), two other check boxes become available for use. Select a slice and then click Explode This Slice to emphasize a slice by pulling it out a short way from the rest of the pie. Figure 7.37 shows a pie with an exploded slice. Figure 7.38 shows the same slice hidden. Select a slice and then click Hide This Slice to turn off the display of a slice and hide extraneous data.

Fig. 7.37

A pie chart with an
exploded slice.

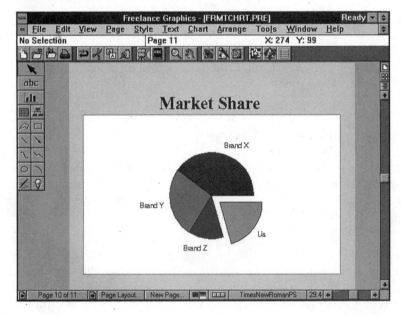

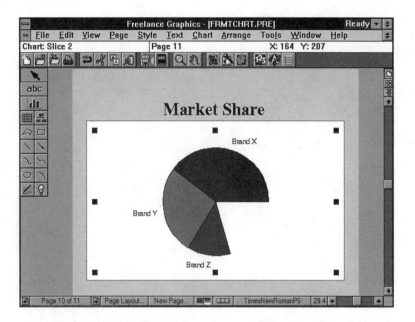

Fig. 7.38

The pie chart with the same slice hidden.

The Start Angle setting, just below the column of pie slices in the Pie Chart Attributes dialog box (refer to fig. 7.36), enables you to rotate the pie. By default, the first pie slice starts at the 3 o'clock position, and other slices are added to the pie in counterclockwise order until the pie is complete. Entering **90**, for example, rotates the entire pie 90 degrees counterclockwise. Figure 7.39 shows two pies side by side. The pie on the right is the same as the pie on the left, but rotated 90 degrees. You may want to rotate a pie when the slice labels conflict with another pie's labels or with another graphic object on the page. You also can change the Start Angle if the slice labels are too long to fit the chart. By rotating the pie, the slices will be at different positions, so the labels will fall at different positions on the chart.

Changing the 3D Depth and Tilt Angle

When you choose to create a 3D Pie from the chart gallery or you turn on the 3D effects for a pie, you can change the depth of the 3D effect by clicking **O**ptions in the Pie Chart Attributes dialog box and then changing one of the settings in a second dialog box, the Pie Chart Options dialog box, that appears. Figure 7.40 shows this dialog box.

Fig. 7.39

The pie on the right, rotated 90 degrees.

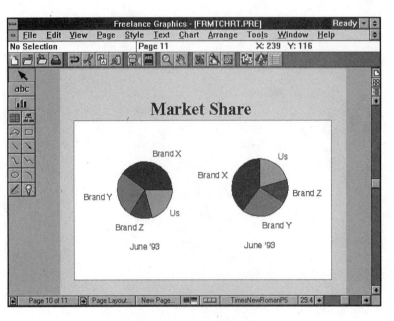

Fig. 7.40

The Pie Chart Options dialog box.

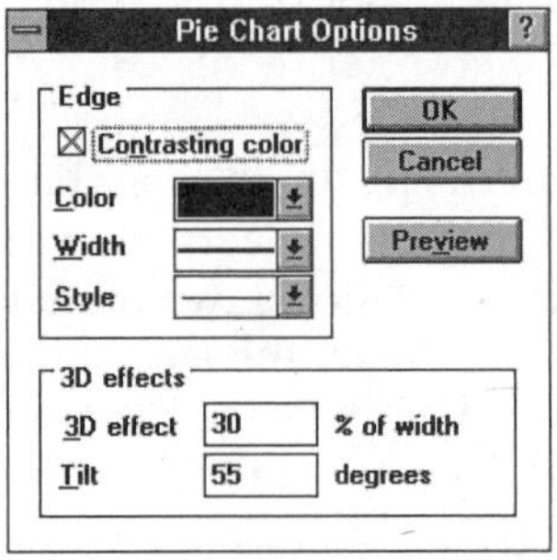

The Edge controls enable you to change the appearance of the edges of all pie slices. To use the Color control, you must click the Contrasting Color check box; otherwise, the edges will be the same colors as the interiors of the slices.

By using the 3D effects controls, you can change the depth of the 3D effect and the tilt of the pie. The **3D Effect** setting is measured as a percentage of the width of the pie (a setting of 50 makes the pie about half as tall as it is wide). The **Tilt** setting enables you to tilt the pie away from you. Zero degrees creates a two-dimensional pie; 89 degrees, the maximum setting (and a useless one), creates a pie that appears to lie flat. The default setting of 55 produces an attractive tilt. Figure 7.41 shows a pie with a 50% 3D effect and a severe 65 degree tilt.

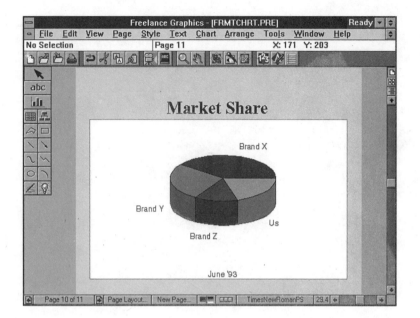

Fig. 7.41

A pie with a 50% 3D
effect and a 65 degree
tilt.

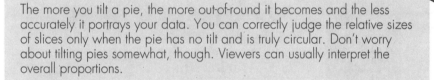

CAUTION

The more you tilt a pie, the more out-of-round it becomes and the less
accurately it portrays your data. You can correctly judge the relative sizes
of slices only when the pie has no tilt and is truly circular. Don't worry
about tilting pies somewhat, though. Viewers can usually interpret the
overall proportions.

When you finish with the Pie Chart Options dialog box, click OK to return to the Pie Chart Attributes dialog box.

Using a Legend or Slice Labels

Freelance offers two ways to identify the slices of a pie. A legend shows
the color or pattern coding you used. Legends are useful when a chart
has two or more pies. Slice labels are placed next to slices. If you have
only a single pie and the labels are short, slice labels are better because
they do not require the viewer to color-match slices with a legend. Figure 7.42 shows a pie with slice labels. Figure 7.43 shows the same pie
with a legend.

Fig. 7.42

A pie chart with slice labels.

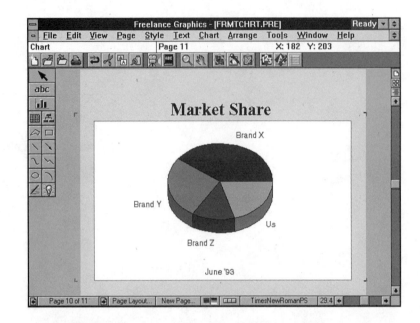

Fig. 7.43

The same pie chart with a legend rather than slice labels.

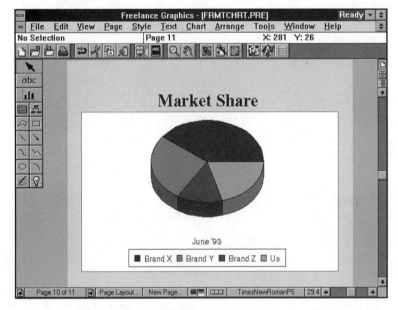

You can decide whether a pie chart will have a legend or slice labels when you choose a pie chart style from the chart gallery. Or you can decide between a legend and slice labels after you choose **Legend** from the **C**hart menu. Click either Use **L**egend or Use **S**lice Labels in the Single Pie Chart Legend dialog box, as shown in figure 7.44.

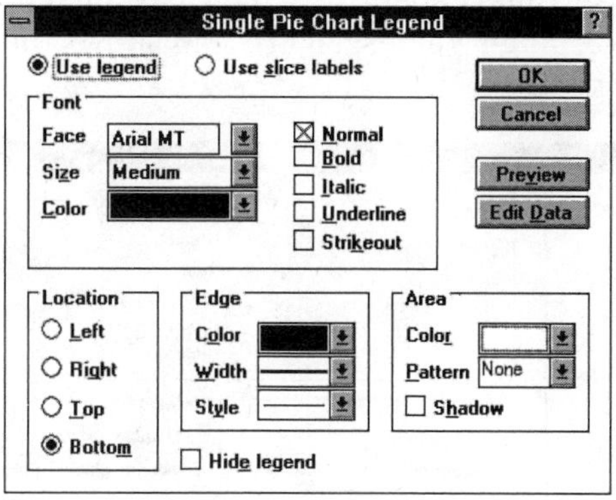

Fig. 7.44

The Single Pie Chart Legend dialog box.

If you choose Use **S**lice Labels, Freelance grays out all other controls in the dialog box. If you choose Use **L**egend instead, you can use the Font, Location, Edge, and Area controls to set the appearance of the legend.

To change the formatting of slice labels, you must choose **P**ie Titles & Labels from the **C**hart menu. The Pie Chart Titles & Labels dialog box appears, as shown in figure 7.45.

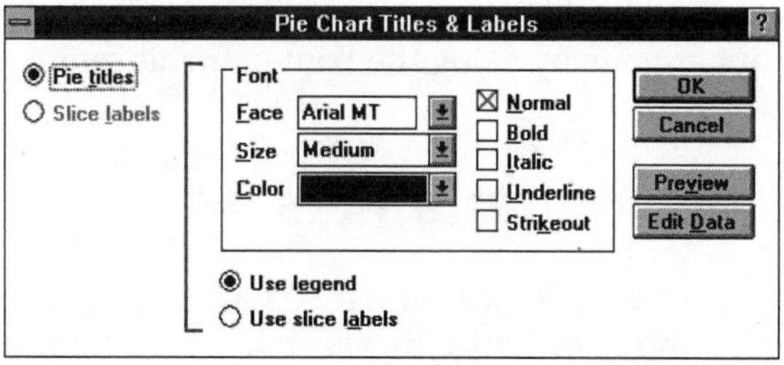

Fig. 7.45

The Pie Chart Titles & Labels dialog box.

Click the Pie Titles button at the left and then use the controls in the middle to change the text formatting of the titles at the top of the pie. Click the Slice **L**abels button and then use the controls at the right to change the text formatting of the slice labels. If you decide that the slice labels you have formatted are still not right, you can always switch to a legend by clicking Use **L**egend at the bottom of this dialog box.

Value Labels

To place the actual number that each slice represents adjacent to the slice label, choose **V**alue Labels from the **C**hart menu and then click the Di**s**play check box under Values. Figure 7.46 shows the Pie Chart Value Labels dialog box.

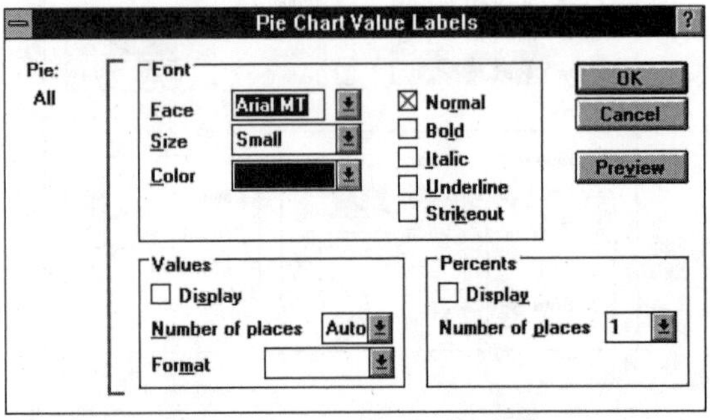

Fig. 7.46

The Pie Chart Value Labels dialog box.

The **N**umber of Places and For**m**at options are the same as those offered for axis labels on bar charts. For detailed information, refer to the section "Formatting Axis Titles and Labels," earlier in this chapter.

To display the percentage that each slice represents, click the Displa**y** check box under Percents. You can display both the actual values and the percentages by checking both boxes. Change the text formatting for the values and percents by using the Font controls mentioned earlier.

Formatting Multiple Pies

When you choose Multiple Pies from the chart gallery, Freelance may not give you the option of using slice labels. Freelance assumes that you will want to use the same colors for corresponding slices in all the pies and that a legend can identify these colors. To create pies with separate colors and slice labels, you must choose **O**ptions from the **C**hart menu and then choose **P**ie from the pop-out menu. The dialog box shown in figure 7.47 appears.

When you choose **S**hared Attributes & Legend, Freelance uses the same color scheme for all pies and places a legend on the chart. When you choose Se**p**arate Attributes (No Legend), however, Freelance enables you to enter separate slice labels for each pie in the Chart Data & Titles dialog box, as well as different colors and different starting angles for each pie. To choose the colors, double-click the pie to bring up the Attributes dialog box and then choose from among the pie chart choices at the left (Pie A, B, C, or D) before choosing a slice color or starting angle. When you choose Separate Attributes, you also can change the attributes of the value labels independently for each pie.

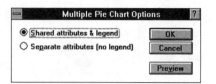

Fig. 7.47

The Multiple Pie Chart Options dialog box.

Formatting High-Low-Close-Open Charts

Formatting high-low-close-open (HLCO) charts is much like formatting standard bar or line charts. HLCO charts have two independent y-axes, though (see fig. 7.48), so dialog boxes often display a pair of buttons that let you specify whether you want to format the Y or Bottom Y axis. After you choose Scale to change the minimum and maximum values, for example, you must click either **Y** or **B**ottom Y to let Freelance know which y-axis you want to scale.

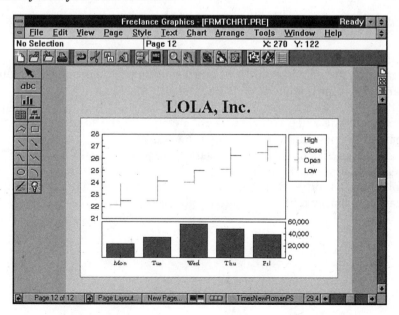

Fig. 7.48

An HLCO chart.

As with all charts, double-click any element within the HLCO chart to access the chart's Attributes dialog box, as shown in figure 7.49. Choose a chart element from the Data Set list at the left and then change the color or width with the Attributes controls. The other settings are grayed.

Fig. 7.49

The HLCO Chart Attributes dialog box.

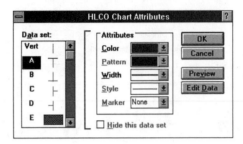

One other setting that is exclusive to HLCO charts appears when you choose Frame from the Chart menu. By using a setting called Height for Volume Bars Frame in the Chart Frame dialog box, you can determine the height for the lower portion of the chart that displays bars as a percentage of the full height of the chart. To make the bar portion of the chart one-quarter of the height of the entire chart, you enter 25%, for example.

Setting a Default Chart

While you are working in a presentation, you can set a chart you have created as the default chart for the presentation. Then, whenever you start a new chart, you can click Use Default Chart in the New Chart Gallery dialog box to use the formatting of the default chart. If the chart contained data when you set it as the default chart, the same data appears in the new chart too. You can then edit the data. When you need to create a series of charts of the same design, for example, you can create the first chart, including entering its data, and set it as the default chart. On other pages in the series, you can then use the default chart and simply edit the data to complete the chart.

To set a chart as the default chart, select the chart and then choose Replace **D**efaults from the **C**hart menu. The chart type and style, all formatting, and any data will be stored as the default chart for the current presentation.

Ungrouping a Chart

A chart on a presentation page is a single object linked to the data on the chart's Chart Data & Titles dialog box. The only way to modify the chart is to change the data or change the formatting of a chart element with the formatting commands and dialog boxes you learned about earlier in this chapter.

You can convert a chart to a collection of drawing objects by ungrouping it so that you can manipulate each individual shape within the chart as if it had been added with the drawing tools of Freelance. After you ungroup a chart, you gain access to each shape within the chart (each bar, line, or pie slice), and you can move, stretch, copy, recolor, and perform many other actions on them just as you can for any graphic shape. You learn about using the drawing tools of Freelance to edit drawing objects in Chapter 13, "Editing Objects."

After you ungroup a chart, however, you lose access to its data. The chart is now simply a picture of a data chart without the numbers. If you have created a chart by linking the chart to data in another file or application, the link is severed. After you ungroup a chart, you can never regroup it.

If a chart is in a "Click here to create chart" block, you must press the Ctrl key and drag the chart away from the block before Freelance lets you ungroup it. You will have no problem ungrouping a chart placed on a page if you didn't use a "Click here..." block, though.

To ungroup the chart, select the chart and then choose **U**ngroup from the **A**rrange menu. A warning message reminds you of the dangers of ungrouping a chart. Click OK to proceed and ungroup the chart. When the chart is ungrouped, handles surround each shape within the chart. Each shape is now a separate drawing object. Click outside the chart to deselect all the objects, and then click any one object to work with it independently. Figure 7.50 shows a chart that has been ungrouped. Notice the handles around each drawing object in the picture.

Fig. 7.50

An ungrouped chart.

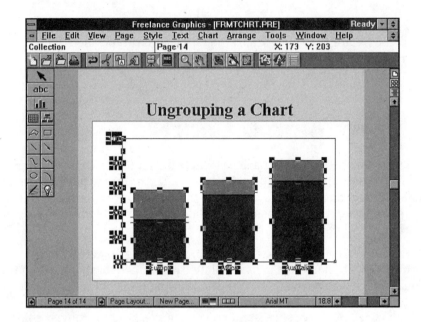

Summary

In this chapter, you learned how to change the appearance of charts that you add to presentation pages. You learned to use the attribute settings to make overall changes and to select individual chart components for more detailed formatting changes.

In the next chapter, you learn to import the data for a chart from another file or from another Windows application.

Importing the Data for a Data Chart

Why retype the numbers for a chart when you can import them into Freelance instead? Retyping is more work and introduces the possibility of human error. By importing the numbers from a file or another program, you can quickly chart data that you keep somewhere else. What's more, you can usually set up a link between the original numbers and the Freelance chart. If the original numbers change, so does your chart.

Importing Data from a Lotus 1-2-3 or Microsoft Excel File

Freelance can access Lotus 1-2-3, Symphony, and Microsoft Excel worksheets and, with a little help from you, selectively pull data into a Chart Data & Titles dialog box. After the data is in the dialog box, one click of the **OK** button will chart the data automatically.

Identifying the Source and Destination for the Data

For an import from 1-2-3 or Excel to work successfully, you must select the data to import in the spreadsheet program and then identify how the data will be used in Freelance. During the import process, you actually see the 1-2-3 or Excel worksheet in a window within Freelance, and you then can identify the parts of the worksheet to use for various parts of the chart. You can mark worksheet cells that contain legend entries, for example, so that the contents of the cells will be used as legend entries in a Freelance chart. You can even set up a link between the 1-2-3 or Excel data and the Freelance data chart so that changes to the 1-2-3 or Excel data will update the chart automatically.

To import data from a 1-2-3 or Excel worksheet, you must open the Chart Data & Titles dialog box for a chart (see fig. 8.1). You get to the Chart Data & Titles dialog box whenever you start a new data chart or double-click an existing data chart. From that window, click **Import**, press F6 (Import), or click the Import Data SmartIcon. When the Import Data File dialog box opens, as shown in figure 8.2, select the type of file to import from the drop-down list of File **Types**, and then use the File **Name** and **Directories** controls to find the file.

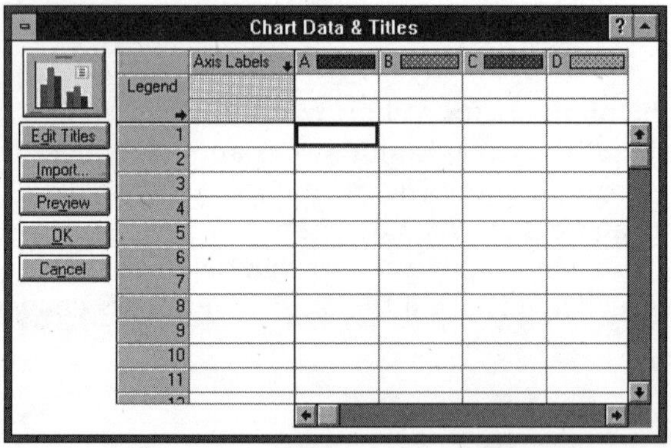

Fig. 8.1

The Chart Data & Titles dialog box for a new data chart.

> **Chart Data & Titles**
>
> Legend
> Axis Labels   A   B   C   D
>
> Edit Titles
> Import...
> Preview
> OK
> Cancel
>
> 1 2 3 4 5 6 7 8 9 10 11

After you select a worksheet file, the Import Data dialog box opens, as shown in figure 8.3. Data from the worksheet you have chosen appears in the dialog box, along with controls on the left that let you identify the cells that contain legends, labels, and chart data. An illustration below these controls shows a sample bar chart and points out the legends and labels.

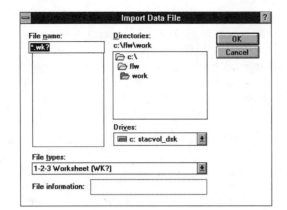

Fig. 8.2

The Import Data File dialog box.

Fig. 8.3

The Import Data dialog box showing the selected worksheet data.

If you have not selected the correct worksheet, click the **F**ile button to return to the Import Data File dialog box so that you can select a different file.

TIP

If you have already used the Import Data dialog box to select a worksheet, the same worksheet will appear in that dialog box the next time you click **I**mport. Freelance assumes that you want to import data from the same worksheet again. To choose a different worksheet, click the **F**ile button to get to the Import Data File dialog box.

When the worksheet data appears in the Import Data dialog box, you can choose the data to import to Freelance. You may want to import only certain sets of numbers, or you may want to import only the row headings from the worksheet to use as legend entries and type the numbers from another source. Imagine that you need to chart the sales results of 10 salespeople whose names happen to appear in a 1-2-3 worksheet. You can import only the names from the worksheet as label entries, so the names will appear along the x-axis and under the bars of a bar chart.

To identify the range of cells that contains legend entries, labels, or chart data, select the range and then click the Copy **L**egends, Copy **L**abels, or Copy **C**hart Data check box. The cells you select will become color coded. For example, the legend entry cells will be outlined in red, the label entry cells will be outlined in green, and the chart data cells will be outlined in blue. These colors are shown in the bar chart diagram within the dialog box.

If you have named ranges in the 1-2-3 or Excel worksheet, you can automatically go to and select a named range by clicking the **R**anges button and then choosing the range name from the list that appears.

If you identify a range of cells as chart data but do not identify which cells hold labels or legends, Freelance will not be able to determine whether the columns in the Chart Data & Titles dialog box should be filled with numbers from worksheet columns or worksheet rows. Freelance asks you for the answer in the Data Orientation dialog box, as shown in figure 8.4.

Fig. 8.4

The Data Orientation dialog box.

Data Orientation	
You have selected a range in this file that will be used for your chart's data.	**OK** / **Cancel**
When you leave this dialog box, this range will appear in the Chart Data & Titles window in the columns labelled A, B, C, ...	
Should the A, B, C, ... columns be made up from	
⦿ the columns or	
○ the rows	
of your selected range?	

Linking the Data

By clicking the Lin**k** Selections check box in the Import Data dialog box before you click OK to import the data, you can create a link between the data in the 1-2-3 or Excel worksheet and the data in Freelance. Once a link is created, the chart will update if the worksheet is changed. You can determine whether this update will be automatic or manual.

Linked data in a Freelance Chart Data & Titles dialog box is shown underlined in light blue.

> To return to the Import Data dialog box to change any of the linking, double-click any data that is linked (underlined in light blue).

To change the type of link established between a worksheet and a chart, select the chart in Current Page view and then choose **Links** from the **Edit** menu. A Links dialog box, similar to the one shown in figure 8.5, shows the current link settings for the selected chart.

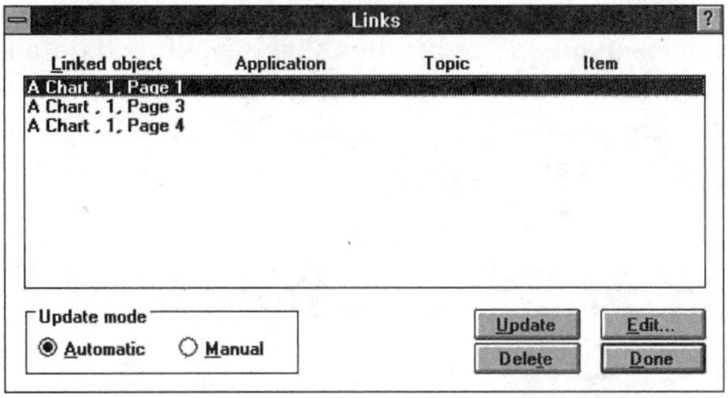

Fig. 8.5

A typical Links dialog box.

With the Update Mode controls, you can choose whether the link will be **Automatic**, updating every time the data changes, or **Manual**, updating only when you click **Update** in the Links dialog box. To delete the link but leave the data for the chart in Freelance, click **Delete**. To edit the link, click **Edit**. The Edit Links dialog box appears (see fig. 8.6).

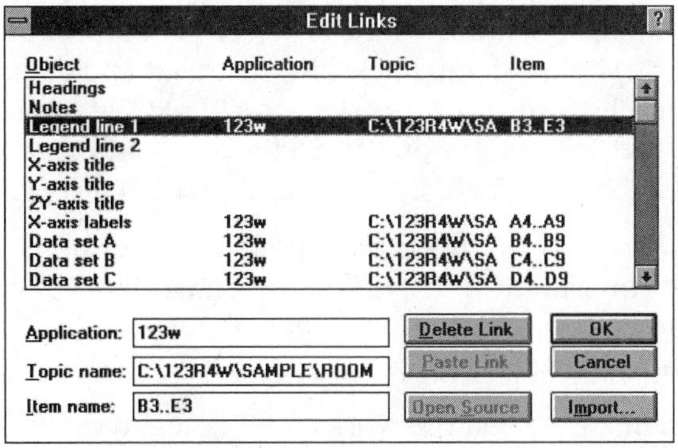

Fig. 8.6

The Edit Links dialog box.

Under **O**bject, you'll find a list of the chart parts that can be linked. If a link exists for that chart part, information about the link is presented also. Application lists the name of the application from which the data was imported. Topic lists the path name and file name to the linked data. Item lists the range from which the data was imported.

Click an object to move its information to the **A**pplication, **T**opic Name, and **I**tem Name text boxes within the dialog box, where the object can be edited. To delete a link but leave the current data in Freelance, click the link and then click **D**elete Link. To create a new link, click an **O**bject that is not already linked and then click **I**mport. When the Import Data dialog box opens, select the data to link and then click OK. In the Edit Links dialog box, click **P**aste Link to show the link on the list. The Open **S**ource button is available only when you have linked data from a Windows application by using Object Linking and Embedding (OLE). Click OK when you finish using the Edit Links dialog box. Then click Done if you have finished changing the links in the chart.

Importing Additional Data to a Freelance Chart

If you need to copy additional data from a worksheet file to a Freelance Chart Data & Titles dialog box, you must copy and paste the data with a special technique.

Click **I**mport in the Chart Data & Titles dialog box and then open the worksheet from which you want to pull data. Then select the data and click OK without clicking the Copy **C**hart Data check box. An information window opens indicating that the selected data will be copied to the Windows Clipboard if you click OK. Go ahead and click OK to copy the data to the Clipboard and return to the Chart Data & Titles dialog box. Position the cell pointer on the first cell where you want the data to appear; then choose **P**aste from the **E**dit menu of Freelance.

This procedure will work only if the data in the worksheet is oriented the same way you want it to appear in the Chart Data & Titles dialog box. If you copy a row of data from a worksheet, the data will be pasted as a row of data in Freelance.

To establish a link between the worksheet data and the Freelance data, or to copy and paste the data and transpose a row of numbers into a column, click P**a**ste Special (rather than **P**aste) from the Freelance Edit menu. When the Edit Paste Special dialog box appears, as shown in figure 8.7, select the data set from the scrollable list of chart parts and then click OK. To link the data, click the **L**ink Data check box before you click OK. If you have selected a worksheet row, the row of numbers will appear as a column in the Chart Data & Titles dialog box.

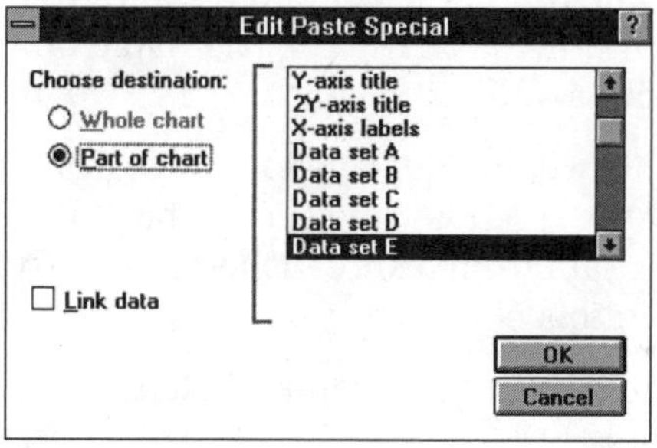

Fig. 8.7

The Edit Paste Special dialog box.

Importing Data from an ASCII File

When the data you need to chart is in an ASCII file, you can import the ASCII file into the Chart Data & Titles dialog box just as you'd import a 1-2-3 or Excel worksheet. Being able to import an ASCII file also makes it possible to import data from a DOS program that is not a Windows application or from an ASCII file downloaded from a mainframe or another large, remote computer. As long as the DOS program or other source can place an ASCII file on your system, you'll be able to chart the numbers in Freelance easily.

The data in an ASCII file must be arranged in columns separated by spaces or tabs. Any text that you want as legend entries or axis labels must be enclosed in quotation marks; otherwise, it will be ignored, and only the numbers will be imported. The following example shows the contents of an ASCII file whose text and numbers can be successfully imported into Freelance:

```
Training Days
Jan. - Apr.

           "Sharon"      "Richard"
"Jan"        13            14
"Feb"        16            19
"Mar"        12            17
"Apr"        18            20
```

To import the ASCII file, click **I**mport in the Chart Data & Titles dialog box and then choose ASCII Numbers (PRN), using the File **T**ypes control near the bottom of the Import Data File dialog box. Use the **D**irectories and File **N**ame controls to find and select the ASCII file. Freelance assumes that the ASCII file will have a PRN extension, but you can change the filter at the top of the list of file names to filter out files with other extensions. Entering ***.TXT** in the File **N**ame box, for example, will display only files with a TXT extension.

The data from the file will be displayed in the Import Data dialog box. Proceed to identify the legends, labels, and chart data as you would if you were importing data from a spreadsheet. Refer to the description of this step earlier in this chapter.

Figure 8.8 shows the data in the sample ASCII file as it is displayed in the Import Data dialog box.

Fig. 8.8

The ASCII data displayed in the Import Data dialog box.

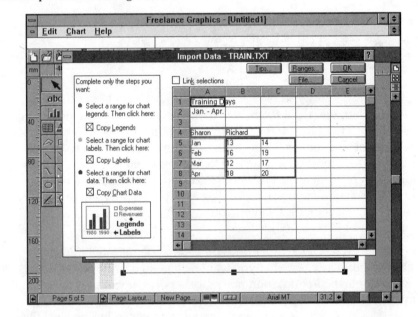

Notice that the column headings have imported into the wrong cells. The first column heading is in cell A4 rather than B4. The second heading is in B4 rather than C4. You can still identify the cells as legends or labels, and they will go into the correct position in the Chart Data & Titles dialog box. Figure 8.8 shows also how ranges of cells have been identified as labels, legends, and chart data. Figure 8.9 shows the data after it is imported into the Chart Data & Titles dialog box.

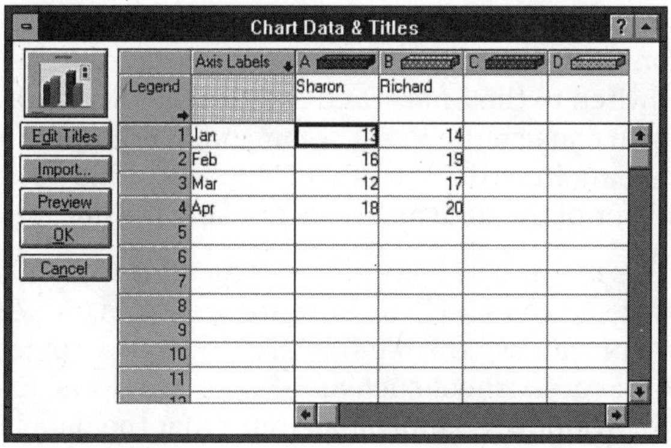

Fig. 8.9

The data after importing into Freelance.

Importing Data from Another Windows Application

When the data you need to chart is in another Windows application, you can easily copy it into the Chart Data & Titles dialog box. With certain other Windows applications, you can even set up an active link between the original data and the data in Freelance. The active link causes the chart in Freelance to update immediately when you make any change to the original data in another application. The active link is called a DDE link. (DDE stands for a Windows capability called Dynamic Data Exchange. DDE is one part of another Windows capability called Object Linking and Embedding, or OLE.)

The benefits of DDE linking are enormous. You don't have to worry about updating a Freelance presentation if any of the data it depends on is updated. Even if you didn't know about a change that somebody made to the 1-2-3 for Windows data on which a Freelance data chart is based, your data chart will still accurately reflect the 1-2-3 for Windows changes.

Copying Data from a Windows Application

To copy data from another Windows application to a Freelance chart when you have no concern whether the chart is updated if the original data changes, you can use the Windows Clipboard with the Copy and

Paste commands. After selecting the data in the other application, use the application's Copy command to copy the data to the Windows Clipboard. Then switch to the Chart Data & Titles dialog box of a Freelance chart. There you can use the **Paste** command in Freelance's **Edit** menu to retrieve the data from the Windows Clipboard. This performs a one-time-only transfer of the data and does not set up a link.

You can use this method to copy and paste a table from a Windows word processor such as Ami Pro, Word for Windows, or WordPerfect for Windows. You can use the method also to copy a range of numbers from a Windows spreadsheet such as 1-2-3 for Windows, Excel, or Quattro Pro for Windows. Simply make sure that the data is set up in the cells of a table, in tab-separated columns, or in the cells of a spreadsheet. Then select the data to chart and use the Copy command in the application's Edit menu to copy the data to the Windows Clipboard.

When you plan to perform a one-time-only copy and paste of data into Freelance, the data in most Windows applications must be arranged the same way you want it to appear in the Freelance Chart Data & Titles dialog box. The data sets that you will represent with lines or sets of bars must be arranged vertically in columns, rather than horizontally in rows. Some Windows applications supply the data to Freelance in such a way that Freelance can ask whether you want to transpose the rows and columns. Spreadsheets are in this category. Figure 8.10 shows a 1-2-3 for Windows worksheet range that can be easily copied to Freelance because each series of numbers is arranged in a column. Figure 8.11 shows the same worksheet with the data arranged in rows. This second worksheet requires an additional procedure that will transpose the rows and columns. You may have to test Windows applications other than spreadsheets to see whether the transposition procedure described next will work.

When the data sets are arranged correctly in columns and you do not need to create a link, follow this procedure:

1. Open the other application containing the data.

2. Select the data to copy to a Freelance Graphics chart.

3. From the Edit menu of the other application, choose the Copy command.

4. Switch to Freelance Graphics for Windows.

5. Position the cell pointer in the Chart Data & Titles dialog box where you want the data to appear. Place the pointer in the gray cell at the top of the Axis Labels column and to the left of the

Legend row if you have also selected the column and row headings in the other application. Place the pointer in the first blank cell if you have selected only the data without selecting the column and row headings.

6. From the **Edit** menu of Freelance, choose **Paste**.

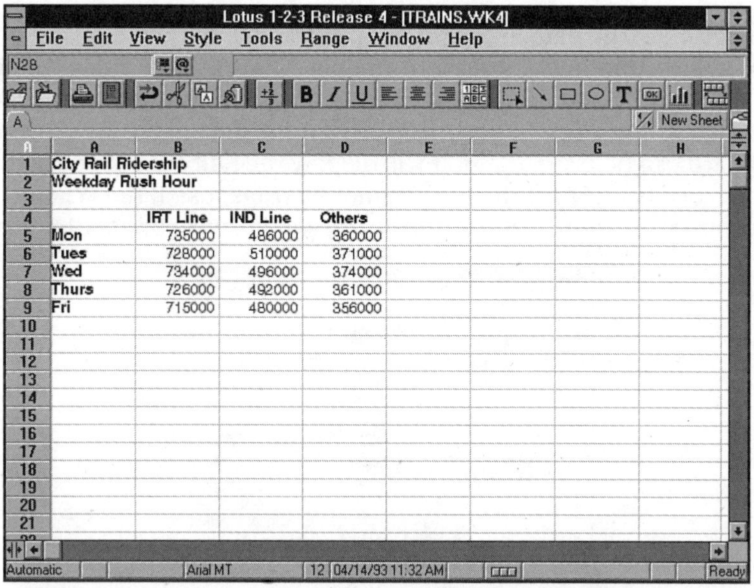

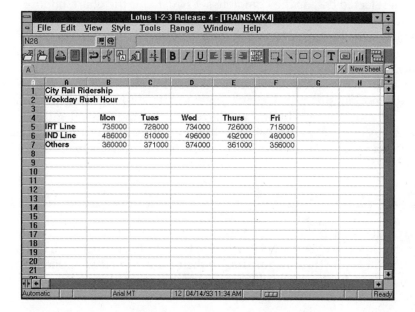

Fig. 8.10

An easily imported worksheet with data arranged in columns.

Fig. 8.11

The same data arranged in worksheet rows; the rows and columns must be transposed.

Transposing the Columns and Rows

If the rows and columns of data in the other application need to be transposed for the Freelance graph, or if you want to link the other application's data with the Freelance chart, you must use the Paste Special command to retrieve the data from the Windows Clipboard.

After selecting the data in the other application and then copying it to the Windows Clipboard, switch to an open Chart Data & Titles dialog box in Freelance and then choose Paste Special from the Edit menu of Freelance. If Freelance has recognized that the data in the Windows Clipboard can be transposed, it will display the Edit Paste Special dialog box (see fig. 8.12). If the data cannot be transposed, the Whole Chart option in the Edit Paste Special dialog box will appear dimmed.

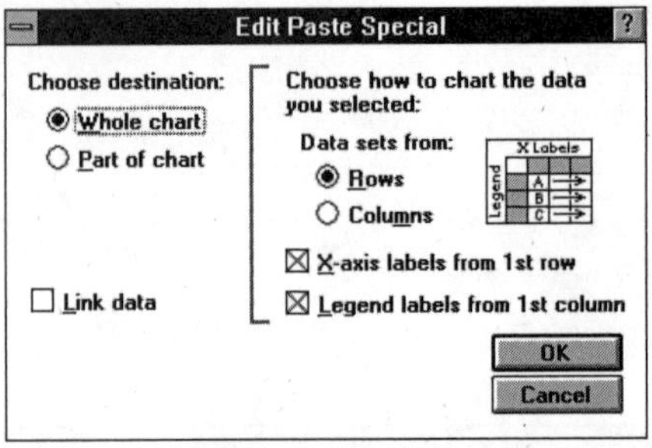

Fig. 8.12

The Edit Paste Special dialog box in Freelance.

If the selected data is the complete set of data for the chart, choose Whole Chart. A set of options at the right within the dialog box lets you specify whether the data sets in the 1-2-3 data are arranged in rows or columns. If the data sets are arranged in columns, Freelance will import them as is to the Chart Data & Titles dialog box. If the data sets are arranged in rows, Freelance will transpose the rows and columns before importing them. Two check boxes in the Edit Paste Special dialog box let you indicate whether you have included the column and row headings in selected data and whether to include them as x-axis labels or legend entries in the Freelance Chart Data & Titles dialog box.

Creating and Editing a DDE Link

To create a link between the other application's data and the Freelance chart, click the Link Data check box in the Edit Paste Special dialog box. After you create the link, updates to the data in the other application will update the Freelance chart if you have automatic updating turned on. If not, you must manually update the link.

To turn on automatic updating of links, choose **Links** from the
Freelance **Edit** menu. The Links dialog box appears (see fig. 8.13).

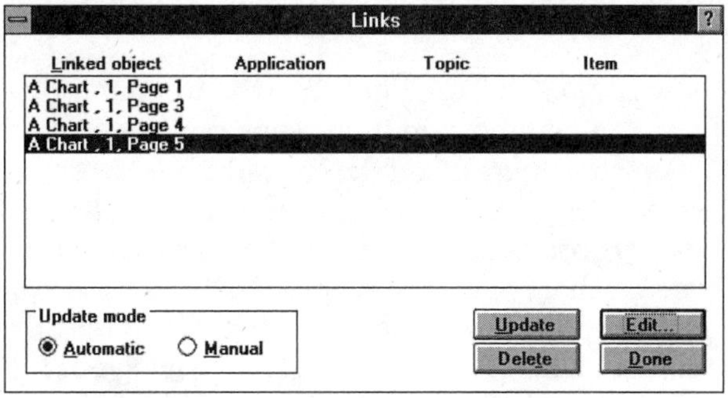

Fig. 8.13

The Links dialog box.

Each row within the dialog box lists a link between a Freelance chart
and another application. Click one of the links and then make sure that
Automatic is selected under Update Mode. To change a link to manual
updating, click **Manual**. To update the link manually, you need to open
this dialog box, select the link to update from the list, click the **Update**
button, and then click **Done**.

To delete a link, select the link and then click Delete. The link will be
broken, but the data will remain as imported in the Freelance Chart
Data & Titles dialog box. If any changes occur to the data in the original
application, they will not be reflected in the Freelance chart, though.

To modify a link, select the link and then click the **Edit** button. The Edit
Links dialog box opens (see fig. 8.14).

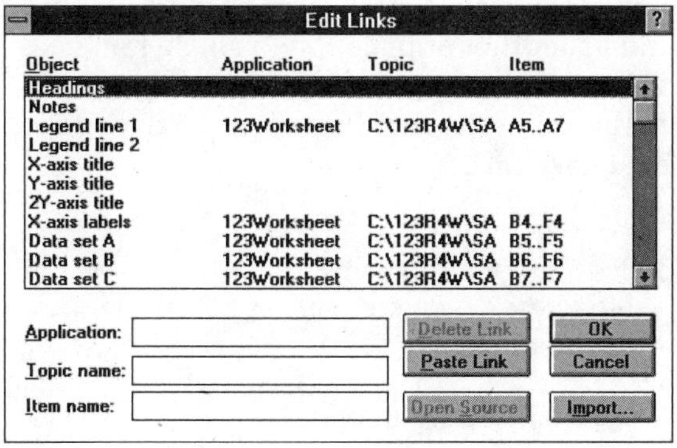

Fig. 8.14

The Edit Links dialog
box.

Each row within the dialog box displays the part of the chart and information about the data with which it is linked, including the Application, Topic (usually the file name), and Item (usually the range address of a spreadsheet).

To change information on a row, click the row and then edit the text in the **A**pplication, **T**opic Name, and **I**tem Name text boxes. With this facility, you can link a chart part to a different range in a worksheet, for example. To selectively delete links between parts of the chart and the data, click the appropriate row and then click **D**elete Link. To create a new link between a chart part that is not linked and data in another application, click Import, select the data when the Import Data dialog box opens, and then click OK. In the Edit Links dialog box, click **P**aste Link to paste the new link into the list.

Importing Data to Part of a Chart

If you select data in another Windows application that contains data for only part of a chart, perhaps a single data set, choose **P**art of Chart from the Edit Paste Special dialog box. The dialog box will show a list of chart parts. By selecting one of these parts, you can determine where the data will go in the Chart Data & Titles dialog box. If you are copying a data set with **P**art of Chart, you must type the Legend or Axis Label data manually. Only **W**hole Chart lets you automatically import x-axis titles and legend entries. Figure 8.15 shows the Edit Paste Special dialog box when you choose **P**art of Chart.

You can use **P**art of Chart when you want to import only a portion of a set of data found in another application (a single range from a 1-2-3 for Windows worksheet, for example). You select the data and then the chart part from the list in the Edit Paste Special dialog box. The data is imported to that chart part.

TIP

Because choosing **P**art of Chart enables you to pull selected data into a selected portion of a chart, you can use this option to consolidate sets of numbers from various applications. You can select data in one file and use **P**art of Chart to paste it into data set A, then select data from a different file and use **P**art of Chart to paste it into data set B, and so on.

When you use **P**art of Chart, you can click the Link Data check box to set a link between the original data and the selected part of the chart.

In one chart, therefore, you can have active links to several different data sources. Changes to any of the sources will be reflected in the Freelance chart.

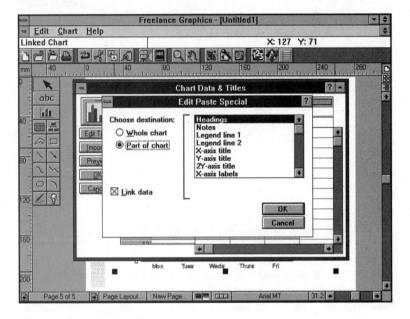

Fig. 8.15

The Edit Paste Special dialog box when **P**art of Chart is selected.

Exercise: Importing a Spreadsheet Range to a Freelance Chart

This exercise demonstrates the task of importing a range of data from a spreadsheet program to a Freelance chart. In this exercise, you use 1-2-3 for Windows, but the exercise works equally well if you use Microsoft Excel or Quattro Pro for Windows.

In the exercise, you import a range from a 1-2-3 worksheet into a Freelance chart. Then you add a range from a different worksheet, setting up links between the data in 1-2-3 and the Freelance chart.

Begin by creating the small worksheet shown in figure 8.16 and choose **F**ile **S**ave to save it in a file.

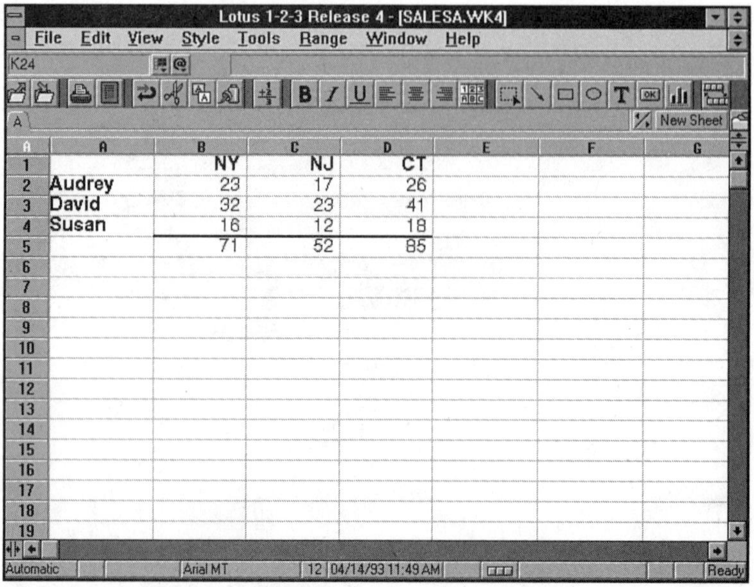

Fig. 8.16

The sample worksheet with data to be graphed in Freelance.

Then select the column and row headings and the numeric data, as shown in figure 8.17. Do not include the cells along the bottom of the worksheet that contain calculations.

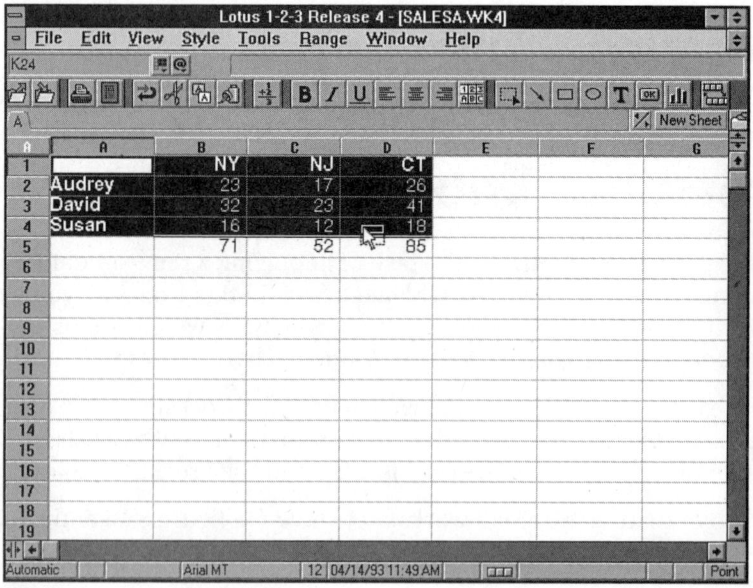

Fig. 8.17

The data selected in the 1-2-3 worksheet.

From the Edit menu of 1-2-3, choose Copy to copy the range to the Windows Clipboard. Then switch to Freelance Graphics and create a chart by following these steps:

1. Click a "Click here to create chart" block to start a chart.

2. In the New Chart Gallery dialog box, choose 3D Bar as the chart type, select any chart style, and then click OK.

3. Place the cursor in the lower of the two gray cells at the upper-left corner of the data area that shows in the Chart Data & Titles dialog box.

You next use Paste Special to import the data from 1-2-3 and create a link. Because each individual's numbers are arranged in a row in the 1-2-3 data, you use the controls in the Edit Paste Special dialog box to transpose the data so that each row of numbers in 1-2-3 will appear in a column in the Chart Data & Titles dialog box. As a result, each set of numbers will be represented by a set of bars of the same color. The legend will indicate the person represented by each color. To use Paste Special, follow these steps:

1. From the Edit menu of Freelance, choose Paste Special.

2. Choose Whole Chart in the Edit Paste Special dialog box to tell Freelance to import all the data in the Windows Clipboard as a complete set of data for a chart.

3. Choose Rows to specify that the data in 1-2-3 be arranged in rows.

4. Make sure that two check boxes—X-Axis Labels from 1st Row and Legend Labels from 1st Column—are checked so that the row and column headings in the 1-2-3 data will import into the Axis Label and Legend cells of the Chart Data & Titles dialog box.

5. Click the Link Data check box to set up a DDE link between the 1-2-3 data and the Freelance chart. Figure 8.18 shows the completed Edit Paste Special dialog box.

6. Click OK. The data is imported into the Chart Data & Titles dialog box, and the rows and columns have been transposed (see fig. 8.19). The blue underlines in the cells indicate that they contain linked data.

Fig. 8.18

The completed Edit Paste Special dialog box.

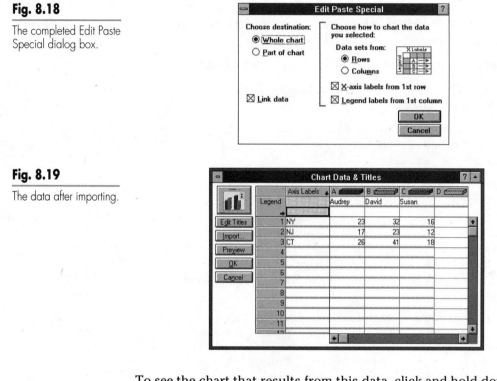

Fig. 8.19

The data after importing.

To see the chart that results from this data, click and hold down the Preview button. After you've seen the chart, release the Preview button to return to the Chart Data & Titles dialog box.

To complete the chart, you need to add more personal data. That person's data is kept in a different worksheet. Take a quick moment to create a new worksheet in 1-2-3 and then enter the data as shown in figure 8.20.

Select only the numbers (do not include the row or column headings) and then use the Copy command to copy them to the Windows Clipboard. Then switch back to Freelance and follow these steps:

1. Choose Paste Special from the Freelance Edit menu.

2. Choose Part of Chart from the Edit Paste Special dialog box and then select Data set D from the list of chart parts.

3. Make sure that the Link Data check box is checked.

4. Click OK.

To complete the data, you need to type the name **Steve** in the Legend cell at the top of data set D (in the cell to the right of Susan). To see the chart that results, click OK. Figure 8.21 shows this chart.

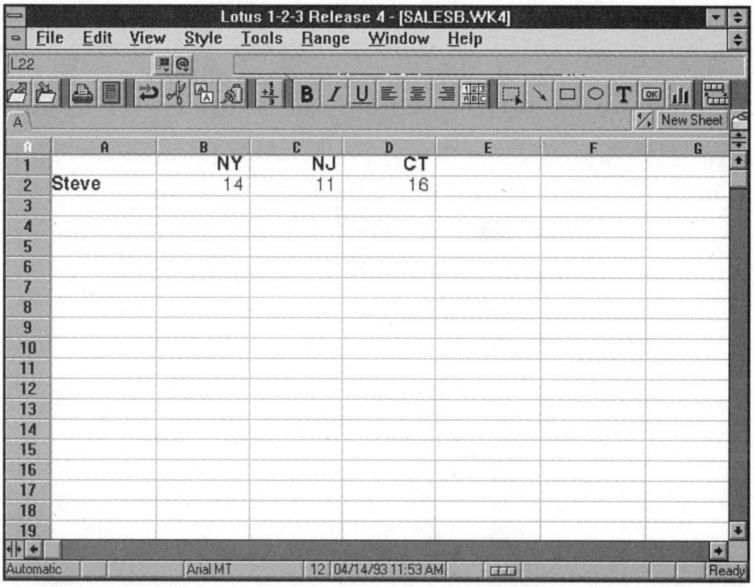

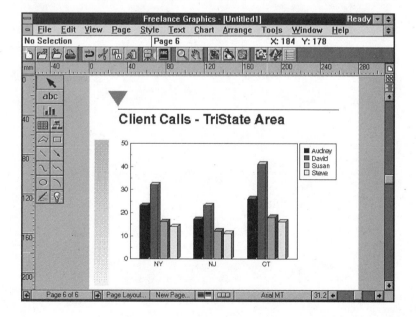

Fig. 8.20

The data for an additional person.

Fig. 8.21

The completed Freelance chart.

Summary

In this chapter, you learned to import the numbers for a Freelance chart from a Lotus 1-2-3 or Microsoft Excel worksheet file and to pull the numbers from an ASCII file generated by any other application. In addition, you learned to copy the numbers for a chart from another Windows application and to set up a live link to the original numbers.

The next chapter shows you how to create a different type of chart, an organization chart.

Creating Organization Charts

Organization charts depict the structure of an organization, showing with boxes and connecting lines who is subordinate to whom in a hierarchy. Also called org, staff, or pyramid charts, organization charts are easy to make and modify. Figure 9.1 shows a sample Freelance organization chart.

Freelance Graphics Release 2.0 for Windows can create an organization chart automatically from a list of names that you type. Earlier versions of the program did not include organization charts as a chart type, so you had to draw an organization chart with the drawing tools of Freelance.

Building an Organization Chart

If you plan to include an organization chart in a presentation, you can add a page for the chart and then select the Organization Chart page layout. A page containing the "Click here to create organization chart" block is displayed, as shown in figure 9.2. Using this approach, you can create a page with the organization chart automatically sized and positioned to fit the "Click here..." block.

Fig. 9.1

A sample Freelance organization chart.

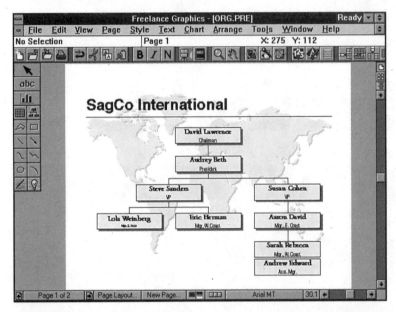

Fig. 9.2

The Organization Chart page layout.

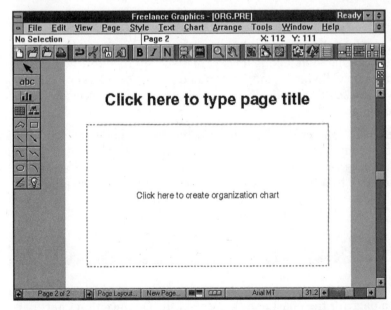

You can add an organization chart to an existing page that may have text or other charts by following either of these steps:

■ Click the Organization Chart icon in the toolbox.

■ Choose **New** from the **C**hart menu and then choose **O**rganization Chart from the pop-out menu of chart types.

The Organization Chart Gallery dialog box appears, as shown in figure 9.3.

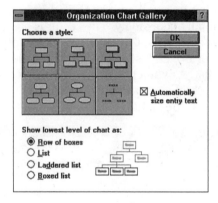

Fig. 9.3

The Organization Chart Gallery dialog box.

Choosing an Organization Chart Style

After you start an organization chart, you use the Organization Chart Gallery dialog box to make some design decisions about the chart before entering any data. After you type names and titles, Freelance draws the chart with the design you've specified.

One of the six chart style buttons is already pressed when this dialog box opens. You may want to click another button to choose a variation on the basic organization, though. With these style buttons, you can choose a chart design with shadowed boxes, three-dimensional boxes, rounded rectangle boxes, elliptical boxes, or no boxes at all. The choice is purely aesthetic, and you can always change it later.

You use the **A**utomatically Size Entry Text check box to determine whether Freelance will automatically resize the text within the boxes if you resize the entire organization chart. Unless you need text of a particular size within the boxes, you should leave this box checked so that Freelance can keep the text proportional to the chart size.

A list of choices at the bottom left of the Organization Chart Gallery dialog box enables you to choose how the lowest level of the chart will be visually depicted. The **R**ow of Boxes option is the most familiar choice (see fig. 9.4), but not necessarily the best. When you choose **R**ow of Boxes, Freelance displays the individuals at the lowest level of the structure as side-by-side boxes, making it clear that they are equals. These groups of boxes require more horizontal space, though. Compounding the problem, the pyramid shape of most organizations places more people at the lowest levels. Therefore, to fit all the people, the boxes and names must be small, and all the other boxes and names in the chart become small accordingly. The result is a chart with small boxes and hard-to-read names. Choosing any of the other choices—**L**ist, La**d**dered List, or **B**oxed List—solves this problem by placing the names in a vertical list. As you choose one of these options, a small diagram in the dialog box demonstrates the choice. Figure 9.5 shows an organization chart with the last level depicted as a laddered list.

Fig. 9.4

The last level of an organization shown as a row of boxes.

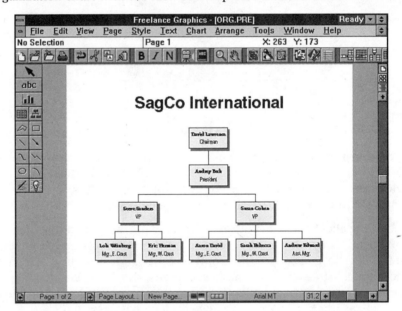

Entering Organization Members

As always with Freelance, the next step after choosing the design of a chart is to enter the data. Freelance opens the Organization Chart Entry List dialog box, as shown in figure 9.6.

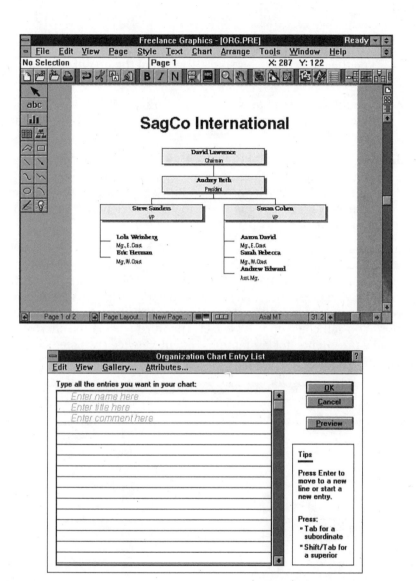

Fig. 9.5

The last level of an organization shown as a laddered list.

Fig. 9.6

The Organization Chart Entry List dialog box.

The dialog box shows a lined text-entry area that looks much like a piece of ruled paper. Within this area, you enter information about the people in the organization, from the top down. Prompts that appear dimmed show you where to enter the name, title, and comments about the head of the organization first. The cursor is at the Enter name here prompt.

To begin entering the organizational structure, follow these steps:

1. Type the name of the person at the top of the organizational structure and press Enter to move to the next line.

2. Type the title of the person and press Enter. This step is optional. You can press Enter without entering a title to get to the comment line.

3. Type a comment about the person, if you want, and then press Enter. Typing a comment is also optional. You can press Enter to skip the comment. The comment line is open for any use, though. You may want to use this space to enter a telephone extension, for example.

You can have only one head of an organization. After you enter information about him or her, the cursor moves down to the next line and to the right one level, as shown in figure 9.7. The subordinates of the first entry (the vice presidents in a standard corporation) are indented one level. Each level of indent is a lower level in the diagram of the organization. You can chart up to 12 levels. The third level in the chart (assistant vice presidents, for example) is indented twice (two steps to the right).

Fig. 9.7

The text-entry area after you enter information about the head of the organization.

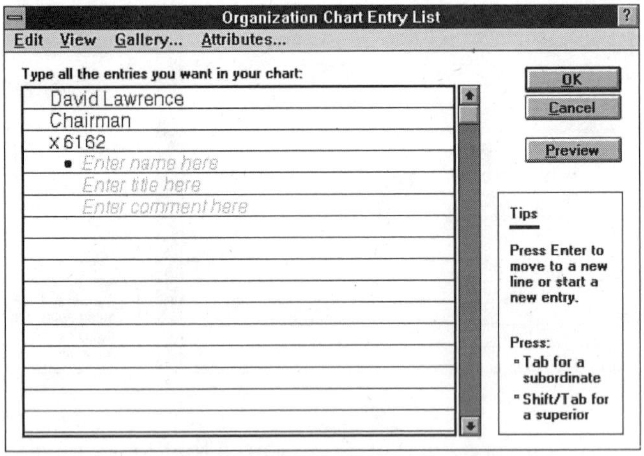

As the tips within the dialog box suggest, before you enter the name of an individual, you can press Tab to make the individual subordinate to the one immediately above in the list. Pressing Tab moves the prompt text one level to the right. You also can press Shift+Tab to move a subordinate up to the level of the individual immediately above in the list.

You can leave an empty box in the structure to fill in later. Just press Enter to pass the prompts for an individual without typing a name, a title, or comments.

Changing the Level of Detail in the Chart

Freelance assumes that you will enter the name, title, and comments about each member of the organization. Your chart may need only names, though, or only names and titles without comments. To remove prompts that you don't need from the entry list, use the **View** menu in the Organization Chart Entry List dialog box.

After you choose **View** from within this dialog box, you can choose **N**ames Only, Names and **T**itles, or **A**ll. The prompts in the text-entry area are automatically readjusted. Figure 9.8 shows the Organization Chart Entry List dialog box when Names and Titles is selected.

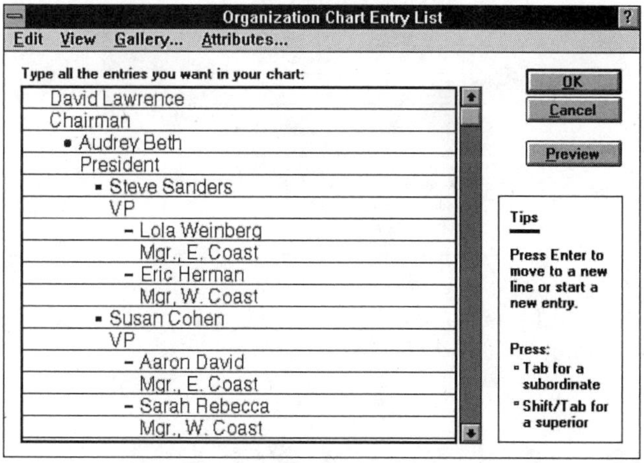

Fig. 9.8

Names and Titles selected.

Selecting a Different Organization Chart Style

Even after you enter the data for an organization chart, you can change its overall style by choosing **G**allery from the menu within the Organization Chart Entry List dialog box. This reopens the Organization Chart

Gallery dialog box. You can select a different combination of settings within the dialog box and then click and hold down the **Preview** button to see the changes before clicking OK to accept them.

Adding a Staff Position

All the members of the organization depicted are in line positions. Each member reports in line to the manager above in the hierarchy. In any organization chart, you can add one special assistant to the head of the organization, and that assistant is in a staff position. Each chart can have only one staff position, and the person in that position must report to the individual at the top of the organization.

To add a staff position, choose **S**taff from the **E**dit menu. The Organization Chart Staff dialog box opens, as shown in figure 9.9. Enter as much information about the individual as you want; then click OK. Figure 9.10 shows the staff position that results from the information you entered.

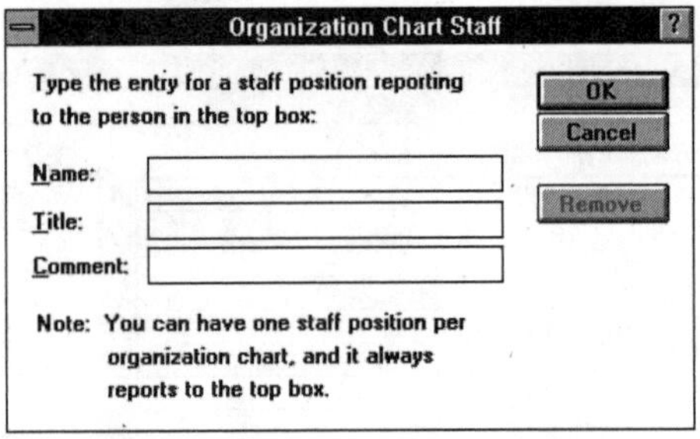

Fig. 9.9

The Organization Chart
Staff dialog box.

To remove a staff position no longer needed, return to the Organization Chart Staff dialog box and click Remove.

Editing the Names, Titles, and Comments

If a personnel replacement requires you to change the information in a box, you can easily edit text in the Organization Chart Entry List dialog box by clicking that text with the mouse. A typing cursor appears where you click, and you can make editing corrections as you would in any text. In fact, you can use all the cursor-movement and text-selection techniques you use when editing any text in Freelance. For example, you can press Home to move the cursor to the beginning of a line, press Shift+End to highlight to the end of the line, and then type new text to replace the highlighted text.

Fig. 9.10

A staff position added to an organization chart.

TIP

When the **A**utomatically Size Entry Text check box is checked, Freelance may wrap part of a name to the next line to better fit all the entries in the chart. A person's second name may appear on the line below the first name, for example. To keep all the name on one line, press Enter once or twice at the end of the name to add blank lines below the name. This "uses" the second and third lines in the box, forcing the name to shrink so that it fits on the first line.

After you have instructed Freelance to draw the chart based on the information provided in the Organization Chart Entry List dialog box, you can make direct changes to the text in the boxes instead of returning to that dialog box. To do so, click the box that holds the text to be modified. You'll see that the chart is selected and the box is *subselected* (large handles appear around the entire chart, and smaller handles appear around the box you clicked). Then click again on the text to place a typing cursor. When the typing cursor appears, you can use all the cursor-movement and text-editing keys to edit the text. You cannot use the text-formatting keys or the commands in the **T**ext menu (such as **B**old) to change the appearance of the text. You must change the attributes of the text in the boxes instead. Changing attributes is covered later in this chapter.

Modifying the Organizational Structure

The Organization Chart Entry List dialog box is not only the place to enter the data shown in the chart, but also the place to make changes in response to hirings, firings, or reorganizations in the structure you are representing. You can insert new members in the organization, delete members who have left the organization, and rearrange the positioning of members in the chart.

Demoting or Promoting Members

An organization member that has no subordinates can be demoted to become the subordinate of the member immediately above on the list. After the member has been demoted, he or she can be promoted back to the previous level. To demote a member, place the cursor anywhere on the member's name, title, or comment, and then press Tab or choose **D**emote from the **E**dit menu within the dialog box. To promote a member that has been demoted, press Shift+Tab or choose **P**romote from the **E**dit menu instead. Figures 9.11 and 9.12 show the "before" and "after" of demoting an individual.

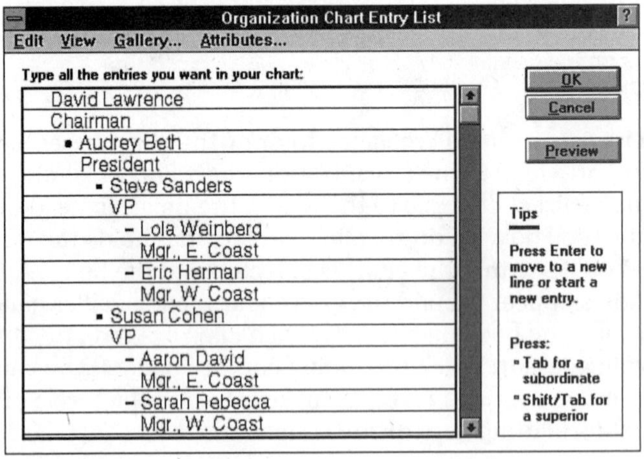

Fig. 9.11

Before demoting an individual.

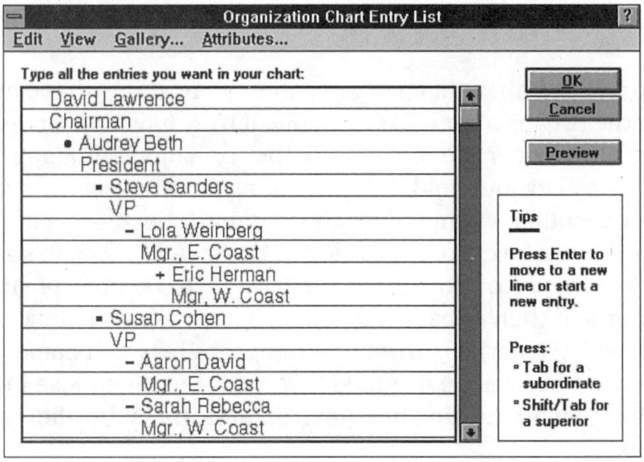

Fig. 9.12

After demoting an individual.

If an organization member has subordinates, the procedure is quite a bit different because you cannot promote or demote a member who has subordinates without also affecting the subordinates. To promote or demote a member with subordinates, you must select the member and the subordinates by clicking the symbol in front of the member's name. When you do, a rectangle appears that encloses the member's information and the information of all the subordinates below the member. You can then press Tab or Shift+Tab to demote or promote the entire group, or you can choose **D**emote or **P**romote from the **E**dit menu. Figure 9.13 shows the selection rectangle that appears when you click the symbol in front of the name Steve Sanders.

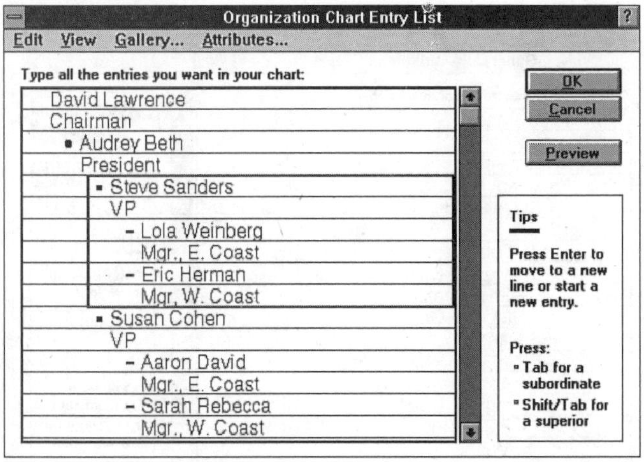

Fig. 9.13

The selection rectangle surrounding Steve Sanders and his subordinates.

Moving Members

You can move members in an organization chart if they have been moved in the organization—for example, if they have been reassigned to a different manager. To move a member or a member along with subordinates, click and hold down the mouse button on the symbol in front of the member's name. The mouse pointer becomes a large triangle pointing to the current position of the member. While still holding down the mouse button, move the triangle to the new position for the member and then release the mouse button. As you move the triangle on the list, a dark horizontal bar appears between names to show where the member will be dropped if you release the mouse button. If the member you are moving has subordinates, the subordinates will be moved too.

When you move a member, he or she stays at the same level in the new position. If a member at the third level is moved (an assistant vice president, for example), the member will appear at the third level when placed below a different second-level member. If there is no second-level member, though, the third-evel member will become a second-level member. You cannot move someone at the third level to the first level. The third-level person will move but will be "promoted" to the second level so that a level is never skipped.

Figure 9.14 demonstrates the moving of a fourth-level member. The member has moved from one third-level supervisor to another. Figures 9.15 and 9.16 show how the organization chart changes when the move is made.

Fig. 9.14

Moving a fourth-level member.

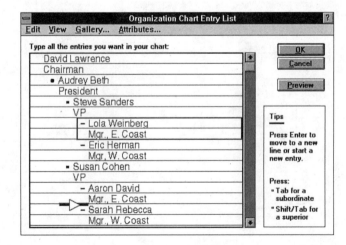

Fig. 9.15

Before moving the fourth-
level member.

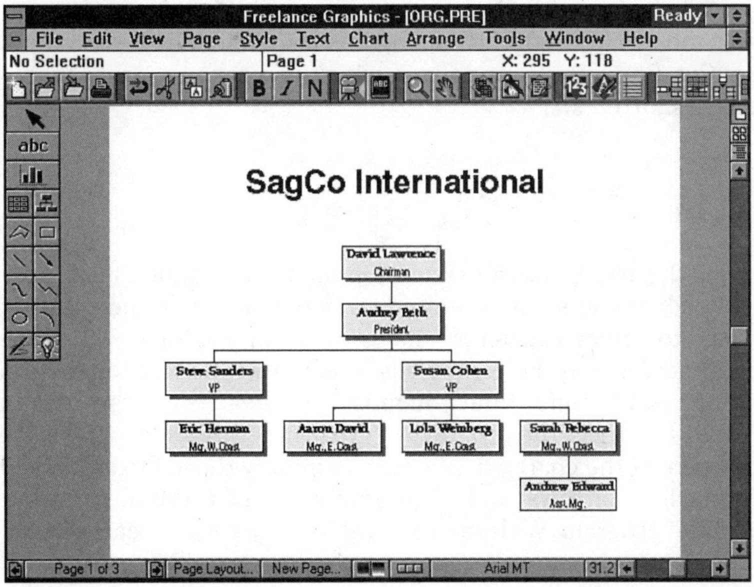

Fig. 9.16

After moving the fourth-
level member.

Inserting, Copying, and Deleting Members

Adding and removing members in an organization chart is far easier than adding and removing members in real life. To insert a new member in the chart, place the cursor on the last line of data for the member immediately above where you want the new member to be, and then press Enter. Press Tab if you want the new member to be a subordinate.

To delete a member or group of members, click the symbol in front of the member's name. A selection box surrounds the member and any subordinates. Press the Del key to permanently clear the members, or press Ctrl+X or Shift+Del to cut the members from the chart. When you use cut rather than delete, you can paste the members back into the chart at another position by moving the pointer to that position, clicking, and then pressing Ctrl+V or Shift+Insert. To copy members and subordinates from one position to another, select their names and press Ctrl+C or Ctrl+Ins. Move the cursor to the destination for the copy, click, and press Ctrl+V or Shift+Insert. The Edit menu within the Organization Chart Entry List dialog box also holds the menu commands Cut, Copy, Paste, and Clear, which you can use rather than keyboard shortcuts.

Making Other Changes

Changing the arrangement of names in the Organization Chart Entry List dialog box offers only a limited array of changes to the chart. You may need to depict a structure that is not a simple, top-down, pyramid shape. Unfortunately, Freelance offers no automatic way to create such nonstandard diagrams. What you must do instead is use the Organization Chart feature of the program to create a few boxes and lines (the central core of the chart); duplicate and modify those boxes; and add additional lines, arrows, and other graphic shapes with the drawing tools of the program. With the drawing tools, you can create virtually any diagram you want.

If you will be adding boxes and lines, you can simply draw them onto the existing chart. But you may want to convert the chart to a collection of drawing objects that you can move, duplicate, and redesign. To convert the chart, select it and then choose Ungroup from the Arrange menu. Freelance warns you that ungrouping the chart will convert it to a collection of drawing objects. Click OK to proceed. Then you can begin working with the individual pieces of the chart (the lines, boxes, and text). Figure 9.17 shows the chart after it has been ungrouped. Notice that each element of the chart has its own set of handles because it is an individual drawing object. Consult Chapter 12, "Drawing Objects," for information about using the drawing tools of Freelance.

Fig. 9.17

An ungrouped organization chart.

Changing the Organization Chart's Attributes

The steps you have completed so far have provided the content and basic design for the chart. To modify the appearance of individual elements of the chart (the boxes, text, connecting lines, or frame), you must change the attributes of the elements.

As always, you must select the element before you can make any changes to it. The easiest ways are to position the pointer on an element and then either double-click the left mouse button or single-click the right mouse button. With both methods, a pop-up menu appears with three choices: Edit, Gallery, and Attributes.

■ Edit opens the Organization Chart Entry List dialog box so that you can make changes to the contents or structure of the chart.

■ Gallery opens the Organization Chart Gallery dialog box so that you can choose a different overall design for the chart.

■ Attributes opens the Organization Chart Attributes dialog box, which enables you to change the appearance of the part of the chart you clicked. Figure 9.18 shows this dialog box.

Fig. 9.18

The Organization Chart
Attributes dialog box.

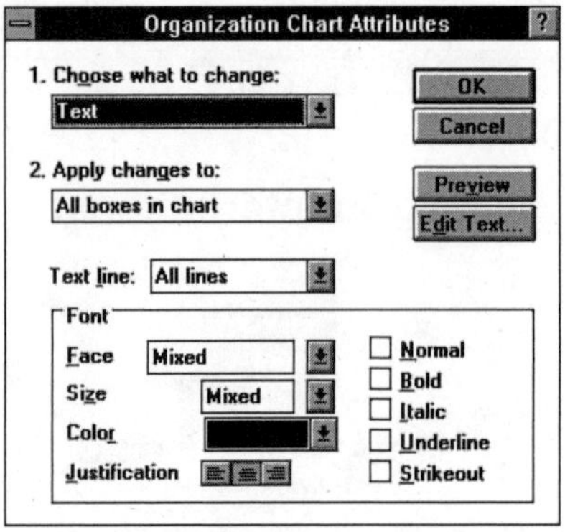

The Organization Chart Attributes dialog box includes two numbered steps. Follow step 1 by clicking the button next to the text box and selecting from the drop-down list the part of the chart you want to change (Text, Boxes, Connecting Lines, or Frame). Then, in step 2, choose the part of the chart to decide which boxes the change should affect. Here are the choices:

All Boxes in Chart	Affects every box in the chart
Current Box	Affects only the subselected box
Current Box & Subordinates	Affects only the subselected box and subordinates of that box
Current Box & Peers	Affects only the subselected box and other boxes on the same level

The lower half of the dialog box is reserved for controls that change the part of the chart you've selected. After you make changes, click and hold down the Preview button to see the results, or click OK to accept the changes and return to the chart.

Clicking the **E**dit Text button takes you directly to the Organization Chart Entry List dialog box so that you can modify the contents or structure of the chart.

Changing the Appearance of Text

To change the appearance of the text within the chart, choose Text from the Choose What To Change list. Then choose whether you want to change all the text in the chart, only the text in the current box, the text in the current box and subordinates, or the text in the current box and other boxes on the same level. An additional option lets you choose whether to change the text in all lines within the boxes, only the name, only the title, or only the comment. You can choose Title, for example, to italicize only the titles of all the organization members shown in the chart.

When you choose to change the text in the chart, controls to change the font of the text fill the lower half of the dialog box, as shown in figure 9.19. You can use these controls to choose a **F**ace, Size, Color, and **J**ustification for the text and to apply character attributes such as boldfacing and underlining.

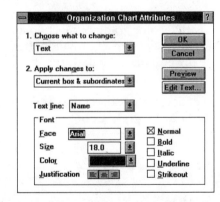

Fig. 9.19

The controls for changing the appearance of text.

CAUTION

Freelance automatically controls the sizing of the text in the boxes if **A**utomatically Size Entry Text is checked in the Organization Chart Gallery dialog box. Overriding the automatic sizing of the text by changing the Si**z**e setting will turn off automatic sizing of the text. The text then remains at its current size even if you change the size of the chart.

Modifying the Look of the Boxes

The organization chart style you chose when you started the organization chart determines the overall design of the boxes in the chart—whether they are plain, three-dimensional, shadowed, or not shown.

The two controls at the bottom of the Organization Chart Attributes dialog box, shown in figure 9.20, enable you to change the Color, Width (thickness), and line Style of the edge of the boxes and the colors of the interior of the boxes.

Fig. 9.20

The controls for changing the look of boxes.

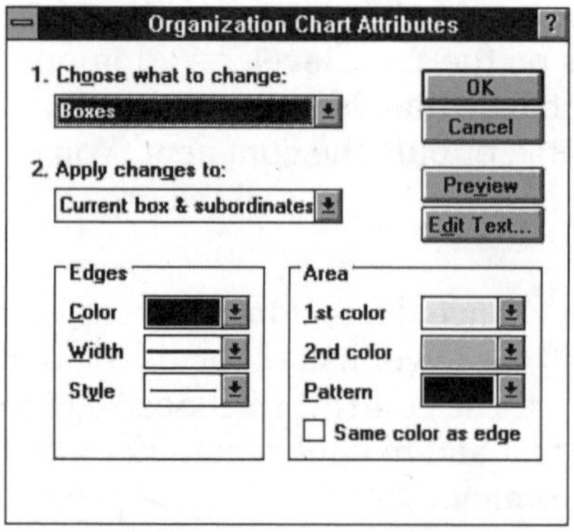

You can fill the boxes with a color gradient by choosing different first and second colors and then selecting a gradient pattern from the list of available patterns. The lower half of the patterns that appear when you click the Pattern pull-down button are gradients.

To quickly create a box filled with a solid color and with no discernible edge, click the Same Color as Edge check box.

Redesigning the Connecting Lines

You can change only the width (thickness), style, and color of lines that connect the boxes in an organization chart. Figure 9.21 shows the controls that are available when you choose to change the connecting lines.

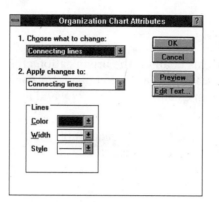

Fig. 9.21

The controls for changing the connecting lines.

Changing the Frame

The default for the organization chart's frame (the rectangle in the background of the chart) specifies no line style and no pattern. Therefore, the frame does not appear. You can turn on the frame and set the appearance of both its edge and its area. Be sure to use a dark frame with light boxes, connecting lines, or text to provide sufficient contrast in the chart. For an interesting effect, you can fill the frame of the chart with a gradient by choosing different first and second colors for the area and then selecting a gradient design for the pattern (see fig. 9.22).

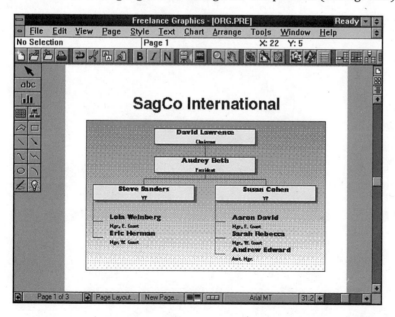

Fig. 9.22

An organization chart with a gradient frame.

Summary

As you learned in this chapter, the organization chart features of Freelance make creating organization diagrams easy. In fact, you can simply enter the names and their hierarchy and let Freelance draw the chart for you.

In the next chapter, you learn to create table charts, which are also new to the latest version of Freelance.

Creating Table Charts

Table charts, a new feature of Freelance Graphics Release 2.0 for Windows, hold text and numbers in a grid of cells. Freelance makes these charts easy to create and modify.

When you start a table chart, you select a design from a visual gallery. After you move from cell to cell, entering text and numbers, you may be perfectly satisfied with the chart you get. But to place on the chart your own design stamp, you can click any cell or click the entire chart and choose formatting from the clearly presented alternatives.

This chapter describes the process of creating, editing, and formatting table charts, and it gives you the chance to practice by creating a table chart. A sample table chart is shown in figure 10.1.

Creating a Table Chart

To start a table chart, you can create a new page that has a table chart "Click here..." block, or you can add a table chart to an existing page in the presentation.

Fig. 10.1

A Freelance table chart.

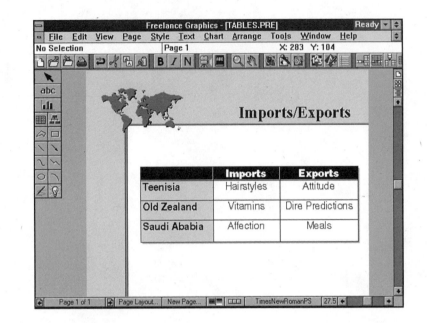

To create a new page with a table chart "Click here..." block, start a new page by clicking the New Page button at the bottom of the Freelance window and then select the Table page layout from the Choose Page Layout dialog box that opens. A page with "Click here to type page title" and "Click here to create table" blocks appears.

 To add a table chart to any page of the presentation, turn to that page and, from the **Chart** menu, choose **N**ew. Then choose **T**able from the pop-out menu of chart types. Yet another way to add a table to a page is to click the Table icon in the toolbox.

No matter which method you use, the Table Gallery dialog box opens, as shown in figure 10.2. You use this dialog box to choose a basic design for the table.

The dialog box shows two numbered steps: Choose a Table Style and Choose Number of Rows and Columns. Default selections have already been made. To accept the default selections, simply click OK. Or follow these steps to set the basic table design:

1. Click one of the six table style buttons that depict basic table designs to choose how the grid lines in the table should appear. You can always return to this dialog box to choose a different table style for a table you've created.

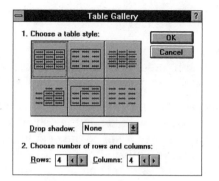

Fig. 10.2

The Table Gallery dialog box.

2. Use the **Dr**op Shadow drop-down list to select the direction in which a background shadow will extend from the table (or choose None to use no drop shadow).

3. Use the increment and decrement buttons next to the **R**ows and **C**olumns prompts to increase or decrease the number of rows and columns in the table. You can always add and delete rows and columns later.

4. Click OK. A blank table chart appears, as shown in figure 10.3.

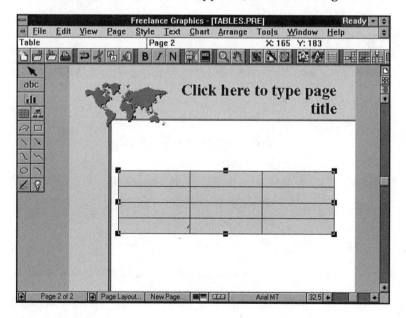

Fig. 10.3

A blank table chart.

Entering and Editing Table Text

When the blank table chart appears, the entire table is selected. To begin entering text and numbers into cells of the table, you must click a cell. This produces a blinking typing cursor in the cell.

As you type, the text automatically wraps words within each cell. Freelance fits as many words as it can in the cell and then increases the row height and moves the cursor to the next line within the row. To avoid word wrapping, you must either make the text smaller or increase the width of the cell. Both techniques are discussed later in this chapter.

After you type an entry, press the Tab key or Ctrl+→ to move one cell to the right, or press ↓ to move one cell down. To start a new line in the current cell, press Enter. To move the cursor to the left, press Shift+Tab or Ctrl+←. To move the cursor to the upper-left corner cell of the table, press Ctrl+Home. To move to the lower-right corner cell, press Ctrl+End. Of course, you can always click any cell with the mouse pointer to move the cursor to that cell. Table 10.1 summarizes the keyboard combinations for moving the cursor in a cell.

Table 10.1 Moving the Cursor in a Table Chart

Key(s)	Action
Tab or Ctrl+→	Moves right one cell
Shift+Tab or Ctrl+←	Moves left one cell
↓	Moves down one cell
↑	Moves up one cell
Ctrl+Home	Moves to upper-left corner cell
Ctrl+End	Moves to lower-right corner cell
End End	Moves to the last cell in the row
End End End	Moves to the end of the first line in the last cell in the row

By default, text is left-aligned in cells, and numbers are right-aligned.

To edit the contents of a cell, click the text in the cell. A typing cursor appears. Then use the standard text-editing keys to revise the existing text. Any text that you highlight in a cell, for example, will be replaced by the new text you type. You can double-click a word to highlight it and then type a replacement word.

Adding and Deleting Columns and Rows

When you first create a table chart, you select the number of rows and columns you'll need. But projects often end up bigger than planned, and table charts can too. Adding more rows or columns to a table chart is easy. Simply follow these steps:

1. Click a cell in the table to insert a typing cursor in the cell next to where you want the new column or row to appear.

2. From the **Chart** menu, choose **Table**.

3. From the pop-out **Table** menu, choose **Insert Column/Row**. The Insert Column/Row dialog box opens, as shown in figure 10.4.

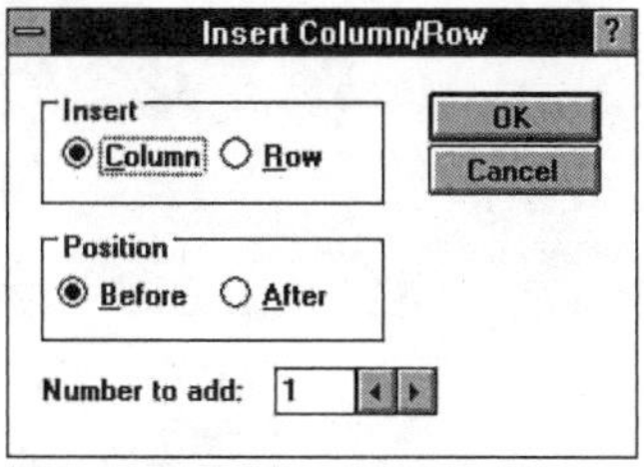

Fig. 10.4

The Insert Column/Row dialog box.

An alternative to steps 2 and 3 is to click the right mouse button and choose Insert/Column Row from the pop-up menu.

TIP

4. Choose whether to insert a **Column** or **Row**.

5. Choose whether the new column or row will appear **B**efore or **A**fter the selected cell. (If you are inserting a row, *after* means below. If you are inserting a column, *after* means to the right.)

6. Use the increment or decrement button to change the number of columns or rows to add; then click OK.

Freelance also comes with a set of SmartIcons that can quickly and easily add and delete columns and rows: Add Column, Delete Column, Add Row, and Delete Row. To use these SmartIcons, click a particular cell to place a typing cursor inside. Then click the appropriate SmartIcon. A new column will appear to the right of the cell; a new row will appear below it. Chapter 23, "Modifying the Default Settings," shows you how to add these SmartIcons.

Resizing Columns and Rows

The easiest way to change the width of a column or the height of a row is to drag the boundary of any cell in the column or row. You can drag the boundary between two columns to the left or right and drag the boundary between two rows up or down. The entire column or row resizes. As you increase the size of columns and rows, the entire table grows or shrinks accordingly. Figure 10.5 demonstrates the process of changing the width of a column.

Fig. 10.5

Dragging the right boundary of a cell to change the width of a column.

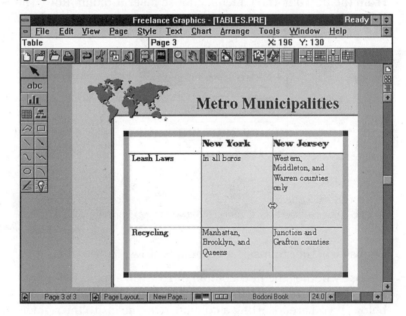

To drag a boundary, place the mouse pointer on the line at the edge of the cell, click and hold down the left mouse button, and then drag. When you click the boundary of the cell, the cursor becomes a double arrow that points in the directions you can drag the boundary.

TIP

By increasing the width of a column that contains word-wrapped text, you may create enough space in each cell of the column for all the text to fit on one line.

To set exact column widths and row heights, you must use the **Size Column/Row** menu command. With this command, you can set all the columns of a table to exactly the same width, for example. To use **Size Column/Row**, click a cell in the column or row to resize, and then choose **T**able from the **Chart** menu. From the pop-out **T**able menu, choose **Size Column/Row**. You also can click a cell, click the right mouse button, and then choose Size Column/Row from the pop-up menu. The Size Column/Row dialog box appears (see fig. 10.6).

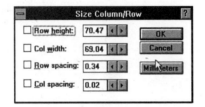

Fig. 10.6

The Size Column/Row dialog box.

Use the increment and decrement buttons next to Row **H**eight and Col **W**idth to change these settings, or highlight the current measurement and type a replacement number. Click the button below Cancel, which displays the name of a measurement unit, to cycle through the following measurement units for the numbers in the dialog box: Inches, Points, Picas, Millimeters, and Centimeters.

Adding Column and Row Spacing

To add some space between successive columns or rows in a table, you must use the **Size Column/Row** menu command. Select the table or click any cell in the table and then, from the **Chart** menu, choose **T**able. From the **T**able pop-out menu, choose **Size Columns/Rows**. You also can click the right mouse button and then choose Size Column/Row from the pop-up menu. If you have selected the entire table rather than a particular cell, **S**ize Columns/Rows is the only command available.

Use the increment and decrement buttons next to **R**ow Spacing and **C**ol Spacing to change the spacing between successive rows and columns. The spacing for all the rows and columns in the table will be adjusted. Figure 10.7 shows a table with the same spacing between both columns and rows.

Fig. 10.7

A table with the same spacing between the columns and rows.

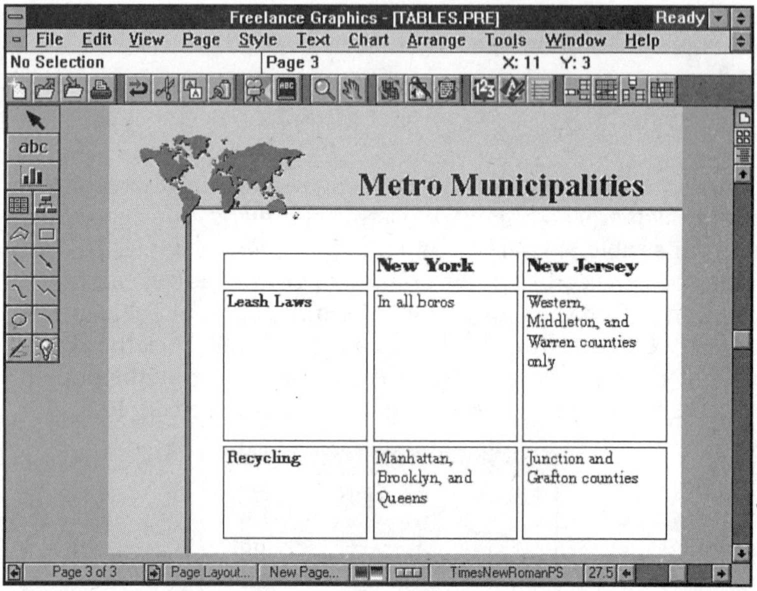

Moving Columns and Rows

You can move columns one position left or right and move rows one position left or right by using the **M**ove Columns/Rows menu command. To do so, click a cell in the column or row that you want to move and then, from the **C**hart menu, choose **T**able. From the **T**able pop-out menu, choose **M**ove Columns/Rows. You also can click the right mouse button and then choose Move Column/Row from the pop-up menu. The Move Column/Row dialog box appears, as shown in figure 10.8.

Fig. 10.8

The Move Column/Row dialog box.

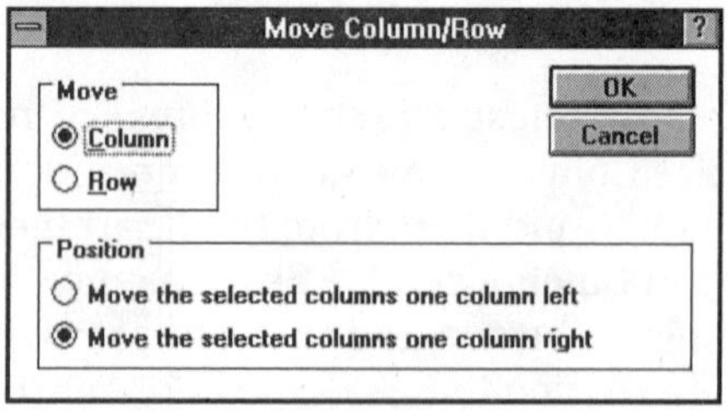

Within the dialog box, use one of the Move options (**C**olumn or **R**ow) to choose whether to move the column or row where the cursor is located. Then use one of the two Position options to choose whether to move the column or row up, down, left, or right. Click OK to finish. The table is then updated.

Resizing the Entire Table

After you have added as many columns and rows as you need and you've stretched them to fit the data, you may need to adjust the overall size of the table to fit the design of the page. By clicking and dragging a side handle (the handles along the four sides of the table), you can make the overall table wider, narrower, taller, or shorter. By dragging a corner handle, you can make the table larger or smaller in two directions simultaneously.

As you change the size of the table, the text and numbers inside do not change size, though. As you widen the table, more text can fit across each cell, so the word wrapping changes. To cause the text size to change proportionately with the table size, press and hold down the Shift key as you drag a corner handle. As the table size increases, the size of the text and numbers in the cells increases too, so the text remains just as you want it, with the same word wrapping. Figure 10.9 shows a table after it has been resized by dragging a corner handle. Notice that the text size remains the same even though the table has been reduced and the word wrapping in the cells has changed. Figure 10.10 shows a table that was resized by holding down the Shift key while dragging a corner handle. Notice that the table shape has remained the same and the text has reduced in size along with the table.

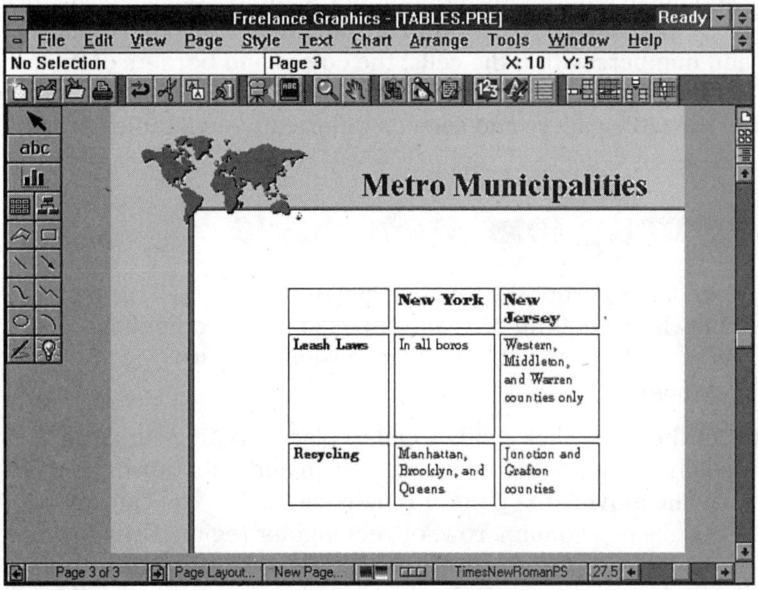

Fig. 10.9

A table resized by dragging a corner handle.

Fig. 10.10

A table resized by shift-dragging a corner handle.

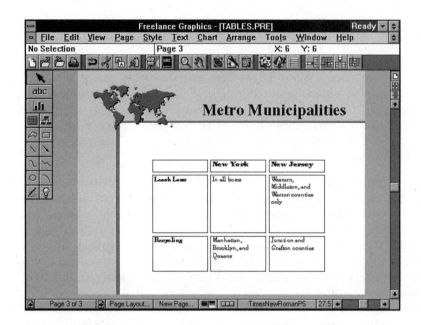

Formatting the Table

After you finish entering the content of the table, you can begin formatting the appearance of the table. You can change the appearance of the text and numbers within the cells, the colors and borders of the cells, and the color and border design of the overall table. You can even return to the table gallery and select a different overall table design.

Formatting Text in the Table

To format all or part of the text in a cell or to format all the text in a group of cells, select the cells and then use the Text Font and Text Size buttons at the bottom of the Freelance window or use the options in the **Text** menu.

To select the cells, click a single cell to place a typing cursor in the cell. Then position the pointer on the cell again and hold down the mouse button while moving the pointer to adjacent cells. You can select a group of cells in a column, row, or rectangular region. Cells that are selected become highlighted. Figure 10.11 shows a selected region of cells in a table.

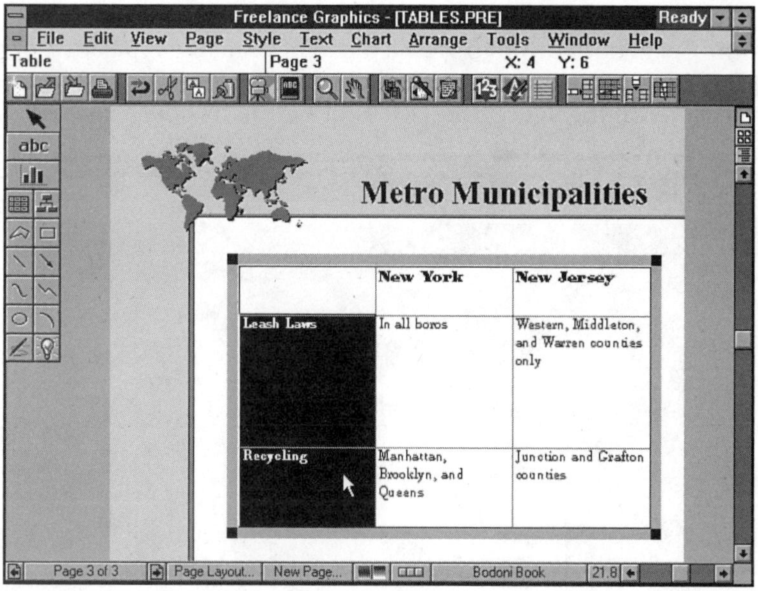

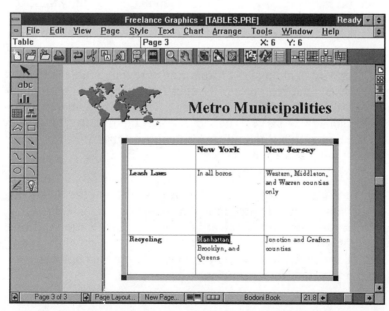

Fig. 10.11

A selected region
of cells.

To select only a portion of text in a single cell (a single word, for example), click at the beginning of the text to select. This places a typing
cursor in the cell. Then drag across the text with the pointer while
holding down the mouse button, or hold down the Shift key while
pressing the right-arrow key. Figure 10.12 shows selected text within
a cell.

Fig. 10.12

Selected text within
a cell.

After you have selected the text or cells that contain text to format, click the Text Font button to view a menu of available typefaces, or the Text Size button to view a list of possible text sizes. Figure 10.13 shows both buttons. In the figure, the Text Font button has been clicked.

Fig. 10.13

The available text fonts.

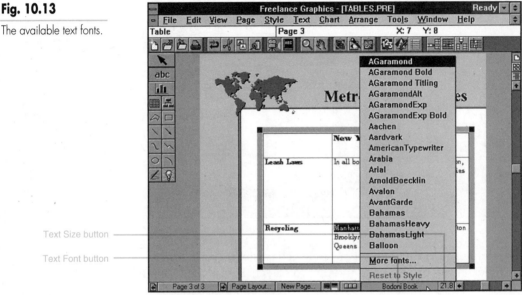

To make other formatting changes, you can use the text-formatting SmartIcons or the controls in the **Text** menu after selecting table text. Choose **B**old, **I**talic, **U**nderline, or **S**trikeout from the menu; or choose **F**ont to change these text attributes and the typeface, point size, and text color too.

Yet another way to change the formatting of text in a table is to select a cell or rectangular region of cells, click the right mouse button, and choose Attributes from the pop-up menu. This method affects all the text in the selected cells. You cannot use this method to change only part of the text within a cell. When you choose Attributes, the Table Attributes dialog box appears, as shown in figure 10.14.

If the **T**ext Attributes option is selected in the dialog box, a full set of text attribute controls appears in the lower portion of the dialog box, including controls for changing the typeface, point size, text color, character attributes, and justification. The four justification buttons depict a paragraph that has been left-, center-, right-, and left- and right-aligned. To preview the changes you make with these controls, click and hold down the Preview button.

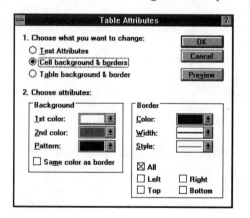

Fig. 10.14

The Table Attributes
dialog box.

Formatting Table Cells

To change the appearance of the cells in a table, select individual cells
or the entire table; then choose Attributes from the Chart menu, or
click the right mouse button and choose Attributes from the pop-up
menu. From the Table Attributes dialog box that appears, choose Cell
Background & Borders. The lower half of the dialog box shows controls
for changing the background color of the selected cells as well as the
color and style of the border surrounding the cells (see fig. 10.15).

Fig. 10.15

The Background and
Border controls.

You use the Background color controls (**1**st Color and **2**nd Color) to
choose two colors to use for a pattern or gradient in the selected cells.
A gradient shows a transition from the 1st color to the 2nd. The **Pattern**
control lets you select a pattern or the shape of the gradient that will
fill the cells. If you select None as the **Pattern**, the cells fill with the 1st
color. To make the 1st color the same color as the border, click the
check box labeled Same Color as Border.

The color controls display the current color of the selected cells. If the selected cells are filled with different colors, a triangle appears rather than a color in the color controls.

You use the Border controls (Color, Width, and Style) to choose the appearance of the line surrounding each selected cell. To draw no border around cells, select None as the Style. After you choose a color, width, and style, you can click the All check box to have the border drawn on all four sides of each selected cell; or you can click Left, Right, Top, or Bottom to draw the border on that side only. To draw a border along the bottom of a row of cells, for example, you select the cells; choose a border color, width, and style; and then click the check box labeled Bottom.

Formatting the Table Background and Border

To format the table background color and the border surrounding the entire table, select the table or any cells in the table and then choose **Attributes** from the **Chart** menu, or click the right mouse button and choose Attributes from the pop-up menu. From the Table Attributes dialog box, choose Table Background & Border. The dialog box shows controls for changing the background and border settings and an additional control for placing a shadow behind the table. Select None to show no shadow, or select Bottom Right, Bottom Left, Top Right, or Top Left to determine the direction in which the shadow should extend from the table. Figure 10.16 shows the Table Attributes dialog box with the Shadow control. Figure 10.17 shows a table chart with a shadow extended to the bottom right. The shadow gives the page a subtle three-dimensional look.

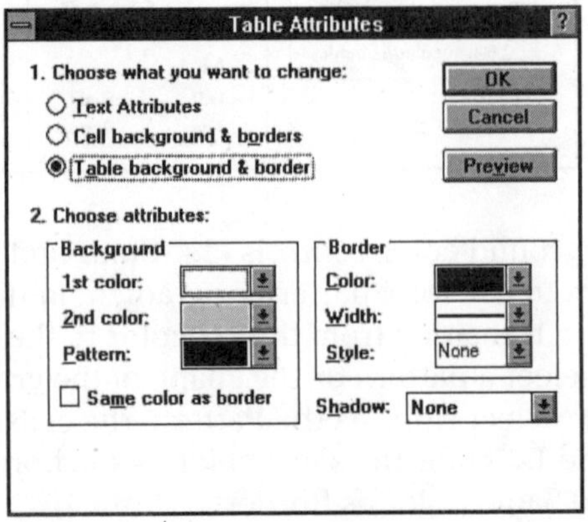

Fig. 10.16

The Table Attributes dialog box when Table Background & Border is selected.

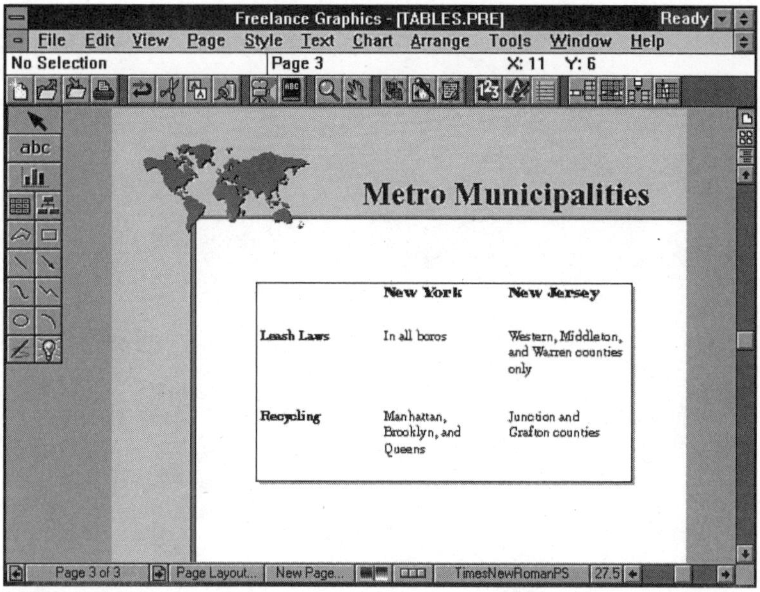

![Freelance Graphics window showing a sample table titled "Metro Municipalities" with columns for New York and New Jersey, and rows for Leash Laws and Recycling.]

Fig. 10.17

A sample table with a shadow.

Selecting a Different Table Design

To select a different overall design for a table, you can return to the Table Gallery dialog box at any time. Simply select the table and then choose **G**allery from the **C**hart menu, or click the right mouse button and choose Gallery from the pop-up menu. You can choose settings from the Table Gallery dialog box and then use Preview to see the effect on the completed table.

CAUTION

The new table design selected from the table gallery may override some of the cell-border formatting you have applied.

Summary

In this chapter, you learned to use the table chart feature of Freelance to create table charts. In Part III of this book, you learned to create data charts, organization charts, and table charts.

In Part IV, you use the drawing tools and commands of Freelance to add other graphic objects and text to presentation pages. The next chapter describes adding and formatting blocks of text.

Adding Text and Graphics to Pages

PART

IV

OUTLINE

Adding and Formatting Text Blocks

Now that you have filled in the "Click here..." blocks on the page layouts you've chosen, something still may be missing from the presentation. You may want to add more text and position it in different places on the page. You may want to change the appearance of some of the text you've already entered. Or you may want to get creative and turn text on some of the pages into design elements by curving the text or combining it with a symbol or an object. This chapter tells you how to add and format the simplest or most elaborate text.

Adding Text Blocks

Clicking "Click here..." text blocks enables you to add text to a page quickly. But you can add additional text to any page by manually creating text blocks after you click the Text icon. You can place a text block anywhere on the page and then set its appearance, but you may find it easier to create a text block, format it in a clear area of the page, and then position the text.

In Freelance, you can create two types of text blocks: wrapping and nonwrapping. The text in a wrapping text block fits neatly within a box that you draw on the page. When the words that you type can no longer fit within the box, they wrap to the next line. Using wrapping text lets you designate the precise area of the screen in which the text should appear. The text in a nonwrapping block starts at a point you designate and runs across to the right until you press Enter to start a new line. Nonwrapping text does not fit in a rectangular area of the page. It just starts at the point you specify. You can easily make nonwrapping text into wrapping text, though.

Creating Wrapping Text Blocks

To create a wrapping text block, you must first outline the boundaries of the text block by drawing a box with the Text icon. Then you can type text into the box.

To make a wrapping text block, follow these steps:

1. Click the Text icon in the toolbox.

2. Place the pointer where you want one corner of the text block to be.

3. Hold down the mouse button and drag diagonally to create a box, as shown in figure 11.1.

Fig. 11.1

Dragging the box that marks the boundaries of a wrapping text block.

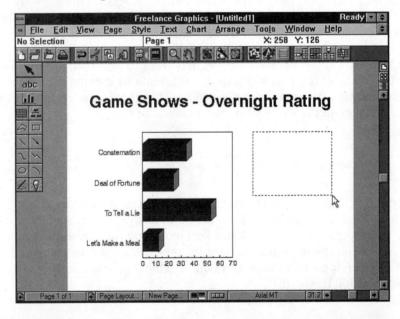

4. Release the mouse button. The text fits into the area you delineated.

5. Type text into the box, as shown in figure 11.2.

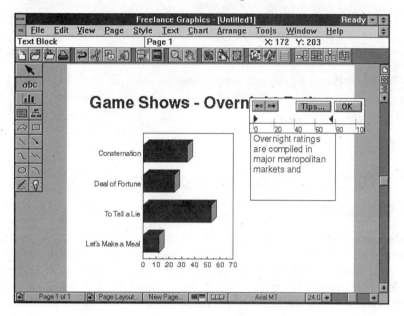

Fig. 11.2

Typing text into a text block.

6. When you finish typing, click OK or click elsewhere on the page.

Creating Nonwrapping Text Blocks

To place a line of text on the page without specifying a box into which it should fit, simply click at the starting point for the text and then begin typing. The text will not wrap to the next line unless you press Enter. Follow these steps to create a nonwrapping text block:

1. Click the Text icon in the toolbox.

2. Click at the point where the text should begin.

3. Begin typing.

4. When the text is complete, click the OK button or click elsewhere on the page.

TIP

You can turn nonwrapping text into wrapping text at any point by simply resizing the nonwrapping text (dragging a handle at a corner of the text block). You can also double-click the text block and then click the **W**ord Wrap check box in the Paragraph Styles dialog box.

NOTE

To delete a text block after creating it, just select the text block by clicking it and then press the Del key. Or you can click the Delete SmartIcon.

Exercise: Creating Wrapping and Nonwrapping Text Blocks

In this exercise, you get the chance to create text blocks that are both wrapping and nonwrapping. If you already have a presentation on-screen, you may want to turn to the end of the presentation and then follow the steps of the exercise. If you do not have a presentation open, then start a new presentation and follow these steps:

1. Click the New Page button at the bottom of the Freelance window to open the New Page dialog box.

2. Select the Basic Layout page layout.

3. Click the "Click here to type page title" text block.

4. Type **Twenty-first Century Eye Wear: Looking Forward** and click anywhere on the page outside the text block. This closes the text block.

5. Click the Text icon in the toolbox and drag a rectangle directly below the title. A text block in edit-text mode appears on the page.

6. Type **Contacts are out and glasses are in as we approach the end of the millennium.** and click anywhere on the page outside the text block. A finished block of wrapping text appears on the page. This text block on your screen may appear different from the text block shown in figure 11.3. Your text will be word-wrapped within the rectangle you dragged.

7. Click the Text icon in the toolbox and click once below the first text block. A nonwrapping text block in edit-text mode appears on the page.

8. Type **With so many styles from which to choose, glasses are no longer utilitarian.** and click anywhere in the blank area of the page. You've just created a nonwrapping text block, and it is selected on the page. Figure 11.3 shows both a wrapping text block and a nonwrapping text block. The SmartMaster set you're using will determine how your screen will look.

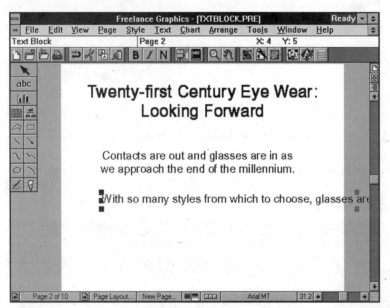

Fig. 11.3

A wrapping text block and a nonwrapping text block.

9. Click and drag the bottom-right corner handle of the nonwrapping text block down and to the left to make a taller, narrower rectangle that fits on the page. This turns a nonwrapping text block into a wrapping text block. Figure 11.4 shows the dragging of a corner handle to resize a nonwrapping block into a wrapping block.

10. Click within the text block at the end of the word utilitarian. The text block goes into edit-text mode.

11. Type **People who never would have thought of wearing glasses in the 1970s and 1980s now have an eye wear wardrobe.** Notice that the text automatically wraps within the text block.

Fig. 11.4

Dragging the text block handle to make a wrapping text block.

12. Click anywhere on the page outside any text block. You now have a Basic Layout page with two wrapping text blocks, as shown in figure 11.5.

Fig. 11.5

Two wrapping text blocks.

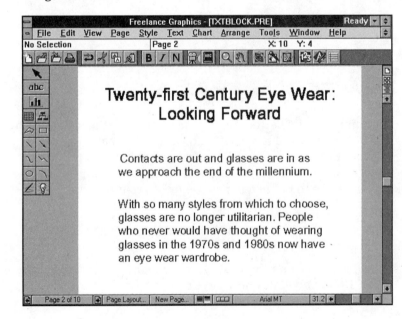

Importing Text into a Text Block

Instead of typing text in a text block, you can import text from another application. If the text is from another Windows application, you can select the text, copy it to the Windows Clipboard, and then paste the text into a presentation page. Follow these steps:

1. In the other Windows application, select the text and then choose **C**opy from the **E**dit menu or press Ctrl+C or Ctrl+Ins. This copies the text to the Windows Clipboard.

2. Switch to Freelance.

3. Click a "Click here..." text block or position the cursor in an existing block at the point where the text should be inserted. If the cursor is not positioned in a text block, the text will be pasted into the presentation page in its own text block.

4. From the **E**dit menu, choose **P**aste, press Ctrl+V or Shift+Ins, or click the Paste SmartIcon.

If the text is in an ASCII file, you can import that file just as easily. Simply follow these steps:

1. Click a "Click here..." text block or position the cursor in an existing block at the point where the text should be inserted. If the cursor is not positioned in a text block, the text will be pasted into the presentation page in its own text block.

2. From the **F**ile menu, choose **I**mport.

3. From the drop-down list of File Types, choose ASCII (PRN).

4. Use the File **N**ame and **D**irectories controls to find and then select the appropriate file name. The File **N**ame control will display only files with a PRN file extension unless you edit the *.PRN filter at the top of the control. The filter *.* displays all files, for example. The filter *.TXT displays only ASCII files that end with the TXT file extension.

Imported text takes on the attributes of the paragraph style that is in effect at the insertion point. You learn about paragraph styles next in this chapter.

Formatting Text Blocks

The difference between editing text and formatting text is simple. When you edit text, you change its content. When you format text, you change its appearance.

The default formatting of the text in a presentation is controlled by the paragraph styles in the SmartMaster set you've chosen. Every SmartMaster set has paragraph styles that apply three different formats to text, although every new text block automatically gets the 1st paragraph style. You can switch a text block to the 2nd or 3rd paragraph style, and you can change the settings of all three paragraph styles.

As an alternative to changing the paragraph styles, you can change the formatting of text by selecting the text and then using the commands in the Text menu. This is called *direct formatting* of text.

Formatting Text Blocks with Paragraph Styles

To change the appearance of a text block, you can choose a different paragraph style for the block (there are three to choose from). Or, if none of the paragraph styles is suitable, you can change the attributes of the paragraph styles.

Choosing a Different Paragraph Style for a Text Block

To change the paragraph style applied to a text block, place a typing cursor in the text block by clicking the text block, pausing for a moment, and clicking again. Then click the Indent button at the top of the text block to change the entire block to the 2nd paragraph style. Click again to switch to the 3rd paragraph style. Clicking the Outdent button returns to the 2nd paragraph style. Clicking again returns to the 1st paragraph style. Figure 11.6 shows the Indent and Outdent buttons.

If you place the typing cursor before the first character of text in the block, you can also press Tab to indent to the next style or press Shift+Tab to outdent to the previous style.

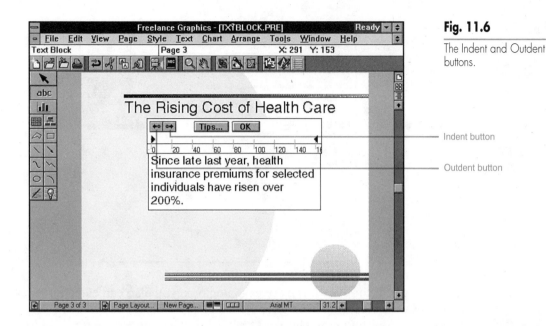

Fig. 11.6

The Indent and Outdent buttons.

Indent button

Outdent button

> Unless the three paragraph styles have different attribute settings, you may see no difference in the text when you apply a different paragraph style.

NOTE

Editing Paragraph Styles

If you don't like how the default paragraph styles that come with a SmartMaster set format a particular text block, you can override them by creating your own paragraph styles. Changing the attributes in the paragraph styles changes the look of only one block of text without affecting the rest of the text in a presentation.

To change the paragraph styles for a text block, you must open the Paragraph Styles dialog box by double-clicking the text block. You also can click a text block with the right mouse button to open the pop-up menu and then choose Paragraph Styles. Either way, the Paragraph Styles dialog box opens, as shown in figure 11.7.

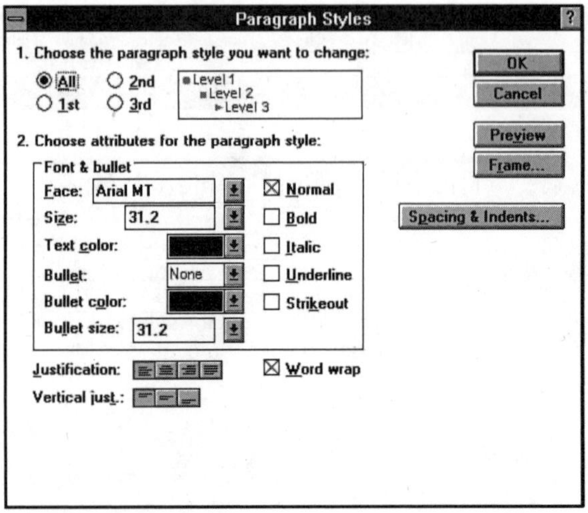

Fig. 11.7

The Paragraph Styles
dialog box.

Paragraph Styles

1. Choose the paragraph style you want to change:

○ **All**   ○ **2nd**   ■ Level 1
○ **1st**   ○ **3rd**   ■ Level 2
          ▶ Level 3

2. Choose attributes for the paragraph style:

┌─ Font & bullet ─────────────────────┐
  Face: Arial MT   ⊠ **Normal**
  Size: 31.2   ☐ **Bold**
  Text color: ☐ **Italic**
  Bullet: None   ☐ **Underline**
  Bullet color: ☐ **Strikeout**
  Bullet size: 31.2

Justification: ⊠ **Word wrap**
Vertical just.:

OK
Cancel
Preview
Frame...
Spacing & Indents...

To get to the Paragraph Styles dialog box, you also can click the Paragraph Styles SmartIcon after selecting a text block, or you can select a text block and then choose **Attributes** ["Click Here..." Text Block] from the **S**tyle menu or choose **P**aragraph Styles from the **T**ext menu.

The Paragraph Styles dialog box contains controls that let you change the text attributes that will be applied by the three paragraph styles. Step 1 is to choose the paragraph style to modify (**1**st, **2**nd, or **3**rd). A diagram to the right of the controls identifies the three paragraph styles. You can apply the same change to all three paragraph styles simultaneously by clicking **A**ll.

Step 2 is to change the settings of the Font & Bullet controls and the horizontal and vertical justification settings. A button at the right side of the dialog box enables you to choose whether the paragraph style will draw a frame around the text block. Another button lets you set the spacing and indents that will be applied by the paragraph style.

Using the **F**ace drop-down list, you can select from among the available typefaces installed in your version of Windows. The Size and Text **C**olor controls let you select a point size and color for the text. The **F**ace and Size controls may display Mixed if you have chosen to change **A**ll paragraph styles and two or more styles use different faces and sizes.

You use the Bull**e**t drop-down list to choose a bullet shape from a display of common shapes. You also can select Symbol from the list if you want to retrieve a symbol from the library and use it as a bullet. The None setting displays no bullet point before a text block. You use Bullet Color and Bullet Size to choose a color and size for the bullet.

Bullets are dramatic punctuation marks that grab your attention. They are such a valuable device for presentations that Freelance has four different page layouts with built-in bulleted text and lists.

Bullets are traditionally round or rectangular, but you can choose numbers, letters, or Roman numerals from the Text Bullet Style pop-up menu. New number and letter bullets automatically progress in numerical or alphabetical order, so for every new paragraph, your text will automatically be bulleted with the next number or letter.

You use the **N**ormal, **B**old, **I**talic, **U**nderline, and Stri**k**eout check boxes to turn on or off these character attributes for all the text in the text block.

The **J**ustification control offers four buttons that you can click to left-justify, center, right-justify, or left- and right-justify text. The button faces show a sample justified paragraph. With the Vertical Just. control, you can vertically justify text so that it is placed along the top edge, in the vertical center, or along the bottom edge of the text block.

The **W**ord Wrap check box turns on or off word wrapping in the text block.

To add a frame around a text block, click the F**r**ame button in the Paragraph Styles dialog box. A frame can add a dramatic highlight to a text block, giving it the appearance of a sign. When you click the F**r**ame button, the Text Frame dialog box appears, as shown in figure 11.8.

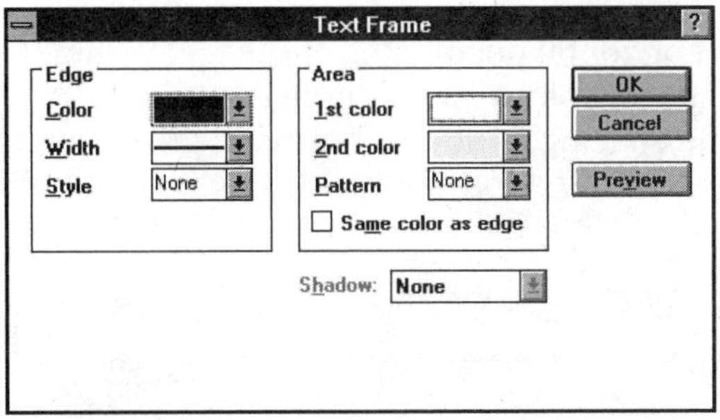

Fig. 11.8

The Text Frame dialog box.

You use the Edge controls to choose a **C**olor, line **W**idth, and line **S**tyle for the edge of the frame surrounding the text block. To see the edge, you must choose a style other than None. When you choose a style, the **S**hadow control becomes active, enabling you to choose a direction in which a subtle background shadow extends from the frame. The Area controls let you choose a **1**st and **2**nd color for the interior of the frame. To determine how these colors will be used, choose a pattern with the **P**attern control. The pattern is displayed in the two colors.

If the pattern is a gradient, the gradient shows a transition from the 1st color to the 2nd color. To make the box a solid color, click the Same Color as Edge check box to make the interior of the box the same color as the edge.

Figure 11.9 shows a text block with a shadowed frame.

Fig. 11.9

A text block with a shadowed frame.

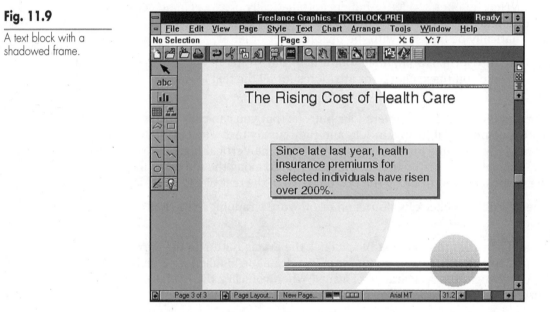

To change the horizontal positioning of the text within the block and to change the spacing between successive lines and successive paragraphs, click the Spacing & Indents button in the Paragraph Styles dialog box. The Spacing & Indents dialog box opens, as shown in figure 11.10.

Fig. 11.10

The Spacing & Indents dialog box.

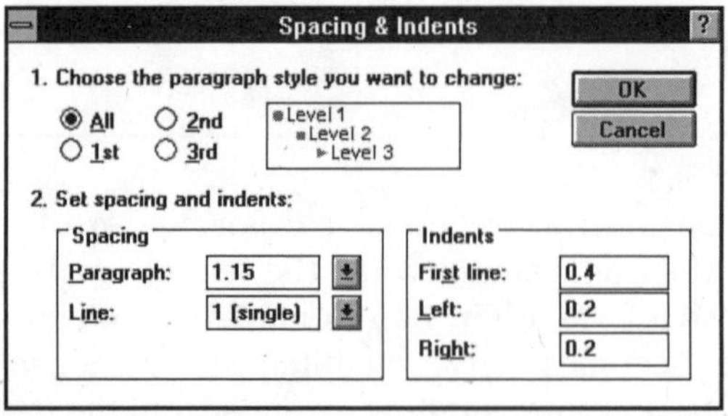

First choose the paragraph style you want to modify, or choose **All** to modify all three paragraph styles at once. Then use the Spacing and Indents controls in step 2 to change the current measurements. The **Paragraph** setting determines the distance between paragraphs. The **Line** setting determines the spacing between successive lines in a paragraph; increase this setting to space out the lines a bit and make the text look a little airier. The **First Line** setting lets you set a special indent for the first line of a paragraph. The **Left** and **Right** settings determine the left and right margins within the text block (the interior distance between the text and the edge of the block).

If you've changed the paragraph styles of text in a "Click here..." block, two additional check boxes appear in the Paragraph Styles dialog box. **Apply to SmartMaster** makes the same change to all other "Click here..." text blocks on all other pages that use the same page layout. **Reset to SmartMaster** removes the changes you've made to the paragraph styles and resets the paragraphs to the default styles in the SmartMaster set.

After modifying any or all of the settings in the Paragraph Styles dialog box, click OK to view the changes.

Exercise: Formatting a Text Block with Paragraph Styles

Before getting started, check the measurement units for the indents. Make sure that the measurement units are set to **Inches** by choosing **Units & Grids** from the View menu to open the Units & Grids dialog box. If the units aren't set to Inches, click the Inches box and click OK. Then follow these steps:

1. Click the New Page button at the bottom of the Freelance window to open the New Page dialog box.

2. Double-click [Blank Page] to make a new page without "Click here..." blocks.

3. Click the Text icon in the toolbox and drag a rectangle on the page. A text block in edit-text mode appears.

    `abc`

4. Type **Worldwide, old styles of eye wear will be new in '96. Look for the reappearance of goggles: lorgnettes, half-glasses, monocles, and pince-nez.** and click OK. Figure 11.11 shows the text block on the page.

Fig. 11.11

The text block added to the page.

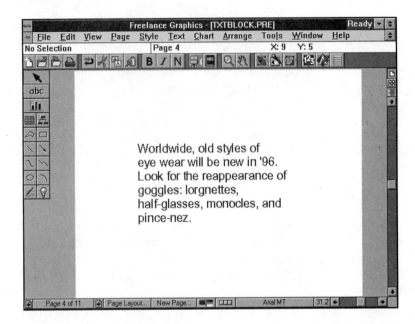

5. Double-click the text block to open the Paragraph Styles dialog box.

Now begin making changes to the styles that control the appearance of the block. Follow these steps:

1. Click the **All** paragraph styles button; in the Font & Bullet box, choose Arial MT as the **Face**, 32 pt. type as the **Size**, and dark blue as the Text **Color**.

2. Click the **Justification** button that sets both left and right justification (the button farthest to the right).

3. Click the Vertical jus**t**. button that centers the text vertically (the middle button).

Figure 11.12 shows the Paragraph Styles dialog box with all the changes.

Change the spacing and indents of the text block by following these steps:

1. Click the S**p**acing & Indents button to open the Spacing & Indents dialog box.

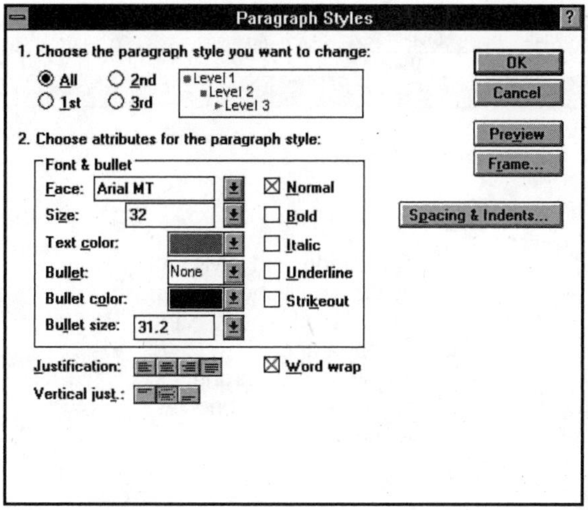

Fig. 11.12

The Paragraph Styles dialog box with all the changes.

2. Click the **1**st paragraph style button.

3. Click the button to the right of **Paragraph Spacing** and choose 1.5 from the drop-down list.

4. Make sure that Li**ne** Spacing is set to 1 (single).

5. Enter **0.5** in the Fir**s**t Line Indents box.

6. Enter **0.5** (inches) in the **Left** and **Righ**t boxes also.

7. Click the **2**nd paragraph style button.

8. Set **P**aragraph Spacing to 2 (double).

9. Set Li**ne** Spacing to 1.5.

10. Enter **0.5** in the Fir**s**t Line Indents box.

11. Enter **1.0** in both the **Left** and Ri**gh**t Indents boxes.

12. Click OK to save your settings and return to the Paragraph Styles dialog box. Figure 11.13 shows the screen now.

Add and format a frame for the text block by following these steps:

1. In the Paragraph Styles dialog box, click F**r**ame to open the Text Frame dialog box.

2. Click the Edge **C**olor pull-down button and choose black from the palette colors.

Fig. 11.13

The text block with revised spacing and indents settings.

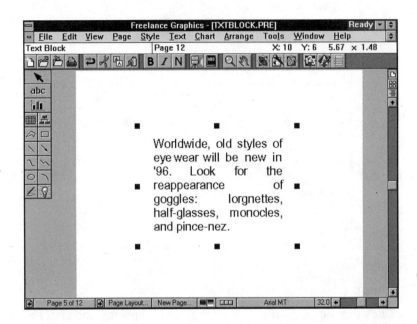

3. Pull down the Edge **W**idth list and choose the widest thickness of line.

4. Pull down the Edge **St**yle list and choose the straight, unbroken line.

5. Pull down the Area **1**st color list and choose a light gray color. Ignore the **2**nd color for this exercise.

6. Pull down the Area **P**attern list and choose the solid pattern (at the upper-left corner).

7. Pull down the **Sh**adow list and choose Bottom Left.

8. Click and hold down the Preview button for a quick preview of the frame. Release the mouse button, and the Text Frame dialog box is redisplayed.

9. Click OK to save the Text Frame settings and return to the Paragraph Styles dialog box.

10. Click OK in the Paragraph Styles dialog box to save all your changes and return to the text block.

Now try using the paragraph styles. Follow these steps:

1. Place the cursor in front of the L in the text `Look for the reap-pearance...` and press Enter. The text block goes into edit-text mode, and the second sentence becomes the beginning of a new paragraph, as shown in figure 11.14.

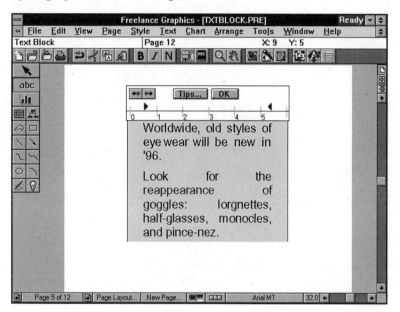

Fig. 11.14

The text block after it becomes two paragraphs.

2. Click the Demote icon once (the right-arrow icon near the Tips button). The text `Look for the reappearance of goggles: lorgnettes, half-glasses, monocles, and pince-nez.` is reformatted in the **2**nd paragraph style with wider margins, wider spacing, and a hanging indent.

3. Click anywhere outside the text block. The final framed text appears on the page with the text block handles showing.

4. If you want to change the size, shape, or placement of the framed text, you can click and drag the text block rectangle until you've adapted it so that it is pleasing to you. Notice that narrowing the text block changes the placement of the text. Click anywhere outside the text block to deselect it when you are through. Figure 11.15 shows the final framed text block.

Fig. 11.15

The final framed text block showing two different paragraph styles.

```
┌──────────────────────────────────────────────────────────────┐
│           Freelance Graphics - [TXTBLOCK.PRE]      Ready ▼ ▲  │
│  File  Edit  View  Page  Style  Text  Chart  Arrange  Tools  Window  Help  ▲  │
│ No Selection            Page 12              X: 11  Y: 4      │
│ [toolbar icons]  B I N                                      ▲ │
│ ┌──────────────────────────────────────────────────────┐ ▢ │
│ ▸   ┌──────────────────────────────────────┐            │    │
│ abc │   Worldwide, old styles of            │            │    │
│ ▮▮  │   eye wear will be new in             │            │    │
│ ▦ ▣ │   '96.                                │            │    │
│ ◿ ▢ │                                       │            │    │
│ ╲ ╲ │   Look      for      the              │            │    │
│ ╲ ╲ │   reappearance     of                 │            │    │
│ ○ ╮ │   goggles: lorgnettes,                │            │    │
│ ◿ 💡│   half-glasses,                        │            │    │
│     │   monocles,         and               │            │    │
│     │   pince-nez.                           │            │    │
│     └──────────────────────────────────────┘            │ ▼  │
│ ◂ Page 5 of 12  ▸ Page Layout...  New Page... ▣▬ ▭▭   Arial MT   31.2 ◂ │
└──────────────────────────────────────────────────────────────┘
```

Changing the Default Paragraph Styles

Each SmartMaster set contains two sets of default paragraph styles: one set for the title page layout and one set for the rest of the page layouts. By changing the default paragraph styles, you can change how every new text block will be formatted because each new text block takes on the attributes of the default paragraph styles. You may want to change the default paragraph styles if you would like every new page title in a presentation to be a different color or a larger size, for example.

Changing the default paragraph styles will not change text blocks that have already been formatted by paragraph styles, though. Nor will it change text blocks that you have formatted by editing their paragraph styles. Changes to the paragraph styles of a text block override the default settings.

abc To revise the default paragraph styles, double-click the Text icon in the toolbox. The Default Paragraph Styles dialog box appears, as shown in figure 11.16.

NOTE

You also can open the Default Paragraph Styles dialog box through the **S**tyle menu. Choose **D**efault Attributes from the **S**tyle menu to open the Style Attributes dialog box. Then click the Text Block icon in the Ob**j**ect Type menu to open the Default Paragraph Styles dialog box.

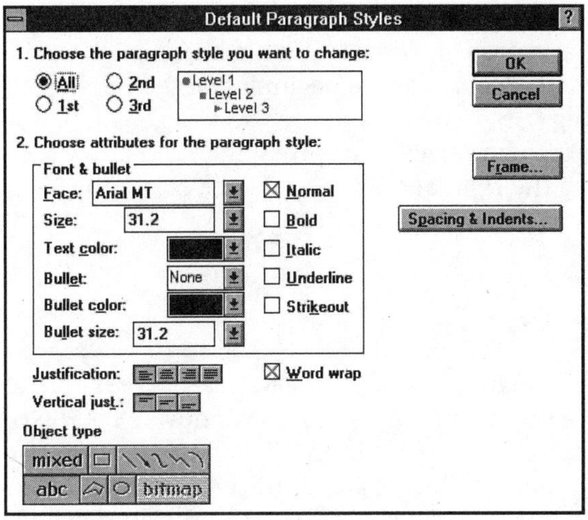

Fig. 11.16

The Default Paragraph Styles dialog box.

You can change the settings in the Default Paragraph Styles dialog box just as though you were changing the settings of the paragraph style for a single text block. The Object Type control at the bottom of the dialog box shows that the abc button has been pressed, indicating that you are changing the defaults for text blocks. When you finish, click OK. Now every new text block will be formatted with the new default paragraph styles. The SmartMaster set still retains the original default paragraph styles, though; when you start a new presentation with this SmartMaster set, the original paragraph styles will be in effect.

Formatting Text Directly

Paragraph styles control the overall look of a text block, but changing them is somewhat involved, as you've seen. Sometimes, if a text block needs only one quick formatting change, you can select the block and then apply a formatting change directly. At other times, you may need to emphasize a few characters or words within the block by changing their styling (boldfacing them or changing their font, for example). To format specific text within a block, you can select only that text and then choose formatting that will override the paragraph style.

Whether you want to quickly format a block of text, a word, or a phrase, you use the same direct formatting techniques. You can use the method that is most comfortable so that if you're a "keyboard" person, you can use the keyboard, and if you're a "mouse" person, you can use a mouse.

To directly format an entire text block, click the block to select it. To directly format a passage of text within a block, click the block, pause a moment, and then click at the beginning of the passage within the block. A typing cursor appears in the text where you have clicked. Drag across the text to be selected, or press and hold down the Shift key while pressing the right-arrow key. Selected text appears in reverse video.

Choosing Text Fonts

After you select text to format, you can use the Text Font and Text Size buttons at the bottom of the Freelance window, click the right mouse button, and then choose Font from the pop-up menu or choose Font from the Text menu. If you've added the Change Font SmartIcon to the SmartIcon palette, you can click it to get to the Font dialog box.

Changing the font and size of text is covered in detail in Chapter 4, "Making Basic Changes to the Presentation."

TIP

Freelance provides a visual way to size the text in a text block. Simply hold down the Shift key, click and hold down the mouse button on a corner handle of the text block, and then drag the handle diagonally. When you release the mouse button, the text resizes according to the next size of the block.

Choosing Text Character Attributes

The fastest way to choose text character attributes is to select the text to format and then use accelerator keys. Table 11.1 lists these keys.

Table 11.1 Accelerator Keys for Text Character Attributes

Character Attribute	Accelerator Key
Bold	Ctrl+B
Italic	Ctrl+I
<u>Underline</u>	Ctrl+U
Normal	Ctrl+N
Undo	Ctrl+Z

The text character attributes may be used alone or in any combination. If you want to reverse an attribute you just chose, press Ctrl+Z to undo the last command or action. If you want to remove all the character attributes you have added, press Ctrl+N to return the text to Normal.

The character attribute SmartIcons are another quick way to choose character attributes. SmartIcons work like toggle switches; you can click them on or off. Click the Text Bold SmartIcon to apply boldface to text, the Text Italic SmartIcon to italicize text, the Text Underline SmartIcon to underline text, or the Text Normal SmartIcon to remove all character attributes from the selected text.

Adding Text Bullets

Adding bullets to text is easy. To add a bullet to only one paragraph in a text block, place the typing cursor anywhere in the paragraph. To add a bullet to every paragraph in a text block, select the text block. Then click the right mouse button to open a pop-up menu. Choose Bullets to open the Text Bullet dialog box, as shown in figure 11.17.

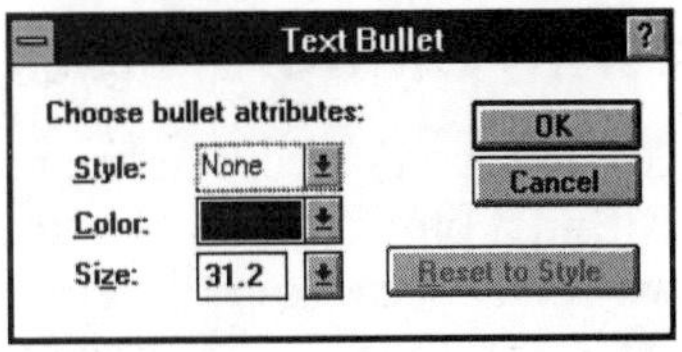

Fig. 11.17

The Text Bullet dialog box.

In this dialog box, choose the style of the text bullet from the **Style** drop-down list and the color of the text bullet from the **Color** drop-down list. Choose the size of the text bullet from the **Size** drop-down list or enter a custom point size, and then click the OK button.

To use a symbol as a bullet, select Symbol from the list of available bullet styles. Then select a symbol from the symbol gallery. A miniature of the symbol will appear as a bullet before each paragraph. Figure 11.18 shows a hand symbol used as a bullet in a text block.

Fig. 11.18

A hand symbol used as
a bullet.

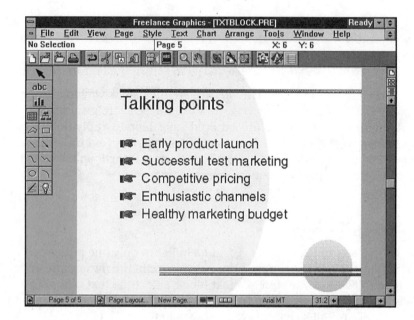

Setting Indents with the Text Block Ruler

 With the text block ruler, Freelance provides an easy, visual method for changing the indents within a block of text. To turn on the text block ruler, you choose **View** Preferences from the **View** menu and then make sure that the **Text Block Ruler** check box is checked. You also can click the Show Text Ruler SmartIcon.

Then, when you place a typing cursor in a text block, the text block ruler appears at the top of the block. Small markers within the ruler indicate the first-line, left, and right indents. To change the indents, you can drag these markers along the ruler. The marker at the right, which indicates the right indent, is a solid triangle. The triangular marker at the left is composed of two smaller halves. Drag the top half to set the first-line indent and drag the bottom half to set the left indent. You can drag the top marker to the left of the bottom marker to set a hanging indent, for example. Figure 11.19 shows the markers in the text block ruler as they are set to create such a hanging indent.

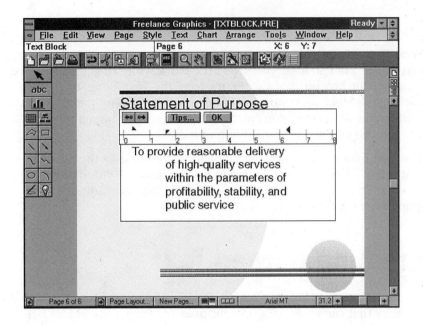

Fig. 11.19

The text block ruler showing a hanging indent.

Justifying Text

The only way to justify text without changing the paragraph style for a block is to use the accelerator keys for justification. Table 11.2 lists these keys. Select the text block and then use the appropriate accelerator key.

Justification affects all the text in a block, even if the block contains more than one paragraph.

Table 11.2 Accelerator Keys for Text Justification

Justification	Accelerator Key
Left-justify	Ctrl+L
Center	Ctrl+E
Right-justify	Ctrl+R

Framing Text

You can frame only an entire text block; you cannot frame selected text within a block. After you select the block, you can access the Text Frame dialog box by choosing Frame from the Text menu, or by right-clicking the block and choosing Frame from the pop-up menu. With the Text Frame dialog box, you can override the default paragraph style and remove a frame or add a different frame.

The Text Frame dialog box that appears is the same as the dialog box that opens when you click Frame in the Paragraph Styles dialog box; the Text Frame controls are described in the section "Editing Paragraph Styles" earlier in this chapter.

Creating Curved Text

Freelance Graphics Release 2.0 for Windows has a new text-formatting capacity that can really jazz up your presentations. Curved text lets you mold text into any shape you want. Or you can choose from among the many predesigned shapes in the Curved Text dialog box. With curved text, you can make text into a design element that stands on its own, or you can even shape the text around an object or a symbol.

You can curve any text block on a presentation page. You can even use the same procedure when editing page layouts to curve a "Click here..." text block. Then text blocks you create by clicking the curved "Click here..." text block will appear with the curve you've created. You learn how to edit page layouts in Chapter 23, "Modifying the Default Settings."

Creating Curved Text with Predesigned Shapes

You don't need to custom-design a text shape to turn your text into something special. Freelance offers so many predesigned text shapes that you can probably find what you want in the extensive menu of curves, ovals, circles, rectangles, squares, and triangles. The only text element that won't curve is a bullet.

To curve text by using one of the predesigned text shapes, click the
text block you want to shape, and then choose Curved Text from the
Text menu to open the Curved Text dialog box (see fig. 11.20). You
also can click the selected text block and then click the Curved Text
SmartIcon to curve text.

NOTE

You cannot curve text that you have created with a "Click here..." text
block unless you press Ctrl and drag the text away from the "Click
here..." block.

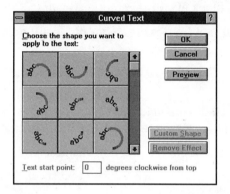

Fig. 11.20

The Curved Text dialog
box.

In the Curved Text dialog box, you can scroll through many predesigned text shapes, click a text shape, and then click Preview
to see how the text will look. If the new text design passes inspection,
click OK.

NOTE

You can edit curved text like any other text. Click the text to enter edit-text
mode. The text reverts to a straight line so that it is easier to edit. Remember to click the right mouse button for quick access to font style, size, and
so on. You cannot underline or strike out curved text, though. When you
finish editing, click OK. The text becomes curved once again.

TIP

To alter the size and shape of curved text, drag the text block by any of
its handles until you have the look you want.

To remove the curving from curved text, click the curved text, open the
Curved Text dialog box, and click **R**emove Effect.

Exercise: Creating Curved Text with a Predesigned Shape

Try curving text around a shape by following these steps:

1. Click the New Page button at the bottom of the Freelance window to open the New Page dialog box.

2. Double-click [Blank Page] to make a new, blank page.

3. Click the Text icon in the toolbox and drag a rectangle on the page. A text block in edit-text mode appears.

4. Type **Traditional frames create an old-fashioned look.** and click OK.

5. Click Curved Text in the Text menu to open the Curved Text dialog box.

6. Scroll through the menu of predesigned shapes until you see the horizontal oval with the text starting at the bottom.

7. Click OK. The text curves into a horizontal oval.

8. Move and enlarge the newly curved text by clicking and dragging the text block by its handles. Figure 11.21 shows the curved text.

Fig. 11.21

Text curved into a predesigned oval.

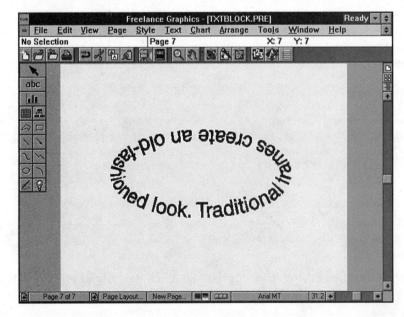

Custom-Shaping Text

None of the predesigned text shapes in the Curved Text dialog box may suit your taste. Perhaps you'd like a text shape that is more spontaneous, irregular, or asymmetrical. You can custom-design curved text to follow exactly the contours you want.

To custom-design curved text, follow these steps:

1. Draw a graphic shape with one of the tools from the toolbox.

2. Create the text block.

3. Select both the graphic shape and the text block. You can select both objects by selecting one object, holding down the Shift key, and selecting the other object.

4. From the **Text** menu, choose Curved Text.

5. Click Custom **S**hape in the Curved Text dialog box.

The text is redrawn, following the edge of the graphic shape you've drawn. The text is also resized so that the text block fits the length of the edge of the graphic shape.

You can leave the graphic shape, or you can delete it to leave behind only the reshaped text.

Exercise: Custom-Shaping Text

First create the text to be custom-shaped by following these steps:

1. Click the New Page button at the bottom of the Freelance window to open the New Page dialog box.

2. Select [Blank Page] to make a new, blank page.

3. Click the Text icon in the toolbox and drag a rectangle on the page. A text block in edit-text mode appears.

4. Type **Ready-mix Eyeglass Tint: New Ocean Shades** and click OK.

Next create the graphic object around which the text will reshape by following these steps:

1. Click the Curve icon in the toolbox.

2. Position the pointer near the left side of the page, press and hold down the mouse button, and drag the pointer to a second spot above and to the right.

3. Release the mouse button to create the first part of the curve.

4. Press and hold down the mouse button again, and then drag the pointer to a third spot below and to the right.

5. Release the mouse button to create a second segment of the curve.

6. Press and hold down the mouse button again, and then drag the pointer to a fourth spot up and to the right.

7. Release the mouse button to create the third curve segment.

8. Click the right mouse button to end the curve. Figure 11.22 shows the completed text block and curve.

Fig. 11.22

The completed text block and curve.

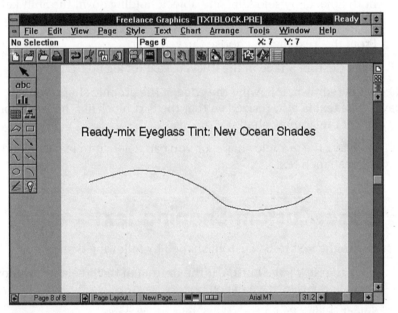

Now shape the text along the curve by following these steps:

1. Select both the curve and the text block by clicking one, holding down the Shift key, and clicking the other.

TIP

Remember that you can always delete the shape and try again by selecting the curve and either choosing Clear from the **E**dit menu or pressing the Del key.

2. From the **Text** menu, choose Curved Text.

3. Choose Custom **S**hape in the Curved Text dialog box. Figure 11.23 shows the final shaped text.

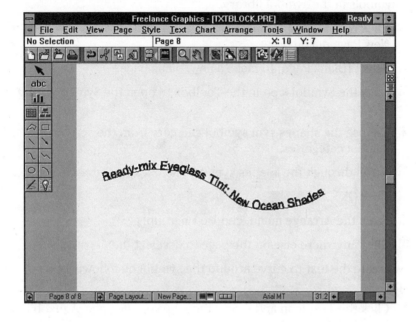

Fig. 11.23

The final shaped text.

Custom-Curving Text around a Symbol

You can also use Freelance to mold text so that it curves around an object to create a unified design statement.

To start, create a text block or select the text block you want to curve. Then click the Symbol icon in the toolbox to open the Add Symbol to Page dialog box. There you can browse through the symbol categories until you find a predesigned symbol you like. Click the symbol and then click OK. The symbol appears on the presentation page. Click and drag the handles to move and size the symbol, if you choose.

For the text to be able to follow the shape of the object, you must ungroup the symbol and then select the principle shape. Then choose Curved Text from the **Text** menu to open the Curved Text dialog box, and choose Custom **S**hape. The text curves to fit the contours of the object on the page.

Exercise: Curving Text around an Object

The following steps show you how to curve text around part of one of the symbols in the symbol library:

1. Click New Page at the bottom of the Freelance window to open the New Page dialog box.

2. Select [Blank Page] to make a new, blank page.

3. Click the Symbol icon in the Toolbox to open the Symbol dialog box.

4. Choose the shapes.sym symbol category from the scrolling list of symbol categories.

5. Scroll through the shapes.sym list and click the hexagon shape.

6. Click OK.

7. From the **Arrange** menu, choose Ungroup.

8. Click anywhere else on the page to deselect the hexagon.

Now create the text to curve around the symbol by following these steps:

1. Click the Text icon and drag a rectangle on the page. A text block in edit-text mode appears.

2. Type **STOP! — Think before you spank your kid. — You're stronger and larger. —** and click OK.

3. Click the hexagon, press and hold down Shift, and click the text block. Figure 11.24 shows both objects selected.

4. From the **Text** menu, choose Curved Text to open the Curved Text dialog box.

5. Click Custom Shape in the Curved Text dialog box. The selected text will shape itself around the hexagon, changing the type size to fit completely around the hexagon. Figure 11.25 shows the final reshaped text.

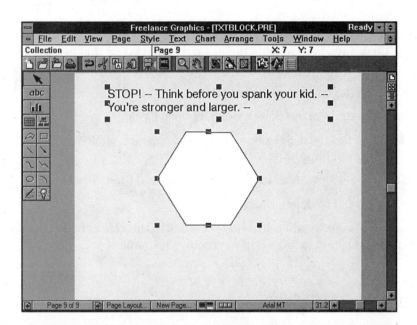

Fig. 11.24

The selected text and hexagon.

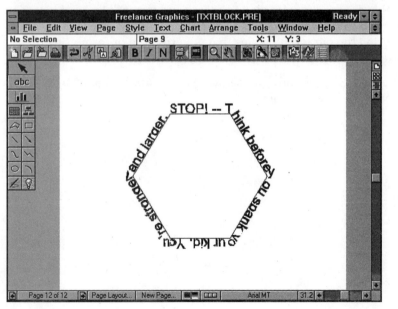

Fig. 11.25

The text shaped around the hexagon.

To remove the hexagon and leave just the text, follow these steps:

1. Click anywhere outside the hexagon and text so that neither is selected.

2. From the **Edit** menu, choose **Select**.

3. From the pop-out **Select** menu, choose **Cycle**.

4. When the Cycle Selection dialog box appears, click **Next** until Polygon/Shape appears in the dialog box.

5. Click **Select** to select only the hexagon and then click OK.

6. Press Del to delete the hexagon.

You might want to add a second text block in the center of the shaped text with the large word STOP to create a dramatic sign.

Summary

In this chapter, you learned to create and format blocks of text. You learned to add text blocks and to change their appearance by either altering the paragraph styles that govern them or formatting them directly.

The next chapter shows you how to add graphic shapes by using the Freelance drawing tools.

Drawing Objects

Page layouts and "Click here..." blocks make it easy to create presentation pages that hold text, charts, and symbols, but often you may need graphic drawings on pages as well. A presentation might not be complete, for example, without a client's logo at the lower corner of each page or without an arrow pointing to an important bar or pie slice. Figure 12.1 shows a presentation page with both a client's logo and a chart annotation. The logo and the arrow were added as drawn objects.

Freelance gives you the tools to draw and edit graphic shapes on the pages of a presentation. The drawing tools are powerful enough to make Freelance an impressive stand-alone drawing program. You can start with a blank page and draw a diagram such as an office floor plan or a map with directions to an event. Figure 12.2 shows such a map drawn on a blank page.

This chapter describes how to add basic graphic shapes by using the drawing tools and how to change the attributes that control the appearance of the objects. It also tells you what you need to know to set up the drawing aids of Freelance, such as the rulers and grid.

The next chapter describes how to use the commands in Freelance for arranging objects or groups of objects. In that chapter, you learn how to align, rotate, and flip objects. You learn also how to make extensive editing changes to individual objects.

Fig. 12.1

A presentation page
with added drawing
objects.

Fig. 12.2

A map drawn with the
Freelance drawing tools.

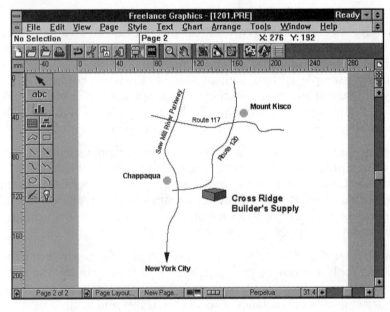

Understanding Drawn Objects

The toolbox holds a set of tools that you can use to draw various graphic shapes, such as lines, rectangles, and circles. After choosing an icon from the toolbox, you must follow the specific drawing procedures that apply to that icon. These procedures are a variation of the general procedures that you follow when using all icons, such as clicking the icon, dragging the pointer to draw the object, clicking the mouse to place points on the page, and releasing the mouse button to finish an object.

Each graphic shape that you add is a separate drawn object on a Freelance page. You can select the objects independently and then move, resize, or edit them. You can also perform a wide range of actions to change the appearance of the objects by using the commands on the **Arrange** menu. You can place a graphic object behind a text block created with a "Click here..." text block, for example. The following chapter covers these commands.

Changing the Attributes of Drawn Objects

After you have drawn an object, you can double-click the object to gain access to the object's attributes dialog box. You can also click the object with the right mouse button and then choose Attributes from the pop-up menu, or you can click the object with the left mouse button and then choose **Attributes** from the **Style** menu. The attributes dialog box for a polygon is shown in figure 12.3.

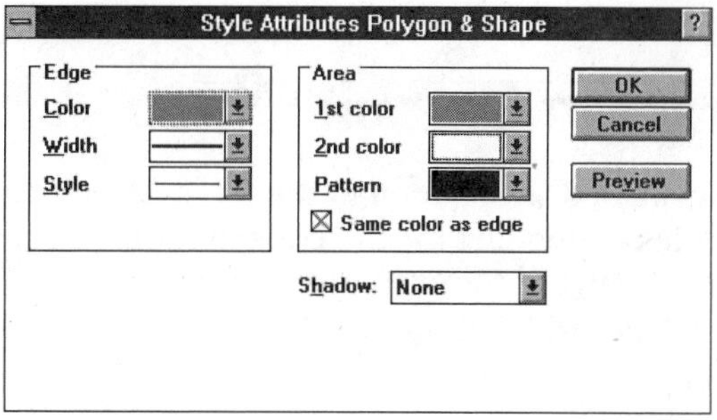

Fig. 12.3

The Style Attributes Polygon & Shape dialog box.

Using the Attributes Dialog Box

Attributes dialog boxes for drawn objects hold settings that enable you to change such basic design aspects of the objects as their edge thickness and interior color. The dialog boxes for most drawn objects have groups of settings labeled Edge and Area. The dialog boxes for some objects have other settings that are applicable to the object type too. The attributes dialog box for a rectangle has a **R**ectangle Rounding setting, for example.

The Edge settings enable you to change the **C**olor, **W**idth, and **S**tyle of the line along the edge of an object. Click the pull-down button to the right of each setting to see the available choices. Choosing None as the **S**tyle setting draws no line along the edge of the object and displays only the interior color.

The Area settings enable you to change the **1**st and **2**nd colors used within the object. If you set the **P**attern to solid (the first choice at the upper-left corner of the menu of patterns), Freelance uses the 1st color to fill the object. If you choose a pattern, the pattern is composed of the 1st and 2nd colors. If the pattern is a gradient, the transition it displays runs from the 1st color to the 2nd. Clicking Sa**m**e Color as Edge fills the object with the Edge color; the object then appears to be made up of a solid color.

After you make changes to the settings in an attributes dialog box, you can click and hold down the Preview button in the dialog box to see the effect of your changes. When you release the mouse button, you return to the dialog box to try different settings or to click OK to accept the current settings.

Any other settings specific to an object type appear below the Edge and Area settings.

Changing the Default Object Attributes

By double-clicking a drawing icon in the toolbox, you can open the default attributes dialog box for the chosen tool. To set the default attributes for rectangles, for example, double-click the Rectangle icon in the toolbox. Figure 12.4 shows the Style Default Attributes Rectangle dialog box.

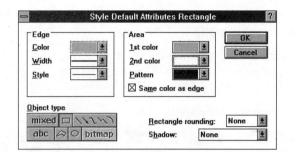

Fig. 12.4

The default attributes dialog box for rectangles.

Changing any of the settings in the default attributes dialog box affects all new objects drawn in the current presentation. Changes to the settings are not carried over to the next presentation you create.

The **O**bject Type buttons in this dialog box show the object type for which you are setting the default attributes. To set the default attributes for a different object type, click the appropriate buttons, or click OK and then double-click a different icon in the toolbox. Clicking Mixed applies the setting changes you make to all object types.

Drawing the Objects

Drawing objects with the drawing tools usually requires choosing an icon from the toolbox, dragging the pointer across the page, and clicking the mouse button. The specific steps you follow depend on the object type. The following sections describe these object types.

Drawing Rectangles and Squares

You draw both rectangles and squares by clicking the Rectangle icon in the toolbox and then dragging the pointer on the page. Simply press and hold down the Shift key while you draw to keep the rectangle a perfect square.

To draw a rectangle, follow these steps:

1. Click the Rectangle icon in the toolbox.

2. Place the pointer where you want one corner of the rectangle to be.

3. Press and hold down the mouse button.

4. Drag the pointer to the other corner of the rectangle. A dashed box marks the rectangle's position.

5. Release the mouse button. The rectangle then appears with the default rectangle attributes. The Rectangle icon in the toolbox is deselected, and the Selector icon is selected.

Figure 12.5 shows the drawing of a rectangle.

Fig. 12.5

Drawing a rectangle.

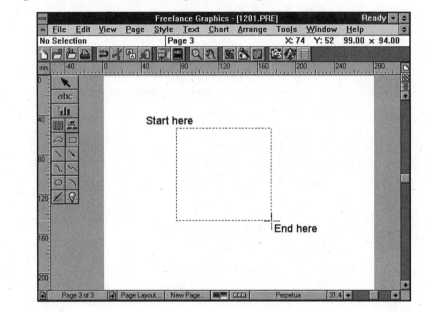

When you double-click the rectangle, the attributes dialog box shown in figure 12.6 appears.

Fig. 12.6

The attributes dialog box for a rectangle.

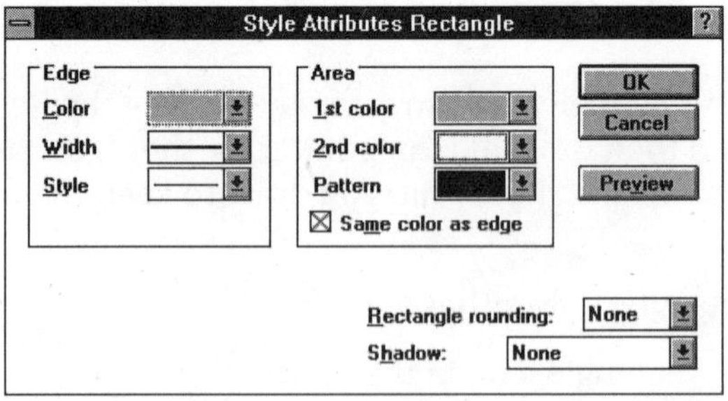

The **R**ectangle rounding setting offers four settings: None, Low, Medium, and High. Figure 12.7 demonstrates each of these settings.

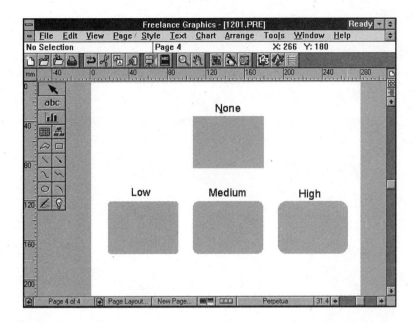

Fig. 12.7

The Rectangle rounding settings.

TIP

By holding down the Shift key as you draw the rectangle, you can constrain its shape to a perfect square.

The **Sh**adow setting enables you to choose a direction in which a subtle shadow should extend behind the rectangle or to display no shadow (None).

Drawing Lines

Drawing lines is just like drawing a line on a piece of paper. With the mouse button pressed, you drag the pointer across the page in a straight line.

To draw a line, follow these steps:

1. Click the Line icon in the toolbox.

2. While holding down the mouse button, use the pointer to draw the line on the page, or click the starting and ending points of the line.

3. Release the mouse button.

To constrain the line to horizontal, diagonal, or vertical, press and hold down Shift while you draw the line.

Figure 12.8 shows the drawing of a line.

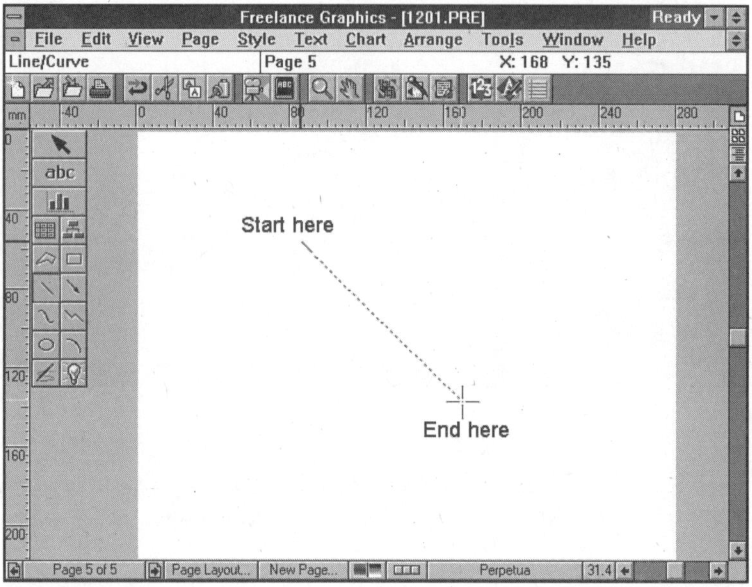

Fig. 12.8

Drawing a line.

By using the Edge settings, you can determine the color, width, and line style of the line. The **Marker** setting enables you to place a graphic shape at the beginning and end of the line; click the pull-down button next to **Marker** to display the available shapes. By changing the **Shadow**

Double-clicking a line brings up the Style Attributes Line & Curve dialog box, as shown in figure 12.9.

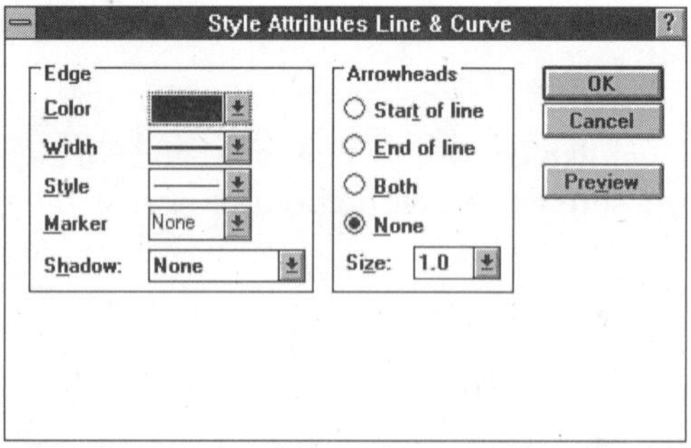

Fig. 12.9

The attributes dialog box for a line.

setting, you can add a shadow behind the line and make the line appear to float above the page.

Because a line has no interior, the Area settings do not appear in the attributes dialog box for lines. By using the Arrowheads settings that are available, you can turn on arrowheads at the **S**tart of Line, **E**nd of Line, **B**oth, or **N**one. The **S**ize setting enables you to change the size of arrowheads you add.

Drawing Arrows

Drawing an arrow is just like drawing a line except that Freelance automatically puts an arrowhead at the end of the line. To draw an arrow, follow these steps:

1. Click the Arrow icon in the toolbox.

2. While holding down the mouse button, use the pointer to draw a line on the page, or click the starting and ending points of the arrow.

3. Release the mouse button.

Figure 12.10 shows a thick arrow with a large arrowhead.

> **TIP**
>
> As with lines, pressing the Shift key as you draw an arrow constrains the arrow to horizontal, diagonal, or vertical.

When you double-click a line, the arrow attributes dialog box looks just like the line attributes dialog box. **E**nd of Line is the automatic setting for Arrowheads. To convert an arrow to a line, choose **N**one for the Arrowheads setting.

Drawing Polylines

Polylines are lines composed of two or more straight segments. To draw a polyline, follow these steps:

1. Click the Polyline icon in the toolbox.

2. Click a point, hold down the mouse button, and draw a line segment. Then click at the end of the segment, hold down the mouse button, and draw the next segment.

3. Click the right mouse button, double-click, or press Esc after you draw the last line segment to finish the polyline.

Fig. 12.10

A large arrowhead.

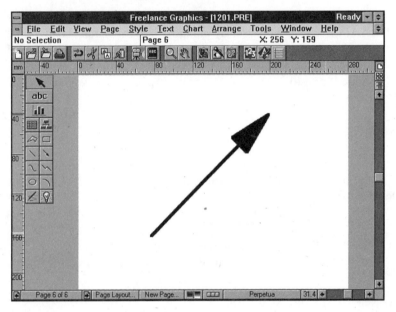

Rather than draw each line segment, you can click at the end of each segment and then right-click the end of the last segment.

Figure 12.11 shows the process of drawing a polyline.

Fig. 12.11

Drawing a polyline.

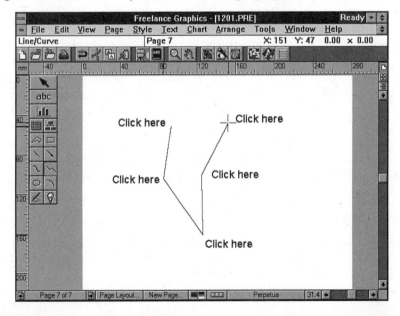

TIP

Holding down the Shift key as you add each segment constrains the segment to a horizontal or vertical line.

Double-clicking the completed polyline brings up the attributes dialog box for polylines, which has the same settings as the attributes dialog box for lines. To learn about these settings, refer to the section "Drawing Lines" earlier in this chapter.

TIP

To delete line segments one by one in the reverse order in which they were drawn, press the Backspace key repeatedly. Each time you press Backspace, Freelance deletes the previous line segment.

To draw an object that has both straight and curved segments, you complete a polyline segment and then use the Curve tool to draw the next segment. A later section in this chapter describes how to use the Curve tool.

Drawing Polygons

Polygons are shapes with three or more straight sides. To draw a polygon, follow these steps:

1. Click the Polygon icon in the toolbox.

2. Click a point, hold down the mouse button, and draw a line segment that serves as a polygon side. Then click at the end of the segment, hold down the mouse button, and draw the next side.

3. Click the right mouse button, double-click, or press Esc after you draw the last side. Freelance joins the ends of the first and last sides to close the polygon.

Rather than draw each side, you can click at the end of each side and then right-click at the end of the last side.

Figure 12.12 shows the process of drawing a polygon.

TIP

Holding down the Shift key as you add each side constrains the segment to horizontal or vertical.

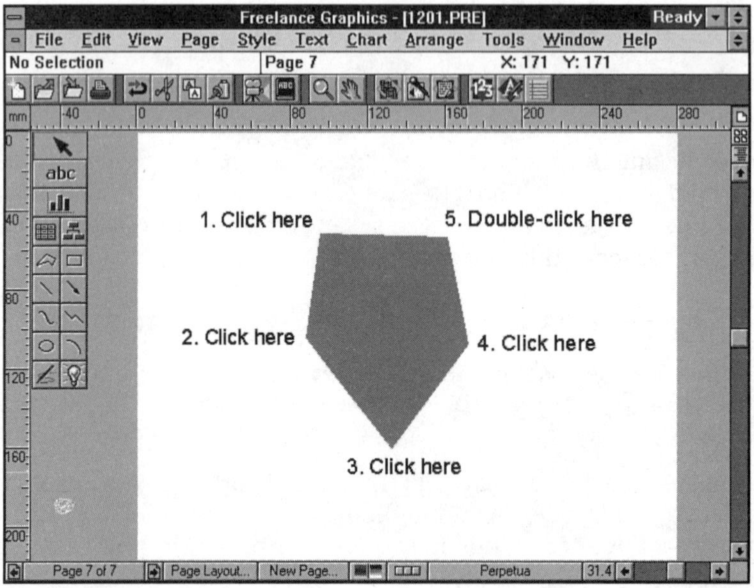

Fig. 12.12

Drawing a polygon.

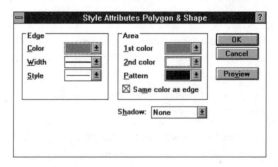

Double-clicking the completed polygon brings up the attributes dialog box for polygons (see fig. 12.13). Polygons have both edges and interior areas, so the dialog box has both Edge and Area settings. You can fill a polygon with a gradient, for example, by choosing different **1**st and **2**nd colors and then choosing a gradient design from the menu of palettes. To place a shadow behind the polygon, use the **Sh**adow setting.

Fig. 12.13

The attributes dialog box for polygons.

TIP

To delete the sides of a polygon one by one in the reverse order in which they were drawn, press the Backspace key repeatedly. Each time you press Backspace, the previous side is deleted.

To draw an object that has both straight and curved sides, you complete a polygon side and then switch to the Curve tool. Switch back to the Polygon tool to complete the polygon. The next section describes the use of the Curve tool.

Drawing Curves

A curve is a continuously curving line that passes through at least three points which you place on the page. Technically, the curve created by the Curve tool is called a Bezier curve because you can change its shape after it is drawn by using special controls at each point along the curve. You learn how to draw the basic curve here. To learn about editing the shape of the curve, refer to Chapter 13, "Editing Objects."

To draw a curve, follow these steps:

1. Click the Curve icon in the toolbox.

2. Click the starting point of the curve.

3. Click the first point that the curve should pass through. A dashed, straight line connects the two points temporarily, as shown in figure 12.14.

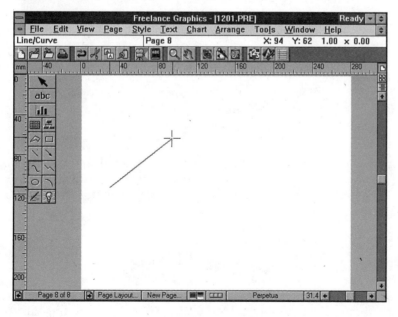

Fig. 12.14

Placing the first two points of the curve.

4. Click the next point that the curve should pass through. A dashed, curved line now passes through the second point to the third, as shown in figure 12.15.

Fig. 12.15

Placing the third point of the curve.

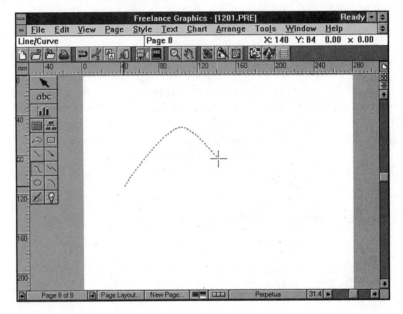

5. Continue clicking points.

6. Click the right mouse button, double-click, or press Esc when you have clicked the ending point for the curve.

TIP

Press Backspace to delete the last point you placed. Continue pressing Backspace to delete earlier points in reverse order.

Double-clicking a completed curve brings up the attributes dialog box for curves. This dialog box holds the same settings as the dialog box for lines. Refer to the earlier section "Drawing Lines" for a description of these controls.

Drawing Circles and Ellipses

After you click the Circle icon in the toolbox, you can draw either a circle or an ellipse. Simply hold down the Shift key while dragging to draw a perfect circle.

To draw circles and ellipses, follow these steps:

1. Click the Circle icon in the toolbox.

2. Click a point on the page and hold down the mouse button.

3. Drag in any direction to size the circle or ellipse.

4. Release the mouse button.

To draw a perfect circle, press the Shift key while dragging the pointer diagonally away from the first point.

Figure 12.16 shows a circle drawn with the Circle tool.

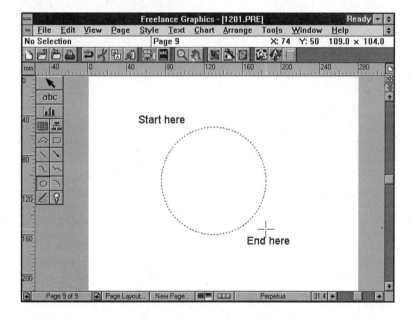

Fig. 12.16

Drawing a circle.

Double-click the circle or ellipse to open the attributes dialog box for the circle (see fig. 12.17). The dialog box contains Edge and Area settings and a **Sh**adow setting.

Fig. 12.17

The attributes dialog box for circles and ellipses.

Drawing Arcs

An arc is a segment of a circle or ellipse. To draw an arc, follow these steps:

1. Click the Arc icon in the toolbox.

2. Click a point on the page, hold down the mouse button, and drag to a second point. A dashed, straight line appears, as shown in figure 12.18.

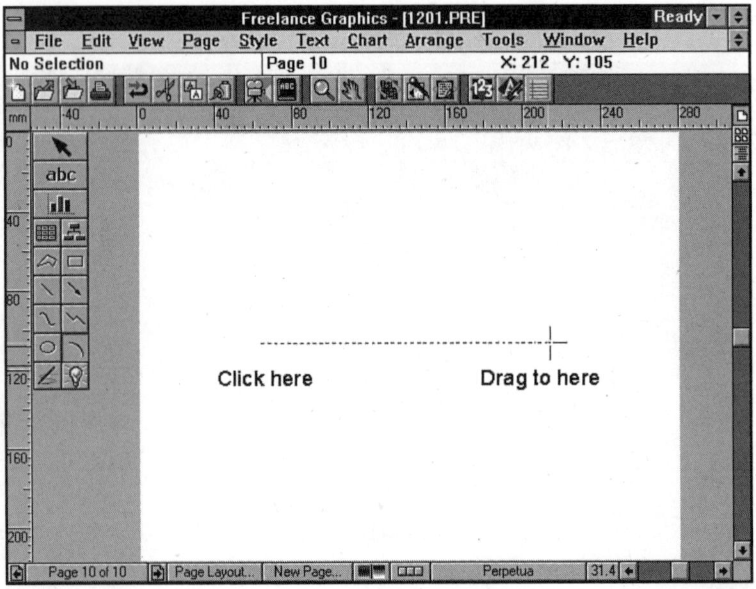

Fig. 12.18

The straight line that appears between the first two points of an arc.

3. Place the pointer anywhere along the line, press and hold down the mouse button, and drag away from the line. A dashed arc then appears, as shown in figure 12.19.

4. Release the mouse button when the arc is correctly shaped.

The arc that forms when you follow these steps is a segment of a circle. To make the arc elliptical (a segment of an ellipse), you must reshape the arc by dragging the side handles.

Double-clicking the arc produces the attributes dialog box for lines and curves. The arc attributes are the same as those for lines and curves. Refer to the earlier section "Drawing Lines" to learn about the settings in this dialog box.

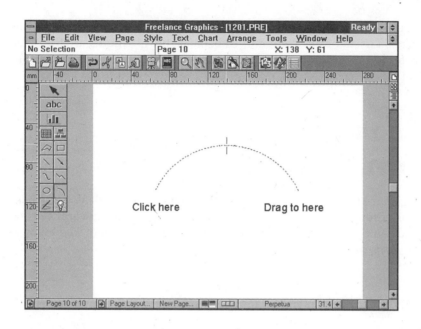

Fig. 12.19

The arc that appears when you drag a point away from the line.

Drawing Freehand

By clicking the Freehand icon and then holding down the mouse button as you drag the pointer around the page, you can draw freehand shapes. Figure 12.20 shows a freehand shape.

Fig. 12.20

Drawing a freehand shape.

Double-clicking the freehand shape produces the same attributes dialog box used for lines and curves because the attributes are the same. Refer to the earlier section "Drawing Lines" to learn about the settings in this dialog box.

Changing the Drawing Environment

Freelance Graphics for Windows offers a number of aids you can use to make drawing objects easier. The program also offers several settings you can change to modify how drawing is accomplished. The following sections discuss these settings.

Using the Drawing Rulers

The drawing rulers are a pair of rulers that run across the top and down the left side of the main page viewing area. As you move the pointer, yellow lines in the rulers display the pointer's position. Blue lines in the rulers display the widest or tallest points of any object or group of objects that is selected. Along the top ruler, for example, blue lines mark the left and right edges of a selected object. Figure 12.21 shows the Freelance window with the drawing rulers turned on.

To turn on or off the drawing rulers, choose View Preferences from the View menu. Then click the **Drawing Ruler** check box.

You also can use the Show Drawing Ruler and Hide Drawing Ruler SmartIcons to perform the same procedures.

To change the units displayed in the drawing ruler, choose **Units & Grids** from the View menu. Then choose **Millimeters, Centimeters, Inches, Points, or Picas.**

Showing Coordinates

When you have **Coordinates** turned on, they display the current X and Y cursor positions in the edit line near the top of the window. When you are drawing an object, the coordinates also show the current size of the object. When you are resizing an object, a second set of numbers shows the change in the width and height of the object. Figure 12.22 shows the coordinates as they look when you are resizing an object. Notice that the object has been stretched so that it is one inch wider.

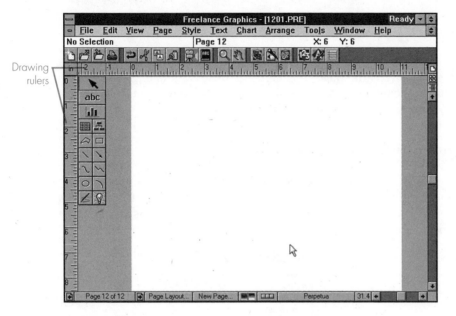

Fig. 12.21

The drawing rulers.

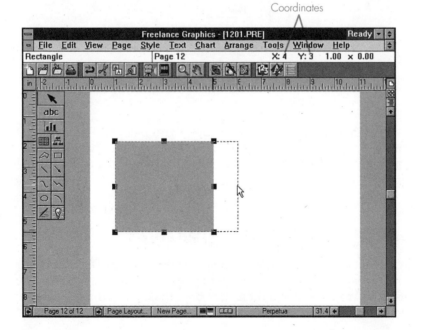

Fig. 12.22

The coordinates displaying the current width and height of the selected object and showing that the object is being stretched one inch.

The units of measurement used by the coordinates are determined by the current Units setting in the Units & Grids dialog box.

Using a Grid

The grid is a series of regularly spaced dots that you can choose to display across the page. You can use these dots to align objects visually. You can also have the pointer snap to the nearest grid dot while you are drawing objects. This makes placing objects a very exact science.

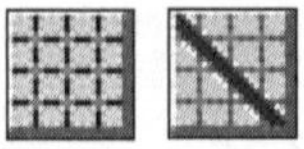

To turn on the grid, choose **U**nits & Grids from the **V**iew menu and then choose **D**isplay Grid in the Units & Grid dialog box that appears (see fig. 12.23). You also can click the Show Grid SmartIcon to show the grid, and the Hide Grid SmartIcon to turn off the grid. The **H**orizontal Space and **V**ertical Space settings enable you to change the spacing between grid points.

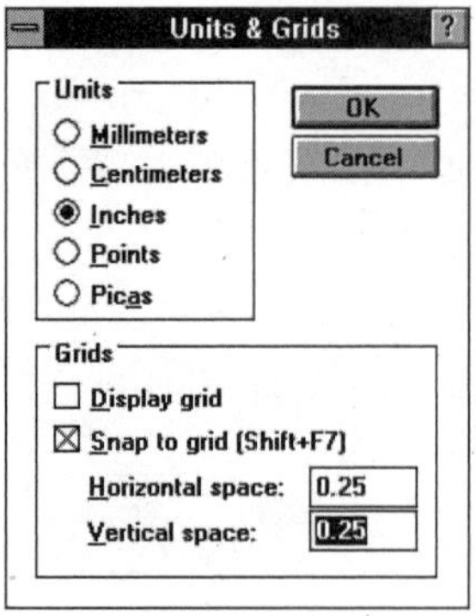

Fig. 12.23

The Units & Grids dialog box.

Units & Grids
Units
○ **M**illimeters
○ **C**entimeters
◉ **I**nches
○ **P**oints
○ Pi**c**as
Grids
☐ **D**isplay grid
☒ **S**nap to grid (Shift+F7)
Horizontal space: 0.25
Vertical space: 0.25
OK   Cancel

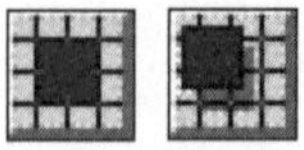

To have the pointer snap to the nearest grid point while you draw, choose **S**nap to Grid or press Shift+F7. You also can click the Turn Grid Snapping On SmartIcon. The Turn Grid Snapping Off SmartIcon does just what its name implies.

Changing the Crosshair Size

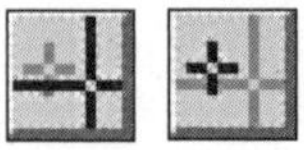

By default, a small crosshair appears while you are drawing objects, but you can have a large crosshair appear. Choose View Preferences from the **V**iew menu and then click **B**ig Crosshair. You also can press

Shift+F4 to switch between a big and small crosshair. A large crosshair can help you align objects. The Big Cursor and Small Cursor SmartIcons also change the size of the crosshair.

Keeping a Drawing Tool Active

By default, the Selector icon is chosen in the toolbox, and the cursor reverts to a pointer the moment you finish drawing an object with a drawing tool. To keep the drawing tool active so that you can easily draw another object of the same type, choose User Setup from the Tools menu and then click Keep Tool Active. Keep Tool Active is one of the Drawing tools settings in the User Setup dialog box. Revert to Pointer returns the cursor to a pointer when you finish drawing an object.

Using Freelance as a Drawing Program

By adding graphic objects to presentation pages, you are already using Freelance as a drawing program, but you also can instruct Freelance to display a blank drawing page every time you start the program. Then, on the blank page, you can add drawing objects just as you would with any software dedicated to drawing.

To have Freelance display a blank page whenever you start the program, follow these steps:

1. From the Tools menu, choose User Setup.

2. Click the check box next to Skip the Standard Startup Dialogs and Bring Up a Blank Page.

3. Click OK.

The next time you start a new presentation or when you next start Freelance, you will see a blank page without the usual dialog boxes that ask you to choose a SmartMaster set and page layout.

Even though you see a blank page, a SmartMaster set is still formatting the presentation. When you create a new page, you must choose [Blank Page] from the list of page layouts to get another blank page. You can always change the SmartMaster set and choose a page layout with a background and "Click here..." blocks by using Choose **S**martMaster Set in the **S**tyle menu and then clicking the Page Layout button.

Summary

In this chapter, you learned to use the drawing tools of Freelance to add basic drawing objects to presentation pages. In the next chapter, you learn to edit and manipulate the objects you've drawn.

Editing Objects

Freelance offers a full arsenal of tools and commands you can use to make editing changes to the objects you have drawn. Most of these commands are in the **A**rrange menu.

With some editing commands such as **G**roup, **P**riority, **A**lign, and **S**pace, you can make basic changes to how objects appear together on the page. Other commands, such as **R**otate, **F**lip, and Con**v**ert, enable you to change the appearance of individual objects. Freelance even includes a special feature, points mode, for modifying the precise shapes of objects.

Selecting Objects

Freelance works according to the consistent practice that you must first select an object and then choose a command that edits the object. Because selecting just the right object to edit is so important when you're working with complex drawings that may contain many objects, Freelance offers several ways to select objects easily and accurately.

Selecting Objects with the Pointer

The simplest way to select a single object is to click it. Handles then appear around a selected object. The simplest way to select more than one object is to hold down the Shift key while you click each object. Handles then appear around each selected object.

Sometimes clicking each object in a drawing can be hard. After you ungroup a complex symbol into dozens of component objects, you may find that clicking each object is virtually impossible. To select multiple objects in this case, use the pointer to draw a box that entirely encloses them. Every object completely within the box is then selected. If part of an object sticks outside the box, the object is not selected.

To draw a selection box, move the pointer to a spot to the left or right of a group of objects and either above or below the group. Then hold down the mouse button and drag the pointer to a spot that is diagonally across the group of objects and outside the group. When you release the mouse button, every object within the selection box is selected. Figure 13.1 shows a selection box being drawn that selects the circle and rectangle, but not the triangle.

Fig. 13.1

Drawing a selection box that selects the circle and rectangle, but not the triangle.

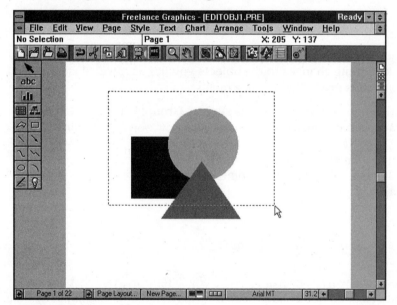

Selecting Objects with the Edit Select Menu

An alternative to selecting objects by clicking them or drawing a selection box is to use a command from the **E**dit **S**elect menu.

These commands enable you to select objects according to a variety of schemes. The following sections discuss the commands in the **Edit Select** menu.

Selecting All Objects

To select all objects on the presentation page, click the Select All SmartIcon, or choose **Select** from the **Edit** menu and then choose **All**. The keyboard alternative is to press F4 (Select All). All objects on the current page are selected, including objects in "Click here..." blocks.

Deselecting All Objects

To deselect all objects on the presentation page, choose **Select** from the **Edit** menu and then choose **None**. This command is helpful after you have ungrouped a complex symbol or drawing. All the objects in an ungrouped drawing are selected. After you deselect them all, you can then select any individual object for editing.

> Another way to deselect a group of objects is to click anywhere on the page—but away from any object. You can even click in the gray area around the page.

TIP

Cycling through the Objects

When you've created a complex drawing with many objects, you may have difficulty distinguishing among the objects, especially if they overlap. By choosing **Select** from the **Edit** menu and then choosing **Cycle**, you can have Freelance highlight each object consecutively; then you can select an object or a combination of objects as you cycle through them.

Freelance cycles through the objects in the order of their priority on-screen. You learn about changing the priority of objects later in this chapter, but usually the priority is the order in which the objects were placed on the page—from first to last. Freelance draws a dashed rectangle around the object and describes it in the Cycle Selection dialog box (see fig. 13.2). Click **Select** to select the currently highlighted object or click **Next** or **Previous** to move to a different object in the cycle.

You can select more than one object as you cycle through them. When an object is selected, the **S**elect button becomes the **D**eselect button so that you can use it to deselect the object. After you select the objects you want, click OK.

Fig. 13.2

The Cycle Selection dialog box.

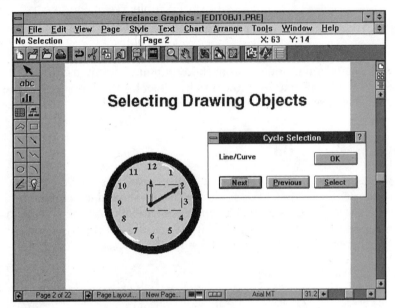

Selecting Like Objects

After you select one object, you can choose any combination of the object's attributes and then select all other objects that have the same combination of attributes. For this task, you choose **S**elect from the **E**dit menu and then choose **L**ike.

When you choose **L**ike, the Select Like Objects dialog box opens, as shown in figure 13.3.

Fig. 13.3

The Select Like Objects dialog box.

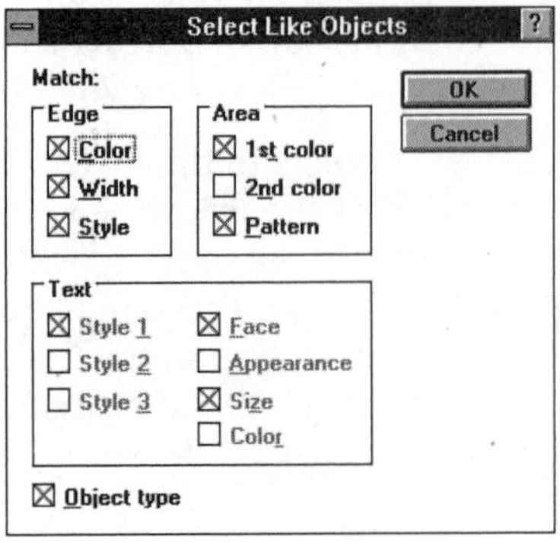

The dialog box is filled with check boxes that represent the different attributes of the object you selected. You can click as many check boxes as you want. Freelance then finds objects whose attributes match the checked attributes. If the object is a graphic shape and you check only the 1st color check box, for example, Freelance selects all other objects that have the same 1st color. If you also click the Edge Style check box, Freelance selects only those objects that have the same 1st color and the same edge style. Click the **O**bject Type check box at the bottom of the dialog box if you want to match only other graphic objects of the same type. When you select a circle, Freelance matches only circles that have the combination of attributes selected. Click OK after you've selected the attributes of the first object, and Freelance then selects all matching objects.

NOTE

If the object that you want to match is text and you've checked a paragraph style check box (Style **1**, Style **2**, or Style **3**), Freelance matches only other entire paragraphs to which the same paragraph style has been applied. If only some text within the paragraph has the same style, the paragraph is not matched.

Selecting Objects inside the Selection Box

By default, when you draw a selection box, all objects that are entirely inside the box are selected. Any objects with parts that stick outside the selection box are not selected. Inside is the default setting when you choose **S**elect from the **E**dit menu. You also can click the Select Inside SmartIcon to choose this command.

Selecting Objects Touching the Selection Box

If you choose **S**elect from the **E**dit menu and then choose Touching, Freelance selects objects that have *any part within* the next selection box you draw, not just the objects that are entirely *inside* the selection box. After you draw the selection box, Freelance returns to its default setting of **I**nside. You must choose Touching again to make the next selection box select all objects inside or touching the box. Figure 13.4 shows three objects that will be selected because they all touch the selection box.

Fig. 13.4

The **T**ouching option
selects all three objects.

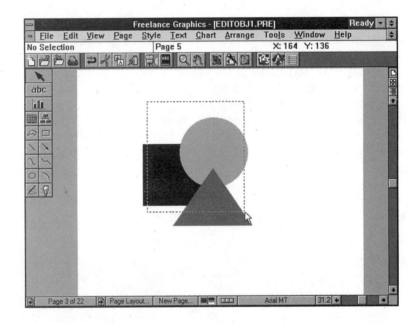

Zooming In

Full-page view gives you the overall picture of a drawing, but zooming
in on only a portion can give you the detail you need. To zoom in closer
on a drawing, choose Zoom **In** from the **View** menu, or click the Zoom
Page SmartIcon and then draw a box around the area of the drawing to
magnify.

With the Zoom **In** command in the **View** menu, you can zoom in
eight times. The Zoom **Out** command zooms out one level. Choosing
Last from the **View** menu returns to the last zoom level you were
using. To return to viewing the full page, choose **F**ull Page from the
View menu or click the View Full Page SmartIcon.

After you zoom in on an area, you can slide the entire page within the
Freelance window to expose parts that were just off the screen. To
move the page, click the Move Page SmartIcon, place the cursor (which
now looks like a hand) on the page, and then hold down the mouse
button and drag the page up, down, left, or right.

Moving and Sizing Objects

The most basic change you can make to an object is to move or size it. You move an object by placing the pointer on it, holding down the left mouse button, and dragging the object to a new location. You size an object by selecting the object, placing the pointer on one of the handles that appear around the object, holding down the left mouse button, and dragging the handle. Most objects resize proportionally, retaining their shape if you hold down the Shift key while you drag a corner handle.

Figure 13.5 shows the two possible results when you size an object. The lower cube on the right is a proportionally enlarged copy of the cube on the left; the copy was made by dragging a corner handle while holding down the Shift key. The upper cube is a copy that was stretched lengthwise by its side handle and flattened by its top handle.

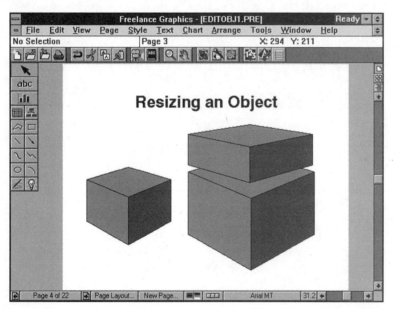

Fig. 13.5

An original object on the left and copies that are sized proportionally and nonproportionally on the right.

Replicating Objects

To make a duplicate of objects on-screen, you can select the object or objects, click **C**opy from the **E**dit menu and then click **P**aste from the

Edit menu. This places a copy of the object on the Windows Clipboard and retrieves the copy from the Windows Clipboard. An easier method is to select the object and then choose **R**eplicate from the **E**dit menu or press Ctrl+F3 (Replicate). You also can click the Replicate SmartIcon. These methods do not overwrite the contents of the Windows Clipboard.

When you use **R**eplicate, a copy of the object appears that is slightly offset from the original. To make the copy appear on top of the original, choose **U**ser Setup from the **Too**ls menu and then click Place Cop**y** on Original.

If you move or resize an object immediately after you replicated it and then use the **R**eplicate command again, the second copy of the object is moved and resized proportionally to the first replication. If the first replication is half the size of the original, for example, the second replication will be half the size of the first replication. Figure 13.6 shows an object that was moved and resized after the first replication and then replicated repeatedly.

Fig. 13.6

Replicating a
replication.

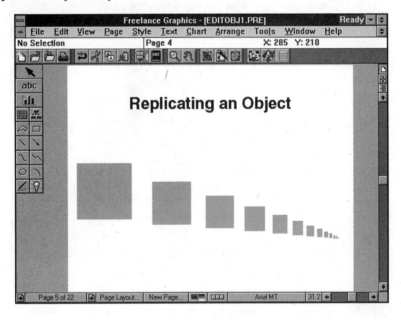

Grouping and Ungrouping Objects

After you arrange a number of objects together to form a picture, you can use the **Group** command to join the objects into one object. Then, when you click the group, only one set of handles appears around the group, as shown on the right side of figure 13.7. You can use the handles to move and size all the objects in the group as though they were one object. When you stretch the group, all objects in the group stretch to the same degree.

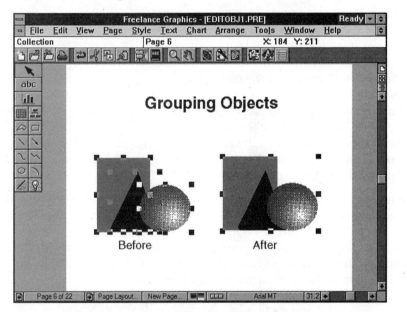

Fig. 13.7

Before and after grouping objects.

To group objects, select all the objects that you want in the group and then choose **Group** from the **Arrange** menu. You also can click the Group SmartIcon.

After you've grouped objects and made a change to the group, you can ungroup the group to select and edit an individual object. To do this, select the group and then choose **Ungroup** from the **Edit** menu or click the Ungroup SmartIcon.

When all the objects in the group are the same type, double-clicking the group opens the attributes dialog box for that object type. When the objects in the group are of different types (such as a polygon, some lines, and a circle), clicking the group brings the Style Attributes Mixed dialog box to the screen (see fig. 13.8).

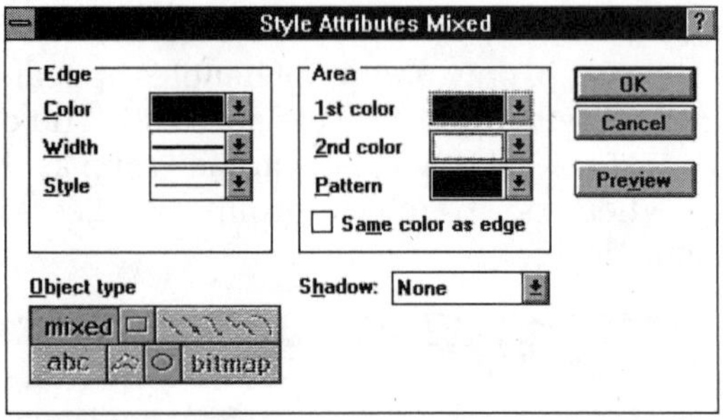

Fig. 13.8

The Style Attributes Mixed dialog box.

The lower-left corner of the dialog box has an **O**bject Type button for each object type in the group. The other **O**bject Type buttons appear dimmed. A button labeled Mixed is already pressed. When the Mixed button is pressed, any changes you make to the Edge and Area attributes affect all objects in the group. To change objects of only one type, click the appropriate **O**bject Type button and then make changes to the settings in the dialog box.

When objects in the group have different attribute settings, a gray triangle appears in the setting for that attribute, as shown in figure 13.9. If you select two objects—one with a red interior and one with a yellow interior, for example—the gray triangle appears in the Area 1st Color setting. The triangle indicates that selected objects have different colors even if they are part of the same group.

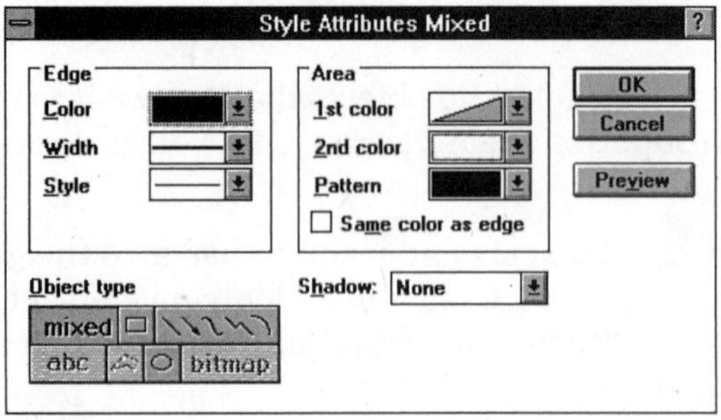

Fig. 13.9

1st Color showing a triangle when the selected objects have different 1st colors.

Changing the Priority of an Object

Drawing objects on-screen is just like placing paper cutouts on a desk-top. The last cutout that you put down will overlap other cutouts already on the desk. But what happens when you place two cutouts on different areas of the desk and then slide them together so that they overlap? Which cutout will end up on top?

When you're working with cutouts, you decide which one overlaps the other. When you're working with Freelance drawing objects, however, the object that was drawn last is the one that overlaps all others. In Freelance terminology, the last object you draw has the highest priority. You can test this concept by drawing three objects of different colors on different areas of a blank page. Then drag the objects together so that they all overlap. You will see that the first drawn object is on the bottom and the most recently drawn object is on top. Freelance maintains this bottom-to-top order for the life of the drawing.

You can change the priority of objects in a drawing, though—moving an object forward or back a level, or moving an object all the way to the top or bottom of the pile. You see the change immediately if the object is already in a pile. You see the change later if the object appears alone and you then move it into a pile. Even the last-drawn object will slide into a pile at the bottom when you use the **Pr**iority command to send it to the bottom. Figure 13.10 shows a collection of objects before and after the sphere is sent back one level.

To change the priority of an object, select the object and choose **Pr**iority from the **Arrange** menu. Then choose one of these choices from the pop-out menu: **T**op, **B**ottom, **S**end Forward One, or **F**all Back One. You also can press Shift+F8 (Send Forward One) or F8 (Fall Back One). The SmartIcons for these commands are Bring to Front, Send to Back, Forward One, and Back One.

Aligning Objects

The Align command gives you the power to align objects relative to one another. To align objects, select all the objects to align and then choose Align from the **Arrange** menu. The Align Objects dialog box appears (see fig. 13.11).

Fig. 13.10

Sending the sphere back one level.

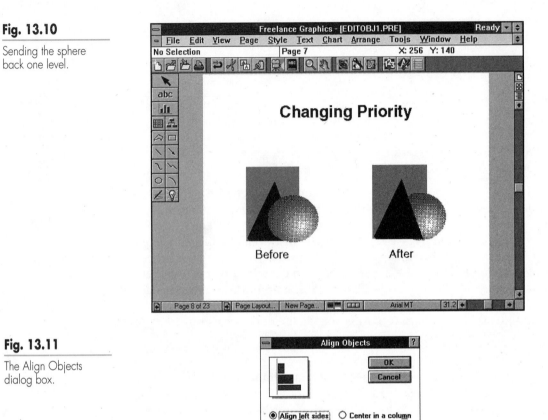

Fig. 13.11

The Align Objects dialog box.

As you click each option in this dialog box, a diagram illustrates the effect of the option. Figures 13.12, 13.13, and 13.14 show the effects of all the options. When you choose to align the sides of objects, they are aligned with the side of the object that extends the most.

In the Align Objects dialog box, you can choose **Center on Page** in addition to any of the other options so that the group of objects are aligned relative to one another and then moved to the center of the page.

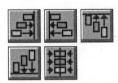

The five align SmartIcons are Align Right, Align Left, Align Top, Align Bottom, and Center in a Column.

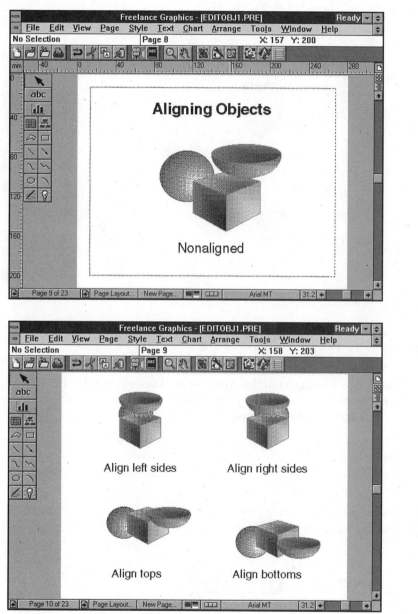

Fig. 13.12

Nonaligned objects.

Fig. 13.13

Aligned objects.

Fig. 13.14

Centered objects.

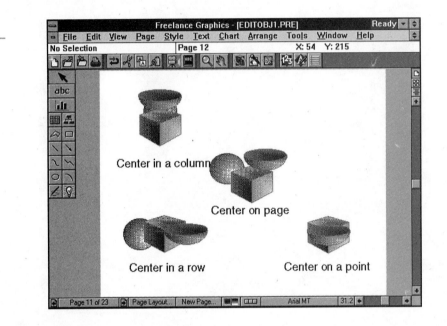

Spacing Objects

The **S**pace command in the **A**rrange menu enables you to evenly space three or more objects on a page. You must select at least three objects for this command to become available.

After you select the objects and choose **S**pace, you can use the Space dialog box to space the objects vertically, horizontally, or both if you click both check boxes. The objects will become evenly spaced, as shown in figure 13.15.

 You also can select the objects and then click one of the following spacing SmartIcons: Space Horizontally or Space Vertically.

Rotating an Object

 To rotate objects around their center, select the object or objects, and then choose **R**otate from the **A**rrange menu or click the Rotate Smart-Icon. The cursor changes shape to show an arrow curving around a plus sign, and the edit line shows the angle of rotation of the objects.

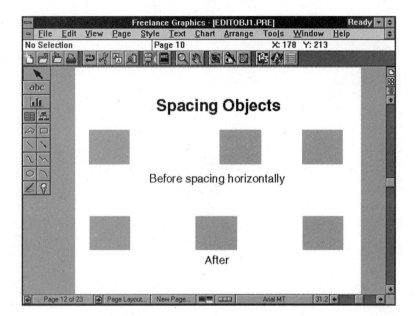

Fig. 13.15

Horizontally spacing three objects.

Place the cursor at a point near the object and drag in a circle around the object in the direction you want to rotate the object. If you have selected one object to rotate, you will see its outline rotate. Figure 13.16 shows an object as it is rotated. When you select two or more objects to rotate, you will see a dashed box rotate, outlining the area of the objects. The objects rotate around a point that is the center of the set of objects.

You can rotate text, but not charts or tables. When you edit a rotated text block, it becomes level temporarily while you are editing the text and then returns to its previous rotation when you finish editing.

By holding down the Shift key as you rotate objects, you can force the objects to rotate in 45 degree increments. Bitmaps can rotate in 90 degree increments only.

TIP

By placing the rotate cursor far away from the object or objects, you gain finer control of the rotation angle when you drag the cursor.

Fig. 13.16

Rotating an object.

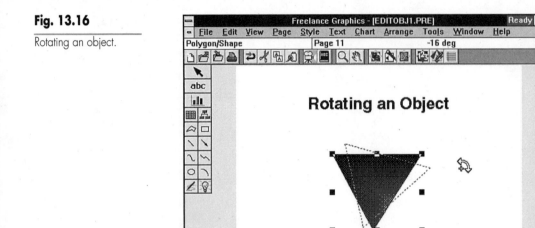

Flipping an Object

Flipping an object turns it upside down or left to right. You can flip only graphic objects. You cannot flip charts, tables, text blocks, linked or embedded objects, or metafiles.

To flip an object, select the object and then choose **F**lip from the **A**rrange menu. From a pop-out menu, you can choose to flip the object **L**eft to Right or **T**op to Bottom. Figure 13.17 shows a picture made from a symbol that has been replicated and then flipped.

 To flip objects, you also can use the two flip SmartIcons: Flip Left to Right and Flip Top to Bottom.

Using Points Mode To Edit Points

Most objects are made up of lines, sides, or curves that connect points. By moving, adding, and deleting points in *points mode*, you can change the shape of the objects.

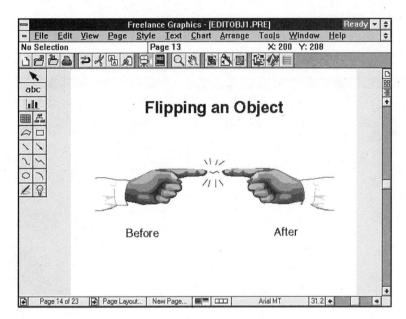

Fig. 13.17

Flipping an object.

To enter points mode, choose Points **M**ode from the **A**rrange menu or press Shift+F6. You also can click the Points Mode SmartIcon. Freelance stays in points mode until you choose Points **M**ode or press Shift+F6 again. While Freelance is in points mode, an Edit Pts indicator appears near the left end of the title bar of the Freelance window, and a check appears next to Points **M**ode in the **A**rrange menu. Freelance also displays an outline cursor with a small, unfilled point inside.

While the program is in points mode, you can work with the points of all drawing objects except rectangles and circles. You must first convert rectangles and circles to lines or polygons by using the Convert command (covered later in this chapter). You cannot edit the points of grouped objects.

Moving Points

When you select a drawing object in points mode, a tiny hollow box appears at each of the object's points. When you click a point to select it, the tiny box becomes filled. After you select a point, you can drag the point just as you would any object—by positioning the pointer on it, holding down the left mouse button, and dragging the mouse. When you release the mouse button, the point is dropped, and the object changes shape accordingly. Figure 13.18 shows a point being moved. Notice the shape of the cursor. Notice also that the selected point shows a filled box. The other points show hollow boxes.

Fig. 13.18

Moving a point in points mode.

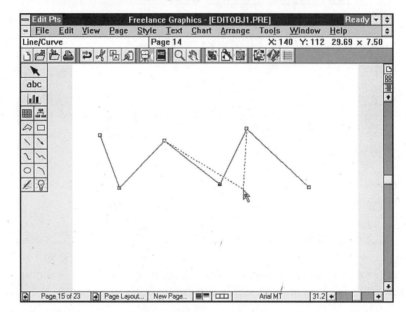

By drawing a selection box around two or more points with the pointer, you can select multiple points. When you drag one of the points, all the selected points move.

Adding Points

In points mode, you can add a point anywhere along the perimeter of a drawing object to gain additional flexibility in changing the shape of the object. To add a point, press the Insert key and then click along the edge of the object where you want the new point to be. Figure 13.19 shows an object before and after a new point is added.

You also can click the Add Point SmartIcon. Or you can choose **E**dit Points from the **A**rrange menu, choose **A**dd Point from the pop-out menu, and then click where you want the new point to be.

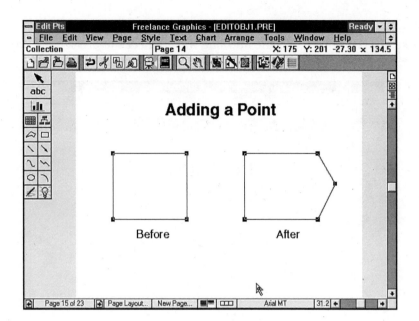

Fig. 13.19

An object before and
after it gets a new point.

Deleting Points

To delete a point you no longer need, select the point and press the Del
key. Or choose **E**dit Points from the **A**rrange menu and then choose
Delete Points from the pop-out menu.

Breaking Objects

While the program is in points mode, you can break a drawing object
into two objects with the **B**reak command. If the object is a polyline,
you can break the polyline into two separate polylines. The original
polyline will still connect the first and last points, but the new polyline
will start at the break point and follow the shape of the original polyline
to the end point. If the object is a polygon, the result will be two separate, smaller polygons.

To break a line, you must select a point along the line. If the line is a
single segment, you must add a point to the line first and then select
that point. You then choose **E**dit Points from the **A**rrange menu and

choose **Break** from the pop-out menu. The original line will connect the first and last points, and the new line will connect the break point and the last point. Figure 13.20 shows a line being broken into two lines.

Fig. 13.20

Breaking a line.

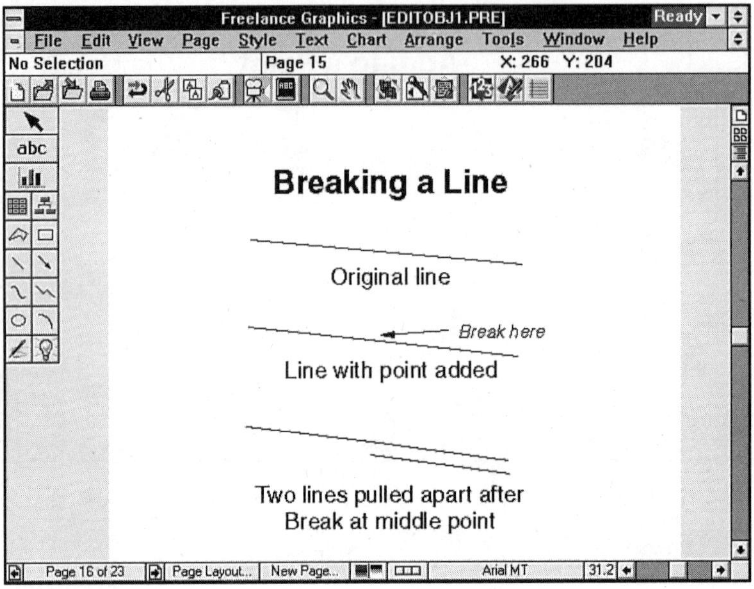

To break a polygon, you must select two points that are separated by other points and then use the **Break** command. The polygon then splits into two objects. The first polygon connects all the points. The second polygon connects the original first point of the polygon, the two selected points, and the points in between the selected points. Figure 13.21 shows a polygon being broken into two polygons.

Changing the Shape of Curves

When the object you select in points mode is a curve or an arc, clicking one of the points along the curve or arc produces a pair of handles at that point. You can drag each handle to change the shape of the curve as it approaches or departs from the point. You also can drag the point as you would drag a point of any object.

When you drag a handle, the handle pulls the bend of the curve. A dashed curve shows how the curve will look when you release the mouse button. When you press Shift and drag a handle, the handle on the other side of the point moves an equal distance in the opposite direction. As a result, the curve remains smooth as it passes through the point. When you press Ctrl and drag a handle, a sharp angle called a *cusp* forms at the point.

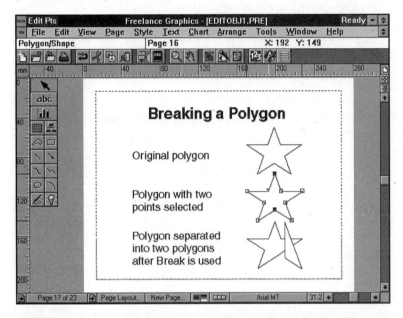

Fig. 13.21

Breaking a polygon.

Figure 13.22 shows a curve with handles at a point and the same curve when one of the handles has been dragged.

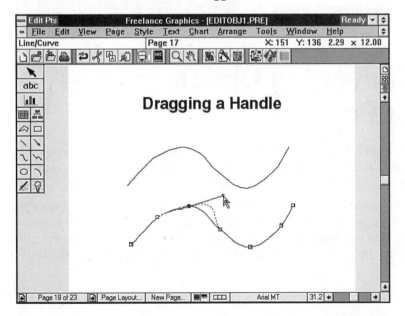

Fig. 13.22

Dragging a handle to change the shape of a curve.

Figure 13.23 shows a curve that has had a handle dragged while the Shift key was pressed. Notice that the opposite handle has moved an equal distance in the opposite direction.

Fig. 13.23

Using Shift and dragging a handle.

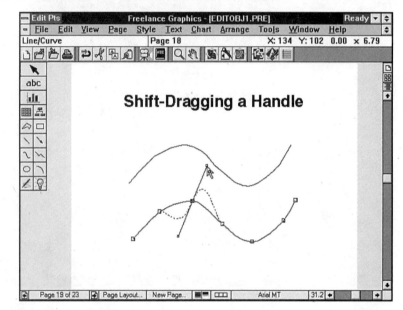

Figure 13.24 shows a curve that has had a handle dragged while the Ctrl key was pressed. Notice that the curve forms a cusp at the selected point.

Converting Objects to Lines or Polygons

You can convert objects to lines or polygons with the Convert command in the **Arrange** menu. You must convert rectangles and circles to lines or polygons before you can edit them in points mode.

When an object is a polygon, you can convert it to a line. Converting a filled polygon removes the fill and disconnects the line between the first and last points of the polygon. In points mode, you can then move the points of the line, add or delete points, or break the line.

Figure 13.25 shows a polygon before and after it is converted to lines. In points mode, the first point was moved away from the last point to show that the lines are no longer connected.

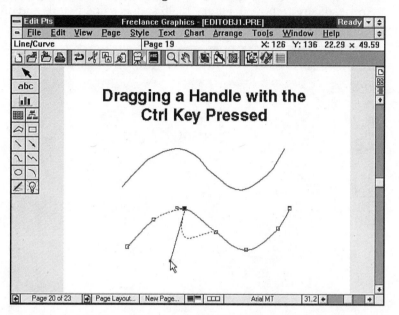

Fig. 13.24

Using Ctrl and dragging a handle.

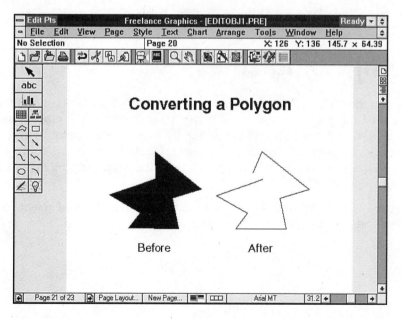

Fig. 13.25

A polygon before and after it is converted to lines.

Converting an object to a polygon connects its first and last points so that the object becomes closed and can be filled with a color, gradient, or pattern. When a line that has arrowheads is converted to a polygon, the arrowheads are removed. Figure 13.26 shows a line before and after being converted to a polygon.

Fig. 13.26

A line before and after it is converted to a polygon.

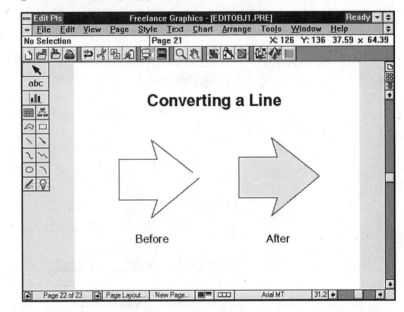

Connecting Lines

To join the ends of lines or curves, you can select the objects and then use the **Connect Lines** command in the **Arrange** menu. The closest two ends of the selected objects are joined by a new line segment. When you select more than one line to connect, Freelance connects each line to the nearest line. When you connect straight line segments, you create a polyline.

Figure 13.27 shows three line segments before and after you select them and use the **Connect Lines** command.

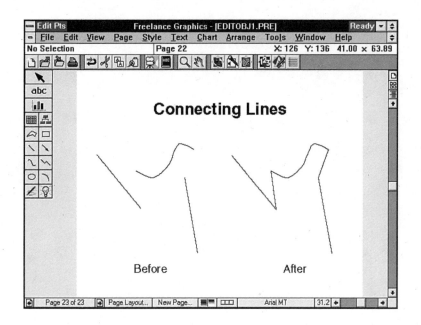

Fig. 13.27

Before and after
connecting lines.

Summary

In this chapter, you learned to change the appearance of a drawing object that you placed on the page by selecting the object and then using an object-editing command.

In the next chapter, you learn to select predrawn pictures from the symbol library that comes with Freelance and add them to presentation pages.

Using Symbols

Rather than draw every picture you need by hand, you can take advantage of the library of pictures that comes with Freelance. These pictures, called symbols, were drawn by professional artists, so they can add polish to any presentation.

In this chapter, you learn to pull the symbols you need from the symbol library and to create your own symbols and add them to the library.

Understanding Symbols

Imagine being the victim of a run-of-the-mill presentation about the economics of shipping oil from Asia—a presentation with text and charts but little else. Even with one of the SmartMaster sets of Freelance, the presentation may still be dull at best. Take a look at figure 14.1 to see how such a presentation can be made more enlightening and entertaining by adding pictures of a ship and an oil refinery. Even without reading the title, the viewer can already key in on the subject simply because of the pictures.

Fig. 14.1

The title page of "The Economics of Asian Oil Shipping."

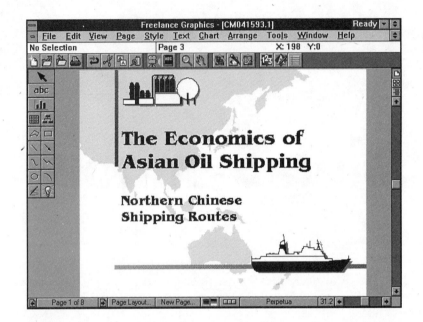

Adding pictures can give any presentation more impact, but original drawings, photos, and copyrighted art cost lots of money and take time to purchase or produce. For these reasons, clip art has long been part of a graphic artist's repertoire. Clip art, in books of pictures and decorative images, is sold to be clipped out and pasted into a page layout copyright-free.

Freelance Graphics has its own library of clip art, called *symbols*. Symbols are copyright-free pictures covering a wide range of subjects. You can use these symbols repeatedly. Figure 14.2 shows just a few of the symbols that come with Freelance Graphics for Windows.

Freelance symbols, no matter how simple or complex, are composed of groups of Freelance drawn objects. Just as you can draw and edit your own art objects in Freelance, professional artists have used Freelance's drawing tools to draw, arrange, and group together objects to make the Freelance symbols. You can also pull out and use only one part of a symbol, or draw additions to the existing symbols with the Freelance drawing tools.

Because you know that Freelance symbols are groups of drawn objects, you can ungroup them to edit their components and modify a symbol to fit your needs. If the symbol is simple, you can select it and change its attributes, such as its edge style and color. If the symbol is more complex, you must ungroup the component objects and then edit each object separately. Figure 14.3 shows a selected symbol before and after it is ungrouped.

Fig. 14.2

A variety of Freelance Graphics symbols (clip art).

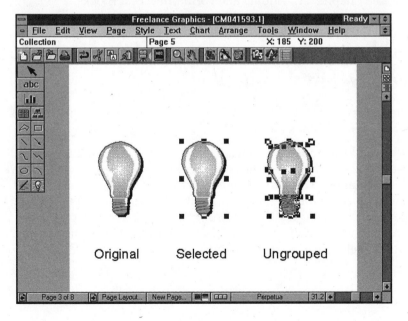

Fig. 14.3

Three forms of the same symbol: original, selected, and ungrouped.

NOTE

Be careful not to use copyrighted art without permission. Computers have made breaking the law—even if it is unintentional—far easier than ever before. Many different packages of clip art exist on disk; some of the packages are copyright-free, and some of them are copyrighted. Using other people's copyrighted art without permission is stealing from them.

Adding a Symbol to a Presentation Page

Symbols can be such an important part of a presentation that two of the page layouts in every SmartMaster set have built-in "Click here to add symbol" blocks. These blocks automatically place and size added symbols. You can add symbols to other presentation pages too. You can then enlarge, reduce, move, or copy the symbols, and change their attributes.

When using Freelance Graphics, you can add anything that is a symbol to a presentation as a text bullet. To learn about using symbols as bullets, see Chapter 11, "Adding and Formatting Text Blocks."

Adding a Symbol with a "Click Here To Add Symbol" Block

The easiest way to add a symbol to a presentation is to click a "Click here..." symbol block (see fig. 14.4).

After you have added a new page to a presentation and chosen the Title or the Bullets & Symbol page layout, click the prompt text "Click here to add symbol." The Add Symbol to Page dialog box appears so that you can browse the categories of symbols in the library (see fig. 14.5). At step 1 (choosing a symbol category), use the scroll bar to scroll through the available categories. For a comprehensive list of the symbols in each category, refer to Appendix B, "The Symbol Library."

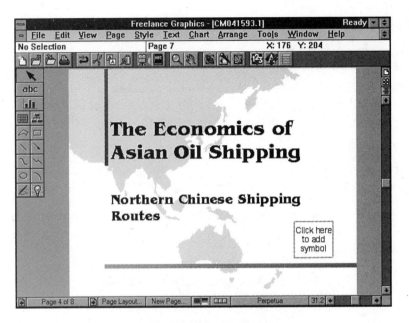

Fig. 14.4

A "Click here to add symbol" block on a title page.

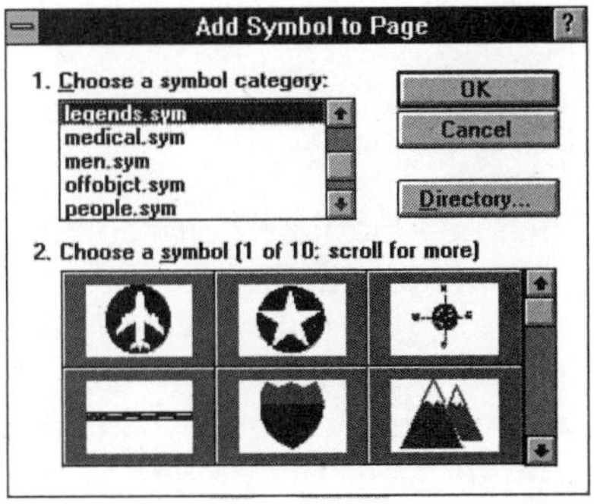

Fig. 14.5

The Add Symbol to Page dialog box.

Click a symbol category, and you see a scrollable display at the bottom of the dialog box of the symbols in that category. Double-click the symbol you want, and it replaces the "Click here to add symbol" block. After you have added the symbol to the "Click here..." block, you can click and drag the symbol block handles to stretch the symbol.

Editing Symbols in "Click Here To Add Symbol" Blocks

Editing the basic attributes of very simple symbols in "Click here to add symbol" blocks is easy. Select the symbol and then choose **Attributes** from the **S**tyle menu. This procedure opens the Style Attributes Polygon & Shape dialog box (see fig. 14.6). In this dialog box, you can edit the **C**olor, **W**idth, and **S**tyle of the symbol's edge. You can also edit the **1**st Color, **2**nd Color, and **P**attern of the symbol's area. To make the interior color of the symbol the same color as the edge, click Sa**m**e Color as Edge. To add a shadow to a symbol, select a shadow from the **S**hadow drop-down list. Click, hold down, and release the Preview button for a quick look at any changes you make; click OK when you have made all the changes you want.

Fig. 14.6

The Style Attributes Polygon & Shape dialog box.

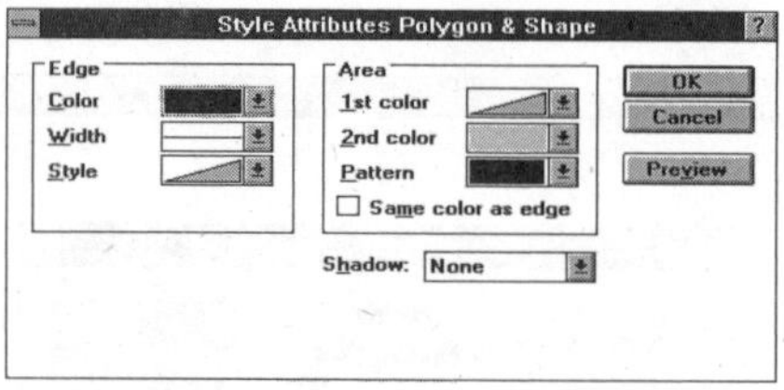

Complex symbols must be ungrouped into component objects so that each object can be edited individually. To ungroup a symbol in a "Click here to add symbol" block, first hold down the Ctrl key and drag the symbol away from the block. Then use the **U**ngroup command in the **A**rrange menu. Handles appear around each object within the symbol. Click anywhere else on the page to deselect all the objects and remove the handles. Then select the object to edit. When you finish editing the symbol, you may want to select all the objects that make up the symbol, and then use the **G**roup command from the **A**rrange menu to rejoin them into one object. To select a group of drawn objects, use the Selector tool to draw a box around the group. All objects that are completely enclosed within the box are selected.

Adding a Symbol to a Presentation Page

You may want to add more symbols to a presentation or add symbols to different pages of the presentation than what is provided by the "Click here to add symbol" blocks. For example, you may want to add a symbol to a chart page.

Adding a symbol to a page is similar to adding a symbol to a "Click here to add symbol" block. Turn to the page where you need the symbol, and then click the Symbol icon in the toolbox. The Add Symbol to Page dialog box appears on-screen. Use this dialog box to select a symbol from the library.

When you add a symbol to a presentation page without using a "Click here to add symbol" block, the symbol usually appears in the lower-left corner of the presentation page. You can then move the symbol and size it as you choose. For step-by-step instructions, see the third part of the three-part exercise in the following section.

TIP

To help you place and align symbols on a presentation page, you may want to display a grid on the Freelance desktop. Choose **U**nits & Grids from the **V**iew menu to open the Units & Grids dialog box. Mark the **D**isplay Grid box and click OK. A grid appears on the desktop. You also can mark the **S**nap to Grid checkbox to have the cursor snap to the nearest grid point while you place or align symbols.

Exercise: Adding Symbols to a Presentation

In this exercise, you get a chance to add a symbol to a page by using both the "Click here to add symbol" block and the Symbol icon in the toolbox.

To begin, create a new presentation, choose the Title page layout, and add text to "Click here..." text blocks by following these steps:

1. From the **File** menu, choose **New** to start a new presentation.

2. Choose the PACIFIC.MAS SmartMaster set from the Choose a Look for Your Presentation dialog box.

3. Choose Title from the Choose Page Layout dialog box.

4. Click the prompt text "Click here to type presentation title," type **The Economics of Asian Oil Shipping**, and click OK.

5. Click the "Click here to type subtitle" block, type **Northern Chinese Shipping Routes**, and click OK.

Next add a symbol to a "Click here to add symbol" block by following these steps:

1. Click the "Click here to add symbol" block. The Add Symbol to Page dialog box appears.

2. Scroll through the list of symbol categories in the upper-left side of the dialog box and click TRANSPOR.SYM. (You also can press T on the keyboard to jump quickly to the first symbol category that starts with the letter T.) The transportation symbols appear in the scrolling symbol menu at the bottom of the dialog box (see fig. 14.7).

Fig. 14.7

The transportation symbols in the symbol library.

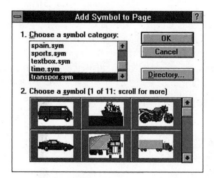

3. Click the small ship and click OK. The small ship is labeled 10 of 11 in the symbol dialog box. The little ship symbol appears in place of the "Click here to add symbol" block (see fig. 14.8).

4. Press the Shift key and then click and drag the corner black handles around the ship to enlarge it so that the page looks like that in figure 14.9. Pressing the Shift key keeps the shape of the symbol constant while it is resized.

Now try adding a symbol elsewhere on the page by following these steps:

1. Click the Symbol icon in the toolbox. The Add Symbol to Page dialog box appears on-screen.

2. Scroll through the list of symbol categories and click INDUSTRY.SYM. A scrolling menu of factory symbols appears.

3. Click to highlight a refinery symbol, number 6 of 8, and click OK. The refinery symbol appears in the lower-left corner of the Basic Layout presentation page (see fig. 4.10).

Fig. 14.8

The Title page layout with text and completed "Click here..." symbol block.

Fig. 14.9

The ship symbol correctly sized.

Fig. 14.10

The title page with text and the ship and refinery symbols added.

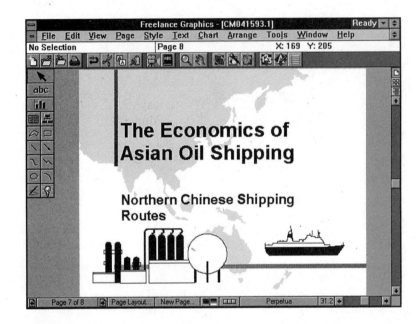

4. Click and drag the refinery symbol above the title, and then size the symbol.

5. Click **S**ave in the **F**ile menu. The Save As dialog box appears.

6. Enter the file name **OILSHIP.PRE** in the File **N**ame entry box and click OK.

Adding a Symbol as a Text Bullet

To use a symbol as a text bullet, click the text with the right mouse button and then choose Bullets from the pop-up menu. Choose Symbol from the list of available bullet styles. Then select a symbol from the symbol gallery. A miniature of the symbol will appear as a bullet before each paragraph.

Adding Art to the Symbol Library

The Freelance symbol library is a collection of symbols, categorized by subject. Each of these categories has an individual file name.

A picture becomes a "symbol" only after it is added to the Freelance Graphics symbol library.

When you find or create new art that you want to use more than once, add the art to the symbol library so that you can quickly retrieve it and add it to a presentation.

You can make all kinds of clip art into symbols. You can add objects drawn in Freelance, edited symbols, charts, and imported bitmap images. Figure 14.11 shows a new symbol created by editing and combining existing Freelance symbols.

Fig. 14.11

A new symbol created with several different Freelance Graphics symbols and a text block.

NOTE

Bitmap images are a type of image made up of tiny dots of color and brightness organized in a grid; each image is controlled by a binary code. An enlarged bitmap image looks something like the dots of a television screen seen at very close range.

To add clip art to the symbol library, access the page containing the graphic object that you want to add to the symbol library. Select the object by clicking it. From the Tools menu, choose **Add** to Symbol Library. This procedure displays the Add To Symbol Library dialog box (see fig. 14.12).

NOTE

If you want to make more than one object into a single symbol, you must first group the objects into one object by holding down the Shift key as you click each object. Then choose **G**roup from the **A**rrange menu.

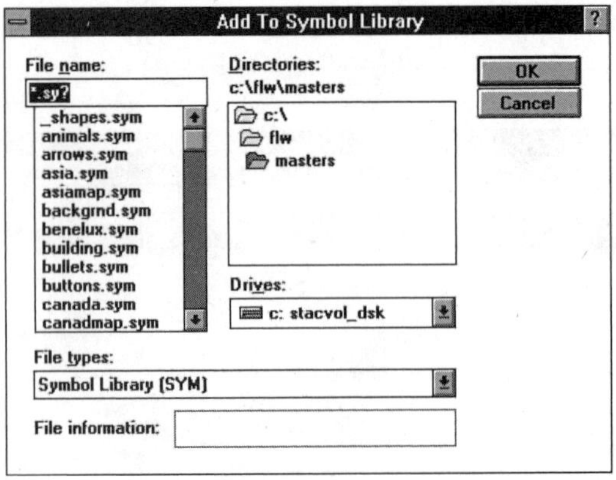

Fig. 14.12

The Add To Symbol Library dialog box.

On the left side of the Add To Symbol Library dialog box is a scrolling list of the file names of all the Freelance Graphics symbol categories. Scroll through the list and click to highlight the symbol category where you want to store your new symbol. Click OK. The object you selected is then added to the highlighted symbol category file.

Adding a New Symbol Category to the Symbol Library

Adding new symbol category files is a great way to keep your symbols organized. You can keep all the symbols pertaining to a subject to- gether in one symbol category file, and you can make special symbol category files for special projects. The more clip art that you acquire from different sources and use in Freelance Graphics presentations, the more useful your new symbol categories become.

To create a new symbol category file, add at least one clip art object or symbol to a blank page in a new presentation; then choose Save **As** from the **F**ile menu to open the Save As dialog box. Select the Symbol Library (SYM) file type from the File **T**ypes list box (see fig. 14.13). Make sure that you use the **D**irectories list box to select the directory in which the SmartMaster sets are stored. (This directory is probably called MASTERS under the FLW directory.) Then enter a File **N**ame of up to eight characters, using the SYM extension, and click OK. The next time you open the symbol library, you will find the new category in the list.

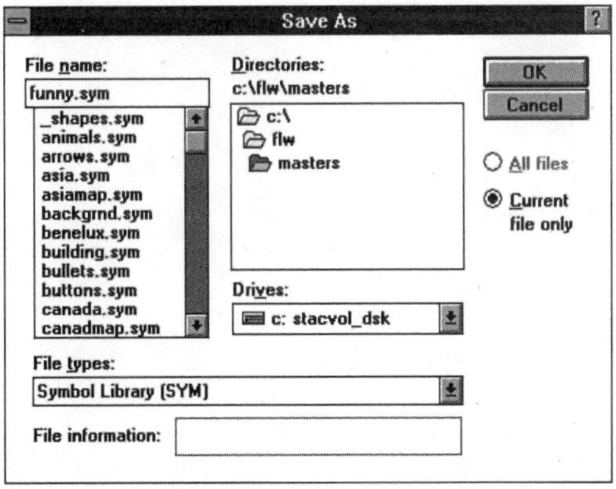

Fig. 14.13

The Save As dialog box with the new symbol category file name FUNNY.SYM.

Summary

In this chapter, you learned to use the symbol library to incorporate predrawn pictures into a presentation. In the next chapter, you learn to add bitmap images to a presentation.

Adding Bitmap Images

The pictures you create when you use the drawing tools of Freelance are composed of an arrangement of objects. You add text, lines, circles, squares, and other graphic shapes to complete a drawing. Each object in the drawing is a discrete, editable item.

The other type of graphic image is a bitmap. A *bitmap* is a pattern of dots of different colors, much like the pattern of dots that makes up a television picture. You cannot create bitmap images in Freelance, but you can add them to a Freelance presentation by importing them from other sources.

Bitmaps are important because they are the type of file generated by scanning software. After you scan a picture with an electronic scanner, the scanning software generates a bitmap file. To incorporate a photograph into a presentation, you must import the bitmap file.

Bitmaps are also the type of file created by paint programs that allow you to produce images on-screen with such tools as paintbrushes and charcoal pencils. Because artists who use paint programs can use the same tools they might use without a computer, a bitmap image can be much more like a painting than an image created from a drawing program.

Bitmap images are stored in a variety of common bitmap file formats. Many paint and scanning programs can generate any or all of the common bitmap file formats. Other programs generate their own exclusive brand of bitmap file format. Fortunately, Freelance can accept most of the popular bitmap file formats you may encounter. Table 15.1 summarizes the bitmap file formats that Freelance can accept.

Table 15.1 Bitmap File Formats Compatible with Freelance Graphics Release 2.0 for Windows

Bitmap Format	Description
Windows/PM Bitmap (BMP)	Used by Windows. The Windows Paint accessory generates BMP files.
Hewlett Packard Graphics Gallery (GAL)	Generated by the Hewlett Packard Graphics Gallery scanning software used to control popular scanners, including the HP ScanJet.
Zsoft PC Paintbrush Bitmap (PCX)	A widely used bitmap file format generated by the Zsoft line of paint programs and others. Most programs that work with bitmap images import and export PCX files. Most scanning programs can export PCX files.
Tag Image (TIF)	Another widely used bitmap file format, sometimes called TIFF (Tagged Image File Format). Most scanning programs can export TIF files.
Targa Bitmap (TGA)	A high-color bitmap-image file generated by the Targa brand graphics adapter and associated software. Targa images are often used to store video pictures.

TIP

If you plan to transfer a presentation from Freelance Graphics for Windows to Freelance Graphics for OS/2, you should import bitmap files as TIF images in Freelance for Windows because Freelance Graphics for OS/2 cannot read PCX or Windows Bitmap (BMP) files. Be aware, though, that color TIF files are converted to shades of gray in Freelance Graphics for OS/2.

Importing a Bitmap

To import a bitmap file, turn to the presentation page where you want the bitmap to appear, and then choose Import from the File menu. Click File Types in the Import File dialog box to display the list of available file types, as shown in figure 15.1.

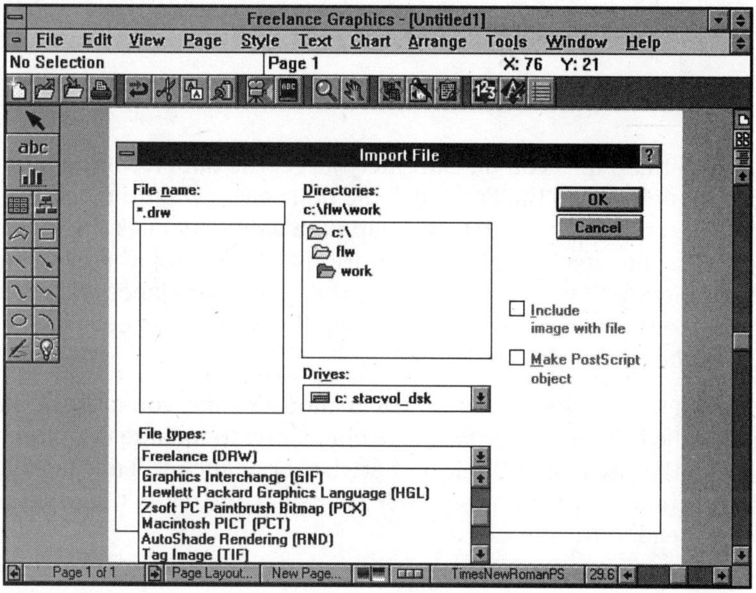

Fig. 15.1

The list of file types in the Import File dialog box.

Select a bitmap-image file type from the list and then use the Directories and File Name list boxes to find the file on your system. The filter line at the top of the list of file names filters out the three-letter file name extension of the file type you've chosen. You can edit the filter, though, to display other files. To see all PCX format files that begin with the letter B, for example, enter **B*.PCX**.

Select a bitmap file from the list and click OK to import the image. The bitmap appears on the page and at the same size the bitmap was created. If the bitmap image is too large to fit the page, the bitmap will be halved in size repeatedly until it fits the page.

A bitmap can be moved and resized just like any other object on the Freelance page. Holding down the Shift key while you drag a corner handle will maintain the proportions of the bitmap as you resize it. Bitmaps change resolution when they are sized, though. As you enlarge or decrease the size of a bitmap, Freelance must use more or fewer dots to form the image; it may, therefore, become less clear. You will have to judge for yourself how the bitmap looks after you resize it. If you are unhappy with the appearance of the picture, select **U**ndo Stretch from the **E**dit menu, click the Undo SmartIcon, or press Ctrl+Z immediately before making another change to the page.

Including the Image Data in the Freelance File

Because Bitmap files can be extremely large, the data from the bitmap file is not included in the Freelance file unless you want the data included. To choose to have the bitmap data included, click the **I**nclude Image with File check box in the Import File dialog box when you import the bitmap. If you do not include the image, Freelance will read in the image data from the separate bitmap file when you need to view the image in the presentation.

If you plan to give the Freelance file to another user, you must be sure to check the **I**nclude Image with File check box to include the bitmap images in the presentation file. Otherwise, Freelance will not be able to find the bitmap images on the other user's system when the program needs to read in the data.

Cropping a Bitmap

You can display any rectangular portion of a bitmap image on a presentation page by using the Crop **B**itmap command. This command enables you to cut out any portions of the picture that you don't want the viewer to see.

To crop a bitmap, select the bitmap in Freelance, as shown in figure 15.2, and then choose Crop **B**itmap from the **A**rrange menu.

A rectangle bounded by handles appears at the corners of the bitmap in the Crop Bitmap window. Drag the handles to position the rectangle over the portion of the bitmap that you want shown (see fig. 15.3). Then click OK. The selected portion of the bitmap fills the space on the page that was previously occupied by the entire bitmap.

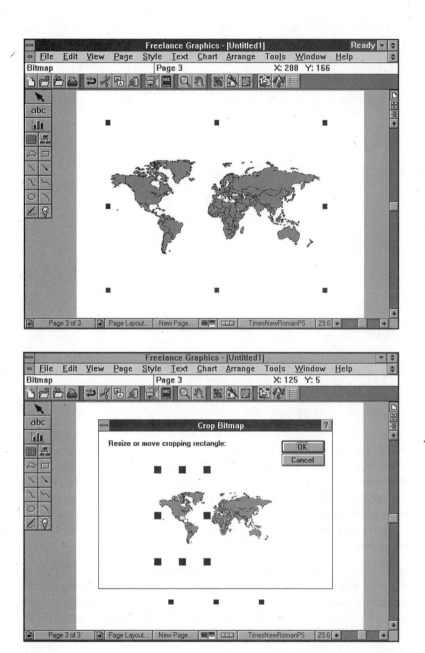

Fig. 15.2

Selecting the bitmap.

Fig. 15.3

The Crop Bitmap window.

Even after you crop a bitmap, the data for the entire bitmap is still available. You can, therefore, select the bitmap and use the Crop **B**itmap command again to choose a different portion of the image or to display the entire image. Figure 15.4 shows the bitmap displayed on the presentation page after the bitmap is cropped.

Fig. 15.4

The cropped bitmap image as it appears on the page.

Modifying the Attributes of a Bitmap

When color bitmaps are printed by Freelance to a color output device, the bitmaps appear in color. When the output device is black and white, Freelance maps color images to shades of gray. To see how a color bitmap will look when printed on a black-and-white printer, switch to the black-and-white color palette for the presentation by clicking the Color/B&W button in the status bar at the bottom of the Freelance window.

Freelance can import black-and-white bitmaps (2-bit), 16-color or gray-scale bitmaps (4-bit), 256-color bitmaps (8-bit), or 1.2-million color bitmaps (24-bit). When you import gray-scale images (various shades of gray with no colors), you can adjust their contrast, brightness, and sharpness. When you import color images, you can change only their contrast and brightness.

Changing the Contrast, Brightness, and Sharpness of a Bitmap

By double-clicking a color or gray-scale bitmap, you can access the Style Attributes Bitmap dialog box (see fig. 15.5). You also can select the bitmap and then choose **A**ttributes [Bitmap] from the **S**tyle menu.

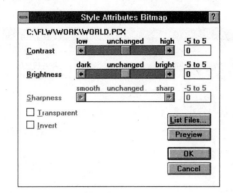

Fig. 15.5

The Style Attributes Bitmap dialog box.

The Style Attributes Bitmap dialog box shows the controls you can use to affect the selected bitmap. Drag the button along each slider to change its setting, or click the arrow buttons at the end of each slider to increment or decrement the setting. Alternatively, you can type a new setting number in the box to the right of the slider.

The **C**ontrast setting changes the ratio of black to white in the image. The **B**rightness setting changes the overall luminosity of the image. The **S**harpness setting changes the clarity of the borders and edges in the bitmap.

After you make changes to these settings, you can use the Preview button to see the changes. If Freelance is unable to find the bitmap file on your system, the program displays the name of the bitmap file on the presentation page. Use the **L**ist Files button to select the appropriate bitmap file on your system for the page.

Making a Bitmap Transparent

Another control in the Style Attributes Bitmap dialog box enables you to make all dots except black dots in the image transparent. Then objects behind the bitmap will show through the bitmap. To make a bitmap transparent, click the **T**ransparent check box. The bitmap's border disappears.

Inverting a Black-and-White Bitmap

If the bitmap is black and white only, you can make all black dots white and all white dots black by clicking the **I**nvert check box in the Style Attributes Bitmap dialog box. You will see a negative of the bitmap. (If the bitmap is already a negative, you will see a correct display of the image.) Figures 15.6 and 15.7 show a bitmap before and after it is inverted.

Fig. 15.6

A bitmap before it is inverted.

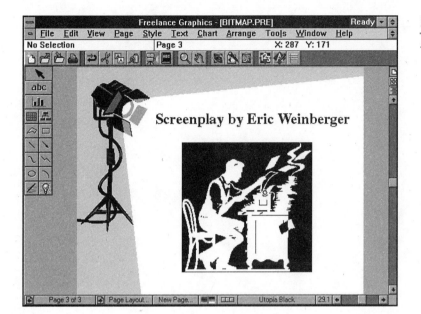

Fig. 15.7

A bitmap after it is inverted.

Summary

In this chapter, you learned to import, crop, and change the attributes of bitmap images that come from painting, bitmap editing, or scanning software. In the next chapter, you learn to import drawing files, charts, and symbols from other graphics programs.

Importing and Exporting Drawings and Charts

Freelance is certainly not the only graphics program that can create drawings. Many drawing programs, such as Micrografx Windows Draw and Adobe Illustrator, have even more sophisticated drawing tools than those in Freelance, so the drawings those programs create have special effects that are impossible to create in Freelance. To enable you to use these sophisticated drawings, you can use the **F**ile **I**mport command of Freelance to import drawing files. The drawings appear on the Freelance page just as if they were created in Freelance.

Freelance also provides a command you can use to export completed presentation pages as graphics files. Then you can incorporate the pages in designs created in other graphics programs, such as bitmap-editing programs or desktop publishing software.

In this chapter, you learn how to import images into and export them from Freelance. You learn also how to import charts and symbols from Harvard Graphics for use in Freelance.

Transferring Graphics between Freelance and Other Windows Applications

Transferring graphics between Freelance and other Windows applications is particularly easy. You can simply select the graphic, choose Copy from the Edit menu, switch to the other application, and choose Paste from the Edit menu. A behind-the-scenes translator in Windows converts the graphic so that its data transfers correctly from one application to another. You can use this technique to import graphics into or export graphics out of Freelance. You can use the copy and paste operations to copy a chart from Freelance into a word processing or desktop publishing document, for example.

Linking a Graphic to a Presentation Page

Windows also enables you to establish a link between a graphic in another application and the graphic in Freelance. The link works both ways, whether you're pulling the graphic from the other application to Freelance or the other way around. To create the link, you must follow these steps:

1. Save to a file the graphic you create in the other application. This step is required, or you will not be able to create a link.

2. Select the graphic in the other application.

3. Choose Copy from the other application's Edit menu.

4. Switch to Freelance.

5. Choose Paste Special from the Edit menu, and the Paste Special dialog box appears. When you choose a format that can be linked, the Link button becomes available.

6. Choose a linkable format from the list of Formats and then click Link. The graphic then appears on the presentation page. You can move and resize the graphic as you would any other graphic. If you edit the graphic in the original application, the changes appear in Freelance too.

When you link a graphic from another application to a Freelance presentation, you must be aware that the data for the graphic still resides in the other application. If you transport the Freelance presentation to another computer, the graphic will not be displayed in the presentation because its data is not stored in the presentation file. You must also transport the file in which the data is stored.

Embedding a Graphic in a Presentation

To ensure that the data for an imported graphic will become part of the Freelance presentation file, you can embed the graphic. You can use embedding only when the other application is a Windows program also. The disadvantage of this approach is that changes you make to the graphic in the original application will not appear in the Freelance presentation. The advantage is that you can still double-click the graphic and then edit it from within Freelance. The original application in which you created the object opens temporarily so that you can use its tools to modify the object.

To embed a graphic from another Windows application, select the graphic and then choose Copy from the application's Edit menu. Switch back to Freelance and choose Paste Special from the Edit menu. One of the formats in the Paste Special dialog box describes the graphic as an object. Choose this format and then click Paste. The object then appears in Freelance.

Figure 16.1 shows a logo for Rorschach Publications that was created in Windows Paintbrush and embedded on a Freelance page with a presentation title and subtitle.

To edit an embedded graphic in its original application, double-click the graphic on the Freelance page. The original application opens with the graphic loaded. Edit the graphic, choose Update, and then choose Exit & Return from the application's File menu.

Fig. 16.1

An embedded logo in Freelance.

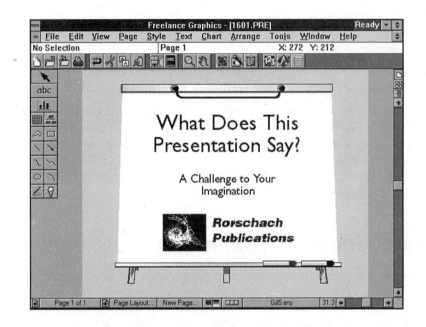

Linking or Embedding a Freelance Presentation Page in Another Application

You can easily copy an individual object from a Freelance page to another application by using Copy in Freelance and Paste in the other application. To link or embed work that you've done in Freelance in another application, however, you must link or embed an entire presentation page. You do this in Page Sorter view.

To link or embed a Freelance page in another application, follow these steps:

1. In Freelance, save the presentation file.

2. Switch to Page Sorter view.

3. Select the page you want to link or embed.

4. From the Freelance Edit menu, choose Copy.

5. Switch to the other application.

6. Place the cursor where you want the Freelance page to appear.

7. From the other application's Edit menu, choose Paste Special.

8. If you want to link the data, choose a format that you can link from the list of formats on the Paste Special menu, such as DDE Link (see fig. 16.2). If DDE Link is not one of the available formats and a Link button appears in the Paste Special dialog box, click each different format until the Link button becomes available for use, and then click Link. To embed the object instead, choose OLE Embed or choose a format that describes the Freelance data as an object. Then click Paste (to embed the data).

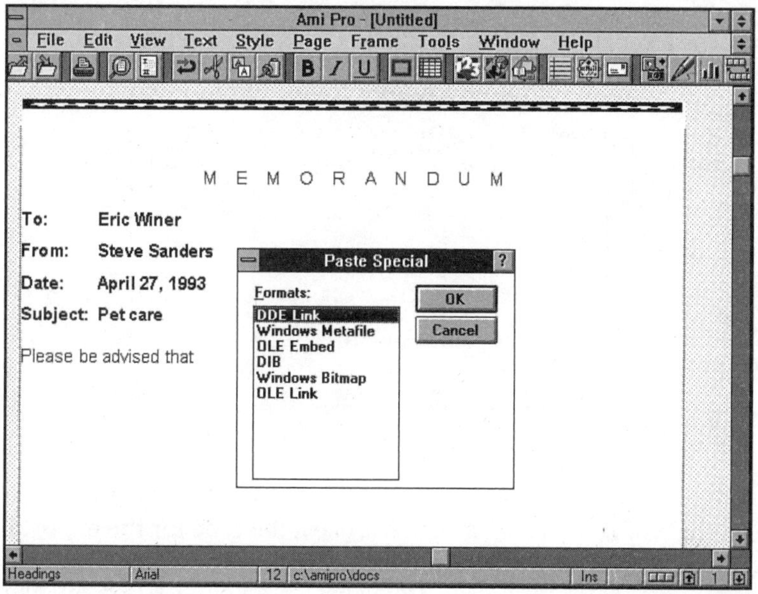

Fig. 16.2

Linking a Freelance page to another application.

When you link a Freelance presentation page to another application, you can edit the presentation page without regard to whether it is linked to another application. Any edits you make will appear in the other application too. The data is stored in Freelance, though; if you transport the file from the other application, the data will not be taken unless you also transport the Freelance presentation file.

When you embed a Freelance page, the data becomes part of the other application's file. To edit the presentation page from within the other application, you double-click the page to open Freelance. If the other application's file has been moved to another computer, you can edit the Freelance presentation page by double-clicking it as long as the other computer also has Freelance installed on it.

Exporting a Presentation Page to a Graphics File

If you want to use a Freelance page in a non-Windows application such as WordPerfect for DOS, you can export the page as a graphics file and then import the file into the other application. You also can export a page to a file for use in a Windows application on another system. After you export the page, you can take the file to the other system and then import it there.

To export a page, turn to the page and choose Export from the File menu. The Export File dialog box opens, as shown in figure 16.3.

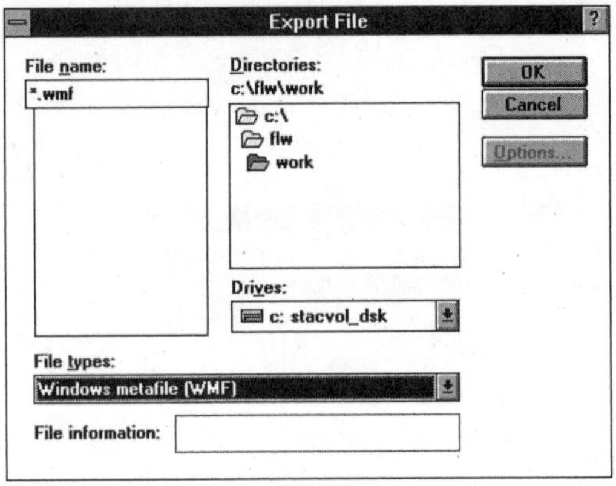

Fig. 16.3

The Export File dialog box.

To use the Export File dialog box, choose a file type for the export file first. Click the pull-down button next to the current file type and then choose a file type from the File Types list. Then enter a DOS file name for the file in the File Name text box. To change the destination for the file, use the Directories and Drives controls to choose a different disk or disk drive and to place the export file in a different DOS directory.

When you click OK, Freelance exports the page to a graphics file with the default set of options for that file type. You can change the options by clicking Options before you click OK, however. When you click Options, an Output Filter Setup dialog box opens. Figure 16.4 shows the dialog box that appears when you choose PCX as the export file type.

Most Output Filter Setup dialog boxes have Format, Resolution, Size, and Color Translation settings.

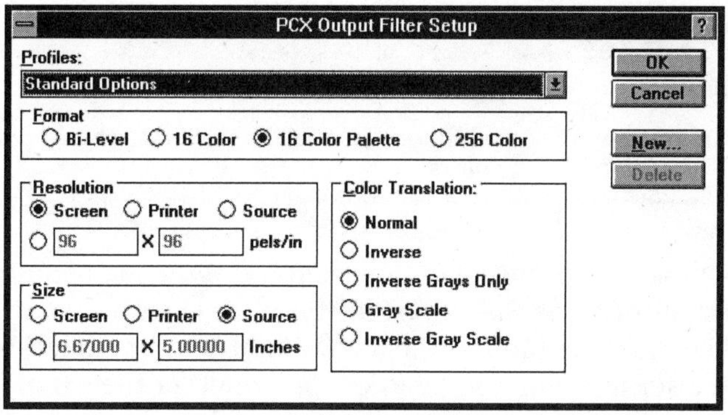

Fig. 16.4

The PCX Output Filter Setup dialog box.

You can use the **F**ormat settings to determine how many colors appear in the export file. Bi-Level shows only black and white, for example.

The **R**esolution settings enable you to choose the density of dots in a bitmap export file. **R**esolution settings do not appear when you are exporting to a vector file type. Choose Screen to match the current resolution of the screen. Choose Printer to match the resolution of the printer that is currently selected in Windows. Choose Source to let Freelance select the optimal resolution. You also can type your own resolution by clicking the button next to the two Pels/In text boxes and then typing a number of horizontal pels (dots) per inch in the first box and the number of vertical pels per inch in the second box.

To limit the size of the image in the output file, use the **S**ize settings. Choose Screen to use the size of the image as it appears on-screen, Printer to limit the image to the size of the current page selected for the current printer, or Source to export the image at the size it is created in Freelance. You can enter a custom size for the image by first clicking the button next to the two text boxes that hold the current size of the image in inches and then typing new horizontal and vertical sizes.

The **C**olor Translation settings tell the output filter to translate the colors shown on a color presentation page when the export file is created. Here are the color translation alternatives:

Option	How Colors Are Translated
Normal	As they are shown in Freelance.
Inverse	To their opposite RGB values.
Inverse Grays Only	Blacks, whites, and shades of gray in the image are inverted to their opposite color. For example, blacks are shown as whites.

(continues)

Option	How Colors Are Translated
Gray Scale	As shades of gray.
Inverse Gray Scale	As shades and then inverted to their opposite colors.

Certain file types have special options settings. When you choose Adobe Illustrator (AI) as the export file type, for example, an output setting called Line Cap Mode appears in the AI Output Filter Setup dialog box. This setting enables you to choose whether the export file has Device line caps (Freelance line endings that Adobe Illustrator supports) or Stroked line caps (Freelance line endings that are not directly supported by Adobe Illustrator but are represented in a style that Adobe Illustrator can accept).

For several export file types, Freelance offers a list of profiles that correspond to several popular applications in which you might use the CGM file. Select a profile to choose an appropriate combination of Options settings. The default profile is called Standard Options. You should check the list of profiles to see whether there is a profile that suits your needs.

If you find yourself using a custom combination of settings often, you can save it in a custom profile. To create a custom profile, choose the settings you want, click **N**ew, and then enter a name for the profile in the **P**rofile Name text box that appears. Then click OK. Only the profiles that you create appear preceded by an asterisk on the list of profiles.

Importing a Graphics File

In the preceding chapter, you learned how to import a bitmap and add it to a presentation page. You also can import graphic drawings that were created in other presentation graphics programs or in drawing and illustration software. These images are composed of collections of drawn objects just as are Freelance images. When you import these images, Freelance converts the objects into Freelance drawn objects.

To import a graphic, choose **I**mport from the **F**ile menu and then choose the import file type from the File **T**ypes drop-down list in the Import File dialog box (see fig. 16.5). If the file type that you choose includes PostScript data and you plan to print the presentation on a PostScript printer or an imagesetter, you may also want to click the

Make PostScript Object button to preserve the image as a PostScript object; otherwise, the drawing is converted to a collection of Freelance drawing objects.

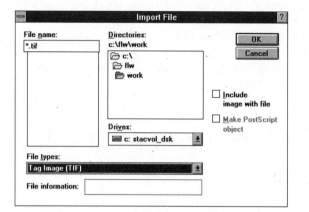

Fig. 16.5

The Import File dialog box.

Importing a Named Chart from 1-2-3 or Symphony

If you have created a named chart in 1-2-3 or Symphony, you can import the chart by choosing Import C**h**art from the Freelance **F**ile menu, selecting the worksheet file that contains the chart (1-2-3 and Symphony worksheet file extensions begin with WK), and then clicking Named **C**harts. Choose the named chart from the drop-down list of charts and then click OK. The chart then appears on the Freelance page.

When you import a named chart from 1-2-3 or Symphony, the chart remains linked to its original data in 1-2-3 or Symphony. Therefore, if you change the data in the other application, the chart changes in Freelance.

Importing a Harvard Graphics Chart

If you have switched to Freelance Graphics for Windows from Harvard Graphics, you can import the Harvard Graphics charts you've created into Freelance presentations. To import a Harvard Graphics chart, choose **I**mport from the **F**ile menu and then choose Harvard Graphics 2.3 Chart (CHT) or Harvard Graphics 3.0 chart (CH3) from the list of file types. Then use the **D**irectories, D**r**ives, and File **N**ame controls to select the chart file. The chart is then imported and converted to a Freelance chart. If the chart you need is in Harvard Graphics for Windows, you must export the Harvard Graphics for Windows file to Harvard Graphics for DOS format. This creates a series of charts. Then you can import one of the charts.

Importing a Harvard Graphics Symbol

If you have used Harvard Graphics in the past and need to use one of the symbols in the Harvard Graphics symbol library to maintain a particular presentation look, you can import a Harvard Graphics symbol file and then select one of the images in it. To import a symbol file, choose **I**mport from the **F**ile menu and then choose either Harvard Graphics 2.3 Symbol (SYM) or Harvard Graphics 3.0 Symbol (SY3) from the list of file types. Then use the **D**irectories, D**r**ives, and File **N**ame controls to choose the symbol file.

Summary

In this chapter, you learned to import graphics from other programs into Freelance and to export Freelance pages to other software.

In the next chapter, you learn to use some of the commands that affect a Freelance presentation as a whole, such as spell checking the presentation.

Working with Presentations

Managing Presentations

After you finish the page-by-page construction of a presentation, you may want to take advantage of some of the tools and commands that Freelance offers for managing the presentation. You can check spelling in the presentation, for example, to remove typographical errors. You can create speaker notes so that the person at the podium can view a miniature of each presentation page, along with printed comments and topics to cover. In addition, you can embed a completed presentation in another Windows application so that the presentation is available from within a document or spreadsheet. You learn how to accomplish all these tasks in this chapter.

Using Spell Check

Freelance does not require, compel, or even suggest that you check the spelling of a completed presentation, but a typo can be most embarrassing when it is exhibited before an audience of your peers. Take a moment to use the program's Spell Check feature before you project your presentation.

As with all computer spell checkers, Freelance's Spell Check warns you only about words that are not found in its dictionary. Spell Check does not detect when you have dropped a word from a sentence or used the wrong word inadvertently (such as *they're* rather than *their*). Be forewarned that a careful proofreading of a presentation is also a good idea.

How Spell Check works depends on the part of the program you are using. The following list summarizes the possibilities:

Activity or View	What Spell Check Checks
Editing text	The word at the typing cursor
Viewing the current page with no text selected	Text on the current page or the entire presentation (your choice)
Page Sorter view	The entire presentation, including text in charts, speaker notes, and metafiles; or the text on the selected page (your choice)
Outliner view	Visible text in the outline (not collapsed text)

To start Spell Check, click the Spell Check SmartIcon, press Ctrl+F2 (Spell Check), or choose **S**pell Check from the Too**l**s menu. A Spell Check dialog box similar to the one in figure 17.1 appears.

Fig. 17.1

The Spell Check dialog box.

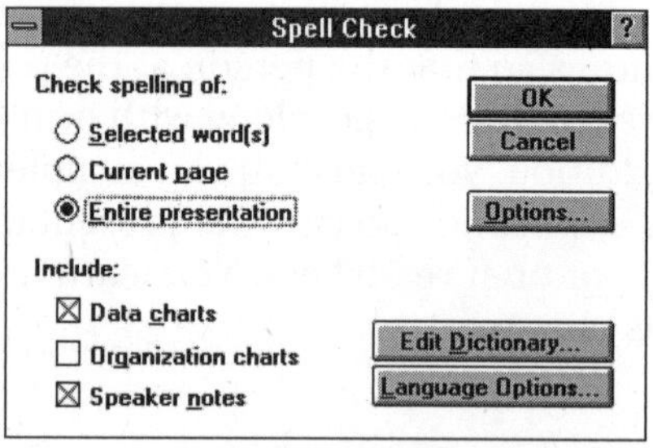

The Spell Check dialog box enables you to determine the scope of the spell checking: whether to check only **S**elected Word(s), text on the Current **P**age, or text throughout the **E**ntire Presentation. You can choose only one option. The dialog box also enables you to specify whether to check the spelling in Data **C**harts, Or**g**anization Charts, and Speaker **N**otes. You can choose any combination of these.

After you click OK, Spell Check finds words that are not in its dictionary, displays each word in context, and suggests alternative spellings (see fig. 17.2). Choose the correct spelling from the list of alternatives and then click Replace to replace only this occurrence of the word, or click Replace All to replace the word wherever it appears in the current presentation. Click Skip if the word is spelled correctly (often when it is a proper name), or click Skip All to ignore all further occurrences of the word. If the word is used frequently in presentations, you may want to add it to the user dictionary by clicking Add To Dictionary. To end the spell checking, click Cancel.

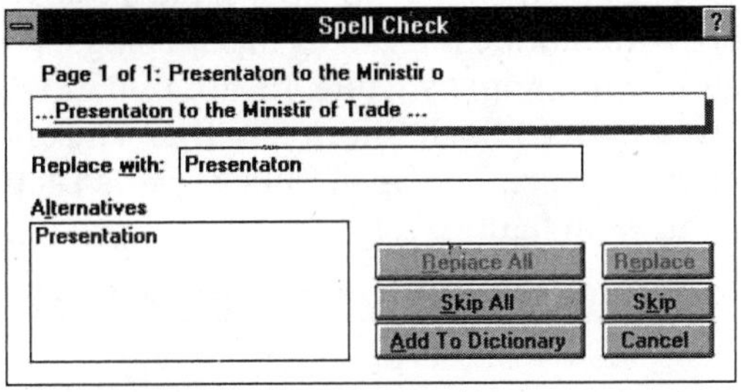

Fig. 17.2

Spell Check in action.

Changing the Spell-Checking Options

By clicking Options in the Spell Check dialog box, you can change how Spell Check works. The Spell Check Options dialog box, shown in figure 17.3, shows four options:

Option	Description
Check for Repeated Words	Finds and flags any words that you may have inadvertently typed twice in succession.
Check Words with Numbers	Checks the spelling of words that contain numbers, such as 2nd or 3rd.
Check Words with Initial Caps	Checks words that start with capital letters. You can turn this option off to prevent Spell Check from flagging proper names as incorrect.
Include User Dictionary Alternatives	Displays words you have entered in the user dictionary as alternative spellings when Spell Check deems they are appropriate.

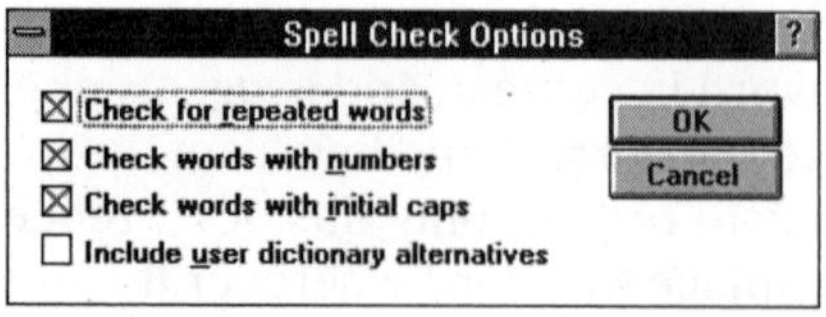

Fig. 17.3

The Spell Check
Options dialog box.

Adding Words to the User Dictionary

You may want to add to the user dictionary any words that are common to your profession, as well as proper names that you frequently
use. These words will not be flagged as misspellings. For example, you
may want to add your company name, its abbreviation, and your own
name. To add words, start Spell Check and then click Edit **Dic**tionary in
the Spell Check dialog box. The Spell Check User's Dictionary dialog
box opens, as shown in figure 17.4.

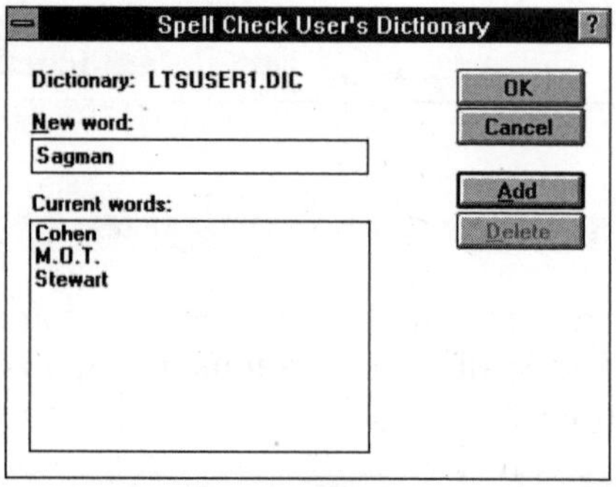

Fig. 17.4

The Spell Check User's
Dictionary dialog box.

To add a new word to the dictionary, type it in the **N**ew Word text box
and then click **A**dd. To delete words, select them from the Current
Words list and then click **D**elete. When you are finished, click OK.

Setting the Spell Check Language

If you have more than one language dictionary installed in your system,
you can change to a different dictionary by clicking the **L**anguage
Options button in the Spell Check dialog box and then selecting the
dictionary from the list that appears.

Switching to a Black-and-White Version of a Presentation

Each SmartMaster set in Freelance Graphics Release 2.0 for Windows comes with a pair of internal palettes that determine all the colors used in a presentation. One palette assigns colors to the various parts of a presentation. The other palette assigns shades of gray instead. You can use the color palette to create color slides or a screen show and then, after the color presentation is complete, temporarily switch to the black & white palette to print the presentation with a black-and-white printer. If you are using a black-and-white printer, you can create the presentation by using the black & white palette to see on-screen how the presentation will look when you print it.

To switch easily from the color palette to the black & white palette, click the Color/B&W button in the status bar at the bottom of the Freelance window or press Alt+F9. Another method is to choose Use Color Palette or Use Black & White Palette from the Style menu.

You can edit the colors in the color palette within each SmartMaster set, but you cannot edit the shades of gray in a black & white palette. You learn about editing color palettes in Chapter 22, "Using and Editing Color Palettes."

Copying Work between Presentations

Freelance makes it easy to copy charts, text blocks, graphic objects, and even entire pages from one presentation to another so that you can easily reuse items rather than re-create them. If a chart that you made for a presentation last month is appropriate for tomorrow's presentation to a different client, for example, you can copy the chart to the new presentation.

To copy a chart, text block, or graphic object from one presentation to another, select the object, and then choose Copy from the Edit menu or click the Copy SmartIcon. Next switch to the other presentation and either choose Paste from the Edit menu or click the Paste SmartIcon.

To have two presentations open at the same time, open first one and then the other. When you click the **Window** menu, a list of all the open presentations appears. Click a presentation name in the list to switch to it. To place two open presentations side by side, click **Tile** in the **Window** menu. To arrange two open presentations so that they overlap one another, click **Cascade**. **Tile** and **Cascade** work only with presentation windows that are maximized or restored. If a presentation is minimized to an icon, it is not affected. Figure 17.5 shows two tiled presentation windows.

Fig. 17.5

Two tiled presentation windows.

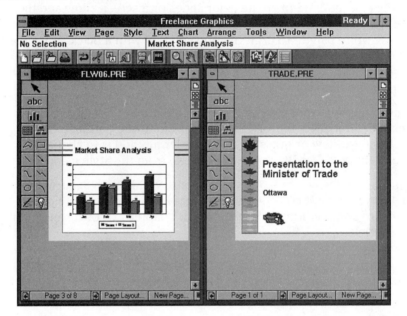

When objects are copied from one presentation to another, they are reformatted by the color palette and page layout of the presentation to which they are copied. A chart copied from one presentation to another may have very different colors when it appears in the second presentation. The content remains the same.

To copy a presentation page between presentations, place two presentations side by side and switch them both to Page Sorter view. Then select a page in one presentation and copy it with the **Edit Copy** command or the Copy SmartIcon. Switch to the second presentation and select the page that the copied page should follow. Then paste the page, using the **Edit Paste** command or the Paste SmartIcon. The page then appears after the selected page in the second presentation and takes on the formatting of the second presentation's SmartMaster set.

Figure 17.6 shows a selected page from one presentation copied to a second presentation. The page design has been changed by the second presentation's SmartMaster set, but the content is the same.

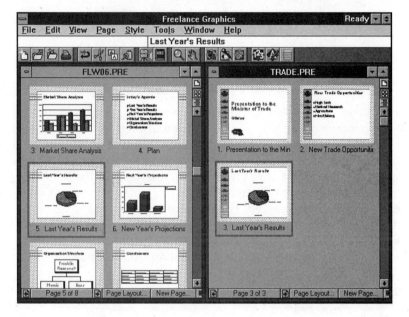

Fig. 17.6

A page copied to a second presentation.

Creating Speaker Notes

You can attach to each page in a presentation a speaker note that contains comments about the page. Speaker notes can come in handy at a lectern, summarizing each slide and offering discussion topics about the slide.

To create a speaker note for a page, turn to the page in Current Page view. Then choose **S**peaker Note from the **P**age menu or click the Speaker Notes SmartIcon. A blank speaker note page that looks like a 3 x 5 card then appears. Figure 17.7 shows a speaker notes page with notes that have been typed in it.

Begin typing notes about the contents of the page, or copy and paste the notes from a presentation page or another Windows application. Every time you press Enter while you type, a bullet appears at the beginning of the new line. To start a new line without a bullet, press Ctrl+Enter.

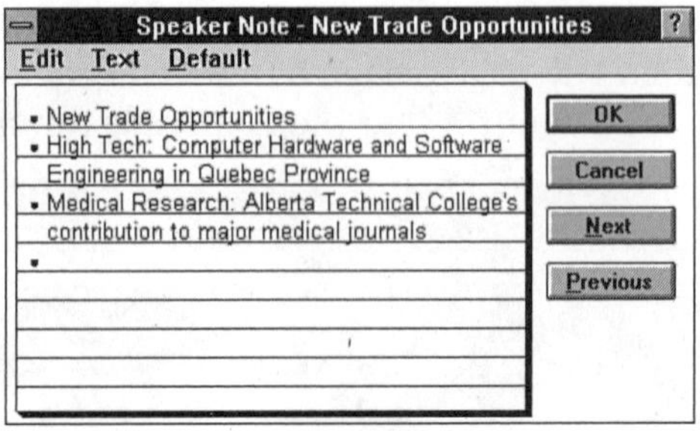

Fig. 17.7

A speaker notes page.

The appearance of the text and bullet is controlled by the settings in the **D**efault menu within the Speaker Note window. The entries in the **D**efault menu enable you to choose a typeface for all the text, a bullet shape, and a text point size. The changes you make to the default settings affect all text you type in other speaker notes. Text that you have already typed is not affected. To change some or all of the text in a particular speaker note, select the text and then use the commands in the **T**ext menu to apply standard character attributes such as boldfacing, or to change the typeface, bullet shape, or text point size.

> **TIP**
>
> To turn off the bullets in a speaker note, choose None as the Bullet style in the **T**ext or **D**efault menu.

The **E**dit menu within the Speaker Note window supplies standard editing commands, such as **C**opy and **P**aste, which you can use on the text inside the window.

To add a speaker note to the next page or to switch to the speaker note for the next page, click **N**ext. To add a speaker note for the previous page or to switch to the speaker note for the previous page, click **P**revious.

When you finish a speaker note in Current Page view, a speaker note icon appears just below the toolbox. When you view the presentation in Page Sorter view, the speaker note icon appears below the page thumbnail. Double-click this icon to view the speaker note. Figure 17.8 shows the speaker note icon for a page; the icon is below the toolbox in Current Page view.

After you finish a presentation, you can print the speaker notes. Freelance prints a small version of the current page and the speaker note on the same page. To print speaker notes, choose **F**ile **P**rint and then choose Spea**k**er Notes from the Print File dialog box. Click the Pr**i**nt button to begin printing.

Speaker note icon

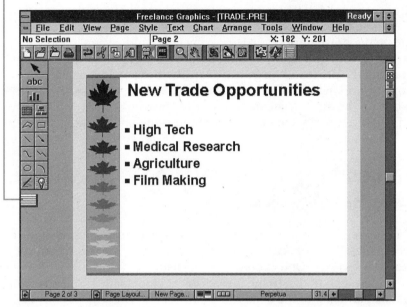

Fig. 17.8

The speaker note icon in Current Page view.

Embedding Presentations in Other Windows Applications

A special feature of Windows 3.1, called Object Linking and Embedding (OLE), gives you the capability of embedding a Freelance presentation in a file within another application that supports OLE (specifically, that can act as an OLE client). After you have created a presentation, you can copy it to another application, where a selected presentation page will appear. Then you can access the Freelance presentation from within the other application by double-clicking the presentation page, and you can take the Freelance presentation wherever the other application's file goes.

Embedding a presentation makes it possible to view a Freelance presentation from within another program. You can embed a Freelance presentation, for example, in a report created in Ami Pro or Word for Windows, two popular Windows word processors. Then you can send the word processor report file to a distant location by mail or modem and know that the presentation is also embedded in the report file. As long as the recipient has Freelance, he or she can view the presentation while examining the report on-screen.

There are two ways to embed a presentation. You can do it from within the other application, which requires that you temporarily switch to Freelance and create the presentation when it is needed. Or you can create the presentation and then copy it to another application, instructing the application to embed the presentation. The first method, creating the presentation from within another application, is best when you are working in a report and you need to create a Freelance presentation on the fly. The second method is preferable when you want to embed in a new document a presentation you have already completed.

Embedding a Presentation from within Another Application

To use Freelance only long enough to create a presentation while you work in another application, you must use the application's Insert Object or Insert New Object command. Consult the application's manual or help system to locate the Insert Object command. The application will display a list of the embedded objects that the applications in your system can provide. Figure 17.9 shows such a list. Freelance Presentation is the object that Freelance provides. To insert a Freelance presentation into the other application (in this case, an Ami Pro document), choose Freelance Presentation and click OK. After a moment, Freelance opens so that you can create a presentation.

When you complete the new presentation, choose Update from the File menu to embed the presentation in the original application. Then choose Exit & Return from the Freelance File menu. The Freelance window closes, and the last page you were working on appears in the other application. With many applications, you can resize the picture of the presentation page. Figure 17.10 shows a presentation page embedded in an Ami Pro document.

TIP

You can switch to Page Sorter view in Freelance and then click a page before using **U**pdate. The page you've selected will be the page that appears in the other application.

TIP

To save a copy of the presentation that you can use when you return to Freelance later, choose Save Copy **A**s from the **F**ile menu.

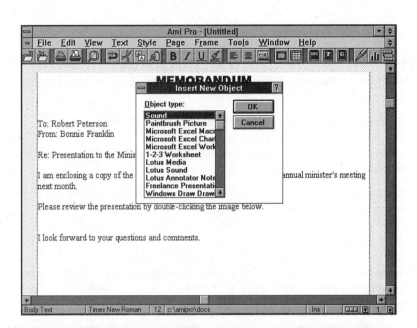

Fig. 17.9

The list of objects you can embed.

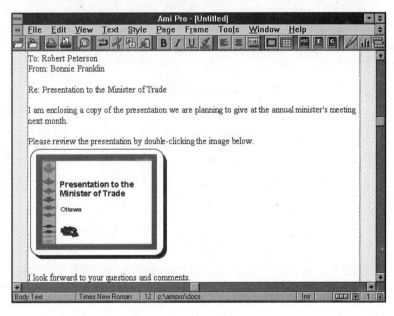

Fig. 17.10

A Freelance presentation embedded in an Ami Pro document.

Embedding an Existing Presentation

The second way to embed a presentation is to copy it as an embedded object to another application. This method allows you to embed an application you've already created.

To embed a presentation, open it in Freelance, switch to Page Sorter view, and click the page you want to see in the other application. Then choose **C**opy from the **E**dit menu. This copies information about the presentation to the Windows Clipboard.

Open or switch to the other application's window and then place the cursor where you would like the image of the selected presentation page to appear. Then choose **P**aste Special from the application's **E**dit menu. When the Paste Special dialog box opens, as shown in figure 17.11, choose Freelance Presentation Object and then click **P**aste. If you're working in Ami Pro, choose OLE Embed in the Paste Special dialog box, as shown in figure 17.12. The selected Freelance presentation page then appears in the other application.

Fig. 17.11

A typical Paste Special dialog box.

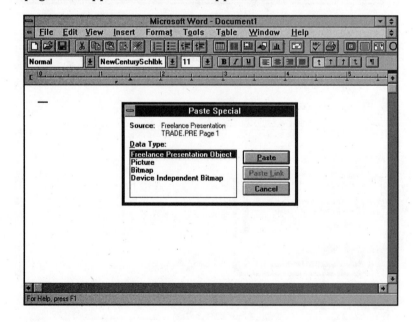

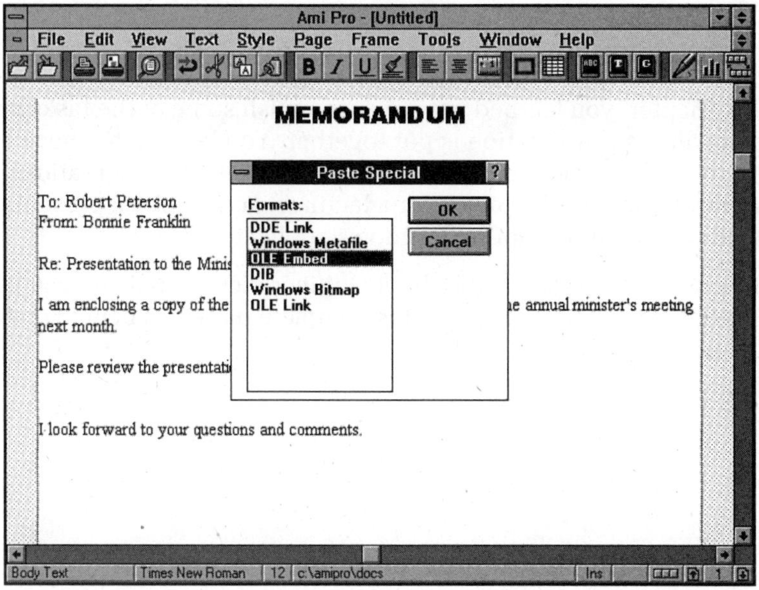

Fig. 17.12

The Paste Special dialog box of Ami Pro.

Using the Embedded Presentation

To provide access to the embedded presentation, the computer that you are using must have Freelance Graphics Release 2.0 for Windows installed. Then you can get to the presentation by double-clicking the presentation page that shows in the other application. Freelance Graphics then opens, and the presentation opens within Freelance. You can view the presentation pages one by one or view the screen show in the presentation. You also can make editing changes to the presentation, using the capabilities of Freelance. These changes are stored in the presentation when you click Update in the Freelance File menu. To finish viewing or editing the presentation, choose Exit & Return from the Freelance File menu.

Summary

In this chapter, you learned how to accomplish some of the tasks carried out after a presentation is put together. You learned to check spelling in the presentation, copy work to and from other presentations, create and print speaker notes for a lecturer, and embed a presentation in a file generated by another Windows application.

In the next chapter, you learn about Outliner view, a tool you can use to reorganize a presentation when it is complete or as it is being created.

Using the Outliner To Organize a Presentation

No top-notch presentation graphics software these days is worth its salt without a built-in, integrated outliner that focuses on the content of a presentation rather than the design.

Many people think in outlines as they gather and organize the thoughts they will express in a presentation. They like to formulate a list of themes, rearrange the flow of ideas toward a conclusion, and then fill in the detail. Freelance's Outliner view is the perfect tool for these people. In an outline, you can create and organize the presentation's text and then switch to Current Page view to concentrate on the design of each page in detail.

Other people will use the Outliner view after they have created presentation pages one by one in Current Page view. The Outliner can filter out charts, drawn objects, and design elements and can display only the presentation text so that the users can edit individual topics and work with the overall flow of concepts instead. Either way, the Outliner view is always available as an alternative view of a presentation.

The other two views, Current Page view and Page Sorter view, offer different functions. Current Page view enables you to work on both the content and design of individual pages. Page Sorter view gives you an overall look at a presentation and enables you to rearrange the order of main topics. Only Outliner view distills the presentation into its text content and gives you the tools to concentrate on the text.

Switching to Outliner View

The Outliner view displays a presentation's text on a representation of a familiar yellow pad. Figure 18.1 shows the Outliner view of a presentation. A page number and page icon in the left margin denote each new page. The text content of the page (text that appears on the page in text blocks) is shown to the right. The image on the page icon informs you of the content of the page. Figure 18.1 shows the different page icon designs.

To switch to Outliner view at any time while working with a presentation, click the Outliner icon that is always present at the right border of the Freelance window (refer to fig. 18.1). You also can choose Outliner from the **View** menu.

Fig. 18.1

The Outliner view of a presentation.

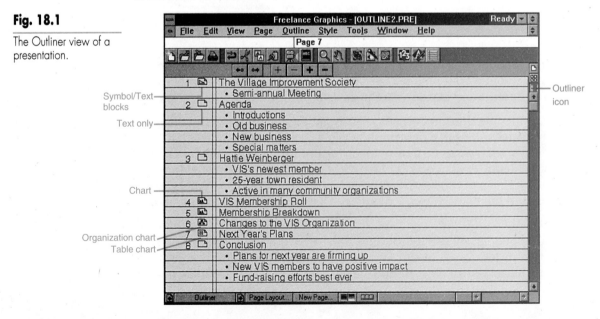

TIP

If you prefer to start a new presentation in Outliner view, you can change the Startup View setting after you choose **U**ser Setup from the Too**l**s menu. Then every time you start a new presentation, the Outliner view is displayed first.

To the right of the page icon, the page title appears. If the page has text blocks, the text in the first two "Click here..." text blocks is shown indented and bulleted beneath the page title (usually beneath the page title and another text block). If the text is in other text blocks added with the Text icon, only the first of these is shown in the Outliner.

All Outliner text is shown in the same typeface (Arial) regardless of its typeface on the presentation page. In fact, you cannot change to a different typeface. This makes it easy to work with the text in Outliner view, but it also means that Outliner view does not represent how text will appear on the final presentation pages.

To return to Current Page view, double-click a page icon to display that page in Current Page view, or place the cursor anywhere in the text for the page and then click the Current Page icon at the right edge of the Freelance window (the first of three icons above the vertical scroll bar). You also can choose **C**urrent Page from the **V**iew menu.

To return to Page Sorter view, click the Page Sorter icon at the right edge of the Freelance window (the second of three icons above the vertical scroll bar) or choose **P**age Sorter from the **V**iew menu. Figure 18.2 shows the Page Sorter view of a presentation.

Adding and Editing Presentation Text

You can edit the text of a presentation page in both Current Page view and Outliner view. While in Outliner view, you can move the cursor and edit text by using all the standard cursor-movement and text-editing keystrokes and commands of Freelance, such as pressing the Del key to delete a character at the cursor position or using the **C**opy and **P**aste commands to copy selected text to and from the Windows Clipboard. Table 18.1 summarizes the cursor-movement keystrokes you can use in Outliner view.

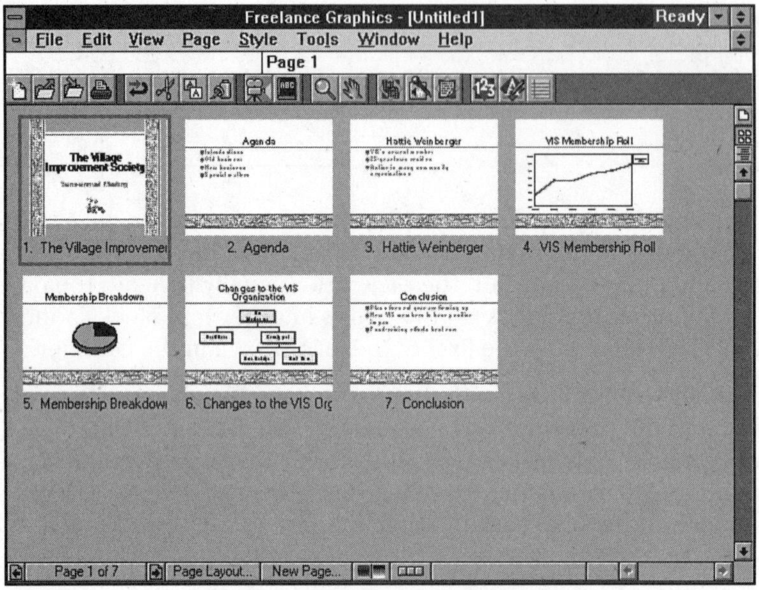

Fig. 18.2

The Page Sorter view of a presentation.

Table 18.1 Cursor-Movement Keystrokes in Outliner View

Keystroke(s)	Action
Home	Moves cursor to the beginning of the current line
End	Moves cursor to the end of the current line
Ctrl+Home	Moves cursor to the beginning of the outline
Ctrl+End	Moves cursor to the end of the outline
PgUp	Moves cursor up one screen
PgDn	Moves cursor down one screen
↑	Moves cursor up one line
↓	Moves cursor down one line
Ctrl+PgUp	Moves cursor to the beginning of the preceding page
Ctrl+PgDn	Moves cursor to the end of the next page
Ctrl+←	Moves cursor left one word
Ctrl+→	Moves cursor right one word

Use the vertical scroll bar at the right edge of the window to scroll the view of the Text in the Outliner.

TIP

Remember that you can replace text by selecting it and then typing new text in its place.

To add new text in the Outliner, move the cursor to the end of an existing line and then press Enter. A new line appears just below the existing line, and the cursor moves to the beginning of the new line. You can then type new text. To indent the new line one level, press Tab before you type the text, or click the Demote icon at the top of the Outliner.

As you create the outline, you can use three levels of indents under the page titles. These levels correspond to the three paragraph styles in the presentation. Text indented to the second level in the Outliner appears in the second paragraph style in Current Page view. Text indented to the third level appears in the third paragraph style. Press Shift+Tab or click the Promote icon to move the text up one level. If the text is already at the first level and you press Shift+Tab, you start a new page, and the text becomes a page title. Figure 18.3 shows both the Promote and Demote icons in Outliner view.

Promote icon ——

Demote icon ——

Fig. 18.3

The Promote and Demote icons in Outliner view.

```
Freelance Graphics - [Untitled1]                    Ready
File  Edit  View  Page  Outline  Style  Tools  Window  Help
                        Page 1

        ←○  ○→  +  −  +  −
1       The Village Improvement Society
          • Semi-annual Meeting
2       Agenda
          • Introductions
          • Old business
          • New business
          • Special matters
3       Hattie Weinberger
          • VIS's newest member
          • 25-year town resident
          • Active in many community organizations
4       VIS Membership Roll
5       Membership Breakdown
6       Changes to the VIS Organization
7       Conclusion
          • Plans for next year are firming up
          • New VIS members to have positive impact
          • Fund-raising efforts best ever

  Outliner     Page Layout...  New Page...
```

To create a new line for more text without giving the new line its own bullet point, press Ctrl+Enter at the end of a line rather than Enter.

Adding, Moving, and Deleting Pages

Outliner view also gives you the freedom to add new presentation pages, move existing pages, and delete pages you no longer need. You learn these procedures in the following sections.

Adding a Page to a Presentation

If you start a new presentation and switch to Outliner view, the number 1 and a blank page icon appear in the left margin. The first page of a presentation always gets the Title page layout. Type the presentation title to the right of the page icon, press Enter, and type the presentation subtitle on the next line. To add the next page, press Enter again and then press Shift+Tab or click the Promote icon.

To add a new page in the middle of a presentation, click on any of the text on a page, as shown in figure 18.4. Then press F7 or choose **N**ew from the **P**age menu. The new page then appears after the page the cursor is on, as shown in figure 18.5. You also can click at the end of the last line of a page, press Enter, and then press Shift+Tab or click the Promote icon.

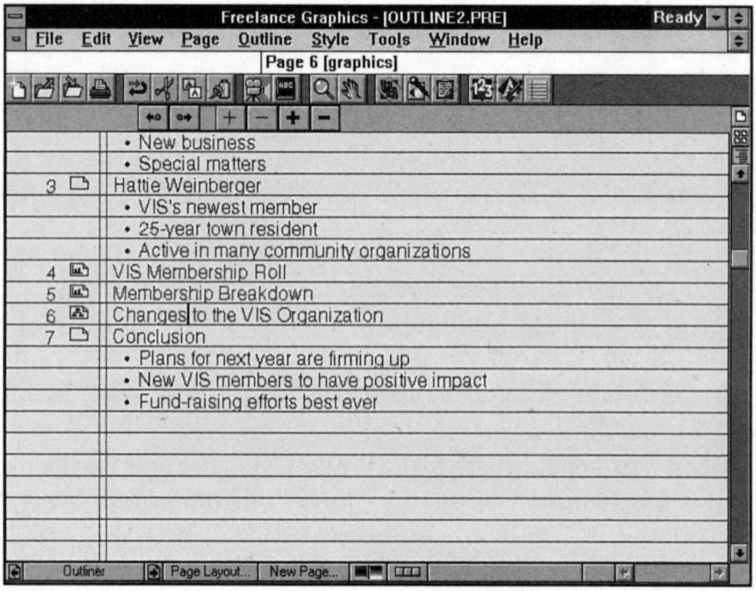

Fig. 18.4

Placing the cursor on a page.

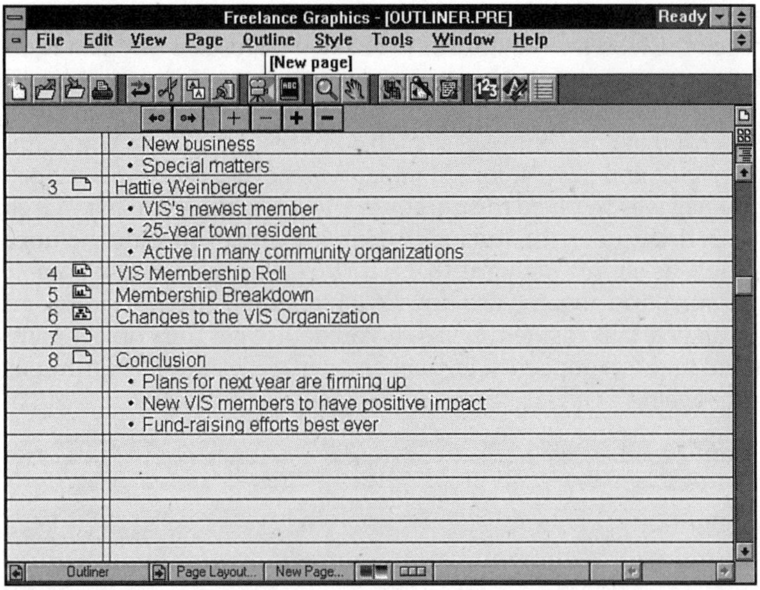

Fig. 18.5

The new page added.

Moving Pages in a Presentation

To move a page or group of pages, you must select the pages first. To select an entire page, click its page icon once. A border surrounds the page, as shown in figure 18.6.

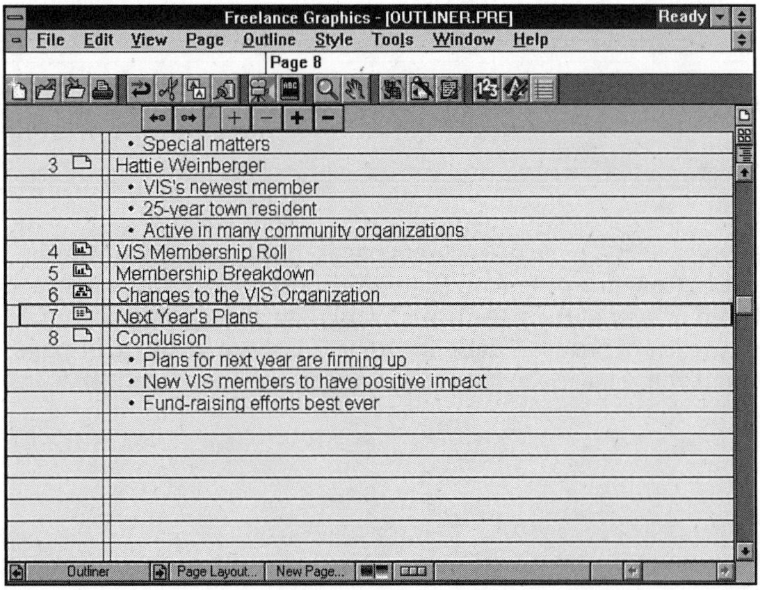

Fig. 18.6

A selected page denoted by a border.

To select adjacent pages in the presentation, press and hold down Shift and click the icon for the next or preceding page. You also can right-click several successive page icons to select more than one page. The border then expands to include these selected pages too. You must click a group of adjacent pages, such as pages 2, 3, and 4. You cannot select page 2 and page 4, for example. Yet another method of selecting several pages is to place the cursor at the left edge of the left margin and then draw a box that includes the page icons you want included in the group, as shown in figure 18.7. The box does not have to completely surround an entry for it to be included; the entry is included if any of its text falls inside the box. If you do not get the correct pages included in the group, click any single page to deselect the group and then try again.

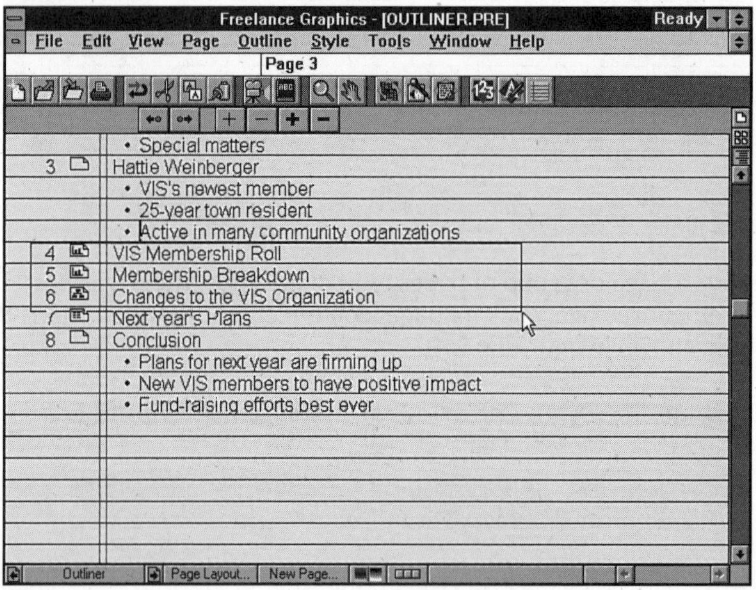

Fig. 18.7

Drawing a box around Outliner entries to select them.

After you select a page or group of pages, click and hold down the mouse button on a page icon (if you've selected a group of pages, click and hold on any of the page icons), and then slide the pointer up and down the list of pages. A dark line appears where the page or pages will end up if you release the mouse button, as shown in figure 18.8.

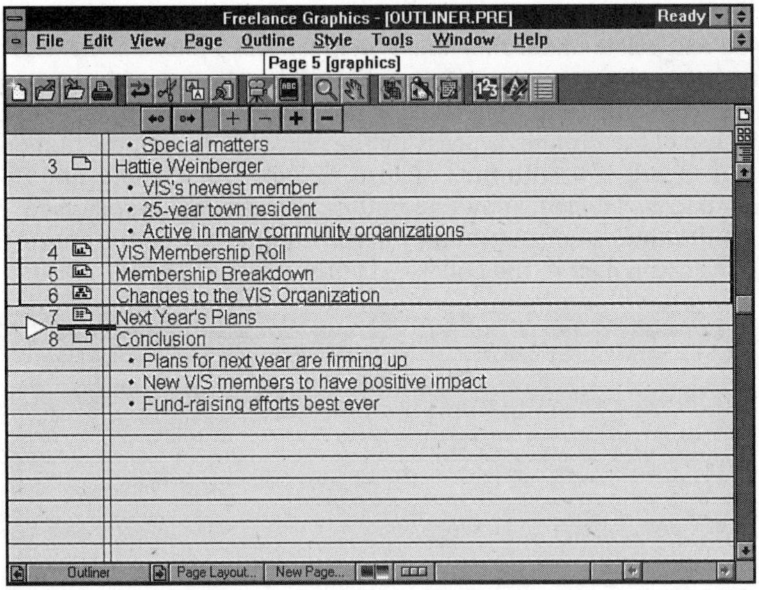

Fig. 18.8

A dark horizontal line identifying the destination for the selected entries.

Deleting Pages from a Presentation

To delete pages you have selected, press the Del key, choose Clear from the **Edit** menu, or click the Cut SmartIcon.

Hiding and Showing Text in the Outliner

If the Outliner is where you will formulate a presentation, you may want to step back a moment and consider the big picture while working on the text for a single page. By collapsing the text at lower levels of the outline, you can view only text at higher levels. You can view only page titles by collapsing all the text underneath, for example, to make quickly reorganizing the presentation's main topics easy.

To collapse the text under any entry in the outline, position the cursor anywhere within the text of the entry and then click the Collapse icon (a thin minus sign) at the top of the outline or press the gray minus key on the numeric keypad of your keyboard. The text under the entry then disappears, and a plus sign appears in the left margin to show that collapsed text exists under this line. When you see a plus sign next to an entry, you can expand the text underneath by placing the cursor anywhere in the entry and then clicking the Expand icon (a thin plus sign) at the top of the outline or pressing the gray plus key on the numeric keypad. Figure 18.9, with the Collapse, Collapse All, Expand, and Expand All icons labeled, shows an outline before a line is collapsed. Figure 18.10 shows a collapsed entry in the outline. Notice the plus sign in the left margin next to the collapsed entry.

Fig. 18.9

A Freelance outline before an entry is collapsed.

Expand icon
Collapse icon
Expand All icon
Collapse All icon

Freelance Graphics - [OUTLINE2.PRE]		Ready
File	Edit	View Page Outline Style Tools Window Help

Page 7

1 The Village Improvement Society
 • Semi-annual Meeting
2 Agenda
 • Introductions
 • Old business
 • New business
 • Special matters
3 Hattie Weinberger
 • VIS's newest member
 • 25-year town resident
 • Active in many community organizations
4 VIS Membership Roll
5 Membership Breakdown
6 Changes to the VIS Organization
7 Next Year's Plans
8 Conclusion
 • Plans for next year are firming up
 • New VIS members to have positive impact
 • Fund-raising efforts best ever

Outliner   Page Layout...   New Page...

To collapse all the text in the outline and leave only the page titles visible, click the Collapse All icon (the bold minus sign) at the top of the outline. To expand all the outline text, click the Expand All icon at the top of the outline (the bold plus sign). The equivalent menu commands—Collapse, Expand, Collapse All, and Expand All—are in the Outline menu.

Printing the Outline

You can print a presentation's outline by choosing **Print** from the **File** menu and then choosing **Outline** as the format. An even faster method is to click the File Print SmartIcon while in Outliner view and then choose **Outline** from the Print File dialog box.

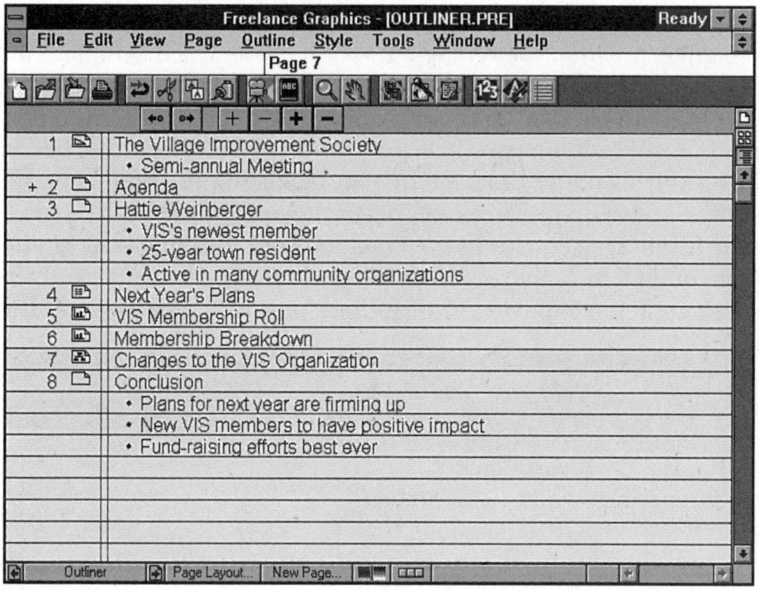

Fig. 18.10

The same outline with the second page collapsed.

When you print an outline, collapsed entries do not print. To print a list of page titles, you can click the Collapse All icon and then click the File Print SmartIcon.

Importing an Outline from a Word Processor

Rather than type an outline in the Outliner, you can create an outline in your favorite word processor and then import the outline into a new presentation's Outliner view. Each outline entry at the first level becomes the title of a new page. Entries indented under the main entry in the word processor become indented entries in Outliner view too.

Importing an Ami Pro Outline

When you use Ami Pro, the Windows word processor from Lotus, copying an outline into Freelance is especially easy. Simply create the outline in Ami Pro, using the outlining features of the software. Then select the outline text and copy it to the Windows Clipboard with the

Edit Copy command. Then switch to the Outliner view of a presentation in Freelance, position the typing cursor on a line in the Outliner, and choose **Paste** from the Freelance **E**dit menu. Level-one entries in the Ami Pro outline become page titles and take on the first paragraph style on presentation pages. Level-two and level-three entries become indented entries under the page title and take on the second and third paragraph styles on presentation pages. Level-four entries and lower become level-three entries in the Freelance outline. Figure 18.11 shows a simple outline in Ami Pro. Figure 18.12 shows the same outline after it has been copied and pasted into Outliner view of a new presentation.

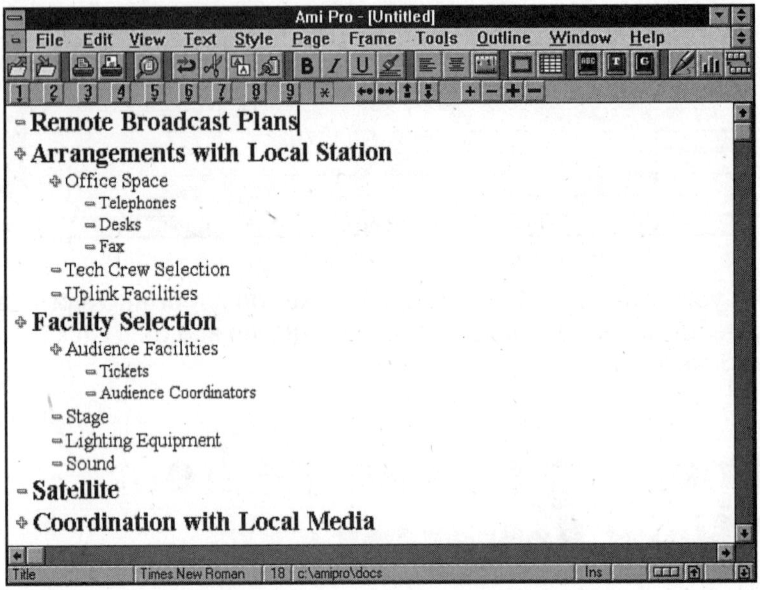

Fig. 18.11

A simple outline in Ami Pro.

Importing a Word for Windows Outline

Only the first two levels of a Word for Windows outline copy and paste properly into Freelance. Level-one entries in a Word for Windows outline become page titles in a Freelance outline. Level-two entries become bulleted text under the page titles. Level-three entries and lower are treated as new page titles, however.

To import text correctly from Word for Windows or any other word processor, export the text from the word processor as an ASCII file and then import the ASCII file into the Freelance Outliner. Each level of text in the ASCII file must be indented by at least two additional spaces at the beginning of the line. Freelance reads the indented ASCII outline and creates a similarly indented outline in Outliner view. Freelance reads only three indented levels of text, however. Levels four and lower become third-level text in Freelance. Blank lines of text in the ASCII file become new blank pages in Outliner view. Note, for example, how an indented outline looks in an ASCII file:

```
East End Recreation
Atlantic Beaches
    Two-Mile Hollow
    Fowler Lane Beach
Local Entertainment
    The Annex Restaurant
    The Swamp Club
Shopping
    Boutiques
    Antiquing
    Gourmet Foods
```

Figure 18.13 shows the same outline when it is imported into Freelance.

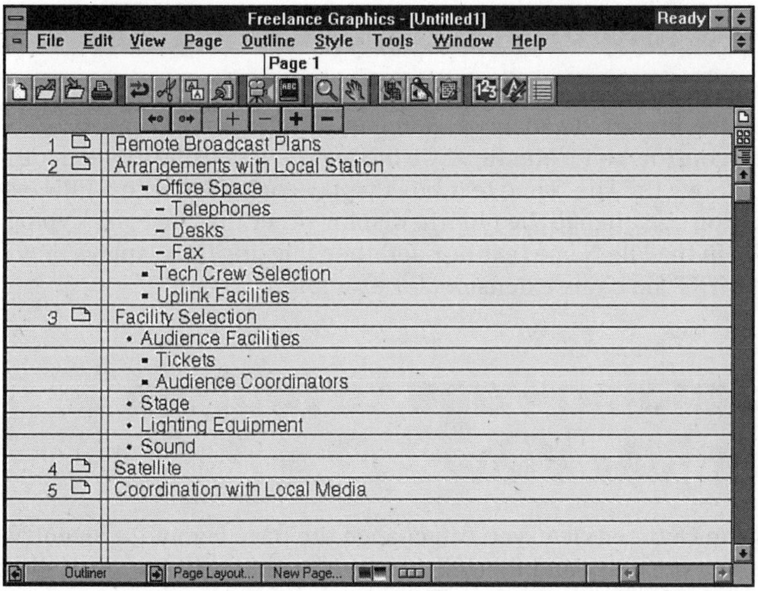

Fig. 18.12

The same outline in Freelance.

Importing an ASCII Outline

To import an ASCII outline file, choose **I**mport from the **F**ile menu. When the Import File dialog box opens, use the **D**irectories and File **N**ame controls to locate the ASCII file and then click OK. By default, the filter above the File **N**ame text box displays only files with a PRN extension. You can change the filter to display other files instead. Typing ***.TXT** in the File **N**ame text box and then clicking OK displays only files with a TXT file name extension, for example.

Changing Page Layouts in Outliner View

While in Outliner view, you can change the page layout for an entry by selecting the entry and then clicking the Page Layout button at the bottom of the Freelance window. The current page layout for the page is highlighted. Choose a different page layout by selecting it from the list.

Making a Second Column of Bulleted Text Entries

When a page in Outliner view has the 2-Column Bullets page layout, the Outliner displays with a special symbol the start of the second column of bullets. You type the text entries for the first column before the symbol, then move the cursor next to the symbol on the line where the second column is to begin, and type the rest of the text entries. After you've entered the text, you can move this symbol by placing the cursor in the line that will be the beginning of the second column and then choosing **M**ake Second Column from the **O**utline menu. The symbol then moves to the left of the line you have selected.

Figure 18.14 shows a 2-Column Bullets page in Current Page view. Figure 18.15 shows the same page in Outliner view.

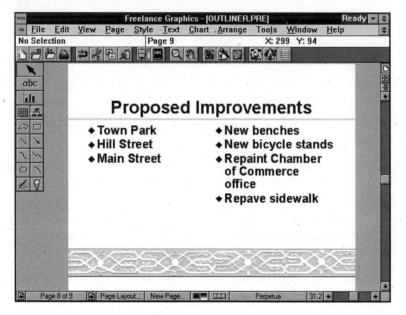

Fig. 18.14

A page with the 2-Column Bullets page layout.

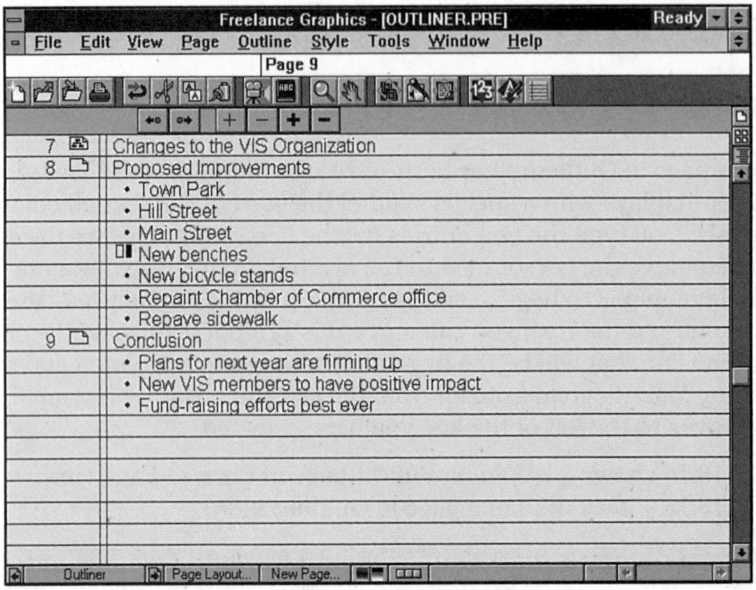

Fig. 18.15

The 2-Column Bullets page in Outliner view.

To create a 2-Column Bullets page while typing an outline, follow these steps:

1. Begin a new page in the outline.

2. Click the Page Layout button and choose the 2-Column Bullets page layout.

3. Type the page title, move the cursor down to the first bullet, and type the left column of bullets. Figure 18.16 shows the text as it appears at this point.

4. After the last bullet in the first column, press the down-arrow key to move the cursor to the line with the new column symbol.

5. Type the second column of bullets. Figure 18.17 shows the completed page in Outliner view. Figure 18.18 shows the page in Current Page view.

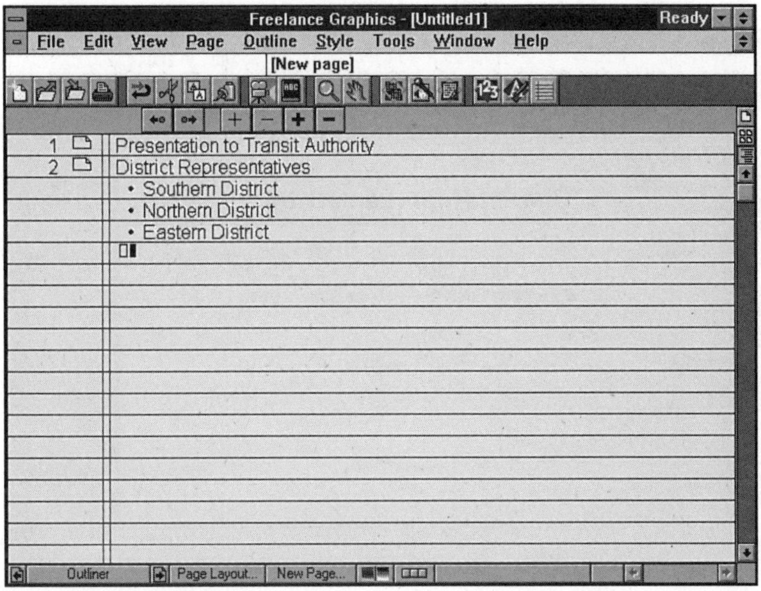

Fig. 18.16

The text for the first column in Outliner view.

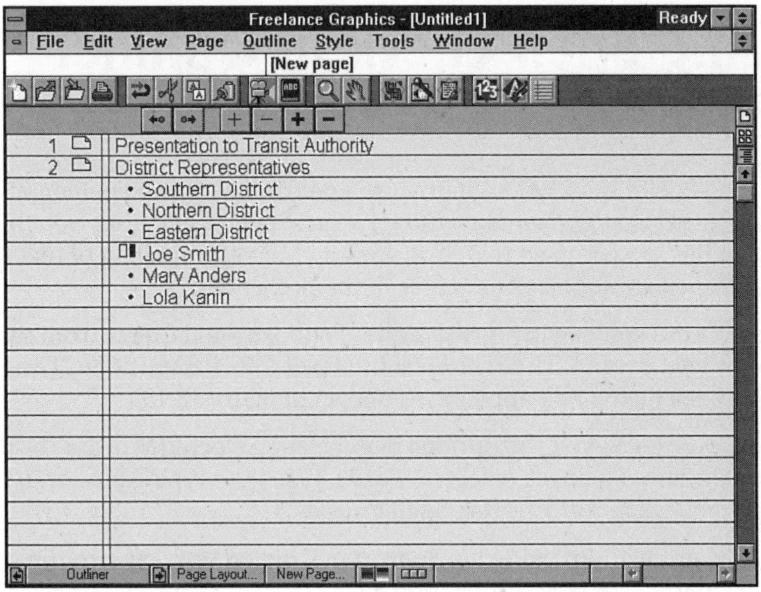

Fig. 18.17

A 2-Column Bullets page in Outliner view.

Fig. 18.18

The 2-Column Bullets page in Current Page view.

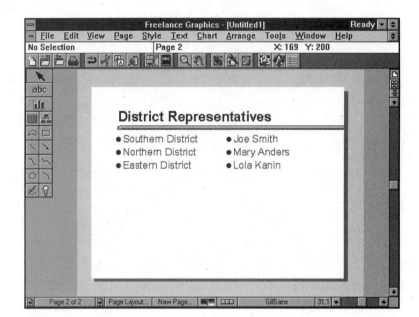

Using Spell Check in Outliner View

By using Spell Check in Outliner view, you can check the spelling of only the text that appears in Outliner view. Spell Check does not check the spelling of collapsed text. Nor does it check the spelling of text in charts, speaker notes, or metafiles in the presentation.

To check the spelling in a presentation, choose **S**pell Check from the Tools menu, press Ctrl+F2, or click the Spell Check SmartIcon. The Spell Check dialog box appears, as shown in figure 18.19.

Spell Check gives you the options of checking **S**elected Word(s) or the entire Outline. To check selected words, place the typing cursor in the word to check before starting Spell Check.

To learn more about using the Spell Check dialog box, refer to the section "Using Spell Check" in Chapter 17.

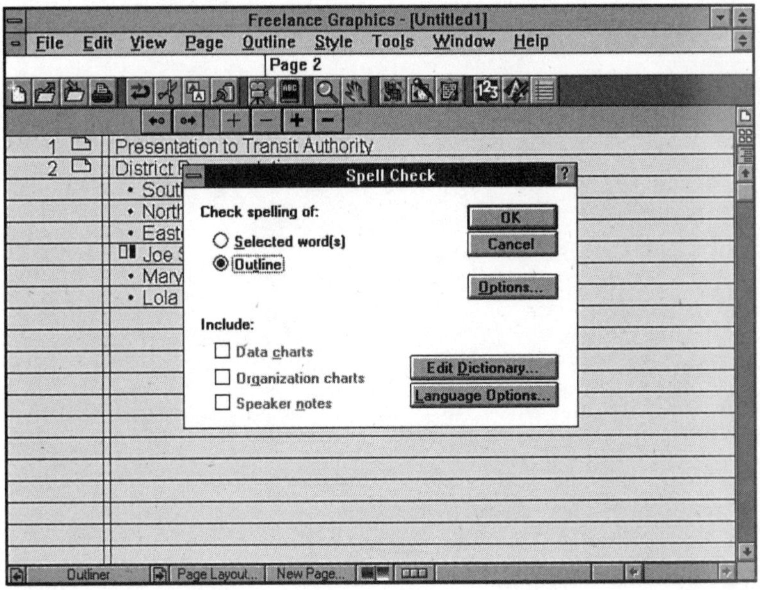

Fig. 18.19

The Spell Check dialog box.

Summary

In this chapter, you learned to display a presentation as an outline in Outliner view. Outliner view enables you to examine and work with the text content of a presentation, filtering out charts, design elements, and graphics.

In the next chapter, you learn to display the presentation as a screen show.

Creating Screen Shows

After you complete all the pages of a presentation, you can print the presentation, send it to a service that will make slides, or display the presentation on-screen as an automated screen show.

A *screen show* is a sequential display of the pages of a presentation. The pages can simply replace one another on-screen, or they can appear with fancy transition effects, such as fades, splits, pans, or rolls.

Screen shows put the liveliness into a presentation that slides simply cannot offer. And when screen shows are projected before an audience with a good-quality computer projector, they can have much of the visual impact of slides too.

In this chapter, you learn to create a slide show by adding transition effects to the pages of a presentation. You learn also how to create bulleted list charts that automatically build on-screen; how to add music, sound, and video to a presentation; and how to add buttons that can give your show interactive possibilities.

Displaying a Presentation as a Screen Show

After you finish a presentation, you can display it as a screen show by simply clicking the Screen Show SmartIcon or pressing Alt+F10. You also can choose **S**creen Show from the **V**iew menu and then choose **R**un from the pop-out menu. When the screen show starts, it advances to the next page each time you click the mouse button, press Enter, or press PgDn. To return to the preceding page, you click the right mouse button, press PgUp, or press the Backspace key. If you have already set up the screen show so that it advances automatically, you can sit back and watch Freelance display page after page at the interval you specified. Table 19.1 summarizes the keystrokes you can use while viewing a screen show.

Table 19.1 The Screen Show Keystrokes

Action	Keystrokes or Mouse Clicks
Move to the next page	Click the left mouse button, press PgDn, or press Enter
Move to the preceding page	Click the right mouse button, press PgUp, or press Backspace
Pause or restart an automatic show	Press spacebar
Cancel screen show and display a list of pages	Press Esc
End screen show	Press Esc and click the Quit Show button in the List Pages dialog box

Changing the Transition Effect

By default, each page of the screen show appears to wipe onto the page from top to bottom. This transition effect, called Top, is only one of 33 transition effects you can program into a screen show.

To change the effect used to draw each page in a screen show, choose **S**creen Show from the **V**iew menu and then choose E**d**it Effects from the pop-out menu. The Edit Screen Show dialog box appears, as shown in figure 19.1.

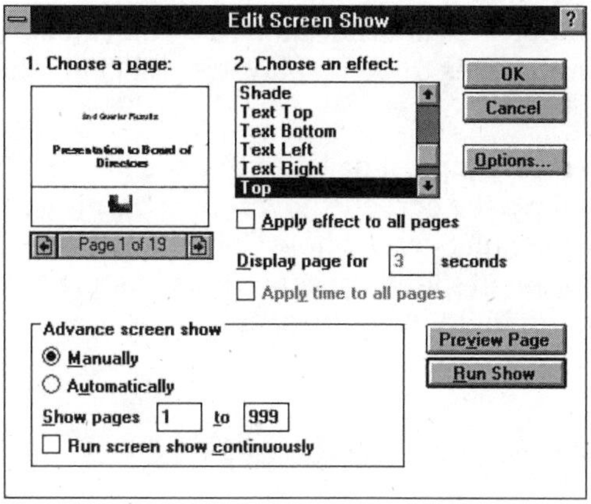

Fig. 19.1

The Edit Screen Show dialog box.

Numbered steps in the dialog box ask you to choose a page and then choose a transition effect for the page. To choose a page in step 1, click the button that displays the current page number and then select a different page from the Choose Screen Show Page dialog box that appears. Or click the left- or right-arrow button to change to the page to which you'll apply the transition effect. To choose an effect, select one from the scrollable list under step 2. Just below the list, a check box (**A**pply Effect to All Pages) enables you to determine whether the effect you choose should be applied to all other pages.

Each page can have a different transition effect, although you may want to limit the variety of transition effects or use the same transition effect repeatedly until you change subjects in the presentation. To preview the transition effect you've chosen for a page, click Preview Page. To run the entire screen show, click **R**un Show.

TIP

By ungrouping a data chart and then selecting one of the four Text transition effects (Text Top, Text Bottom, Text Left, or Text Right) for the page containing the chart, you can have the axis, legend, and value labels of a chart "fly in" one by one to build the chart on-screen.

With the Advance Screen Show controls, you can determine whether the show should proceed to the next page **M**anually (when the left mouse button is clicked, PgDn is pressed, or Enter is pressed) or Automatically (after the number of seconds set in the text box next to **D**isplay Page for *n* Seconds). To change the default setting of 3 seconds, replace that number with another number. You can make the new setting the time for all pages to be displayed by clicking the Apply Time to All Pages check box.

To see only a certain range of pages, enter the first and last pages after **S**how Pages. To have the screen show repeat continuously until you press Esc, click the Run Screen Show **C**ontinuously check box. That option is ideal for unattended presentations in store windows, at trade shows booths, or in building lobbies.

Setting Screen Show Options

In the Edit Screen Show dialog box, you can click **O**ptions to make three overall changes to the way the screen show will work. The Screen Show Options dialog box appears (see fig. 19.2). These three options are discussed in the following sections.

Fig. 19.2

The Screen Show Options dialog box.

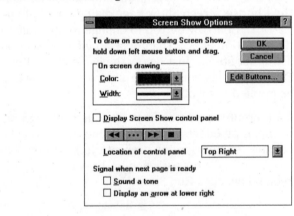

Drawing On-Screen

While a screen show is in progress, you can hold down the mouse button and drag the mouse to draw on a page on-screen. The On Screen Drawing controls in the Screen Show Options dialog box enable you to set the **C**olor and **W**idth of the line you draw.

You can draw on a screen show to point out certain parts of a chart or diagram, or to underline key text points that merit special emphasis.

Using the Control Panel

Placing a control panel on-screen during a screen show gives you a set of controls that you can use to change pages during the screen show. After you click the **D**isplay Screen Show Control Panel check box, you can select one of the preset locations for the control panel by using the Location of Control panel drop-down list. Figure 19.3 shows a presentation page during a screen show with a control panel at the top right.

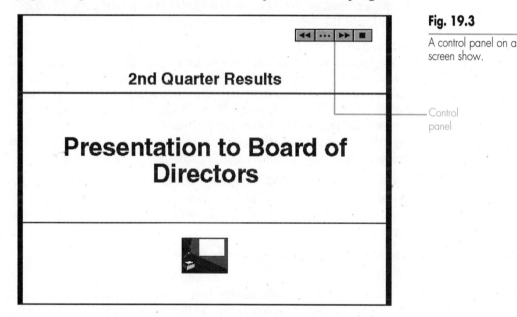

Fig. 19.3

A control panel on a screen show.

Control panel

Click the button containing double left arrows to turn back a page. Click the button containing double right arrows to turn forward a page. Click the button with three dots to get a list of pages that you can jump to in the screen show. Or click the square to end the screen show.

Having Freelance Signal When the Next Page Is Ready

If the images in your presentation are complicated or if the hard disk of your computer is slow, the next page may take a moment to be loaded and available. Freelance can signal with a tone or an arrow at the lower right of the screen when the next page is ready to be displayed. By waiting for the tone or arrow, you can avoid the embarrassment of waiting with an audience for the next page to appear. You can click the **S**ound a Tone check box or the Display an **A**rrow at Lower Right check box. You can even click both check boxes to have both events occur.

Adding Automatic Build Pages

If your presentation includes a bulleted list, you can have Freelance create a *build* that will add each item in the bulleted list sequentially during a screen show. As each new bulleted item appears, it is highlighted, and the items already on the page appear dimmed.

To create a build, Freelance takes a page with a bulleted list and creates a sequence of pages in front of it that gradually add the bulleted items. These are called *child pages*, and the original page is called a *parent page*. The first page in the sequence shows the page title and the first item only. The next page shows the page title, the first item dimmed, and the second item highlighted. The next page shows the page title, the first two items dimmed, and the third item highlighted. Freelance will add as many pages as you have bulleted items.

Figure 19.4 shows a two-page presentation in Page Sorter view. Figure 19.5 shows the same presentation after a build was created from the original second page. Figure 19.6 shows the last in the series of build pages.

Fortunately, creating a build in Freelance is completely automatic. Simply follow these steps:

1. Create a page with a bulleted list. (Use the Bulleted List, Bullets & Chart, or Bullets & Symbol page layout.)

2. Turn to the page in Current Page view or select the page in Page Sorter view.

3. From the **P**age menu, choose Create Build. Freelance informs you with a message box when the build is complete. The program also tells you how many child pages were created from the parent page.

After the pages of a build are added to a presentation, they are just like any other page in the presentation. They can be moved in the presentation or individually edited. You may want to place a different drawing or chart on each page of the build. The drawing or chart will be re-placed by the next drawing or chart when the screen show advances to the next page of the build.

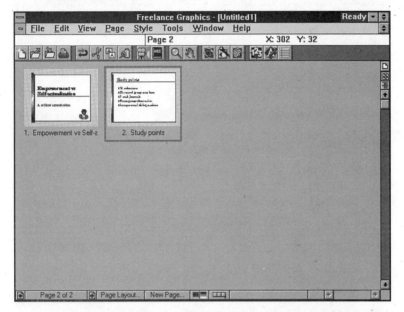

Fig. 19.4

A two-page presentation before the build is created.

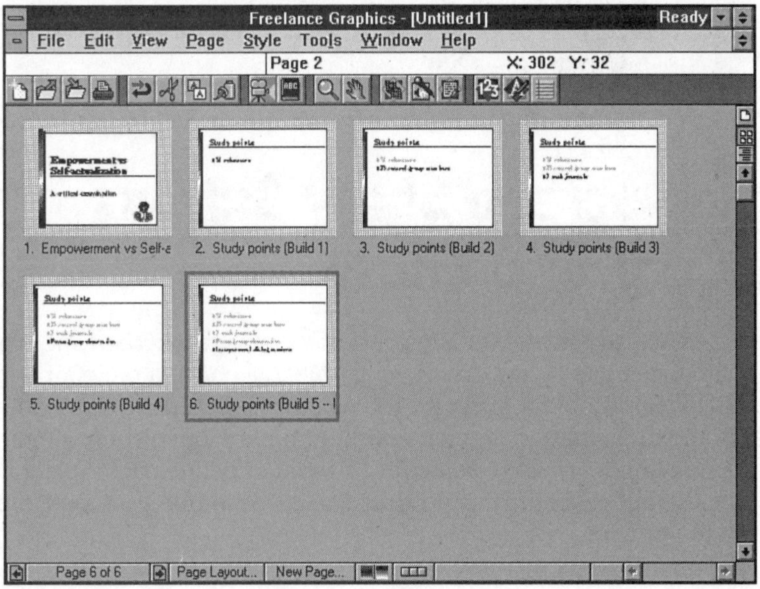

Fig. 19.5

The presentation with a build created from the original second page.

Fig. 19.6

The final build page.

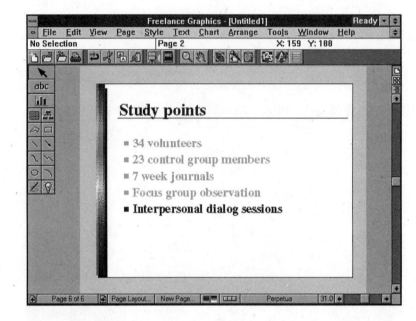

TIP

You can create a bulleted list of sections for a presentation, create a build from the list of sections, and then move individual pages from the build to the front of each part of the presentation to serve as section headings for sequences of slides.

Using Screen Show Buttons To Control a Show

You can make any object on any presentation page a screen show button. The object can be text, a drawing object, a chart, a table, or a symbol. Clicking that object during a screen show will turn to a specific page in the presentation; launch another application; or play a multimedia sound, video, or movie selection. You must define each object that you want to act as a button, and then select the action you want the button to perform.

To define an object as a button, select the object, choose **S**creen Show from the **V**iew menu, and then choose **C**reate/Edit Button from the pop-out menu. Or you can select the object and click the Screen Show Buttons SmartIcon. Either way, the Create/Edit Screen Show Button dialog box appears, as shown in figure 19.7.

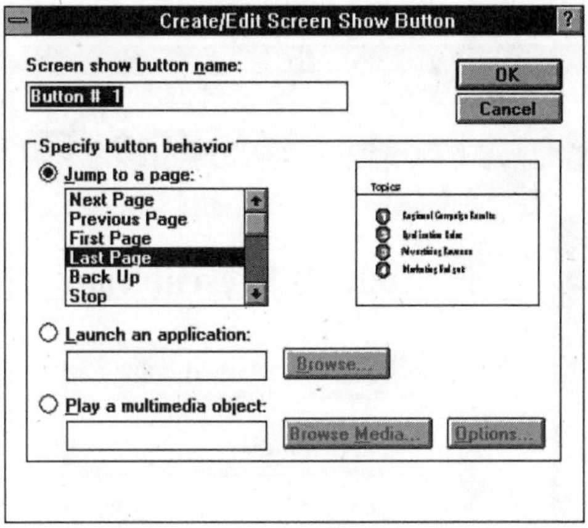

Create/Edit Screen Show Button

Screen show button name:

Button # 1

OK
Cancel

Specify button behavior

● **J**ump to a page:

Next Page
Previous Page
First Page
Last Page
Back Up
Stop

Topics

Regional Campaign Results
April Auction Sales
Advertising Expenses
Marketing Budget

○ **L**aunch an application:

Browse...

○ **P**lay a multimedia object:

Browse Media... Options...

Fig. 19.7

The Create/Edit Screen Show Button dialog box.

Replace the default numbered button name with any other button name you want, and then click one of the three buttons below to select the action that will be performed when you click the button during a screen show: **J**ump to a Page, **L**aunch an Application, or **P**lay a Multimedia Object. These options are discussed in the following sections.

Jumping to a Page

To have the screen show jump to a specific page when you click a button, click **J**ump to a Page and then select the page from the scrollable list. The first several items in the list let you move to another page relative to the current page. Later in the list, you can select a page by name to jump to. The picture to the right of the list shows the page you select from the list.

Here is a sample use for buttons in a presentation: you may want to create a master index for the presentation near the beginning and define each main topic in the list as a button. Then, at any point during the presentation, you can return to the index page and then click a topic name to jump to the first page of that section of the presentation. To make returning to the index page easy, you can create on each page a button that will jump to the index page (perhaps a small drawing of an index in a lower corner). Figure 19.8 shows such a list of topics on an early page of the presentation. Notice that each topic is on a symbol of a three-dimensional button that has been defined as a screen show button. By clicking the button, you can have Freelance turn to the first page of that topic in the presentation.

Fig. 19.8

A list of buttons you can use to turn to topics in the presentation.

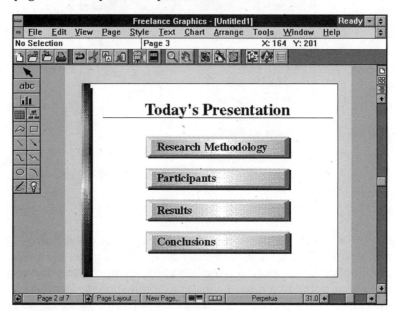

TIP

You can ungroup a data chart and then make each bar, line, or pie slice a button that can lead to a page of additional information about the data.

Launching an Application

To have a button launch another application, click Launch an Application in the Create/Edit Screen Show Button dialog box. The application can be another Windows program or a standard DOS program or batch file. If you know the name of the application's main program file or the batch file and DOS directory in which the application resides, you can type the path name and file name in the text box below Launch an Application. A more error-free way to enter the application's file name is to click **Browse** to the right of the text box and then use the File **Name** and **Directories** controls in the Find Application to Launch dialog box to find the application's EXE, COM, or BAT file (see fig. 19.9).

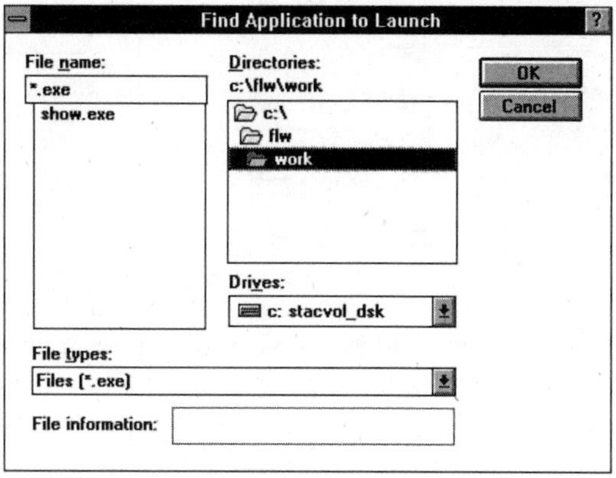

Find Application to Launch	?

File name:
`*.exe`
show.exe

Directories:
c:\flw\work
🗁 c:\
🗁 flw
📂 work

OK
Cancel

Drives:
💾 c: stacvol_dsk

File types:
Files [*.exe]

File information:

Fig. 19.9

The Find Application to Launch dialog box.

When you click a button that launches another application, the other application opens in Windows. When you quit the other application, you return to the screen show in progress.

TIP

You may want to define a button next to a chart that will open the original spreadsheet file on which the chart is based so that you can make modifications to the numbers in the worksheet. If the chart is linked to the worksheet, the chart will reflect the changes to the numbers.

Playing a Multimedia Object

The third choice in the Create/Edit Screen Show Button dialog box enables you to choose a multimedia object to play. A multimedia object can be a sound file, MIDI music file, or movie file.

When you click **P**lay a Multimedia Object, you can click Browse **Media** for assistance in finding the object. The Lotus Media Manager dialog box opens, as shown in figure 19.10.

First select a file type from the File **T**ypes pull-down list. The list includes Wave Files (sound files that require a sound board to play), MIDI Files (data files that control MIDI music synthesizers), and Movies (animated objects or video clips).

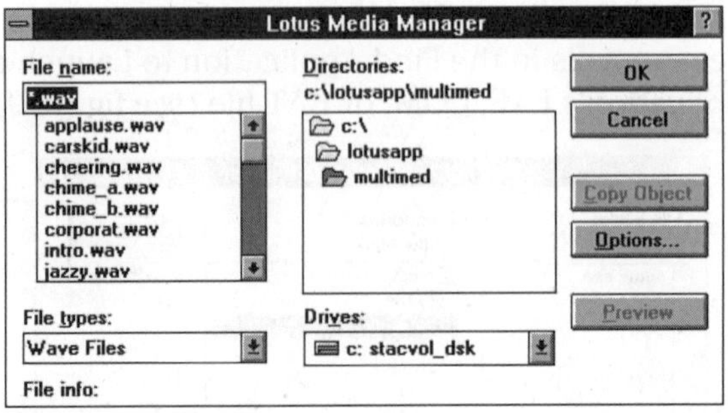

Fig. 19.10

The Lotus Media
Manager dialog box.

Wave files are digital audio files that you can play if you have a sound board installed in your system. Many sound boards available as plug-in devices can reproduce the music and sound effects stored in WAV files. With most of these sound boards, you can use a microphone to record WAV files. You can incorporate the voice of an associate or member of your company within a presentation, for example.

MIDI files are digital data files that can control music synthesizers hooked to your system through a MIDI port. Today's synthesizers can reproduce the sounds of an entire orchestra or band, so you can incorporate sophisticated digital music into a presentation if you have keyboards or synthesizer sound modules that can play MIDI data.

Movies are digital video clips or animations that can bring action to the screen. Two Lotus animation files come with Freelance: MMGLOBE.LSM (a spinning globe) and MMLASER.LSM (a laser that burns across a page). They are stored in the MULTIMED subdirectory under the LOTUSAPP directory on your hard disk. If you have Microsoft Multimedia Movies or Microsoft Video for Windows clips (MMM or AVI files) or you have Digital Video Interactive (DVI) video clips, you also can play them in a screen show.

After you select a file type, use the File **N**ame and **D**irectories controls to find the multimedia file on your system. You can click **P**review to see or hear the multimedia file. Click **O**ptions to view the Media Manager Options dialog box so that you can decide how many times to play the multimedia file. You can choose the following Play Options: Play **O**nce, **P**lay *n* Times (play a specified number of times), or Play **C**ontinuously.

Under File Options in the Media Manager Options dialog box, you can choose either **R**efer to File or **E**mbed File. Choosing **R**efer to File does not copy the data for the multimedia objects into the presentation file.

Instead, the data is read from the disk files and played whenever necessary. As a result, the same multimedia files must be available on a system to which you transfer a screen show in order for the multimedia files to be playable. Choosing **E**mbed File copies the multimedia data into the Freelance presentation file. This makes a presentation with multimedia data that you can transport to another PC. But it also creates very large presentation files because the presentation files have the multimedia data embedded inside.

After you select a multimedia object to play, you can click the **O**ptions button in the Create/Edit Screen Show Button dialog box to choose where on-screen the multimedia object will play.

> **TIP**
>
> Two of the SmartMaster sets that come with Freelance include multimedia movies: MMGLOBE.MAS and MMLASER.MAS. These animated movies move only when the presentation is viewed in a screen show.

Producing a Multimedia Show: Sound, Animation, Video, Music

One way to include a sound, movie, or video clip in a presentation is to assign a preexisting multimedia object to a button. You have already learned how to create buttons that will play multimedia objects whenever the buttons are pressed during a screen show. You also can add a multimedia object to a presentation page that will play whenever the page is viewed in a screen show.

You might want to add music that begins when the title page appears, for example, or add a voice-over from the chairman of the board when a profitability data chart appears on-screen. If you have the hardware needed to get a video clip into your system, you can even play a video clip of the chairman of the board with both sound and picture.

Freelance comes with two special Windows programs that enable you to create and add to pages the multimedia objects that will play during a screen show. Lotus Sound is a small program expressly designed to record and incorporate sound into other Windows applications, such as Freelance. Lotus Media Manager, a program you became acquainted with when you learned to create multimedia buttons, will play sound, movie, and video clips that you have recorded and saved on disk in files. With other Windows software, you can record video and animated movie clips.

Recording a Sound with Lotus Sound

If your PC is equipped with a microphone and a sound board that can record sound, you can use Lotus Sound to record audio clips while creating a page for a presentation. You can save each of these clips in a file on disk. You can also embed each clip in the Freelance file so that the clip becomes an integral part of the presentation. An icon for the sound will appear on the presentation page in Current Page view. Double-click the icon, and the sound will play. When the page appears in a screen show, the sound will play automatically.

To record a sound while creating a presentation, click the Launch Lotus Sound SmartIcon, or choose Insert Object from the Edit menu and then select Lotus Sound from the list of object types. The Lotus Sound dialog box opens, as shown in figure 19.11.

Fig. 19.11

The Lotus Sound dialog box.

The controls in this dialog box look much like the controls on a tape recorder. To start recording, click the Record button and then speak into the microphone. To end recording, click the Stop button that appears in place of the Play/Pause button. After you record a sound, you can play the sound by clicking the Play/Pause button, pause the sound by clicking the Play/Pause button again, or fast-forward or rewind the "tape" by clicking the FF or Rew button. To erase the current sound and start again, click the Erase button.

As the sound plays, the slider at the top of the controls moves to the right. You can quickly move to any point in the sound by dragging the slider left or right. To add to the recording, place the slider in the sound where the new recording should begin, and then click the Record button. To remove excess blank space or unwanted sounds at the end of a recording, move the slider to the desired end point in the sound and click the Record button twice.

When you finish recording a sound, choose Update from the File menu to embed the sound in the Freelance page. Then choose Exit & Return from the File menu to return to the Freelance page. The Lotus Sound icon will appear on the presentation page. Double-click this icon to play the sound.

Before you exit Lotus Sound, you can save the sound you've recorded on disk in a WAV file by choosing Save **As** from the Lotus Sound **F**ile menu and then entering a file name with a WAV extension. That way, you can use the sound later in Freelance or in other Windows applications.

Setting the Play Options for a Lotus Sound Object

After you have added a multimedia object to a presentation page, you can determine how the object will be played in a screen show by selecting the object and then choosing Lotus Media O**b**ject from the **E**dit menu. A pop-out menu gives you four choices. Choose **P**lay to preview the object. Choose **E**dit to open the Lotus Media Manager so that you can choose a different object. Choose P**r**int Options to set whether the object's icon will print when you print the presentation pages. Or choose Play Options to open the Play Options dialog box (see fig. 19.12).

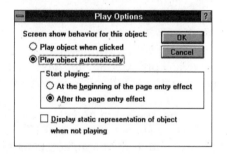

Fig. 19.12

The Play Options dialog box.

The Play Options dialog box provides two choices. Choose Play Object When **C**licked to play the object only if you click its icon during the screen show. Or choose Play Object **A**utomatically. If you play the object automatically, you can set whether the object will play before the transition effect that will display the page begins (At the **B**eginning of the Page Entry Effect) or after the page has fully appeared (After the Page Entry Effect). You also can decide whether to display the presentation's icon when the object is not playing; just click the check box next to **D**isplay Static Representation of Object When Not Playing. Click OK when you finish choosing the play options.

You can set different play options for each multimedia object in a screen show.

Embedding an Existing Multimedia Object

To play preexisting sounds, MIDI music files, or video and animation clips in a screen show, you can embed these files in the Freelance presentation. When you embed a multimedia file, the multimedia data is copied to the Freelance file. You do not need to copy the multimedia files to another computer when you move the screen show file because the data is already within the Freelance file. If the original sound, music, or video clip changes, though, the update will not be reflected in the Freelance screen show. You will be required to embed the revised multimedia object in the Freelance show, replacing the original.

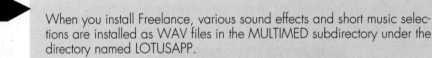

TIP

When you install Freelance, various sound effects and short music selections are installed as WAV files in the MULTIMED subdirectory under the directory named LOTUSAPP.

Fortunately, Freelance comes with a Windows application, the Media Manager, which can preview preexisting multimedia files as well as embed them in a Freelance presentation. To use the Media Manager, click the Launch Media Manager SmartIcon or choose **Insert Object** and then select Lotus Media from the list of object types. The Lotus Media Manager dialog box opens, as shown in figure 19.13. The following sections explain how to select a multimedia object, change the options of a multimedia object, change the icon of a multimedia object, and paste the object in a presentation.

Selecting the Multimedia Object

To use the Media Manager, select the file type you want from the File **Types** pull-down list. Then use the File **Name** and **Directories** controls to navigate to the file you want. Select the file from the list and then click **Preview** to hear or view the file. If the file is the one you want, click **Copy** Object to copy the multimedia object to the Windows Clipboard. Then click OK to close the Lotus Media Manager dialog box.

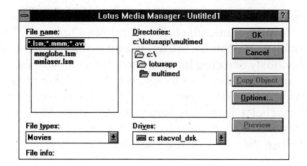

Fig. 19.13

The Lotus Media
Manager dialog box.

Changing the Options of the Multimedia Object

To change how the multimedia object will play and how it will be
stored, click **O**ptions in the Lotus Media Manager dialog box.
The Media Manager Options dialog box appears (see fig. 19.14).

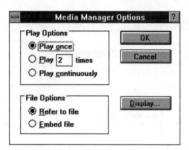

Fig. 19.14

The Media Manager
Options dialog box.

Use the controls under Play Options to determine how many times the
object will play. Select an option under File Options to set whether the
object should be embedded in the presentation file (which may increase the size of the Freelance PRE file considerably) or referred to
(the object remains in its own file on disk). If the object is referred to,
you must be sure to copy it to another computer (such as a portable
computer) along with the presentation file if you want the multimedia
object to play in a screen show.

Changing the Icon of the Multimedia Object

By clicking **D**isplay in the Media Manager Options dialog box, you can
change how the icon for the multimedia object will appear on the presentation page. When the Display Options dialog box opens, choose
Default for this media type to see the default icon for a sound, MIDI, or

video clip object. Choose Metafile from Clipboard if you have copied a particular Windows metafile to the Windows Clipboard. You can use this option to customize the appearance of the icon on the page. Choose Previously Selected Image if you changed the icon and you want to return to the previous image. When you finish changing the display options, click OK to return to the Media Manager Options dialog box. Then click OK again to return to the Media Manager dialog box. Now you can click Copy Object to copy the object to the Windows Clipboard and close the Lotus Media Manager dialog box.

Pasting the Object in the Presentation

To complete the work of embedding a multimedia object, turn to the page where the object should appear; then choose Paste Special from the Edit menu. The Paste Special dialog box opens, as shown in figure 19.15.

Fig. 19.15

The Paste Special dialog box.

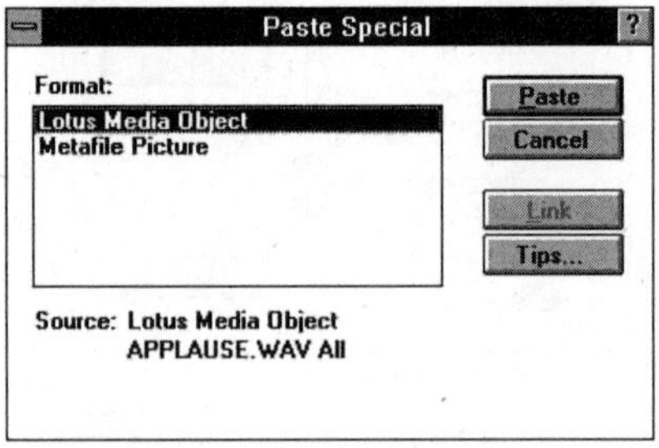

From the list of formats, select Lotus Media Object. Note that a description of the multimedia object appears in the dialog box, too. Then click Paste. The Paste Special dialog box closes, and an icon for the embedded multimedia object appears on the presentation page, as shown in figure 19.16.

Creating a Screen Show for DOS

By preparing a stand-alone version of a Freelance Graphics for Windows screen show, you can create a screen show that you can run with the DOS program SHOW.EXE. To run the screen show, you do not need Freelance Graphics for Windows on the system or even Windows. Displaying a stand-alone version of a screen show from DOS is helpful when you plan to display the screen show from a portable computer, especially if the portable has limited disk space. You can quickly copy a screen show and the DOS program that runs the screen show to the portable computer without having to install Windows and Freelance Graphics for Windows.

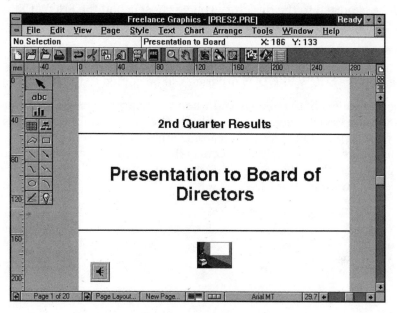

Fig. 19.16

The embedded multimedia object on a presentation page.

To create a stand-alone version of a screen show, choose **S**creen Show from the **V**iew menu and then choose **P**repare Standalone from the pop-out menu. The Export Screen Show dialog box appears, as shown in figure 19.17.

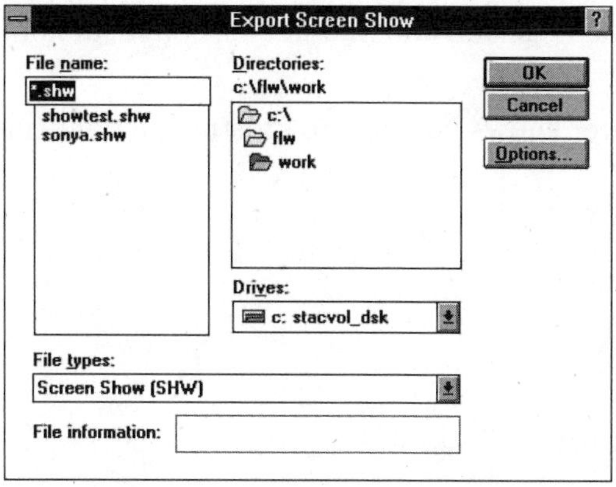

Fig. 19.17

The Export Screen Show dialog box.

If you will be running the screen show on a PC system that has an EGA display adapter rather than a VGA adapter, click **O**ptions in the dialog box and then click **E**GA. Otherwise, select the directory to which the screen show file will be exported, type a DOS file name for the show in the File **N**ame text box, and click OK. The files that make up the show will be exported to the directory you've chosen, and the SHOW.EXE DOS program will be copied to the same directory.

To export a screen show directly to a floppy disk, select the disk by using the D**ri**ves control, name the show file, and click OK. The show files and the SHOW.EXE DOS program will be copied to the floppy disk.

The show files that are generated when you export a screen show may be read by the DOS version of Freelance Graphics and Freelance Plus, so you can play the screen show from within those two DOS applications. Many of the transition effects in the Freelance Graphics for Windows screen show file will be similar to those used in Freelance Plus or Freelance Graphics for DOS.

CAUTION

When you export a screen show as a stand-alone file, the multimedia objects in the presentation will not play, and screen show buttons will not work or appear.

Summary

In this chapter, you learned to display a presentation as an on-screen show. You learned to add transition effects to an existing show; add screen show buttons that can jump to pages; launch other applications; play multimedia files; and add multimedia sound, animation, video, and music to a screen show.

The next chapter shows you how to create paper and slide versions of a presentation.

Creating Output

When it comes time to create a permanent version of a presentation, Freelance offers a number of choices. You can print the pages on a standard printer to create a paper copy of the presentation. If you have slide-making equipment, you can record the presentation on film that can be made into slides. If you need slides but don't have a film recorder, you can send a completed presentation by disk or modem to a slide service bureau that will return developed slides.

In this chapter, you learn how to create printed and film output of a presentation.

Printing Presentation Pages

You can print a presentation in a number of ways. You can print one presentation page per printed page, of course, but you can also print the presentation as speaker notes, audience notes, or handouts. Speaker notes show a miniature of the page on the top half of a printed page and, on the lower half, whatever speaker notes you entered by using the Speaker Notes command in the Page menu. Audience notes show the presentation page on the top half of a printed page with blank space below for audience members to write their own notes. Handouts have two, four, or six presentation pages on each printed page so that audience members can leave the presentation with a miniaturized, but still readable, version of the presentation.

Before you print the presentation pages as a sequence of standard pages, you should check the Printer Setup and Page Setup settings.

Using Printer Setup

When you build a presentation in Freelance, the presentation is customized for the printer that is currently the selected printer in Windows. To change the selected printer, you must use the Windows Control Panel. If you have a Hewlett-Packard LaserJet III printer, for example, then HP LaserJet Series III is probably the currently selected printer in Windows. When you print from any Windows application, the presentation is printed correctly on the HP LaserJet III. If you are printing the presentation on a printer other than the currently selected Windows printer, you can choose that printer in the Printer Setup dialog box, as shown in figure 20.1. Suppose that you routinely use a laser printer to print word-processed pages, but you want to print the Freelance presentation on a special color printer. You can use Printer Setup to customize the presentation for the color printer without having to change from the black-and-white laser printer in Windows.

Fig. 20.1

The Printer Setup dialog box.

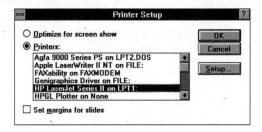

To get to the Printer Setup dialog box, choose Printer Setup from the File menu. Then choose a printer from the scrollable list of printers. Freelance automatically adjusts the pages to match the capabilities of the printer selection. The printer selection remains in effect only during the current session with Freelance. When you use Freelance the next time, the current Freelance printer is reset to the current Windows printer. The printers shown are the printers that are currently installed in your version of Windows. To install a new printer driver, you must use the Windows Control Panel.

To change the current settings for the printer you have selected, click Setup in the Printer Setup dialog box. Another dialog box with settings specific for the printer, such as the resolution and paper source, appears.

If you are displaying the presentation as a screen show rather than printing it, click **O**ptimize for Screen Show. Even though you are not planning to print, the **O**ptimize for Screen Show setting is in the Printer Setup dialog box. Choosing **O**ptimize changes the length-to-width ratio of the page (the aspect ratio) so that it matches the length-to-width ratio of the screen. **O**ptimize also causes the Edit Screen Show dialog box to appear when you click **P**rint.

If you are creating slides, click the Set **M**argins for Slides check box. This sets an appropriate aspect ratio for 35mm slides. You also can find this same check box in the File Page Setup dialog box.

Changing the Page Setup

The File Page Setup dialog box, shown in figure 20.2, enables you to set up a header for the top and a footer for the bottom of every printed page. This dialog box also enables you to set the orientation and margins of the pages.

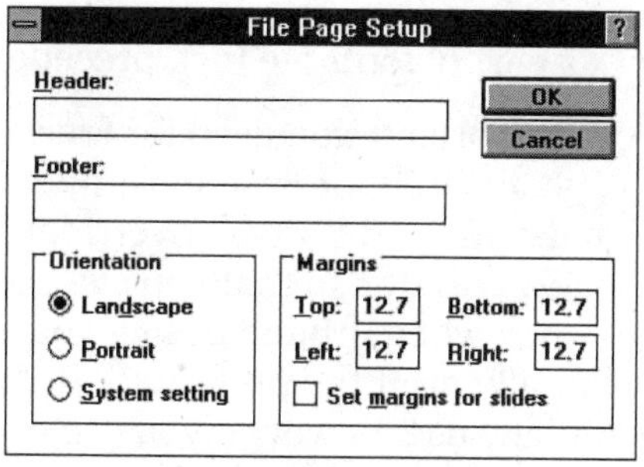

Fig. 20.2

The File Page Setup dialog box.

To set up headers and footers, you simply enter text and codes in the **H**eader and **F**ooter text boxes. You can enter up to 512 characters. Any text that you enter by itself appears left-aligned on the page with the 8-point Arial MT typeface. If Adobe Type Manager is not installed, the closest equivalent font is used.

To enter a page number, type a number sign (#) in the **H**eader or **F**ooter text box. To start sequential numbering with a specific number, enter two number signs followed by the starting number. To start page numbering at page 15, for example, enter **##15** in a text box. This feature is helpful when a presentation is a continuation of a previously printed presentation.

To enter the current date on a page, type an @ in a text box.

Each header and footer can have three parts; the first is left-aligned, the second is centered, and the third is right-aligned. To enter all three parts, separate them with vertical bars. To have the word *Confidential* appear at the bottom left, the page number at the bottom middle, and the date at the bottom right, for example, you enter the following in the Footer text box:

Confidential¦#¦@

You can type a vertical bar without preceding it with an entry to move the next entry to the next horizontal position. You enter ¦# in the Header text box to center a page number at the top of each page, for example.

To split a header or footer into more than one line, enter a tilde (˜) in the text where the line should be split. To have *Confidential* on the first line and *Eyes Only* on the second line, for example, you enter the following:

Confidential˜Eyes Only

To enter a #, @, or ˜ as part of footnote text, precede it with a backslash.

If you want to change the orientation used for Freelance presentation pages, click Lan**d**scape, **P**ortrait, or **S**ystem Setting in the File Page Setup dialog box. Lan**d**scape and **P**ortrait override the current setting for the selected Windows printer so that you can see on-screen how the presentation will look when printed even if you are not using the printer that will eventually print the presentation. If you are using the printer you will eventually use, however, you can click **S**ystem Setting. The current orientation for the selected Windows printer will be used.

To adjust the margins on the presentation pages, use the **T**op, **B**ottom, **L**eft, and **R**ight settings under Margins. These settings automatically adjust any pages you have already created. The contents of the pages scale down smaller if you enter larger margins, for example. The margin setting is measured in the unit selected in Units & Grids from the **V**iew menu.

If you are creating slides, you can click the Set **M**argins for Slides check box. Freelance then uses the margin settings appropriate for 35mm slides.

Printing the Pages

After you check Printer Setup and Page Setup, you can choose **Print** from the **File** menu to print the presentation. You also can click the File Print SmartIcon. The Print File dialog box opens, as shown in figure 20.3.

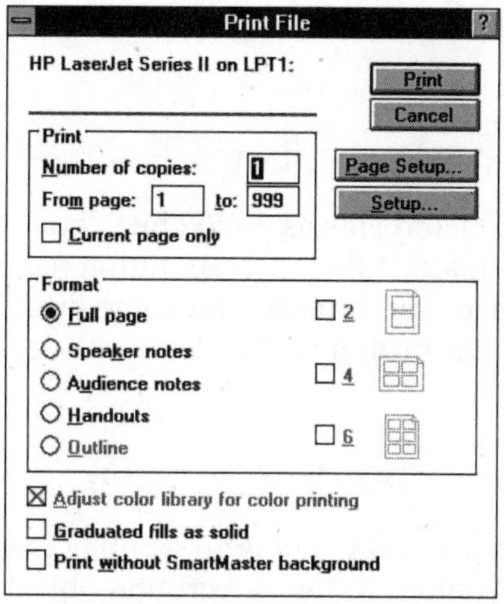

Fig. 20.3

The Print File dialog box.

Use **Number** of Copies and Fro**m** Page *n* **to** *n* to determine which pages and how many copies to print. To print only the selected page, click the **C**urrent Page Only check box. To print the full presentation pages, choose **F**ull Page as the Format setting.

The **P**age Setup button leads to the Page Setup dialog box, in case you need to make last-minute changes to those settings. The **S**etup button leads to the Printer Setup dialog box for last-minute changes to the printer settings.

Choose a format from the list of formats (**O**utline is available only if you are in Outliner view) and then make any adjustments you need to the three check boxes at the bottom, which are discussed in the following sections. Finally, click **P**rint to start the printing.

Adjusting the Color Library for Color Printing

If a color printer is the current Windows printer or you have used the **F**ile Printer Setup command to select a color printer as the current printer for the presentation, Freelance automatically uses a special color palette that is optimized for the selected color printer. This palette helps match the printed output with the colors you see on-screen. You will want to deselect the **A**djust Color Library for Color Printing check box only if you have modified the color library. The adjusted color libraries that Freelance provides are not changed if you adjust the color library for a presentation. You also might want to try turning off the color adjustment if the colors print much lighter than you expected.

Printing Graduated Fills as Solid

By clicking the **G**raduated Fills as Solid check box, you can have Freelance print graduated fills on presentation pages as solid colors. Graduated fills take longer to print, and some printers are incapable of printing graduated fills or don't print them well.

Printing without the SmartMaster Background

To print only the text, charts, and graphic objects you've placed on presentation pages (and not the background objects that are part of the SmartMaster set), you can click the Print **w**ithout SmartMaster Background check box.

Figure 20.4 shows a page from a presentation. Figure 20.5 shows how the page is printed when you choose Print **w**ithout SmartMaster Background.

Printing Speaker Notes

By choosing Spea**k**er Notes as the Format setting in the Print File dialog box, you can instruct Freelance to print speaker notes' versions of the presentation pages. These pages display a reduced version of a presentation page on the top half of the printed page and display the speaker notes you have entered in large print on the lower half of the printed page.

 To enter the speaker notes, you must choose **S**peaker Notes from the **P**age menu or click the Speaker Notes SmartIcon while you are in Current Page or Page Sorter view.

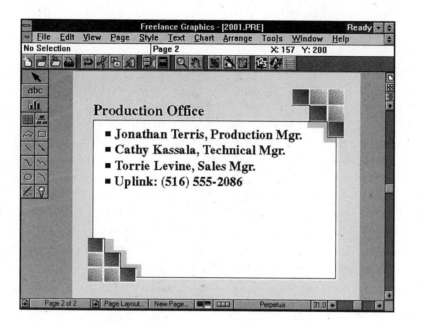

Fig. 20.4

A sample presentation page.

Printing Audience Notes

By choosing **Au**dience Notes as the Format setting in the Print File dialog box, you can have Freelance print a reduced-size version of the presentation page on the top half of the printed page and leave the lower half of the page blank. Audience members can use this space to jot down their own notes about the presentation page.

Printing Handouts

By choosing **H**andouts as the Format setting in the Print File dialog box, you can instruct Freelance to print two, four, or six reduced-size presentation pages on each printed page. You can print a complete presentation in miniature on just a few pages. Handouts can be excellent "leave behinds" for audience members. Figure 20.6 shows a handout with four presentation pages.

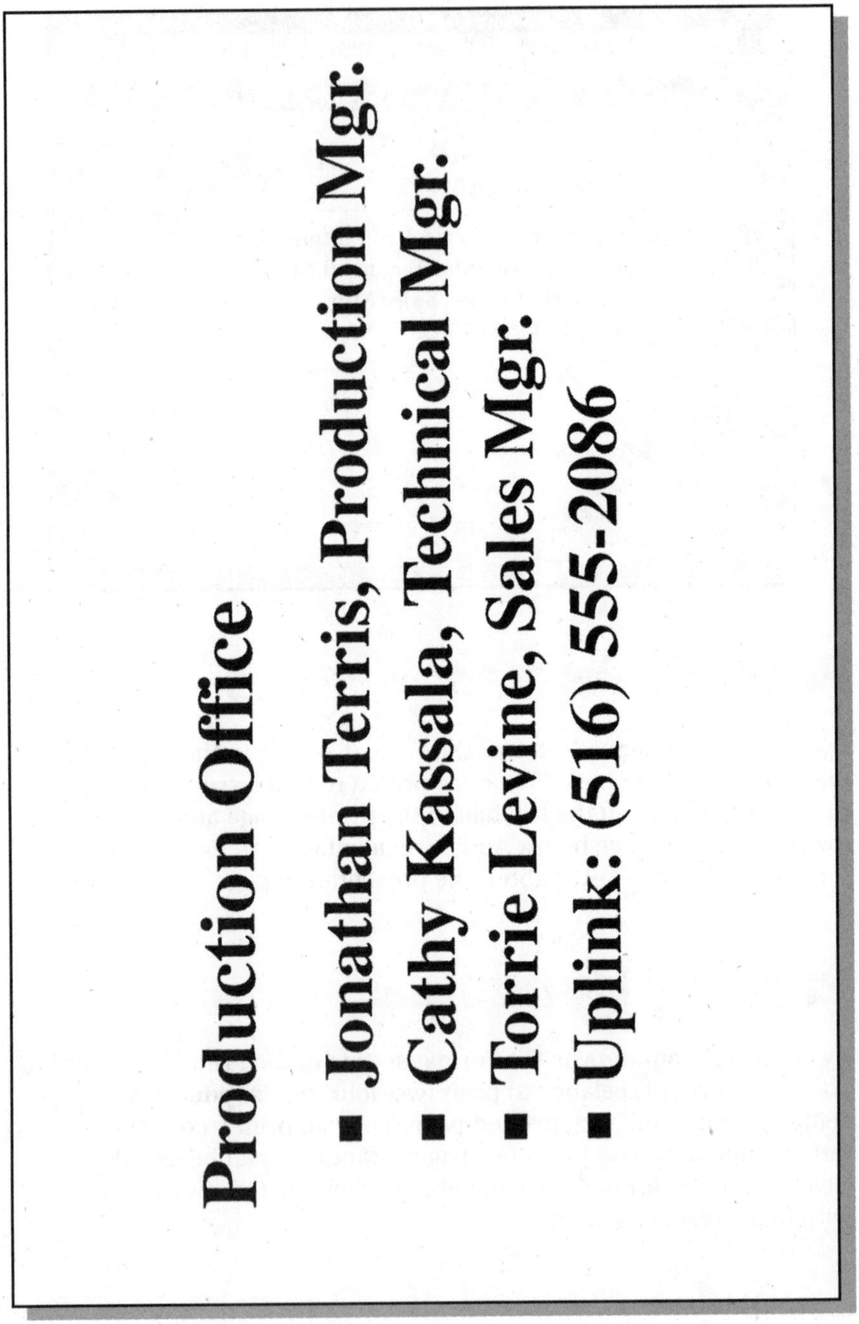

Fig. 20.5

The sample page printed without the SmartMaster background.

Production Office

- **Jonathan Terris, Production Mgr.**
- **Cathy Kassala, Technical Mgr.**
- **Torrie Levine, Sales Mgr.**
- **Uplink: (516) 555-2086**

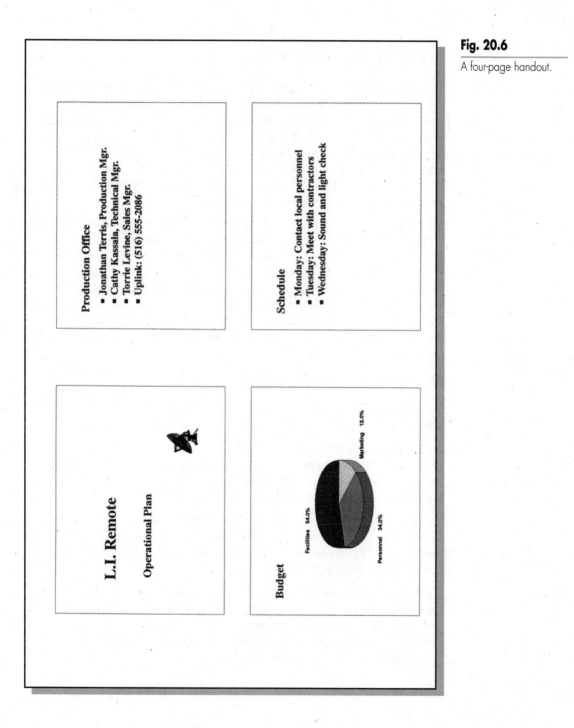

Fig. 20.6

A four-page handout.

Creating Slides

Freelance provides the capability for creating 35mm slides. Slides have the advantage of very high resolution; their detail is extremely fine, their text looks razor sharp, and their colors and color gradients are rich and smooth. Slides, like printed pages, are static, though. You cannot animate slides as you can pages in a screen show; nor can you add sound, music, or video clips by using the multimedia capabilities of Windows and Freelance. Another major disadvantage of slides is that you cannot edit their contents at the very last second.

To create slides, you must have slide-recording equipment (often called a film recorder) that records the pages of a presentation onto 35mm film. After the film is recorded, you develop it as you would develop pictures photographed with a camera. If you do not have slide-recording equipment, you can send a file generated by Freelance to a service that records and develops the slides for you and returns them the same day or overnight. You can even use a modem to send the slide file by telephone to a slide service bureau so that you can get the slides back quickly.

How you set Freelance to create slides depends on how you will have the slides made. If you have a film recorder, you must use the correct Windows printer driver for the film recorder and then print to the film recorder just as if you were printing to any other output device.

If you use a matrix film recorder, you can install the Stingray SCODL driver into Windows and then select Stingray SCODL as the current printer. This driver converts Freelance output into a SCODL file that you can send to a matrix camera.

If you are working with a service bureau, the bureau can tell you the format it accepts. Many service bureaus accept Freelance presentation files (PRE files). Others require you to save a presentation in an Encapsulated PostScript (EPS) file.

If you plan to use the Autographix service center, you can take advantage of the Autographix slide driver and modem communications software that comes with Freelance. This software automatically creates the file used by Autographix and sends the file to the nearest Autographix service center by modem.

Setting Freelance for Creating Slides

Whenever you plan to create slides, you should click the Set **M**argins for Slides check box in the File Page Setup dialog box or in the Printer Setup dialog box. Freelance then adjusts the aspect ratio of the presentation pages so that it matches the aspect ratio of 35mm slides. You should turn on Set **M**argins for Slides whether you are recording the slides yourself or having a service bureau make the slides for you.

After you click Set **M**argins for Slides, you can choose **V**iew Preferences from the **V**iew menu and then, for Show Page Borders, choose **M**argins. Freelance then displays a dashed line on each page at the slide margins so that you can keep graphic elements within the margins while you create the page.

Printing a Presentation to an Encapsulated PostScript File

If the service bureau you use asks for an Encapsulated PostScript file (an EPS file), you need to print the presentation as an EPS file. Check with the service bureau about which Windows printer driver you should use and then follow these steps:

1. Switch to the Windows Control Panel.

2. Double-click the Printers icon. The Printers dialog box appears.

3. Install or select the appropriate Windows PostScript printer driver.

4. Click **C**onnect.

5. From the **P**orts list, choose FILE and then click OK.

6. Click Se**t** as Default Printer in the Printers dialog box.

7. Click Close.

8. Switch back to Freelance.

9. From the **F**ile menu, choose Printer Setup.

10. Select the PostScript printer from the list of Printers and click OK.

11. From the **F**ile menu, choose **P**rint and then **F**ull Page.

12. When Windows prompts you for the **O**utput File Name, enter a DOS file name with an EPS extension into the text box.

EPS files can be very large, so you may have to compress the EPS file with a file compression utility such as PKZIP to fit on a disk for transport to a service bureau.

Using the Autographix Slide Service

When you install Freelance, one of the options during the installation process enables you to install all the files you will need in order to use the Autographix service center. If you have not installed the Autographix slide files, you can return to the install program at any time. After the install program is complete, you must follow these steps to add Autographix support to your system:

1. Close Freelance if it is running.

2. Open the Windows Control Panel and double-click the Printers icon.

3. Click **A**dd in the Printers dialog box.

4. From the **L**ist of Printers, click Install Unlisted or Updated Printer.

5. Click the **I**nstall button.

6. In the Install Driver dialog box, type the full Windows path—for example, **C:\WINDOWS**. Then click OK.

7. In the Add Unlisted or Updated Printer dialog box, click Autographix 4.1 and then click OK.

8. If the Install Driver window appears, insert the requested Microsoft Windows disk into the disk drive, type the path to the disk drive (for example, **A:**), and then click OK. If a newer PostScript driver is already installed, Windows asks whether you want to overwrite it. Click No.

9. Click **C**onnect and choose FILE from the list of **P**orts. Then click OK.

10. Click **S**etup.

11. Choose a paper size of 8.5 x 11 inches, click **L**andscape, and then click **O**ptions.

12. Choose Note as the paper size.

13. Click **A**dvanced to display the Advanced Options dialog box.

14. Choose Bitmap [Type 3] for **S**end to Printer As. Under Graphics, change Halftone Frequency to 60 and Halftone Angle to 45. Then click OK.

15. Click OK to return to the Printers dialog box and then click Close. The Freelance Autographix support is now ready for use.

After you have installed the Autographix printer driver, you can print presentations to a file in the format Autographix can interpret. Then you can use the included communications software and a modem to send the file to the Autographix service center.

To print a presentation to an Autographix file, follow these steps:

1. In the Printer Setup dialog box, choose Autographix 4.1 as the printer.

2. In the same dialog box, make sure that you choose Set **M**argins for Slides.

3. Choose **P**rint from the **F**ile menu and then choose **F**ull Page as the Format. Make sure that you deselect **A**djust Color Library for Color Printing (if necessary).

4. Click **P**rint.

5. Enter the name of the output file that you want, and add a CPS file extension.

The final steps are to prepare an Autographix work order for the presentation and then to send the presentation with the ToAGX communications software. To prepare the work order, follow these steps:

1. Switch to the Windows Program Manager.

2. Double-click the Autographix Slide Service icon in the Lotus Applications Program Group. The ToAGX-Windows window then opens. A list of files in the default directory appears. To change the directory, use **S**witch Directories from the **F**ile menu.

3. Click **M**ix Instructions and specify the number of slides, transparencies, prints, or laser prints you want.

4. Click **O**rder Instructions and specify the instructions you want for the return of the completed work.

5. Click **B**illing Info and enter your billing address, credit card information, or account information.

6. Click Send to send the file to Autographix. The software compresses the output files and sends them to Autographix with the communications settings established in the **S**etup menu.

Summary

In this chapter, you learned to create printed output of your presentations in a number of formats. You learned to print standard presentation pages, speaker notes, audience notes, and handouts. You learned also how to go about creating 35mm slides for a presentation.

In the next three chapters, you learn how to customize Freelance by setting up SmartMaster sets, color palettes, and default settings for your own use.

Customizing Freelance Graphics

PART

VI

OUTLINE

Editing SmartMaster Sets
Using and Editing Color Palettes
Modifying the Default Settings

Editing SmartMaster Sets

As you learned in the early chapters of this book, SmartMaster sets are the key to the ease of using Freelance Graphics for Windows. SmartMaster sets provide both the background design for a presentation and the page layouts that hold the placement of "Click here..." blocks.

The dozens of SmartMaster sets that come with Freelance provide a wealth of professional presentation designs, but you still may want to create your own SmartMaster sets too. By making your own SmartMaster set, you can create a template for future presentations that includes your organization's logo, colors, and a design that picks up on the common themes of the presentations you give. If your organization is involved with real estate, for example, the SmartMaster set that you design might contain images of homes, blueprints, and office buildings. In addition, its colors and text fonts could reflect those used in your company logo, business cards, and signs.

In this chapter, you learn to customize existing SmartMaster sets and to create your own SmartMaster sets with special backgrounds and page designs. You learn also to edit a SmartMaster set so that it adds a graphic element to the background of all pages in a single presentation.

Understanding SmartMaster Sets

Each SmartMaster set contains 2 background designs, 11 page layouts, and 2 palettes. It is the combination of a background design, a page layout, and a palette that gives each presentation page its look.

Background designs are arrangements of graphic shapes, drawings, symbols, and even text that appear in the background of every page in the presentation. The uniformity of the backgrounds throughout the presentation gives the presentation a consistent, professional appearance. One of the two background designs, the Title page background, is used for any page that gets the Title page layout. The other background design, the Basic Layout background, is used for the other 10 page layouts (and any additional layouts you create). The Title page background and Basic Layout are slightly different. Figures 21.1 and 21.2 show the Title Page background and the Basic Layout background of the Spotlite SmartMaster set.

The 11 page layouts in each SmartMaster set contain different combinations and arrangements of "Click here..." blocks. You click these blocks to quickly add text, charts, symbols, and tables to a presentation. The combination of blocks on a page determines what the completed page will hold. The 1 Chart page layout has two "Click here..." blocks, for example. One block, a "Click here..." text block, positions and formats a page title. The other block, a "Click here..." chart block, positions a chart. Figure 21.3 shows the 1 Chart page layout.

The two palettes in each SmartMaster set, one that is color and one that is black and white, control the colors or gray shades of all the text, charts, symbols, tables, and graphic objects placed on pages either by clicking "Click here..." blocks or by moving them manually with the tools in the toolbox. You can use the color palette to see how screen shows, slides, or pages printed with a color printer will look. You can use the black-and-white palette to see how pages printed on a black-and-white printer will look. The palettes, which have the same name as the SmartMaster set, are contained in the SmartMaster set. To switch from one palette to the other while working on a presentation, click the Color/B&W button near the bottom of the Freelance window.

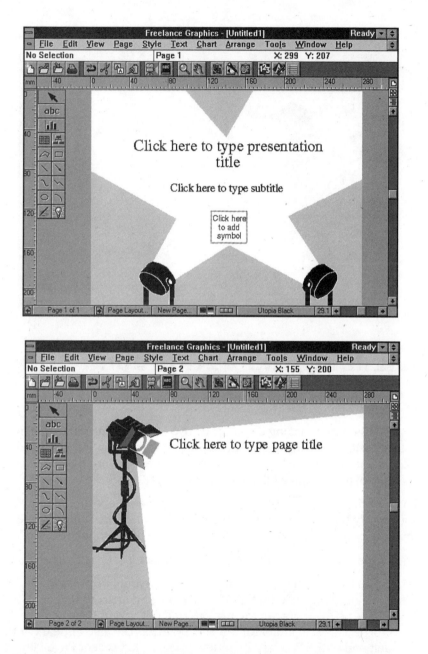

Fig. 21.1

The Title page background.

Fig. 21.2

The Basic Layout background.

In the rest of this chapter, you learn how to edit the backgrounds and page layouts and how to save the revised SmartMaster set as a new file. You learn how to edit color palettes in Chapter 22, "Using and Editing Color Palettes."

Fig. 21.3

The 1 Chart page layout.

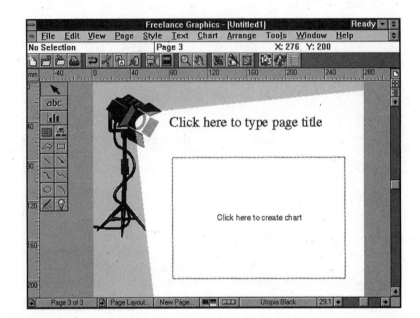

Changing the Background of a Presentation

You may find that making a change or two to the background design of an existing SmartMaster set adds just the customization you need. Adding your company logo to the upper corner of every page is one example of a customized design change.

To make the change to every presentation page except the title page, you modify the Basic Layout background. To make the same change to the Title page, you must modify the Title page background too.

To change a background design, follow these steps:

1. From the Edit menu, choose Edit Page Layouts or press Shift+F9. You also can click the Edit Page Layouts SmartIcon. Diagonal stripes appear across the background of Current Page or Page Sorter view. An indicator labeled SmartMaster also appears at the left end of the Freelance window title bar. In Current Page view, two additional buttons, the Return and Explain buttons, appear on the left.

Figure 21.4 shows Freelance in Current Page view after you choose
Edit Page Layouts. Figure 21.5 shows Freelance in Page Sorter
view after you choose Edit Page layouts. All 11 layouts appear in
the Page Sorter view window.

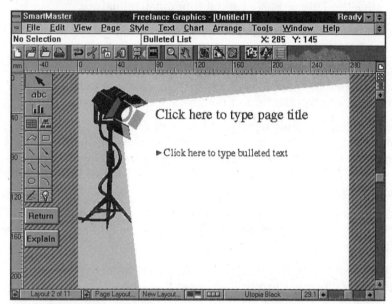

Fig. 21.4

The Freelance window
when in Edit Page
Layouts mode and
Current Page view.

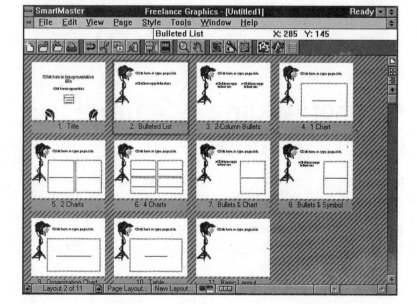

Fig. 21.5

The Freelance window
when in Edit Page
Layouts mode and Page
Sorter view.

2. To see a pop-up list of layouts when Freelance is in Current Page view, click the button at the lower-left corner of the window that lists the current layout number. Then choose either Title or Basic Layout from the list. If Freelance is in Page Sorter view, double-click the Title or Basic Layout thumbnail miniature.

3. Make whatever change you want to the design of the graphic objects on the page.

You can draw a logo or add a symbol from the symbol library, for example. If a bitmap graphic or drawn picture that you want exists in a file on disk, use the **File Import** command to import the file.

When you finish editing the layout you have chosen, you can switch to another layout by clicking the button at the lower left that displays the current layout number and then choosing a different layout from the list. Or you can switch to Page Sorter view and double-click the layout you want to edit.

To finish editing the page layouts, click the Return button under the toolbox, choose Edit Presentation Pages from the **Edit** menu, or press Shift+F9 again.

For information about editing page layouts, click the Explain button under the toolbox in Current Page view.

NOTE

To change the color of the presentation background, you must use the **B**ackground command from the **P**age menu. You learn about changing the background color later in this chapter.

Exercise: Adding a Symbol to the Background

In this exercise, you get the chance to add a symbol from the symbol library to the corner of all the pages of a presentation. By adding the symbol to the Basic Layout background, you don't have to add the symbol to each page manually.

To begin, follow these steps:

1. Start a new presentation by choosing **New** from the **File** menu.

2. Double-click the BULLETS.MAS SmartMaster set in the Choose a Look for Your Presentation dialog box.

3. Double-click the Basic Layout page layout in the Choose Page Layout dialog box. The Basic Layout has only one "Click here..." text block. Figure 21.6 shows the page in Current Page view.

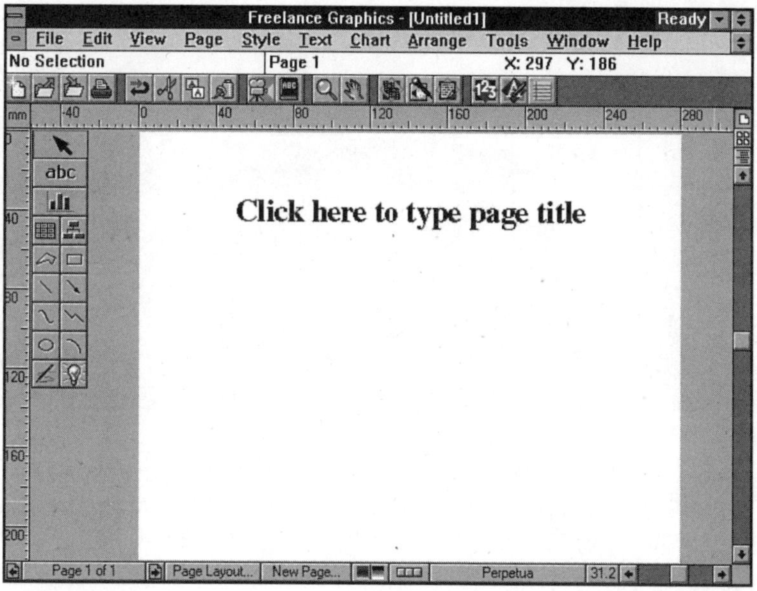

Fig. 21.6

The Basic Layout page layout of the Bullets SmartMaster set.

Then enter Edit Page Layouts mode by choosing **Edit Edit Page Layouts**, pressing Shift+F9, or clicking the Edit Page Layouts SmartIcon.

You can click the Page Layout button (displaying Layout 11 of 11) to examine the list of page layouts you can edit. A check appears next to the Basic Layout to indicate that you will be editing the design of the Basic Layout background.

To add the symbol, follow these steps:

1. Click the Symbol icon in the toolbox.

2. Scroll through the list of symbol categories in the Add Symbol to Page dialog box and then select BUILDING.SYM.

3. Choose the symbol of a house (the third symbol in the top row) and click OK. The house symbol appears on the page, as shown in figure 21.7.

Fig. 21.7

The house symbol as it appears on the page.

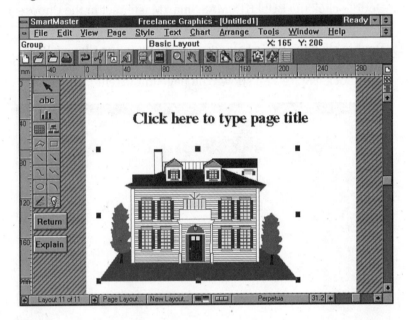

4. Press and hold down the Shift key and drag a corner handle of the symbol toward the center to reduce the symbol's size. Then drag the symbol to the upper-right corner of the page. It may overlap the text block on the page. Use figure 21.8 as a guide.

5. Drag the "Click here..." text block to the left so that it is clear of the house symbol. Figure 21.9 shows the revised positioning of the text block.

6. Switch to Page Sorter view by clicking the Page Sorter icon. Notice that the symbol you placed on the Basic Layout page appears on every page layout except the Title page layout. Notice also that the "Click here..." text block has been moved to the left on all the pages too.

All changes you have made to the Basic Layout page layout have flowed through to all the other page layouts except the Title page layout. You must edit the Title page layout separately.

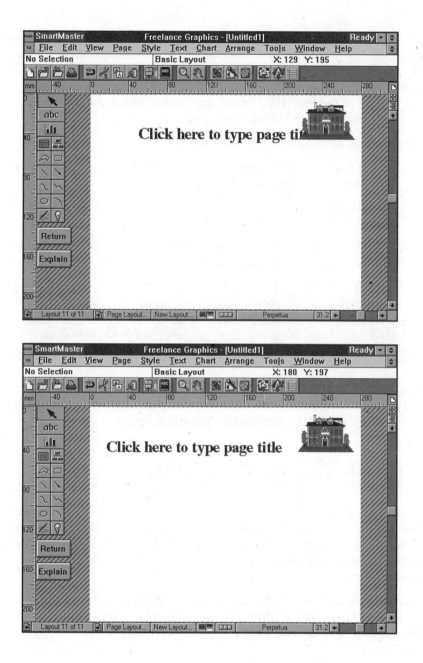

Fig. 21.8

The symbol correctly positioned on the page.

Fig. 21.9

Moving the page title text block.

To return to the presentation, choose Edit Presentation Pages from the **E**dit menu or press Shift+F9. The changes you made will affect the current presentation only. If you use the Bullets SmartMaster set to create a new presentation, the house symbol does not appear. To make the change to the SmartMaster set permanent, you must save the SmartMaster set by following these steps:

1. Choose Save **A**s from the **F**ile menu.

2. In the Save As dialog box, choose SmartMaster Set (MAS) from the File **T**ypes pull-down list.

3. Use the **D**irectories control to navigate to the MASTERS subdirectory under \FLW.

4. Highlight *.MAS in the File Name text box, type a DOS file name for the SmartMaster set, and click OK.

TIP

By following the Freelance convention of switching to Page Sorter view before you save a SmartMaster set, you can ensure that the SmartMaster set will be in Page Sorter view when you choose **F**ile **O**pen to open a SmartMaster set for editing.

The new SmartMaster set with a revision to the design of the page backgrounds appears on the list when you next start a new presentation and are prompted to choose a SmartMaster set.

Modifying a SmartMaster Set

Adding an object to the background of a SmartMaster set is only one of the modifications you can make to a SmartMaster set. You can also edit "Click here..." blocks to change their size and position, add new "Click here..." blocks, add new page layouts, and change the colors of the presentation.

To make any of these changes, you must edit the page layouts of a SmartMaster set. While editing the page layouts, you can make any other design change you want to a SmartMaster set too.

Switching to Edit Page Layouts Mode

Freelance offers two ways to enter the Edit Page Layouts mode. One method is to open a presentation and then choose Edit Page Layouts from the Edit menu or press Shift+F9. You have already used this method. The other method is to open a SmartMaster set by using Open from the File menu. To try this second approach, follow these steps:

1. From the File menu, choose Open.

2. From the pull-down list of file types, choose SmartMaster Set (MAS).

3. Use the Directories control in the Open File dialog box to navigate to the MASTERS subdirectory under the \FLW directory.

4. Choose a SmartMaster set from the list and click OK. The SmartMaster set opens in Edit Page Layouts mode.

To show that you are in Edit Page Layouts mode, Freelance displays in the title bar indicator SmartMaster. Diagonal lines also cross the background of the Freelance window. If Freelance is in Current Page view, Return and Explain buttons appear under the toolbox.

Editing Page Layouts

After you have entered Edit Page Layouts mode, you may want to switch to Page Sorter view to get a bird's-eye view on all the page layouts. In this view, the name of each layout appears under the thumbnail miniature of the layout. Figure 21.10 shows the page layouts in Page Sorter view.

First examine the Basic Layout page layout (page layout #11). The graphic objects and "Click here..." blocks on the Basic Layout page layout are also on all other page layouts, except the Title page layout, which has its own design. To modify the appearance of the SmartMaster set, you should start at the Basic Layout page layout. You can double-click its thumbnail miniature to view it in Current Page view.

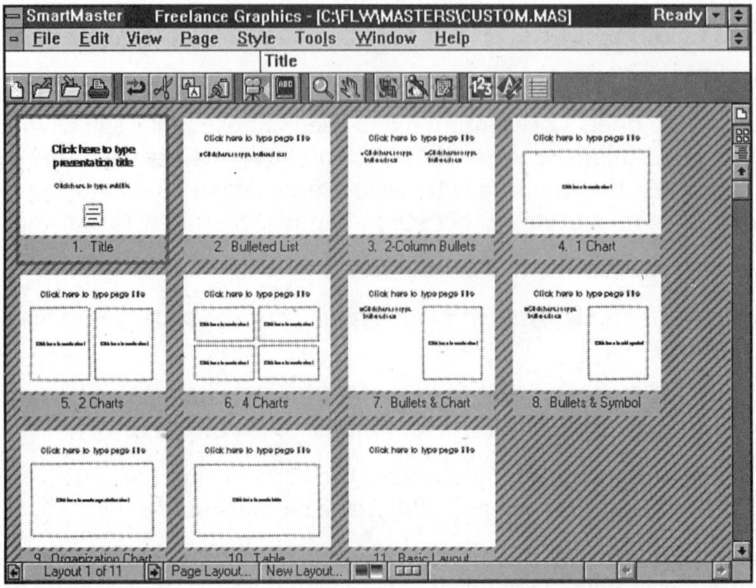

Fig. 21.10

The page layouts in
Page Sorter view.

When the Basic Layout page layout appears in Current Page view, you can move, resize, or edit existing "Click here..." blocks, add new "Click here..." blocks, or edit the drawing objects that form the background design.

The drawing objects in the background are usually grouped together, so you must click the group and then choose Ungroup from the Arrange menu. Then you can edit the individual objects in the same way that you edit any drawing object in Current Page view.

To change the appearance of additional "Click here..." blocks on other page layouts, turn to the page layout by clicking the Page Layout button at the lower-left corner of the Freelance window (the button displaying the current layout number) and then choosing a layout from the pop-up list. You also can click the left or right arrow buttons to move to the next or previous page layout. Another way to choose a different page layout is to switch to Page Sorter view and then double-click the thumbnail of the page layout.

After the page layout appears in Current Page view, you can move, resize, or edit "Click here..." blocks, add additional "Click here..." blocks, or add graphic shapes that appear on pages to which you apply this page layout.

When you finish editing page layouts, choose Edit Presentation Pages from the **E**dit menu, press Alt+F9, or click the Return button that appears below the toolbox in Current Page view.

Editing "Click here..." Text Blocks

You can move and resize existing "Click here..." text blocks in page layouts by selecting and dragging them or by dragging their handles just the way you move or resize any text block.

To change the prompt text that appears in a "Click here..." block, click the block, pause, and then click again to place a typing cursor inside the block. Then edit the text and type a new prompt. You can change "Click here to type page title" to "Click here and then type the name of this page," for example.

To add a new text block, follow these steps:

1. Click the Text icon in the toolbox.

   abc

2. With the pointer, draw a box on-screen that marks the boundaries of the "Click here..." text block and then click OK.

3. Double-click the text block, choose **A**ttributes [Text Block] from the **S**tyle menu, or click the Paragraph Styles SmartIcon. The Paragraph Styles dialog box appears, as shown in figure 21.11.

Fig. 21.11

The Paragraph Styles dialog box.

Paragraph Styles

1. Choose the paragraph style you want to change:

   ⦿ **A**ll   ○ **2**nd   ● Level 1
   ○ **1**st   ○ **3**rd   ▪ Level 2
                              ▸ Level 3

   [OK]
   [Cancel]
   [Preview]
   [Frame...]

2. Choose attributes for the paragraph style:

   Font & bullet

   Face: Arial MT   ☒ **N**ormal
   Size: 31.2   ☐ **B**old
   Text **c**olor: ☐ **I**talic
   Bullet: None   ☐ **U**nderline
   Bullet c**o**lor: ☐ Stri**k**eout
   B**u**llet size: 31.2

   [Spacing & Indents...]

   Justification: ☒ **W**ord wrap
   Vertical just.:

   ☐ Make **t**his a "Click here..." text block

   Prompt te**x**t:
   [Click here to add text]

4. Use the settings in the Paragraph Styles dialog box to establish a look for the three paragraph styles in the text block. First choose the paragraph style from the first set of controls and then change the attributes settings for that style. You also can change the frame for the block by clicking Frame or change the spacing and indentions for the block by clicking Spacing & Indents. To learn more about using the Paragraph Styles dialog box, see Chapter 11, "Adding and Formatting Text Blocks."

5. After you set all the attributes for the "Click here..." text block's paragraph styles, make sure that the Make This a "Click here..." Text Block check box is checked, and then edit the prompt text in the text box below the check box, if you want. If you do not mark the Make This a "Click here..." Text Block check box, the text that you enter in the text block then appears on every page that uses the page layout you are editing. The Make This a "Click here..." Text Block check box and the Prompt Text text box appear only because Freelance is in Edit Page Layouts mode.

6. Click OK. The prompt text appears in the text block.

7. Click OK again to finish and place the "Click here..." text block on the page.

After the text block is on the page, you can still drag the handles of the block to change its size. When you use the "Click here..." text block while creating presentation pages, the text that you enter will word-wrap within the block you create.

Editing "Click here..." Blocks for Charts, Tables, and Symbols

To change the size and placement of the charts, tables, and symbols that you create with "Click here..." blocks, you change the size and position of the "Click here..." blocks in the page layouts.

While in Edit Page Layouts mode, change to the page layout. Click and drag the "Click here..." blocks to any position on the page.

To change the appearance of the "Click here..." block or to change the type of "Click here..." block, double-click the block to open the Styles Attributes Rectangle dialog box, as shown in figure 21.12.

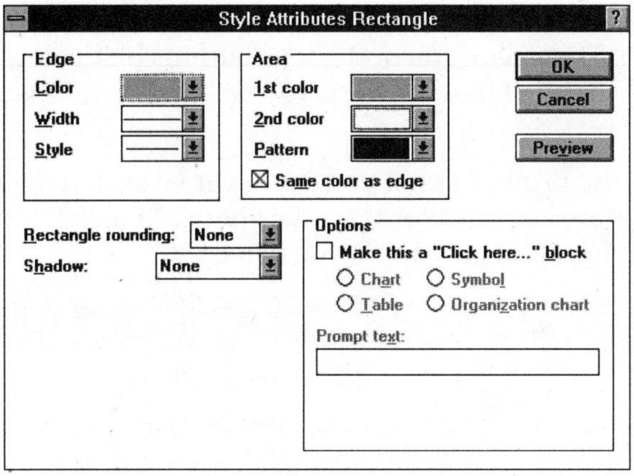

Fig. 21.12

The Style Attributes Rectangle dialog box.

Changing any of the settings in this dialog box changes the appearance of the rectangle that is part of the "Click here..." block. Changing the settings does not change the appearance of the chart, table, or symbol that you create by clicking the "Click here..." block, however. You can convert a "Click here..." block from one type to another by clicking one of the four buttons in the Options group of settings at the lower-right corner of the dialog box.

After you click a button, you can edit the prompt text in the text block below the Options area, but be sure to heed the warning just below the text block and include the suggested keyword within the prompt text. The presence of the keyword in the prompt informs Freelance of the type of "Click here..." block it is when you are creating presentation pages. If the keyword Symbol appears in the prompt, then clicking the "Click here..." block opens the Add Symbol to Page dialog box so that you can choose a symbol from the symbol library.

To create a new "Click here..." block on a page, follow these steps:

1. Click the Rectangle icon in the toolbox.

2. Draw a rectangle on the page that marks the position and size of the "Click here..." block.

3. Double-click the rectangle or choose **A**ttributes [Rectangle] from the **S**tyle menu. The Style Attributes Rectangle dialog box appears.

4. Make sure that the Make This a "Click here..." **B**lock check box is marked. Then click one of the four buttons just below to determine the type of block (Ch**a**rt, **T**able, Symbol, or Organization chart).

5. Modify the prompt text if you want, but be sure to include the appropriate keyword for the "Click here..." block type. The following list shows the keywords you can use:

If the Block Should Create	Be Sure To Include
Data chart	Chart or graph
Organization chart	Organization chart
Symbol	Symbol
Table chart	Table

TIP

By creating a custom SmartMaster set for a certain presentation and then customizing the prompt text in "Click here..." blocks, you can guide the creator of the presentation in placing certain elements on certain pages. You can create a text block prompt, for example, that instructs the user to "Click here to create Quarterly Sales Graph."

Creating a New Page Layout

All the SmartMaster sets that come with Freelance have 11 page layouts, and the same 11 page layout names are used in all SmartMaster sets. Therefore, when you apply a different SmartMaster set to a presentation, the new set can reformat the presentation because it has the same page layout names. The page that has the 1 Chart layout gets the design of the 1 Chart page layout in whatever SmartMaster set is chosen.

You can create additional page layouts of your own and give them unique names to accomplish specific page designs, but if you apply a different SmartMaster set that does not have a page layout of the same name, then the page is not formatted by the SmartMaster set. The content of the page will be placed on a blank page with no special formatting.

To create your own custom page design and save it in a new page layout, switch to Edit Page Layouts mode and then click the New Layout button at the bottom of the window. The New Layout dialog box appears, as shown in figure 21.13.

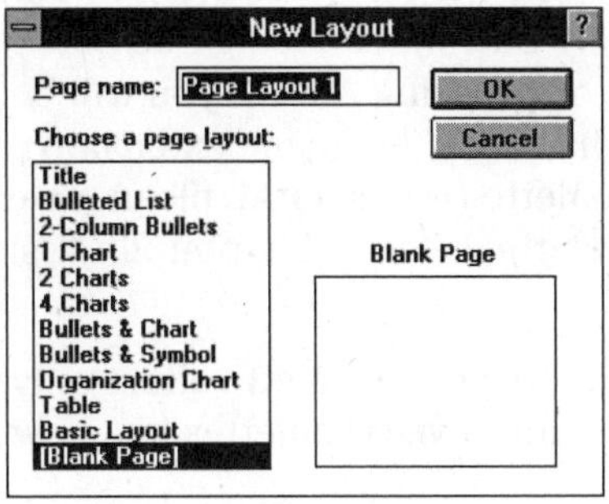

New Layout

Page name: Page Layout 1

Choose a page layout:

Title
Bulleted List
2-Column Bullets
1 Chart
2 Charts
4 Charts
Bullets & Chart
Bullets & Symbol
Organization Chart
Table
Basic Layout
[Blank Page]

Blank Page

OK

Cancel

Fig. 21.13

The New Layout dialog box.

Enter a new page name in the **P**age Name text box and click the Basic Layout page layout to start with the design elements found on every page. Then click OK.

TIP

A shortcut to creating a new page layout is to click the Duplicate Page SmartIcon or press Alt+F7 to duplicate the currently selected page layout. Then you can edit the duplicate.

Add "Click here..." blocks and other design elements. Then switch to Page Sorter view, choose Save **A**s from the **F**ile menu, and save the file as a SmartMaster set file type. If you opened the SmartMaster set with the **F**ile **O**pen command, you can choose **S**ave from the **F**ile menu to update the current SmartMaster set with the changes.

Changing Presentation Colors

The colors of all objects in a presentation are controlled by one of the two palettes. One palette contains colors; the other palette has black, white, and shades of gray. Each SmartMaster set contains both palettes.

Changing the Color of Presentation Objects

You do not need to be in Edit Page Layouts mode to modify the color palettes. You can edit a palette by simply choosing Edit Palette from the Style menu at any time. When you switch to black and white by clicking the Color/B&W button, choosing Use Black & White Palette from the Style menu, or pressing Alt+F9, you will be editing the black-and-white palette (it has a BW file name extension). Otherwise, you will be editing the color palette (it has a PAL file name extension). To learn how to edit a color palette, refer to Chapter 22, "Using and Editing Color Palettes."

The changes you make to a color palette affect only the current presentation unless you save the revised palettes in a new SmartMaster set.

Changing the Background Color

To change the color of the background of pages in a presentation, choose Background from the Page menu. The Page Background dialog box appears (see fig. 21.14).

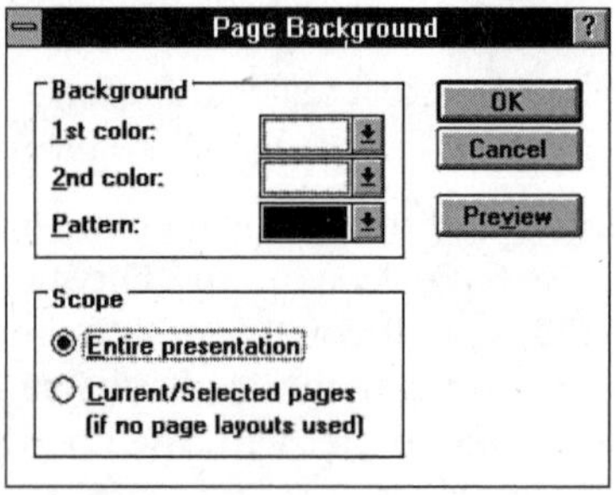

Fig. 21.14

The Page Background dialog box.

To choose a solid background color, change the 1st color by clicking the pull-down button and then clicking a color from the presentation's color palette. To create a gradient background, choose a 1st color and a 2nd color and then choose a gradient pattern from the menu of available patterns.

The color change you make affects all the pages in the presentation unless you have selected a page (or more than one page in Page Sorter view) that has no page layout. If the pages you have selected have a page layout of None, you can click Current/Selected Pages to change the background color of only the selected pages.

Exercise: Creating a Custom SmartMaster Set

In this exercise, you use many of the skills presented in this chapter to create a customized SmartMaster set for your needs. The SmartMaster set must have a blue background (your company color) and your company logo on each page and must include a presentation file number at the lower-left corner, for record-keeping purposes.

To begin the exercise, you open the SmartMaster set called CUSTOM.MAS. This SmartMaster set is a generic design that includes all 11 page layouts, so it is a good place to start when you want to design a new SmartMaster set almost from scratch.

Opening a SmartMaster Set

To open a SmartMaster set for editing, you attach it to a new presentation and then switch to Edit Page Layouts mode, or you can open the SmartMaster set with **File Open**. The second method is a little more direct, so follow these steps to use it:

1. From the **File** menu, choose **Open**. If you have just started Freelance, you can press Esc first to close the Choose a Look for Your Presentation dialog box.

2. In the Open File dialog box, choose SmartMaster Set (MAS) from the pull-down list of file types.

3. From the **Directories** display, double-click the open folder FLW. Then double-click the closed folder MASTERS to open it (this opens the C:\FLW\MASTERS directory). If your SmartMaster sets are in a different directory, navigate to it by using the **Directories** control.

4. Scroll through the list of SmartMaster sets, find CUSTOM.MAS, and double-click it.

The page layouts of the SmartMaster set should appear in Page Sorter view unless someone before you has modified the Custom SmartMaster set. If Freelance is not in Page Sorter view, click the Page Sorter icon. Then, if necessary, switch to Edit Page Layouts mode by pressing Shift+F9. Figure 21.15 shows the Custom SmartMaster set in Page Sorter view. Notice that the indicator in the title bar reads SmartMaster to inform you that Freelance is in Edit Page Layouts mode.

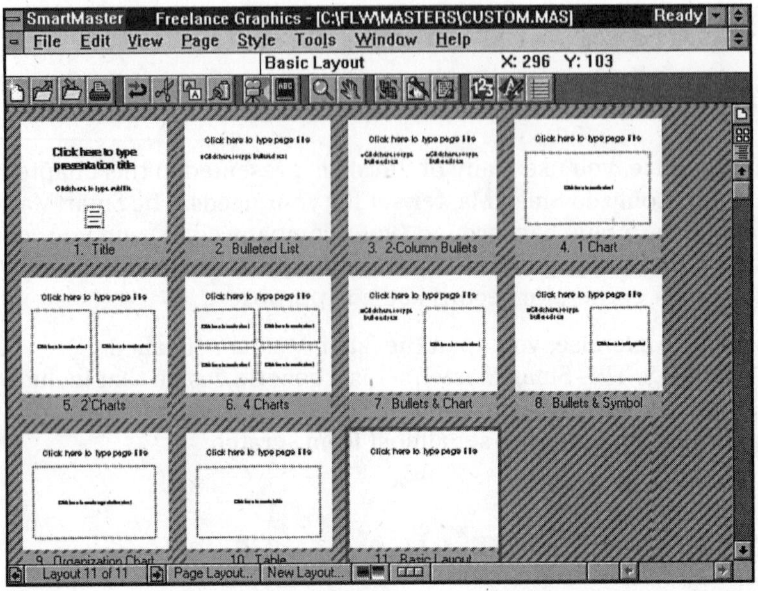

Fig. 21.15

The Custom
SmartMaster set in
Page Sorter view.

Changing the Background Color

Your first editing step is to change the background color. After you
choose the background color you want, you can coordinate the colors
of foreground objects, tables, and charts. To set the background color,
follow these steps:

1. From the **P**age menu, choose **B**ackground. The Page Background
   dialog box appears, as shown in figure 21.16.

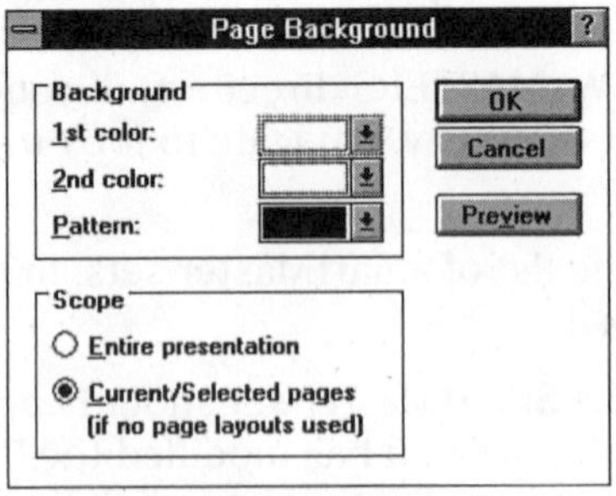

Fig. 21.16

The Page Background
dialog box.

2. In the Page Background dialog box, click the current **1**st color.
   The color palette is displayed.

3. Click the color Blue. It should be the third color in the first column. You can click and hold down the mouse button as you drag the pointer from color to color. When the pointer is on Blue, Palette color: blue appears at the top of the color palette window.

4. Click the current **2**nd color and then choose one of the blacks from the sixth or seventh row of colors in the color palette. (You may be tempted to pick the black in the first row of colors, but do not. You may want to change this black to another color later because it controls the color of text in the presentation. Changing this color to another color would change the background color too.)

5. Click the current **P**attern and choose the vertical gradient in the display of patterns (it should be the sixth pattern in the first column).

6. Make sure that the setting for Scope is **E**ntire Presentation.

7. Click OK. You will see the background color change in all 11 page layouts.

Editing the Color Palette

To make the text readable against the blue background, you must change its color from black to a light shade, perhaps a light yellow or white. The most efficient way to make such a change is to edit the color palette. To do so, follow these steps:

1. From the **S**tyle menu, choose **E**dit Palette. The Edit Palette dialog box appears, as shown in figure 21.17.

   The first three colors in the top row of the palette colors determine the color of text in the presentation.

2. Click the first color and then click the color under **M**odify Color.

3. In the color library display, click White.

4. Click the second color in the first row of the color palette and then click the color under **M**odify Color.

5. In the color library display, click Parchment (the lightest shade of yellow).

6. Click the third color in the first row of the color palette and then click the color under **M**odify Color once again.

Fig. 21.17

The Edit Palette dialog box.

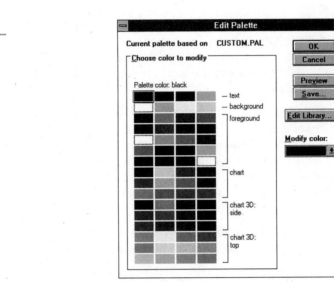

7. Click White once again.

8. Click OK in the Edit Palette dialog box. The titles of all page layouts become white, the subtitles are parchment, and the chart text color is white. When you save the SmartMaster set, the revised palette is saved with it.

Adding a Logo to the Background

Next, you add a logo to the background of presentation pages. To add the logo to every page, you need to place the logo on both the Title page layout and the Basic Layout page layout. When you place the logo on the Basic Layout page layout, the logo appears on every other page layout except the Title page layout.

To switch to the Title page layout, double-click it in Page Sorter view. The Title page layout then appears in Current Page view, as shown in figure 21.18.

To make room for the logo, left-align the title and subtitle "Click here..." blocks. Text that you type into the blocks will be left-aligned too. To left-align the blocks, follow these steps:

1. Click the "Click here to type presentation title" block to select it.

2. Click the right mouse button and then click Attributes from the pop-up menu. (Attributes is the only choice.)

3. In the Paragraph Styles dialog box that appears, click the left-aligned **J**ustification button and then click OK. From this dialog box, you also can make other changes to the appearance of the text on the title page, such as choosing a different typeface and point size. You should make similar changes to the text throughout the presentation to ensure consistency, though. For this exercise, leave the other attributes of the text unchanged.

4. Repeat steps 1 through 3 for the subtitle "Click here..." block.

5. Next drag the two blocks to the left a little to make still more room on the right. You can select both blocks and then use the **Arrange Align** command to align their left sides.

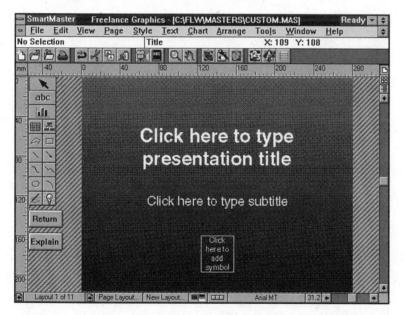

Fig. 21.18

The Title page layout in Current Page view.

Finally, you add the logo to the page layout. If your company logo is in a separate file on disk, you can import the file and then place it on the page. If you have already created your company logo, you may have added it to the symbol library so that you can easily retrieve the logo in situations such as this. To simulate a logo stored in the symbol library, choose another symbol from the symbol library by following these steps:

1. Click the Symbol icon in the toolbox.

2. Choose the symbol category FLAGS.SYM.

3. Scroll to the bottom of the display of symbols and select symbol 44 of 44, the white flag.

4. Click OK.

5. Reposition and resize the symbol so that it fits to the right of the titles.

Because you have added a preset logo to the presentation title page, you no longer need the "Click here to add symbol" block. Select it and press Del to remove it. Figure 21.19 shows the Title page layout at this point.

Fig. 21.19

The edited Title page layout.

Adding a "Click here..." Text Block

While still editing the Title page layout, you need to make one last change. By adding a "Click here..." text block in the lower-left corner of the page, you can prompt the author of the presentation to enter a presentation number for cataloging purposes.

To create this "Click here..." text block, follow these steps:

1. Click the Text icon in the toolbox.

   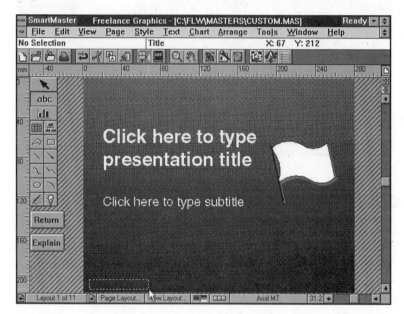

2. With the pointer, drag a small text block that can contain one line of text in the lower-left corner of the page, as shown in figure 21.20.

Fig. 21.20

Dragging to create the boundaries of a "Click here..." text block.

3. Click OK without typing any prompt text in the text block.

4. Double-click the empty text block to open the Paragraph Styles dialog box.

5. Change the point size of the text to 18 points by clicking the current setting next to Size and then selecting 18.

6. Click the check box next to Make This a "Click here..." Text Block.

7. Edit the prompt text below to read "Click here to add presentation number."

8. Click OK to place the edited "Click here..." text block on the page. Figure 21.21 shows the completed Title page layout.

Fig. 21.21

The completed Title
page layout.

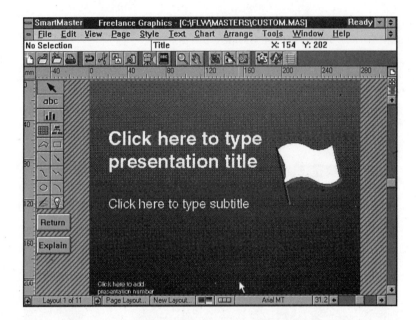

Adding the Logo to the Basic Layout

To have the logo appear on every other page in the presentation, you must place the logo on the Basic Layout page layout. To switch to the Basic Layout page layout, click the button that reads Layout 1 of 11 and then select `11. Basic Layout` from the pop-up list of page layouts.

Follow these steps to left-align the title and move it to the left to make room for the logo.

1. Select the "Click here to type page title" block.

2. Click the right mouse button.

3. Choose Attributes from the pop-up menu.

4. Click the left-align **J**ustification button.

5. Click OK.

6. Drag the text block a little to the left to make room for the logo at the right.

Then select the flag logo from the symbol library by following these steps:

1. Click the Symbol icon in the toolbox.

2. Choose FLAGS.SYM as the symbol category.

3. Scroll through the display of symbols and choose the white flag symbol again.

4. Resize and drag the flag into position to the right of the page title.

To see the edited SmartMaster set as a whole, switch to Page Sorter view by clicking the Page Sorter icon. Notice that the flag appears on every page in the presentation. Figure 21.22 shows the SmartMaster set as it appears in Page Sorter view.

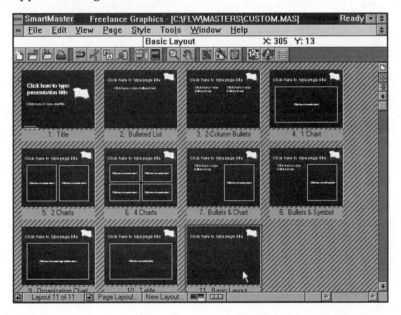

Fig. 21.22

The completed SmartMaster set in Page Sorter view.

The last step is to save the SmartMaster set with a new name. You want to avoid overwriting the unmodified Custom SmartMaster set so that you always have it as a starting point for future custom SmartMaster sets. Follow these steps:

1. From the File menu in Page Sorter view, choose Save **As**.

2. Choose SmartMaster Set (MAS) as the File **Type**.

3. In the File **Name** text box, enter a DOS file name for the SmartMaster set and then click OK. The edited SmartMaster set will be saved as a new set in the MASTERS directory. When you next start a new presentation, it will appear as one of the SmartMaster set choices.

4. To leave Edit Page Layouts mode, press Alt+F9 or choose **Edit** Edit Presentatio**n** Pages.

Summary

In this chapter, you learned how to customize existing SmartMaster sets and create SmartMaster sets of your own. In the next chapter, you learn to edit the color palettes that control the colors of all elements of your presentations.

Using and Editing Color Palettes

Even though Freelance can display and print a stunning 256 colors, the fact is that most presentations are printed in black and white. That is why Freelance Graphics 2.0 for Windows includes a black-and-white palette in each SmartMaster set. The black-and-white palette displays the presentation in the same black and white and in shades of gray both on-screen and when printed.

But if you are fortunate enough to have a color printer or you create slides from your Freelance presentations, you may want to know how the Freelance color palettes work. You need to know about color palettes if you intend to create your own SmartMaster sets with custom color schemes that match the colors used by your organization or a client.

If you are happy with the colors of the SmartMaster sets that come with Freelance or a customized SmartMaster set that has been provided for you, you may never need to learn about color palettes. After all, the colors in the SmartMaster sets have been coordinated by professional artists, and most of us would have difficulties creating better colors.

Understanding the SmartMaster Color Palettes

Each SmartMaster set has two, built-in color palettes. One palette chooses colors for the background of each page and for each of the objects on the page. The other chooses shades of gray instead. You can easily switch between the two palettes by clicking the Color/B&W button in the status bar at the bottom of the Freelance window. You can also switch palettes by pressing Alt+F9 or by choosing either Use **B**lack & White Palette or Use **C**olor Palette from the **S**tyle menu. Figure 22.1 shows the Style menu.

Fig. 22.1

The **S**tyle menu.

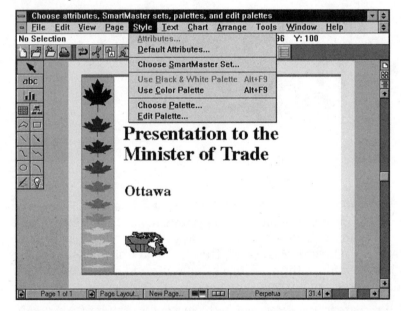

Each palette has 64 positions that control the colors of 64 different parts of a presentation. The color in position 3, for example, is used for all text in data charts (the titles, axis titles, value labels, legend entries, and all other text in the chart). The color in position 22 is used for bullets, lines, and arrows. When you choose a different SmartMaster set, the new colors in positions 3 and 22 determine the new colors of data chart text as well as bullets, lines, and arrows. Most other positions in the palette have new colors too, so that the presentation gets a complete color overhaul.

Later in this chapter, you learn which parts of a presentation are controlled by each position in the color palettes and how to change the colors.

Selecting an Existing Palette

In addition to the two palettes that are built into each SmartMaster set, Freelance comes with a handful of additional palettes you can attach to any presentation. When you choose Choose **P**alette from the **S**tyle menu or click the Choose Palette SmartIcon, you find six color palettes or five black-and-white palettes in the Choose Palette dialog box (see fig. 22.2). Whether you see the color palettes or the black-and-white palettes in the Choose Palette dialog box depends on whether you were viewing the presentation with a color or black-and-white palette.

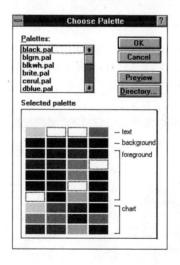

Fig. 22.2

The Choose Palette dialog box.

The palettes that come with Freelance are stored in the same directory in which the SmartMaster sets are stored, usually C:\FLW\MASTERS. Color palettes have a PAL extension. Black-and-white palettes have a BW extension.

Editing a Color Palette

Many people feel no need to modify any of the colors in a Freelance color palette. The color palettes in the SmartMaster sets tastefully coordinate the entire combination of colors used in their presentation.

If you create your own SmartMaster set with a custom background design and logo, however, you will also want to create a pair of palettes, both color and black and white, that either creates a pleasing combination of colors or matches the specific color scheme used for all the printed materials that you generate (in letterheads, logos, and insignias).

When you edit a palette, the colors in the presentation to which the palette is attached change, and any new presentations that you create with the palette show the revised colors. However, presentations that were created with the old version of the palette do not change, unless you specifically choose the revised color palette by using the Choose Palette command.

TIP

After you modify the color palette for a presentation, you can return to the original colors by again selecting the original SmartMaster set.

You may want to start with one of the preexisting color palettes that come with Freelance so that you have a set of colors to edit. Then choose **E**dit Palette from the **S**tyle menu. The Edit Palette dialog box appears (see fig. 22.3).

Fig. 22.3

The Edit Palette dialog box.

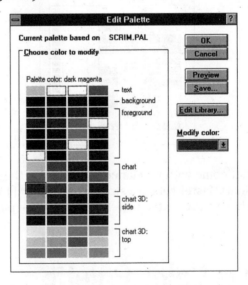

The name of the current color palette appears near the top of the dialog box. Below are the 64 positions that correspond to different parts of the presentation. A color is shown in each position. To see the name of the color in each position, click the color once. The name appears just above the colors. The six categories of positions are identified to the right of the colors, starting with text.

To modify a color, first click the color and then click either the color below **M**odify Color or the pull-down button next to **M**odify Color. Click any of the 256 colors or shades of gray in the color library that appears (see fig. 22.4).

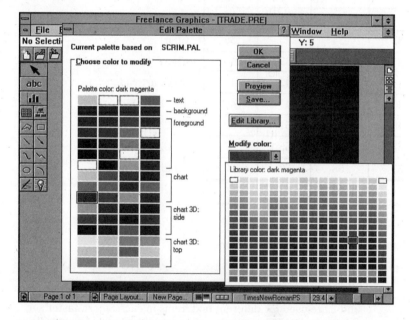

Fig. 22.4

The entire library of 256 colors.

After you modify colors in the color palette, you can click the Preview button to see the effect on the current presentation. When you are satisfied, click **S**ave, enter a new file name for the palette, and then click OK. Click OK in the Edit Palette dialog box to return to the current presentation.

Tables 22.1 and 22.2 identify the presentation element that is controlled by each of the positions in a chart palette. Match the number in table 22.1 to the description of the number in table 22.2.

Table 22.1 The Color Palette Positions

1	2	3	4	Text
5	6	7	8	Background
9	10	11	12	Foreground
13	14	15	16	Foreground
17	18	19	20	Foreground
21	22	23	24	Foreground
25	26	27	28	Foreground
29	30	31	32	Chart
33	34	35	36	Chart
37	38	39	40	Chart
41	42	43	44	3D Chart: Side
45	46	47	48	3D Chart: Side
49	50	51	52	3D Chart: Side
53	54	55	56	3D Chart: Top
57	58	59	60	3D Chart: Top
61	62	63	64	3D Chart: Top

Table 22.2 Descriptions of Positions

Text Colors

1–2   Color assignments differ in each SmartMaster set. Positions 1 and 2 are used for different text items in each SmartMaster set. For example, the color in position 1 might be used for page titles, and the color in position 2 might be used for subtitles.

3   Data chart text (titles, axis titles, labels and values, legends, notes, and number grid).

4   Color of faded text on build pages.

Background Colors

5–8   Color assignments vary in each SmartMaster set.

Foreground Colors

9–14   Color assignments differ in each SmartMaster set.

15   Drawing object area and edge.

16   Frame edge (for charts, legend frames, headings and notes, and number grids) and background edge (for data charts and organization charts).

17   Frame area (for text, "Click here..." blocks, data chart text, legends, headings, and notes) and background area (for data charts, number grids, and organization charts).

18   Organization chart boxes, text table background, and cell background.

19   3D organization chart sides.

20   3D organization chart bottoms.

21   Shadows of objects, data charts, text tables, and organization charts.

22   Bullets, lines, and arrows.

23   Connecting lines in organization charts.

24   3D data chart floors.

25   Data chart grids and grid lines in a number grid.

26   Edges (for bar charts, pie charts, area charts, 3D area/line charts, and organization chart boxes).

27   Text table borders and cell borders.

28   3D data chart walls.

Data Chart Colors

29–40   Data series A through L. After series L, the colors repeat.

3D Charts: Side Colors

41–52   Data series A through L. After series L, the colors repeat.

3D Charts: Top Colors

53–64   Data series A through L. After series L, the colors repeat.

If you change the data chart colors in positions 29–40, you must also choose corresponding side and top colors in positions 41–52 and 53–64 so that the sides and tops of 3D bars match the fronts. For example, if you choose a medium yellow for position 29 (the front of data series A bars), you may want to choose a dark yellow for position 41 (the side of data series A bars) and a bright yellow for position 53 (the top of data series A bars).

Editing the Library Colors

Each palette that shows colors rather than shades of gray displays 64 of the 256 colors in the color library. If none of the colors in the color library is an exact match of the color you need, you can edit any existing color.

Changes to the color library are part of the current color palette only. If you do not save the palette, the changes appear only in the current presentation. If you save the palette as a separate file, you can use the revised color library in other presentations.

To edit the color library, choose Edit Palette from the **S**tyle menu and then click **E**dit Library. The Edit Library dialog box appears (see fig. 22.5).

Fig. 22.5

The Edit Library
dialog box.

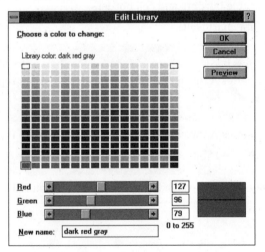

The entire array of 256 colors appears in this dialog box. It also has three sliders that enable you to vary the amount of red, green, and blue in the currently selected color. Click any color that you want to modify, and then drag the button in each slider or change the value in the text box to the right of each slider (enter a number from 0 and 255). You see the result of the changes that you make in the color swatch to the right.

After you modify a color, you may want to edit its name in the **New Name** text box at the bottom of the dialog box. You can then click another color to modify.

Summary

In this chapter, you learned to customize the color library and color palettes that determine the colors or shades of gray that appear in each presentation. You may need this information only if you create custom presentation designs.

In the next chapter, you learn to customize the way Freelance works as a whole, setting the basic operation and defaults for many of the program's features.

23

CHAPTER

Modifying the Default Settings

The default settings for Freelance are initially set so that you can be productive from the moment you have the program installed. But as you become more familiar with Freelance, you may want to change some of these settings to fit the way you like to work.

In this chapter, you learn to customize the settings for the Freelance window, some of the tools and commands, and the SmartIcon palette.

Setting the View Preferences

By changing the Freelance View Preferences, you can change settings that determine how some of the elements in the Freelance window look. You can decide whether the function key panel displays at the bottom of the window, for example, or whether the margins on the page should be delineated.

To access the View Preferences dialog box, select **View Preferences** from the **View** menu. The View Preferences dialog box appears, as shown in figure 23.1.

Fig. 23.1

The View Preferences dialog box.

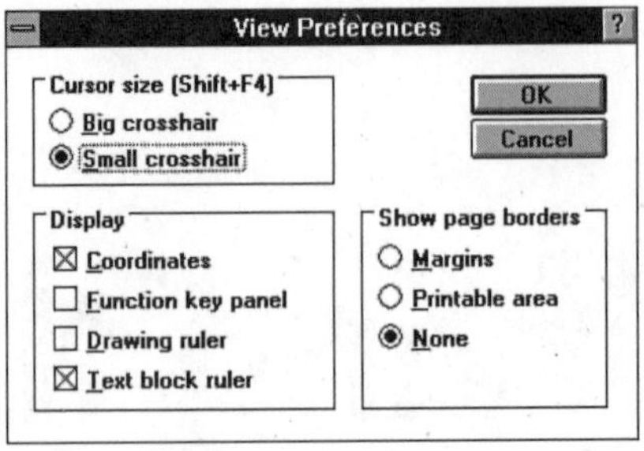

The View Preferences dialog box shows three groups of controls. The Cursor Size controls enable you to change the size of the drawing cursor when you are using the drawing tools of Freelance. Click one of the two options or press Shift+F4 to toggle between **B**ig Crosshair and **S**mall Crosshair.

The Display controls enable you to turn on and off four visual displays by clicking the check box next to each control. Choose the **C**oordinates option to display the current distance of the cursor from the upper-left corner of the page; this distance is displayed in the current units, as set in the Units & Grids dialog box. Choose the **F**unction Key Panel setting to display the function key panel along the bottom edge of the Freelance window. This panel displays the function-key shortcuts that are available. Pressing the Alt, Ctrl, and Shift keys displays the alternative function-key combinations in the function key panel. Choose the **D**rawing Ruler setting to display the drawing ruler across the top and down the left side of the display in Current Page view. The units in the ruler are set in the Units & Grids dialog box. Choose the **T**ext Block Ruler setting to display the text block ruler at the top of selected text blocks. Figure 23.2 shows all four of these elements.

The Show Page Borders controls enable you to turn on the display of a dashed line that shows the current **M**argins (as set in the Page Setup dialog box) or the **P**rintable Area (as determined by the printer selected in the Printer Setup dialog box). The third choice, **N**one, displays no page borders.

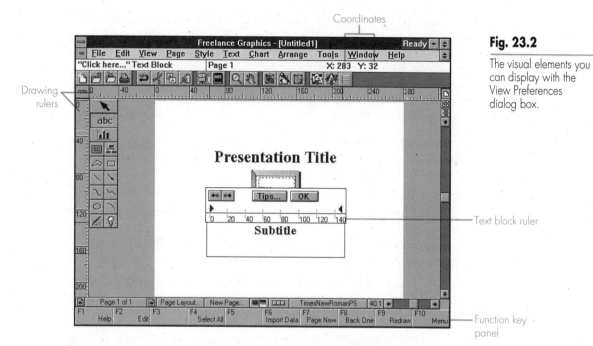

Fig. 23.2

The visual elements you can display with the View Preferences dialog box.

Changing the User Setup

The User Setup command in the Tools menu leads to the User Setup dialog box with its many controls for changing the way Freelance works. Figure 23.3 shows the User Setup dialog box.

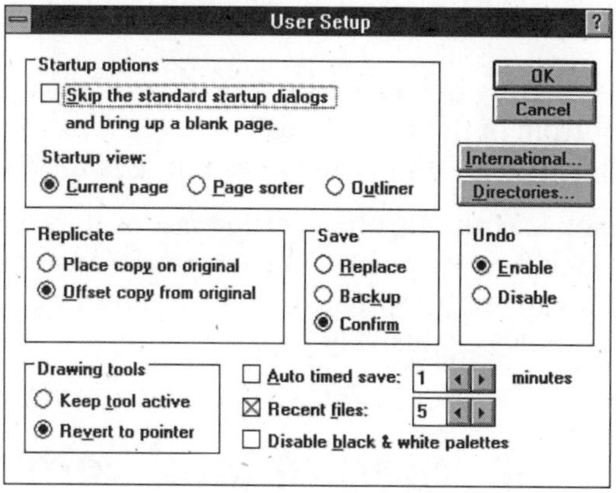

Fig. 23.3

The User Setup dialog box.

The Startup Options settings determine the screen that Freelance presents when you first start the program. Click **S**kip the Standard Startup Dialogs and Bring Up a Blank Page to skip the two dialog boxes that ask you to choose a SmartMaster set and a page layout. Freelance shows a blank page instead. The three mutually exclusive Startup View buttons enable you to start up the program in **C**urrent Page view, **P**age Sorter view, or **O**utliner view.

The Replicate options enable you to determine whether the copies of objects created when you choose the **R**eplicate command will appear on top of or offset from the original.

With the Save options, you can determine whether a presentation that you save replaces the existing saved presentation (**R**eplace), replaces the existing saved presentation and creates a backup copy of the previous saved version (Bac**k**up), or prompts you to indicate whether to replace or back up whenever you save a presentation (Confir**m**).

The Undo options enable you to disable Undo. The default, **E**nable, is almost always preferable because you can undo the last 10 actions by clicking the Undo SmartIcon or choosing Undo from the **E**dit menu.

By using the Drawing Tools options, you can decide whether the current drawing tool you are using should remain active when you finish with it (Keep **T**ool Active) or whether the tool should become inactive in favor of the pointer (Revert to Pointer).

The Auto Timed Save setting automatically saves a copy of the current presentation at the interval you set with the increment or decrement buttons. You must click the check box next to Auto Timed Save to turn it on.

The Recent **F**iles setting determines the number of files that are displayed at the bottom of the **F**ile menu. These are files that you worked on recently. Clicking any of the file names reopens the file.

The Disable **B**lack & White Palettes setting makes it impossible to switch to the black & white palette in each SmartMaster set. Turn this option on only if you are printing to a color printer or generating color slides or screen shows exclusively.

Changing the International Settings

Clicking **I**nternational in the User Setup dialog box leads to the International User Setup dialog box (see fig. 23.4). This dialog box contains controls for changing how times, dates, numbers, and currency are displayed in Freelance. The defaults shown are the current International settings for Windows. To change the Windows settings, you can double-click International in the Windows Control Panel. Any changes that you make to the settings in Freelance override the Windows International settings. They will be used in Freelance only.

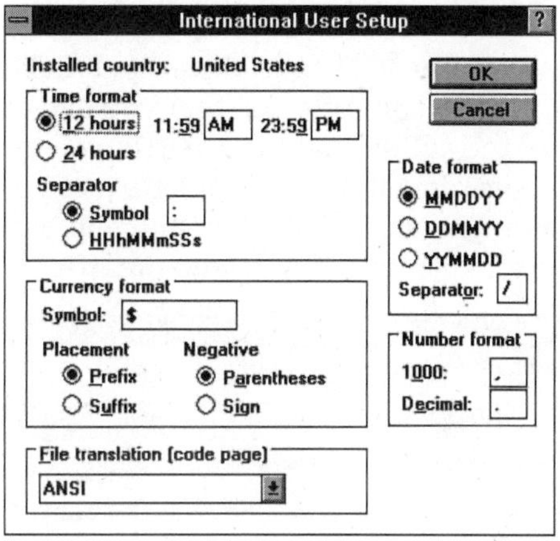

Fig. 23.4

The International User Setup dialog box.

Changing the Default Directories

Clicking **d**irectories in the User Setup dialog box leads to the User Setup Directories dialog box, as shown in figure 23.5.

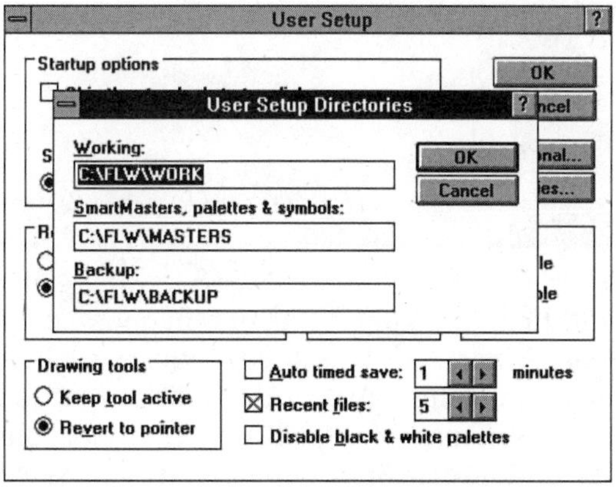

Fig. 23.5

The User Setup Directories dialog box.

The **W**orking directory is the directory in which your saved presentations are stored. The **S**martMasters, Palettes & Symbols directory is the directory in which these elements are installed during the Freelance installation process. The **B**ackup directory is the directory in which backup copies of presentations are saved when you choose Bac**k**up while saving a presentation.

Using SmartIcons

To make choosing commands especially easy, Freelance provides a set of on-screen icons, called SmartIcons, that you can click. Each icon shows a picture of the action that the SmartIcon performs. By default, the SmartIcons appear in a horizontal palette just below the edit line in the Freelance window, but you can place them in other positions on the window too. Figure 23.6 shows the default SmartIcon palette.

Fig. 23.6

The default SmartIcon palette just below the edit line.

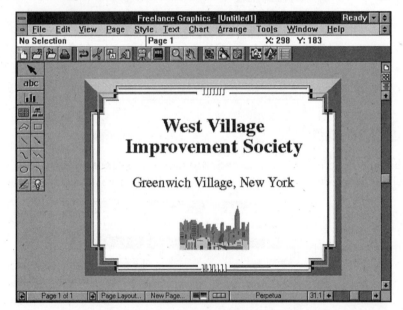

The default SmartIcon palette represents the most common actions you perform in Freelance, such as saving your work in a file, but SmartIcons represent many other commands and actions too. You can add these SmartIcons from the library of SmartIcons to the current palette, or create additional SmartIcon palettes and switch from one palette to another as you perform different types of work in Freelance. For example, you can create a SmartIcon palette containing SmartIcons you can use while drawing and editing objects. You can create a second

SmartIcon palette full of icons that are useful while you create and edit data charts. Then you can easily switch from one SmartIcon palette to another while you work in Freelance.

To find out the name of a SmartIcon, click it with the right mouse button. The name appears in the title bar of the Freelance window. By holding down the right mouse button and sliding the mouse along the SmartIcon palette, you can see the name of each SmartIcon.

Choosing a SmartIcon Palette

After you create a new SmartIcon palette, its name appears in a pop-up menu when you click the SmartIcon button in the status bar at the bottom of the Freelance window. Select the SmartIcon palette that you want from this list. The pop-up menu also provides a command that hides the SmartIcons if you have no need for them. Hiding SmartIcons leaves more space on-screen for the presentation pages.

Another way to choose one of the SmartIcon palettes you've created is to choose SmartIcons from the Tools menu or click the Customize SmartIcons SmartIcon. Either way, the SmartIcons dialog box is displayed (see fig. 23.7).

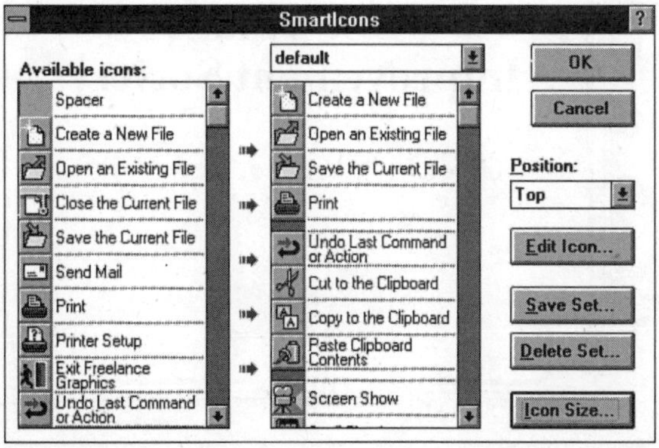

Fig. 23.7

The SmartIcons dialog box.

The name of the current SmartIcon palette appears in a text box near the top of the dialog box. To change palettes, pull down the menu of sets and then choose a different palette from the list.

Yet another way to change SmartIcon palettes is to click the Next Icon Set SmartIcon. This switches to the next SmartIcon palette on the list.

Changing the SmartIcon Palette Position

By default, the current SmartIcon palette appears across the top of the Freelance window. You can move the SmartIcon palette to another position on-screen, however, or place the palette in a floating window that you can move around the screen.

To change the position of the SmartIcon palette, choose SmartIcons from the Tools menu and then pull down the menu under **Position**. The possible settings are Floating, Left, Right, Top, or Bottom.

Choose Floating to place the SmartIcons in a small window on-screen, as shown in figure 23.8. You can drag the borders of the window to stretch the window. The SmartIcons then rearrange inside. To move the window, drag the very small title bar that runs vertically along the left end of the floating SmartIcon palette window. To close the window and hide the SmartIcons, click the white button in the title bar.

Fig. 23.8

The SmartIcons in a floating window.

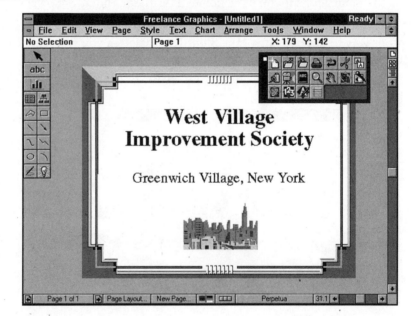

Adding and Deleting SmartIcons

The default SmartIcon palette shows only a small sample of the available SmartIcons. To make choosing commands that you frequently use easy, you may want to choose other SmartIcons from the library of SmartIcons.

To add or delete SmartIcons, choose SmartIcons from the Tools menu or click the Customize SmartIcons SmartIcon. The SmartIcons dialog box opens (refer to fig. 23.7).

The scrollable list of SmartIcons on the left holds all the SmartIcons built into Freelance. The column of SmartIcons to the right is the current SmartIcon palette. To add a SmartIcon to the current palette, find the icon on the list at the left and then drag it to a position in the column on the right. The SmartIcon then appears in the column. By dragging the Spacer at the top of the list of available SmartIcons over to the right, you can add spaces that can separate SmartIcons into logical groups. To delete a SmartIcon from the current palette, drag it off the right column of SmartIcons and out of the SmartIcon window.

TIP

To rearrange the order of SmartIcons in the palette at any time without using the SmartIcons dialog box, you can press and hold down Ctrl and drag a SmartIcon from one position to another while you are in any Freelance view.

To save the revised SmartIcon palette, click the **S**ave Set button, type a name for the palette in the **N**ame of Set text box, and type a DOS file name for the palette (SmartIcons automatically get the extension SMI) in the **F**ile Name text box. Then click OK.

To delete a SmartIcon palette, click the **D**elete Set button and choose the palette to delete from the list. Then click OK.

Changing the Size of the SmartIcons

You can change the size of the SmartIcons if they are too large or too small to be useful. Click the **I**con Size button in the SmartIcons dialog box and choose **S**mall (EGA), **M**edium (VGA), or **L**arge (Super VGA). Then click OK. A sample SmartIcon at the right shows the currently chosen SmartIcon size.

Creating a SmartIcon To Load an Application or Insert an Object

The SmartIcons built into Freelance carry out Freelance commands and load other Lotus Windows applications. To create SmartIcons that can load other programs or insert OLE objects, click Edit Icon in the SmartIcons dialog box. The Edit Icon dialog box opens, as shown in figure 23.9.

Fig. 23.9

The Edit Icon dialog box.

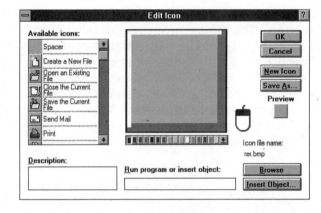

To base the new SmartIcon on an existing SmartIcon, choose the SmartIcon from the list at the left and then enter a name for the new SmartIcon when prompted. To create a brand new SmartIcon, click the New Icon button and enter a name for the SmartIcon when prompted. Then you can draw the picture that will appear on the SmartIcon's face, enter a description for the SmartIcon that will appear in the Freelance title bar, and enter the program name to be started or the OLE object to be inserted.

To draw the picture for the face of the SmartIcon, click a color on the display of colors with one of the mouse buttons. You can click another color with the other mouse button. Then drag across the large button face that is displayed in the dialog box or click specific dots on the button face. Click either mouse button to place a dot of the color assigned to that button. Continue clicking dots or dragging until you have created the picture you want. To choose from among more colors, click the pull-down button at the right end of the color display. A preview at the right edge of the dialog box shows the SmartIcon in progress.

When you complete the SmartIcon picture, type a brief description of the SmartIcon in the **Description** text box. Then click the **Browse** button to find a program's file name or a batch file name to associate with the SmartIcon, or click **Insert Object** to select an object type to associate. Later, when you click the SmartIcon, either the designated program starts or another application launches so that you can create an OLE embedded object.

To finish editing the icon, click OK to leave the Edit Icon dialog box and then click OK again to leave the SmartIcons dialog box. To save the SmartIcon with a new name, click the Save **As** button and then enter the new name before clicking OK to leave the Edit Icon dialog box. When you next add SmartIcons to a SmartIcon palette, you will find the new SmartIcon you have created on the list of available SmartIcons.

Summary

In this chapter, you learned how to change the custom settings that affect how the Freelance window appears and how some of the Freelance commands and tools perform. You learned also how to use and modify the SmartIcons.

SmartMaster Sets

The samples in this appendix show the designs of the 66 SmartMaster sets that come with Freelance Graphics Release 2.0 for Windows. Each sample displays the Bullets & Chart page layout, so you can see the background design, the text, and a chart. Many of the sets have graduated backgrounds, bitmaps, and symbols that you cannot see in these black-and-white illustrations. Examples are GRADATE1.MAS, NEO2.MAS, NIGHTSKY.MAS, and SHIMMER.MAS. To see the full effects of all the designs, refer to your Freelance Graphics documentation or view them on-screen.

Fig. A.1

A sample page from the 1993.MAS SmartMaster set.

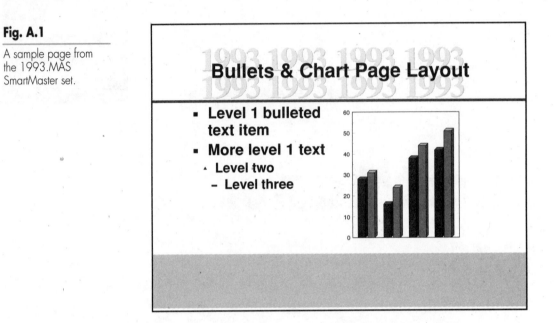

Fig. A.2

A sample page from the 3LINE.MAS SmartMaster set.

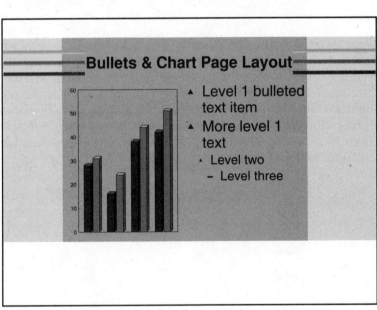

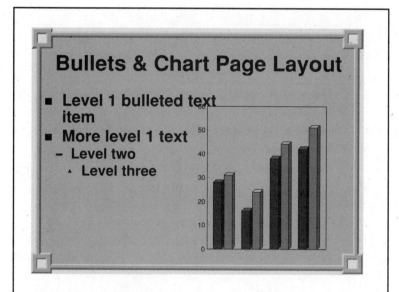

Fig. A.3

A sample page from the 4SQUARE.MAS SmartMaster set.

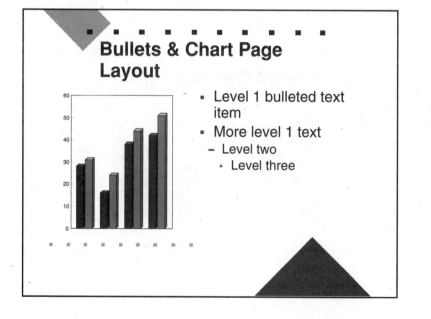

Fig. A.4

A sample page from the ABSTRACT.MAS SmartMaster set.

Fig. A.5

A sample page from the ANGLES.MAS SmartMaster set.

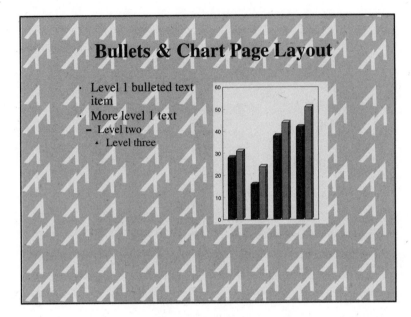

Fig. A.6

A sample page from the BASICLIN.MAS SmartMaster set.

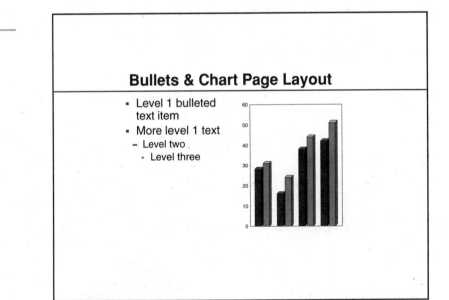

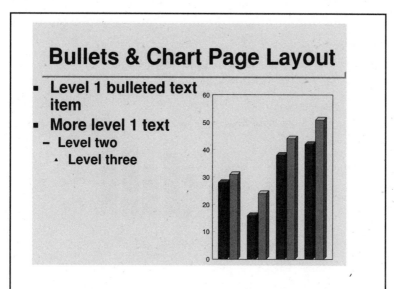

Fig. A.7

A sample page from the BEVRULE.MAS SmartMaster set.

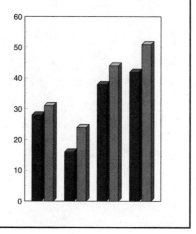

Fig. A.8

A sample page from the BLANK.MAS SmartMaster set.

Fig. A.9

A sample page from the BLOCKLIN.MAS SmartMaster set.

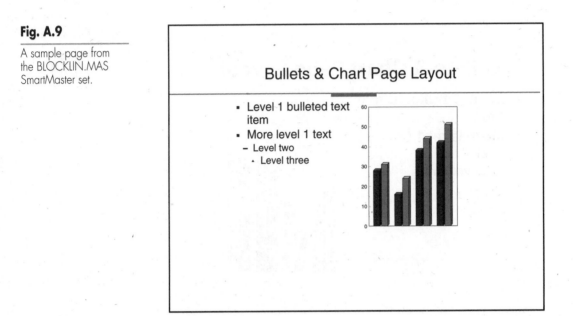

Fig. A.10

A sample page from the BLOCKS.MAS SmartMaster set.

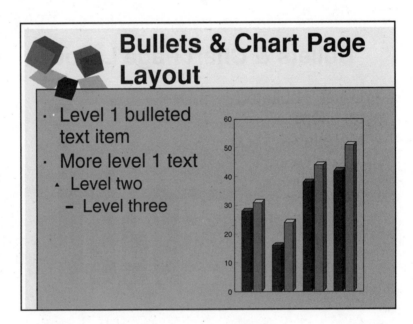

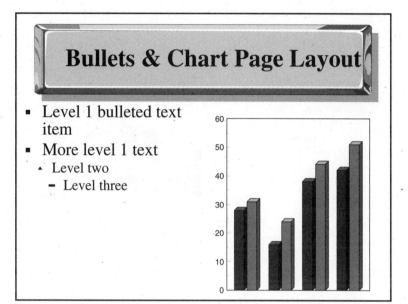

Fig. A.13

A sample page from
the BUTTONS.MAS
SmartMaster set.

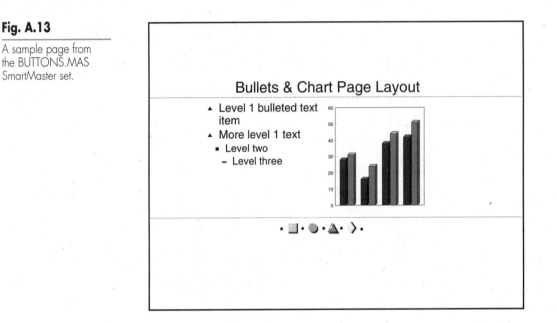

Fig. A.14

A sample page from
the CANADA.MAS
SmartMaster set.

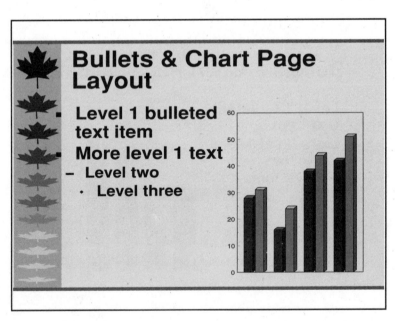

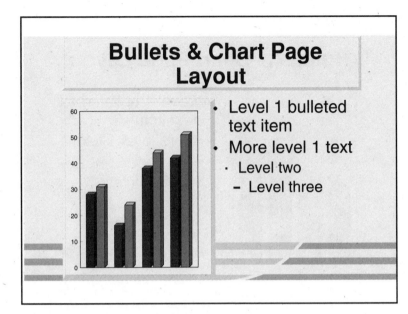

Fig. A.15

A sample page from the CIRCLE.MAS SmartMaster set.

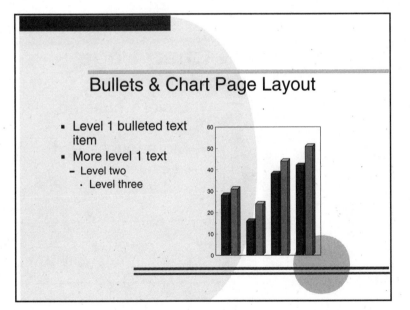

Fig. A.16

A sample page from the CORPORAT.MAS SmartMaster set.

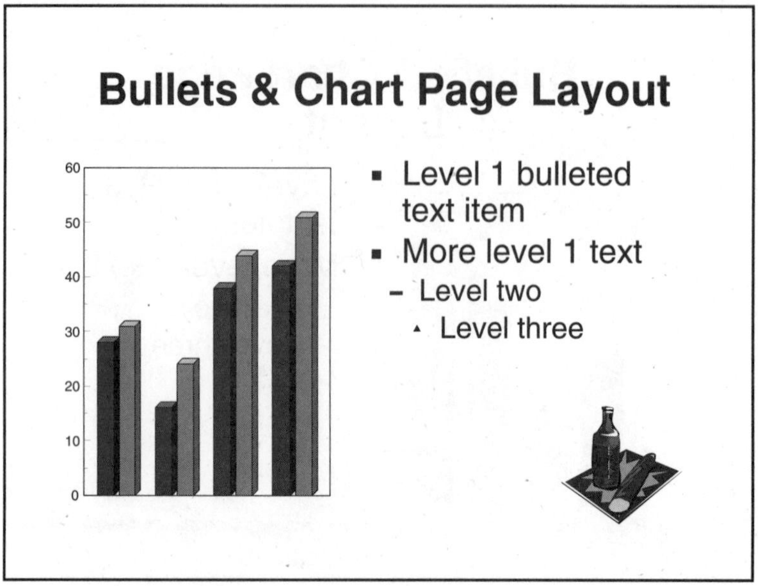

Fig. A.17

A sample page from the CUISINE.MAS SmartMaster set.

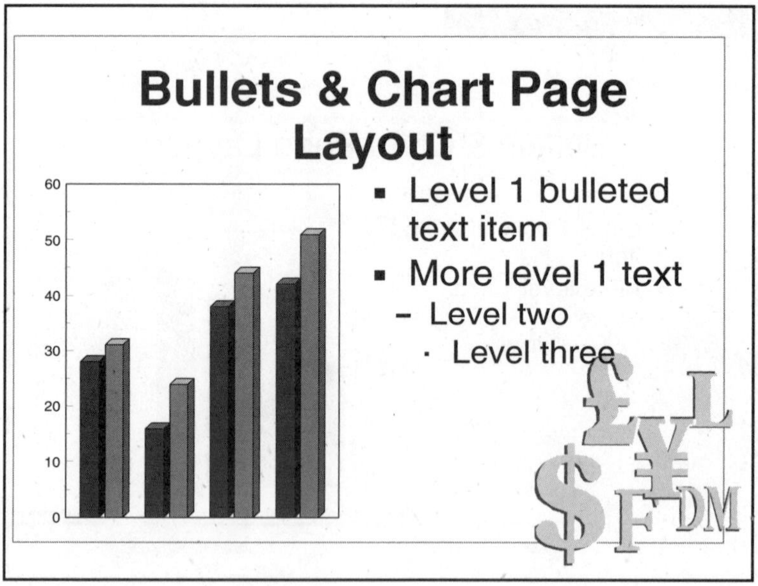

Fig. A.18

A sample page from the CURRENCY.MAS SmartMaster set.

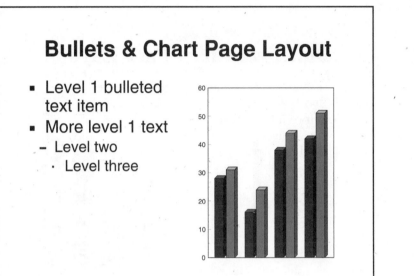

Fig. A.19

A sample page from
the CUSTOM.MAS
SmartMaster set.

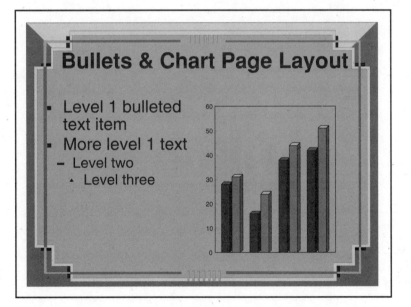

Fig. A.20

A sample page from
the DECO.MAS
SmartMaster set.

Fig. A.21

A sample page from the
DOTLINE1.MAS
SmartMaster set.

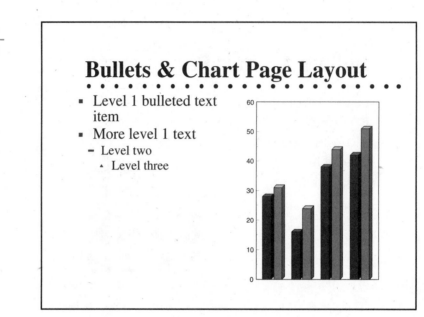

Fig. A.22

A sample page from the
DOTLINE2.MAS
SmartMaster set.

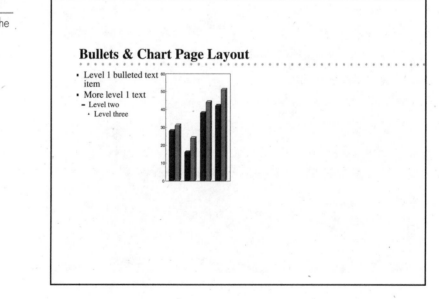

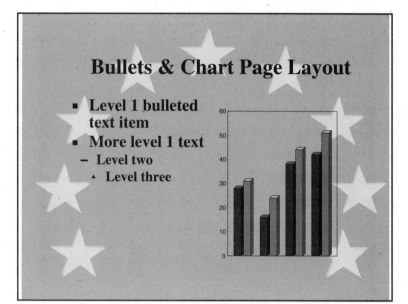

Fig. A.23

A sample page from the
EEC.MAS SmartMaster
set.

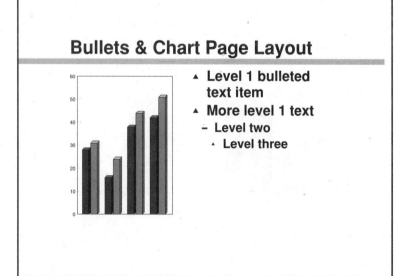

Fig. A.24

A sample page from the
ELEGANCE.MAS
SmartMaster set.

Fig. A.25

A sample page from
the EUROPE.MAS
SmartMaster set.

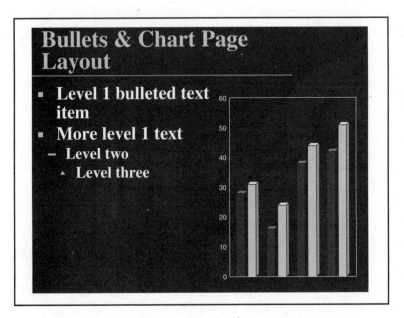

Fig. A.26

A sample page from
the FINANCE.MAS
SmartMaster set.

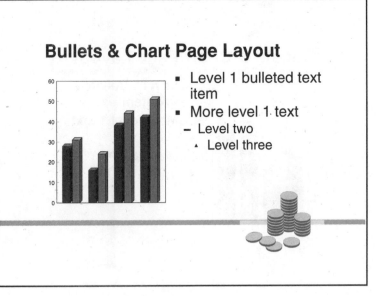

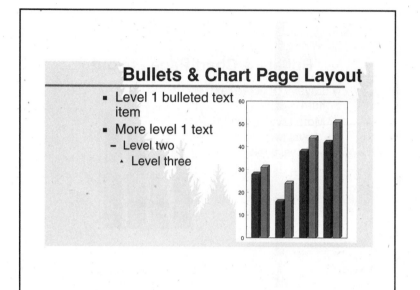

Fig. A.27

A sample page from
the FOREST.MAS
SmartMaster set.

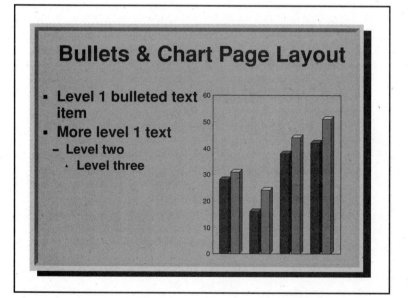

Fig. A.28

A sample page from
the FRAME.MAS
SmartMaster set.

Fig. A.29

A sample page from the GRADATE1.MAS SmartMaster set.

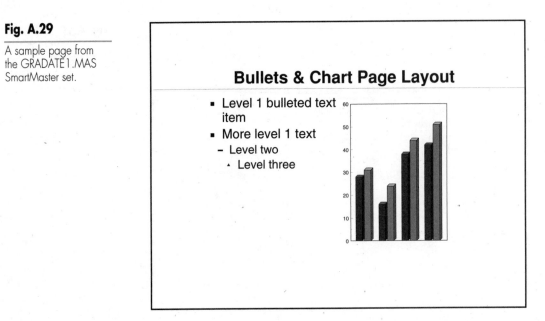

Fig. A.30

A sample page from the GRADATE2.MAS SmartMaster set.

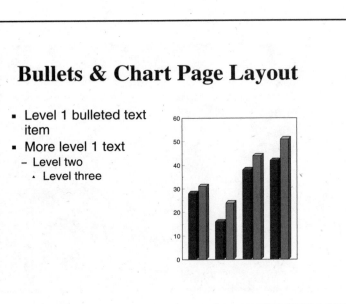

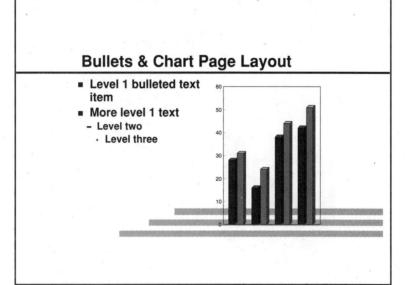

Fig. A.31

A sample page from
the GRADLINE.MAS
SmartMaster set.

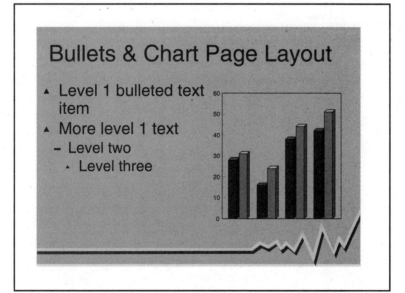

Fig. A.32

A sample page from
the GRAPHLIN.MAS
SmartMaster set.

Fig. A.33

A sample page from the JAPAN.MAS SmartMaster set.

Bullets & Chart Page Layout
60
50
40
30
20
10
0
Level 1 bulleted text item
More level 1 text
Level two
Level three

Fig. A.34

A sample page from the JFLAG.MAS SmartMaster set.

Bullets & Chart Page Layout
Level 1 bulleted text item
More level 1 text
Level two
Level three
60
50
40
30
20
10
0

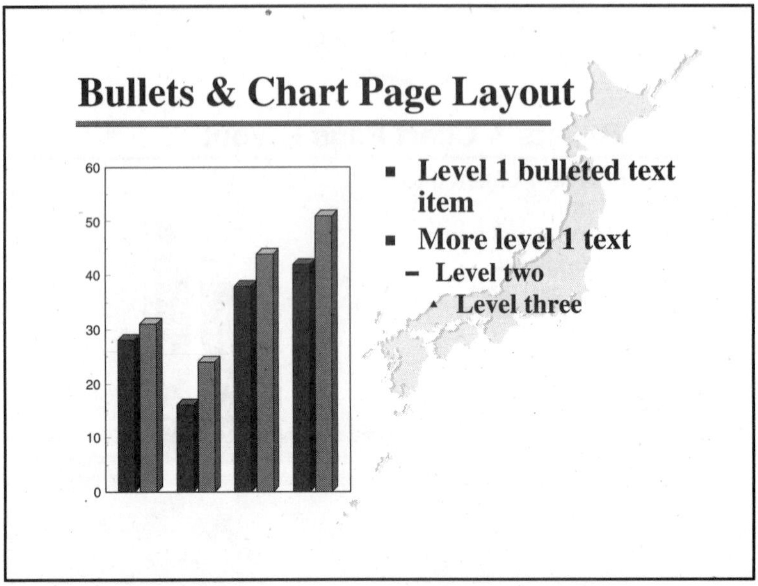

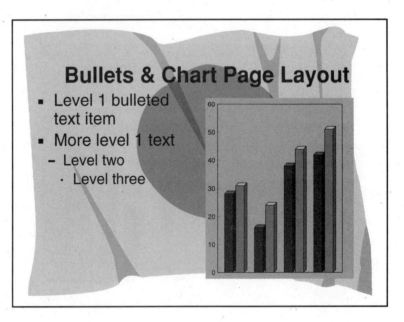

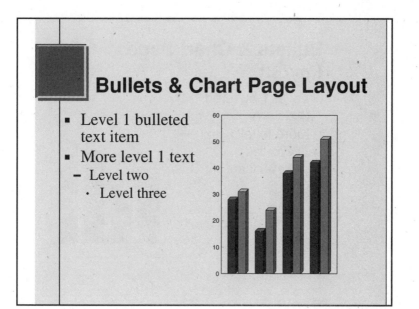

Fig. A.35

A sample page from the MARBLE.MAS SmartMaster set.

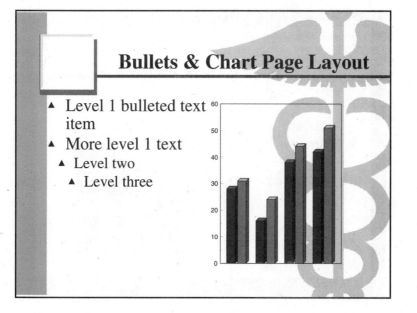

Fig. A.36

A sample page from the MEDICAL.MAS SmartMaster set.

Fig. A.37

A sample page from the MMGLOBE.MAS SmartMaster set.

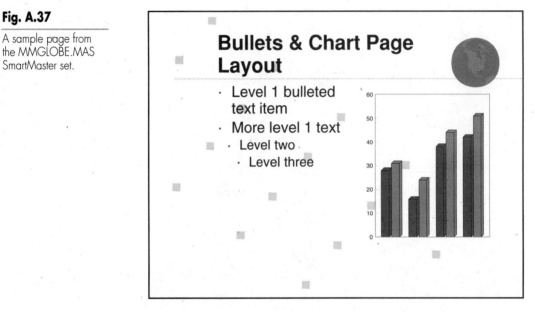

Fig. A.38

A sample page from the MMLASER.MAS SmartMaster set.

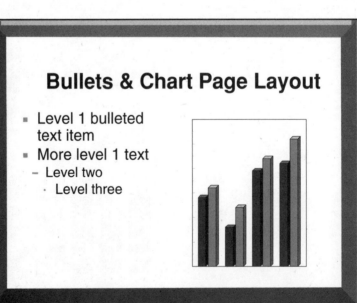

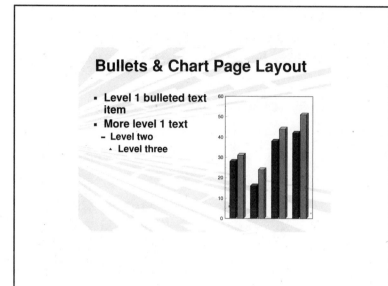

Fig. A.39

A sample page from the MOTION.MAS SmartMaster set.

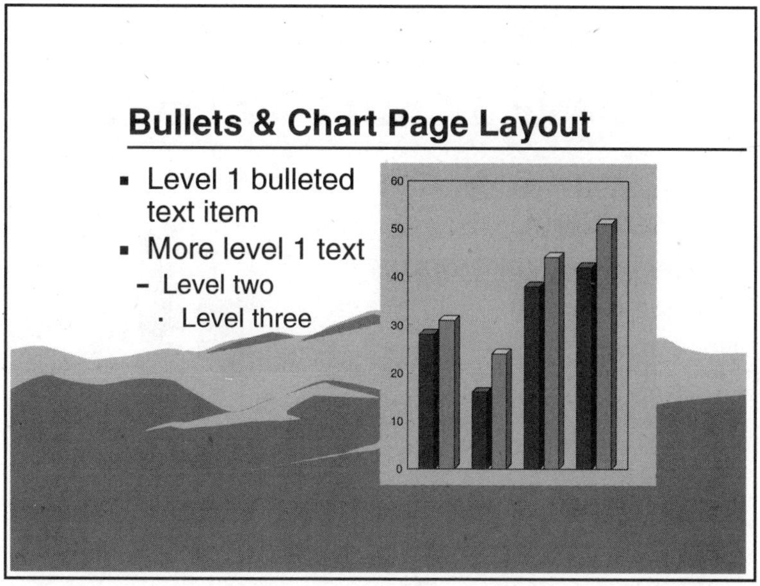

Fig. A.40

A sample page from the MOUNTAIN.MAS SmartMaster set.

Fig. A.41

A sample page from
the NEO2.MAS
SmartMaster set.

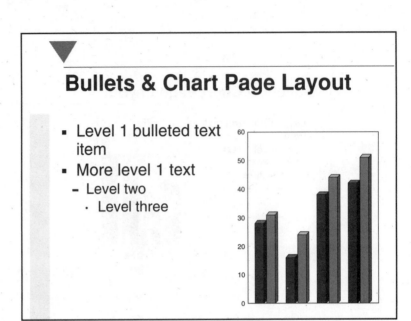

Fig. A.42

A sample page from
the NIGHTSKY.MAS
SmartMaster set.

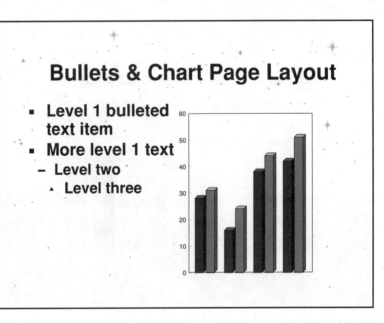

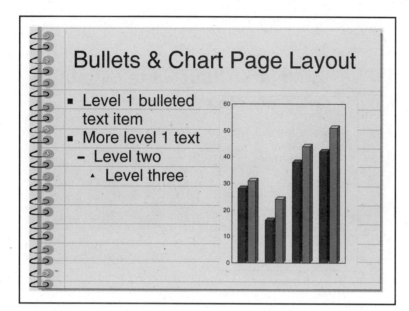

Fig. A.43

A sample page from
the NOTEBOOK.MAS
SmartMaster set.

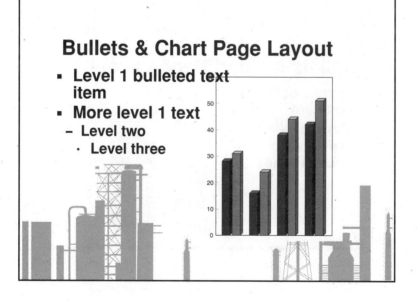

Fig. A.44

A sample page from
the OILREFIN.MAS
SmartMaster set.

Fig. A.45

A sample page from
the ORNATE2.MAS
SmartMaster set.

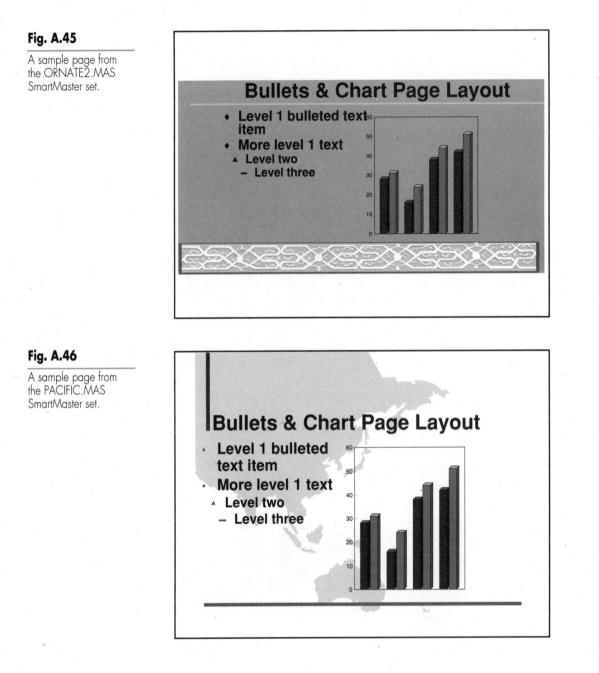

Fig. A.46

A sample page from
the PACIFIC.MAS
SmartMaster set.

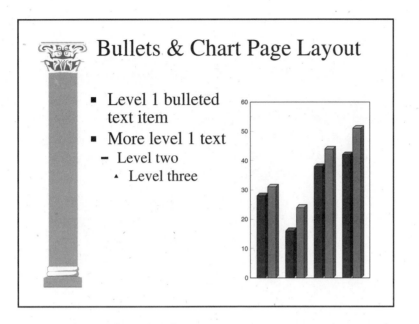

Fig. A.47

A sample page from
the PILLAR.MAS
SmartMaster set.

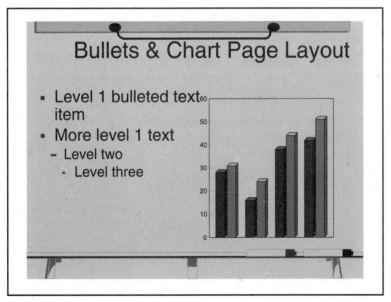

Fig. A.48

A sample page from
the PRESENT.MAS
SmartMaster set.

Fig. A.49

A sample page from the RAINBOW.MAS SmartMaster set.

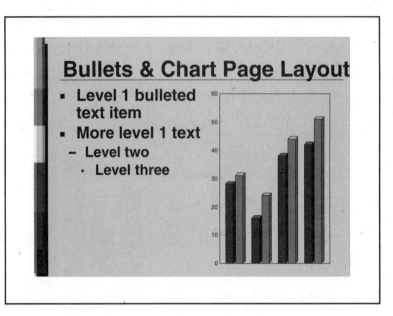

Fig. A.50

A sample page from the SCRIM.MAS SmartMaster set.

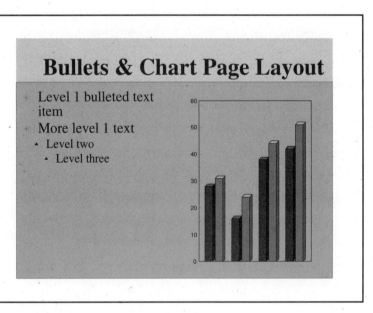

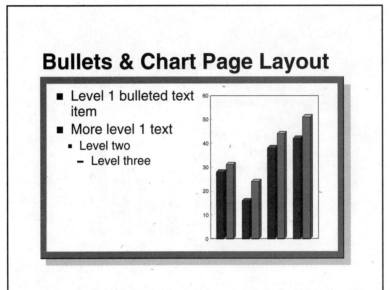

Fig. A.51

A sample page from
the SHADOWBX.MAS
SmartMaster set.

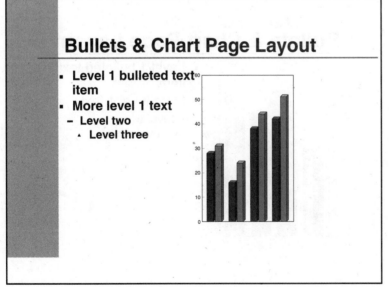

Fig. A.52

A sample page from
the SHIMMER.MAS
SmartMaster set.

Fig. A.53

A sample page from
the SHIP.MAS
SmartMaster set.

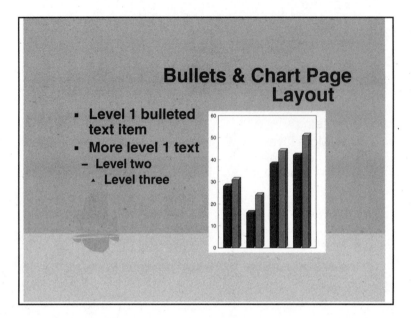

Fig. A.54

A sample page from
the SKETCH.MAS
SmartMaster set.

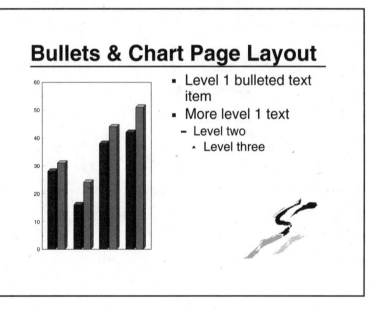

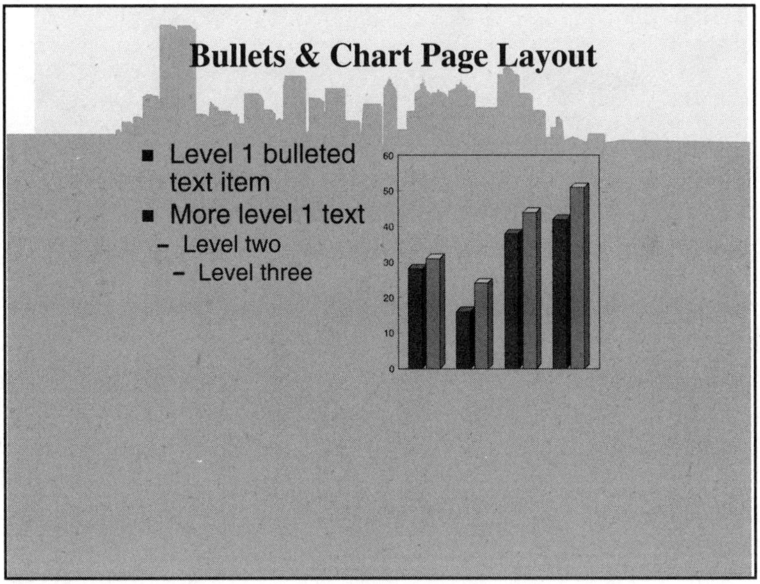

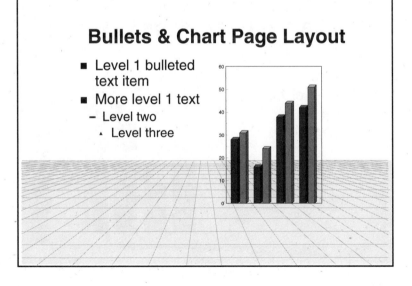

Fig. A.55

A sample page from the SKYLINE.MAS SmartMaster set.

Fig. A.56

A sample page from the SPACE.MAS SmartMaster set.

Fig. A.57

A sample page from
the SPOTLITE.MAS
SmartMaster set.

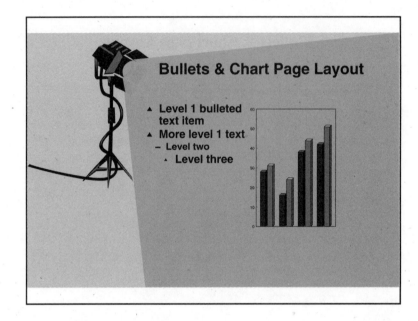

Fig. A.58

A sample page from
the STACK.MAS
SmartMaster set.

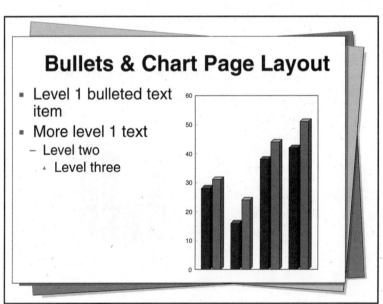

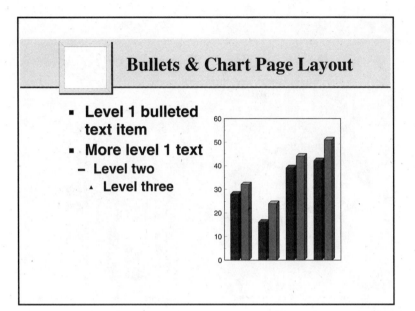

Fig. A.60

A sample page from the TILES.MAS SmartMaster set.

Fig. A.61

A sample page from the TUBE.MAS Smart-Master set.

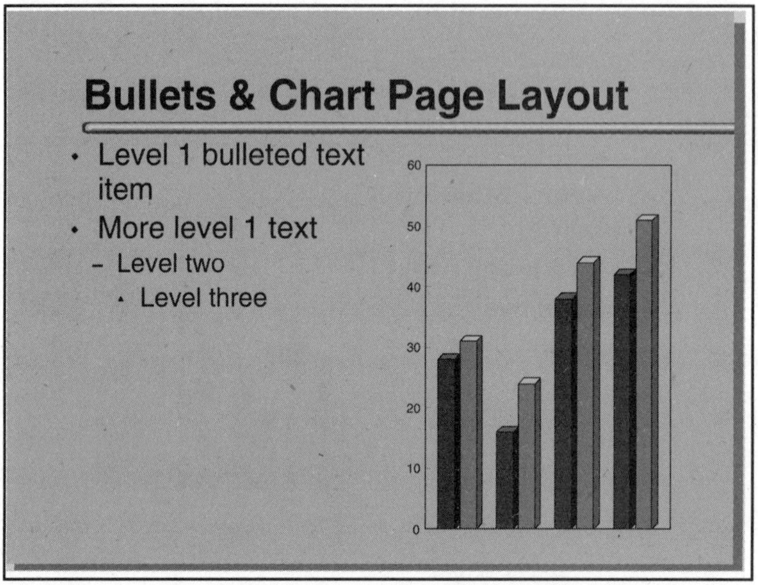

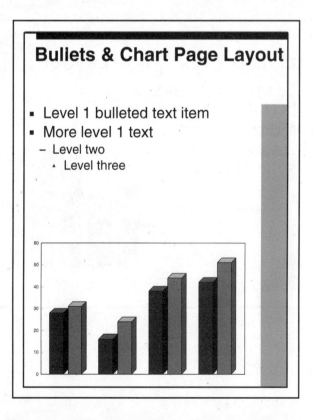

Fig. A.62

A sample page from the VERTBAR.MAS SmartMaster set.

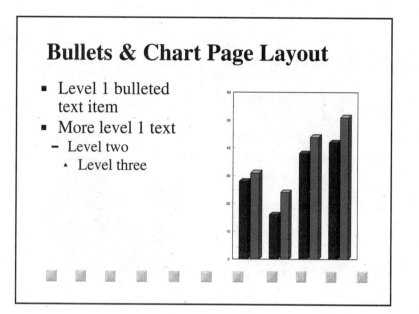

Bullets & Chart Page Layout
Level 1 bulleted text item
More level 1 text
Level two
Level three
60
50
40
30
20
10
0

Fig. A.63

A sample page from the WAFFLE.MAS SmartMaster set.

Bullets & Chart Page Layout
Level 1 bulleted text item
More level 1 text
Level two
Level three
60
50
40
30
20
10
0

Fig. A.64

A sample page from the WAVE.MAS SmartMaster set.

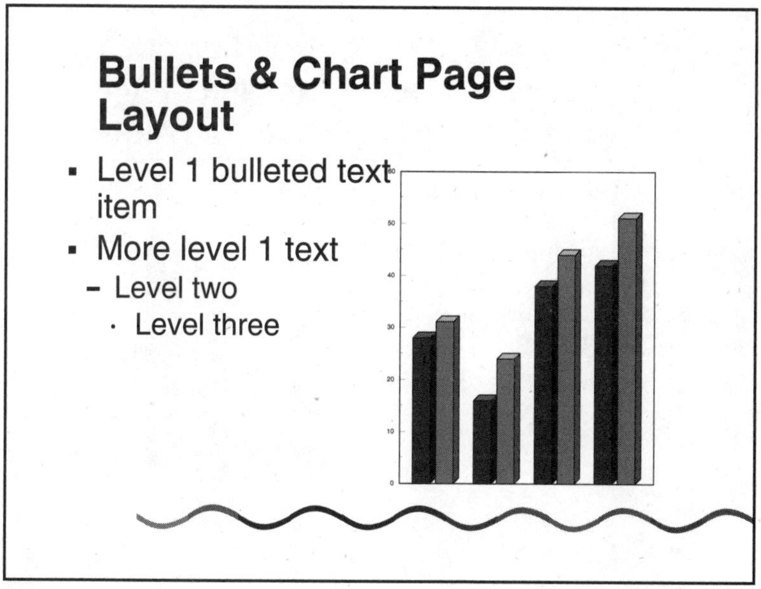

Fig. A.65

A sample page from the WORLD1.MAS SmartMaster set.

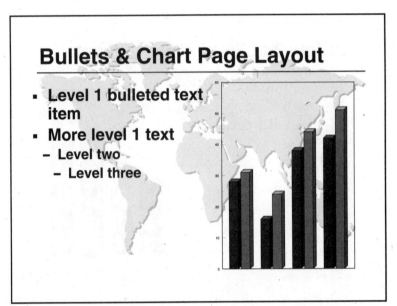

Fig. A.66

A sample page from the WORLD2.MAS SmartMaster set.

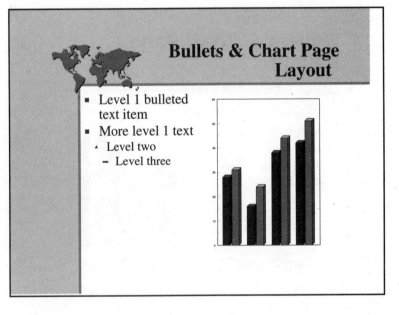

The Symbol Library

This appendix displays the symbols that are available in the symbol library in Freelance Graphics Release 2.0 for Windows. The categories are displayed alphabetically by name both here and in Freelance. The symbols within each category are shown in the same order in which they appear in the library.

ANIMALS (ANIMALS.SYM)

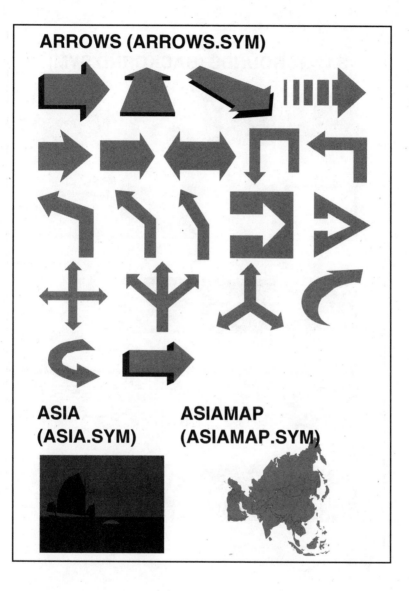

ARROWS (ARROWS.SYM)

**ASIA
(ASIA.SYM)**

**ASIAMAP
(ASIAMAP.SYM)**

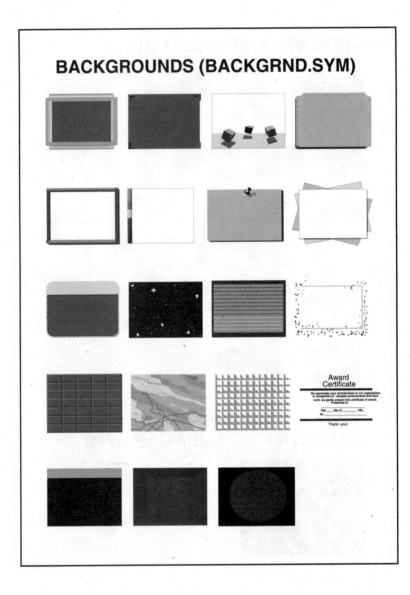

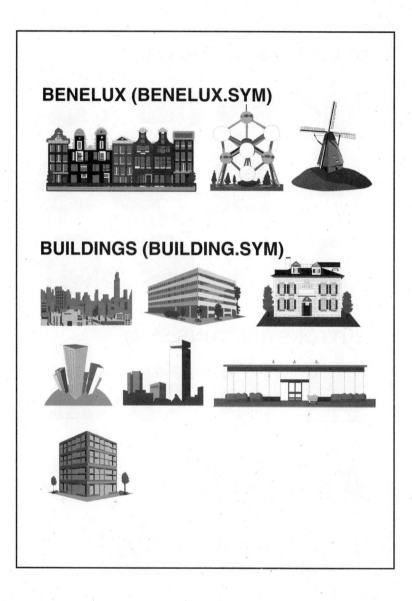

BENELUX (BENELUX.SYM)

BUILDINGS (BUILDING.SYM)

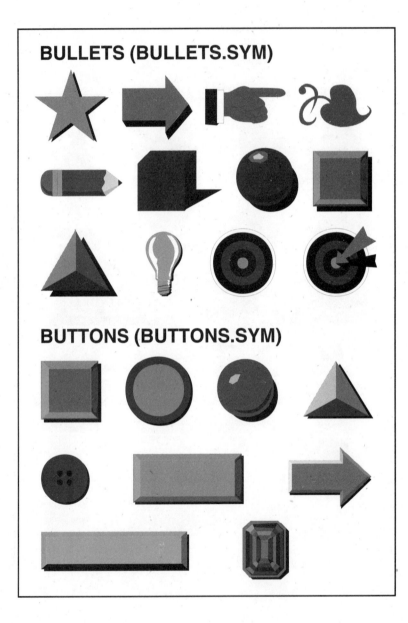

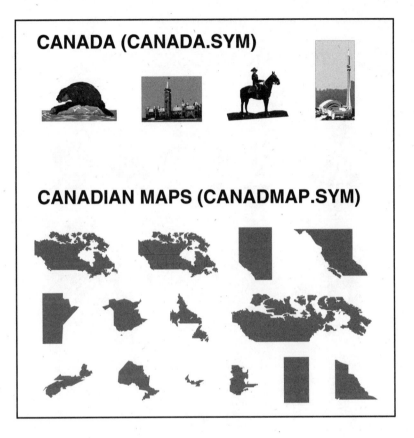

CANADA (CANADA.SYM)

CANADIAN MAPS (CANADMAP.SYM)

COMMON OBJECTS (COMMOBJT.SYM)

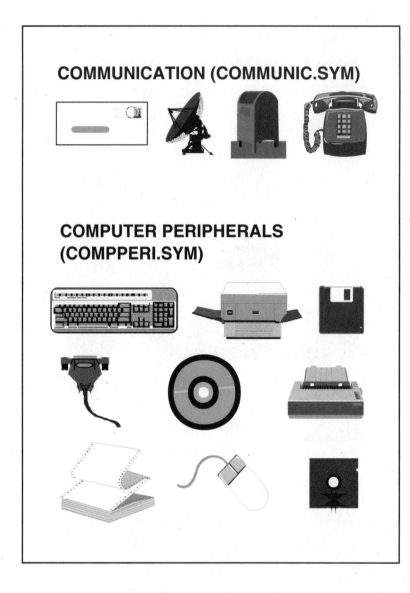

COMMUNICATION (COMMUNIC.SYM)

**COMPUTER PERIPHERALS
(COMPPERI.SYM)**

COMPUTERS (COMPUTER.SYM)

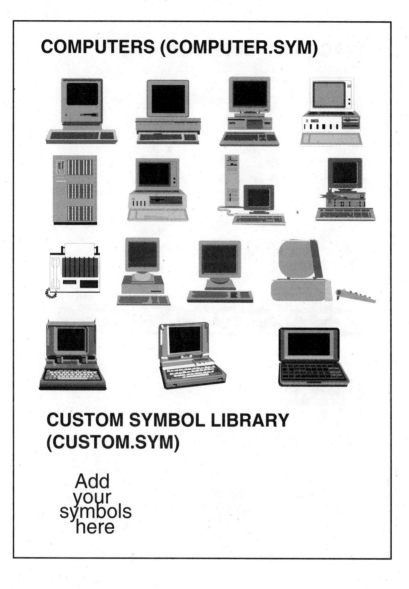

CUSTOM SYMBOL LIBRARY (CUSTOM.SYM)

Add
your
symbols
here

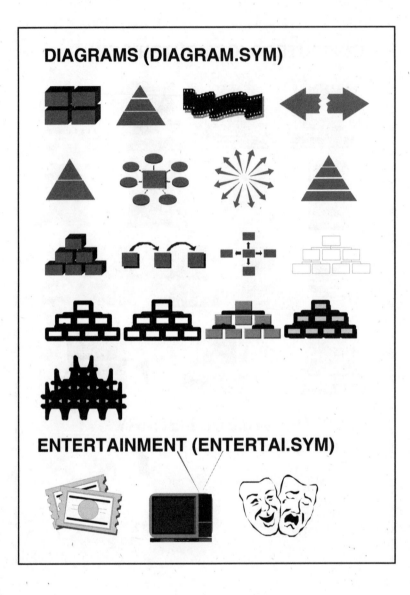

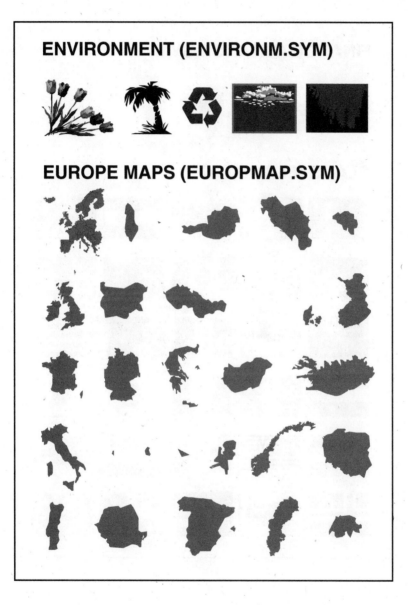

ENVIRONMENT (ENVIRONM.SYM)

EUROPE MAPS (EUROPMAP.SYM)

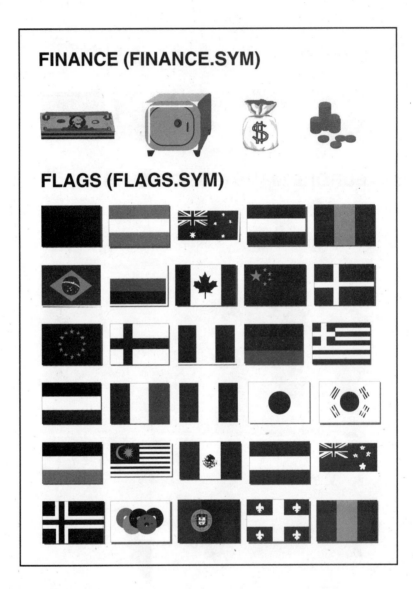

FLAGS (cont.) (FLAGS.SYM)

FLOW CHARTING (FLOWCHRT.SYM)

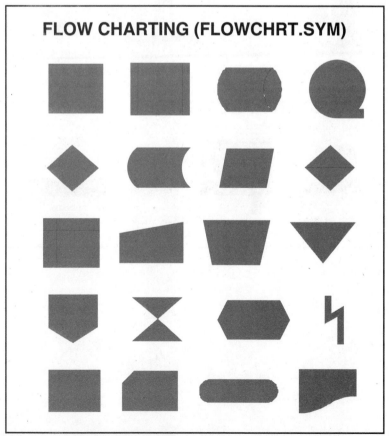

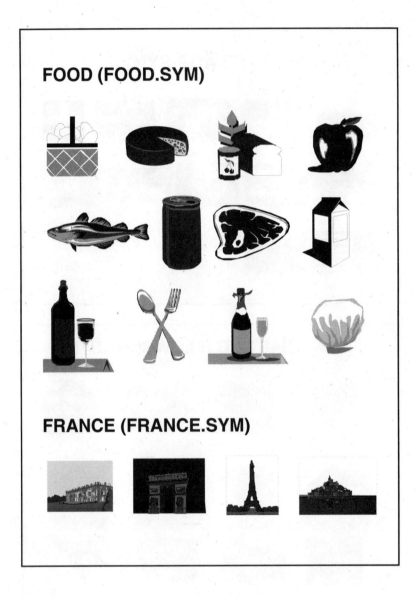

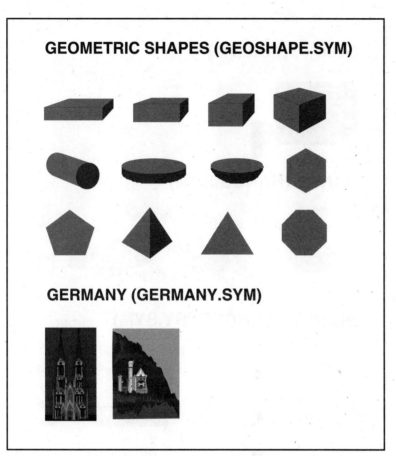

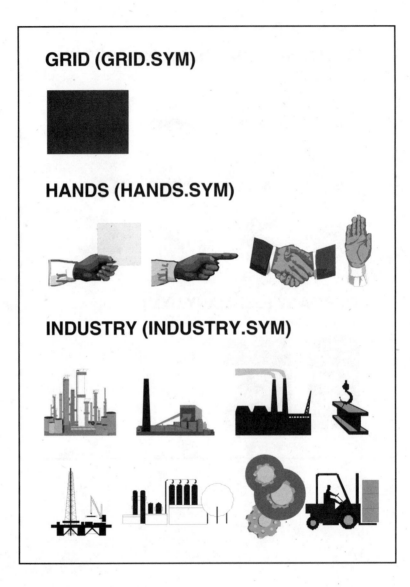

ITALY (ITALY.SYM)

MAP LEGENDS (LEGENDS.SYM)

MEDICAL IMAGES (MEDICAL.SYM)

MEN (MEN.SYM)

OFFICE OBJECTS (OFFOBJCT.SYM)

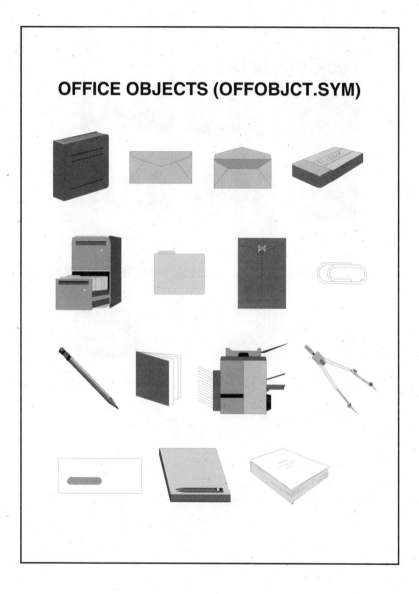

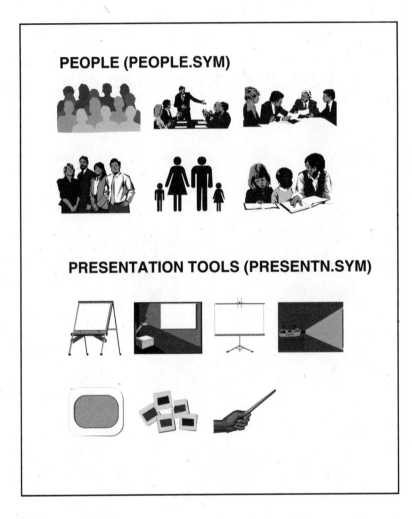

PUZZLE (PUZZLE.SYM)

SCIENCE (SCIENCE.SYM)

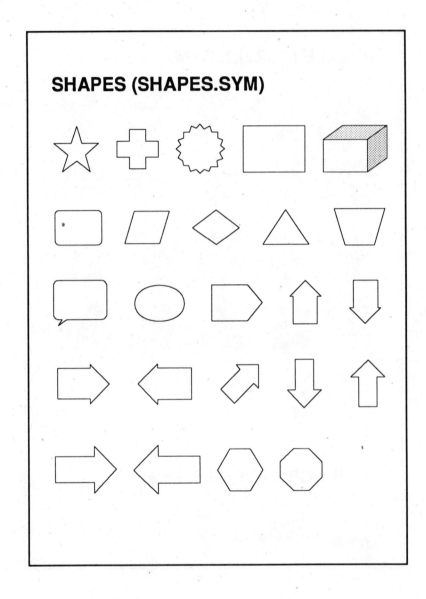

SPAIN (SPAIN.SYM)

SPORTS (SPORTS.SYM)

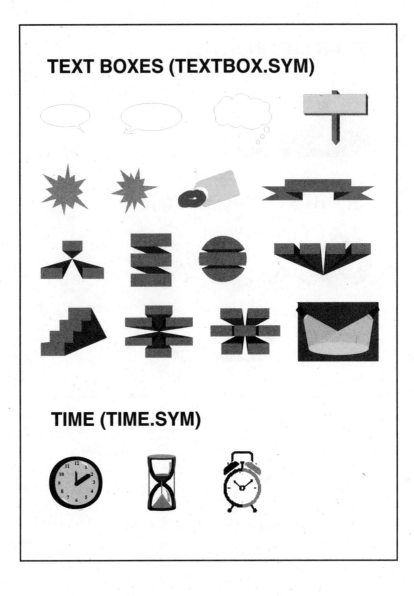

TRANSPORTATION (TRANSPOR.SYM)

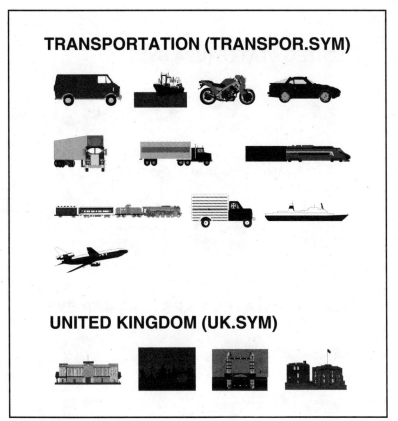

UNITED KINGDOM (UK.SYM)

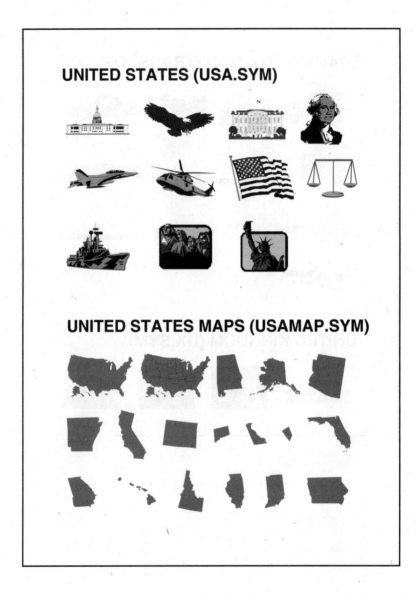

UNITED STATES (USA.SYM)

UNITED STATES MAPS (USAMAP.SYM)

UNITED STATES MAPS cont.
(USAMAP.SYM)

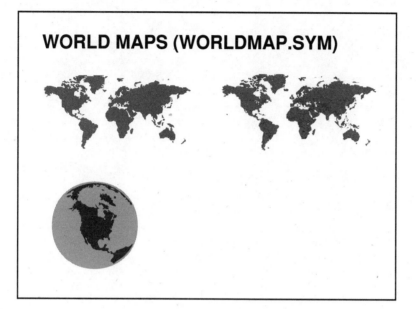

WORLD MAPS (WORLDMAP.SYM)

V

W

X-Z